Library of
Davidson College

Richard L. Weaver, II
*Bowling Green State University*

# UNDERSTANDING BUSINESS COMMUNICATION

Prentice-Hall, Inc., Englewood Cliffs, New Jersey 07632

*Library of Congress Cataloging in Publication Data*

Weaver, Richard L.
   Understanding business communication.

   Includes index.
   1. Communication in management.  I. Title.
HF5718.W416  1985      658.4'5    84-15042
ISBN  0-13-936998-8

Editorial/production supervision
and interior design: **Marjorie Borden**
Cover design: **Wanda Lubelska**
Manufacturing buyer: **Barbara Kelly Kittle**

© 1985 by Prentice-Hall, Inc., Englewood Cliffs, New Jersey 07632

All rights reserved. No part of this book may be reproduced,
in any form or by any means,
without permission in writing from the publisher.

Printed in the United States of America

10  9  8  7  6  5  4  3  2  1

ISBN 0-13-936998-8 01

Prentice-Hall International, Inc., *London*
Prentice-Hall of Australia Pty. Limited, *Sydney*
Editora Prentice-Hall do Brasil, Ltda., *Rio de Janeiro*
Prentice-Hall Canada Inc., *Toronto*
Prentice-Hall of India Private Limited, *New Delhi*
Prentice-Hall of Japan, Inc., *Tokyo*
Prentice-Hall of Southeast Asia Pte. Ltd., *Singapore*
Whitehall Books Limited, *Wellington, New Zealand*

*to*

Scott
Jacquelynn
Anthony
Joanna

*—partners in the business of communicating*

# Contents

|  |  | Preface | ix |
|---|---|---|---|
|  |  | Acknowledgments | xi |
| one |  | Communication in Business | 1 |

*A systems approach,* **3**
*Communication and the system,* **3**
*Levels of communication,* **7**
*Other forms of communication,* **15**
*Effective communication—the payoff,* **20**
*Summary,* **22**

| two |  | Communication Process and Principles | 24 |
|---|---|---|---|

*The communication process: an overview?,* **25**
*Communication as transaction,* **27**
*Axioms of communication,* **29**
*Maslow's need hierarchy?,* **31**
*McGregor's Theory X and Theory Y,* **34**

*The intrapersonal process,* **36**
*The social context,* **38**
*Interpersonal processes,* **39**
*Summary,* **44**

three    Listening                                              46

*Importance of listening,* **47**
*Nature of listening,* **49**
*Listening and feedback,* **54**
*Improving listening,* **57**
*Summary,* **60**

four     Language Needs                                         63

*An overview of language,* **64**
*Characteristics of language,* **68**
*Summary,* **77**

five     Nonverbal Communication                                79

*What is the nature of nonverbal communication?,* **80**
*What functions does nonverbal communication serve?,* **80**
*What are the types of nonverbal communication?,* **82**
*Summary,* **93**

six      Barriers in Business Communication                     96

*Selective attention,* **97**
*Selective retention,* **100**
*Bipolar thinking,* **103**
*Evaluative thinking,* **104**
*Additional barriers,* **106**
*Overcoming barriers,* **108**
*Summary,* **110**

seven    Profiting from Conflict Management                    113

*The profits of conflict,* **114**
*Old view of conflict versus new view,* **115**
*The stages of conflict,* **116**
*Alternative approaches to conflict,* **122**
*A method for resolving conflict,* **124**
*Summary,* **129**

Contents    vii

**eight**   **Visual and Graphic Communication**    *131*

*Values of visual aids,* **132**
*Using visual aids,* **133**
*Graphic aids in written reports,* **139**
*Visual aids in oral reports,* **142**
*Summary,* **146**

**nine**    **The Interview**    *148*

*Purposes of interviews,* **149**
*Types of interviews,* **150**
*Role and responsibility of the interviewer,* **155**
*Role and responsibility of the interviewee,* **159**
*Listening,* **164**
*Questioning,* **165**
*Structuring the interview,* **168**
*Summary,* **170**

**ten**   **Getting a Job**   *173*

*Evaluating yourself,* **174**
*Preparing a résumé,* **176**
*Getting job information,* **181**
*Applying for jobs,* **184**
*Interviewing for jobs,* **188**
*Summary,* **198**

**eleven**   **Meetings, Conferences, and Committees**   *200*

*Why groups?,* **201**
*Characteristics of groups,* **203**
*Ideal conditions,* **208**
*Group problem solving,* **209**
*Membership functions,* **213**
*Leadership functions,* **216**
*Improving meetings, conferences, and committees,* **218**
*Dealing with conflict in groups,* **221**
*Summary,* **222**

**twelve**   **Oral Reports**   *225*

*Definition,* **226**
*Development,* **226**
*Delivery,* **239**

*Evaluation,* **245**
*Summary,* **246**

| | | |
|---|---|---|
| thirteen | **Persuasive Presentations** | *248* |

*Attitudes, beliefs, and values,* **248**
*Emotional support,* **253**
*Logical support,* **258**
*Support from credibility,* **262**
*Resisting the persuasion of others,* **265**
*Summary,* **267**

| | | |
|---|---|---|
| fourteen | **Writing Principles** | *269* |

*Generating ideas,* **270**
*Words: a summary,* **271**
*Sentences,* **276**
*Paragraphs,* **281**
*Compositions,* **285**
*Summary,* **288**

| | | |
|---|---|---|
| fifteen | **Business Letters** | *290* |

*Advantages and disadvantages,* **291**
*Basic qualities,* **293**
*Beginnings and endings,* **298**
*Metacommunication,* **303**
*Different kinds of letters,* **308**
*Summary,* **325**

| | | |
|---|---|---|
| sixteen | **Business Reports and Memoranda** | *327* |

*Purposes,* **327**
*Preparation,* **328**
*Qualities,* **332**
*Structure and format,* **333**
*Style,* **341**
*Short reports,* **341**
*Summary,* **344**

| | |
|---|---|
| **Glossary** | *347* |
| **Index** | *359* |

# Preface

Effective communication is the backbone of business. In their book Peters and Waterman say, "The intensity of communications is unmistakable in the excellent companies." After discussing informality, name tags, open door policies, and physical configurations, they ask, "What does it add up to? Lots of communication."*

*Understanding Business Communication* is designed to help in the understanding and practice of those kinds of communication most crucial to growth and success in business. It operates on the assumption that communication skill is as important as technical competence.

The strength of this book lies in its direct, straightforward approach. What are the basic understandings and needs of those entering business for the first time? What are the basic skills to be acquired? Using recent research, practical suggestions, and numerous relevant examples related to areas essential to communication within businesses, this book puts the student and reader first.

Both oral and written communication are discussed. After Chapter 1, "Communication in Business," sets the stage, the various processes and

---

*Thomas J. Peters and Robert H. Waterman, Jr., *In Search of Excellence: Lessons from America's Best-Run Companies* (New York: Harper & Row, 1982), p. 122.

principles are considered in Chapter 2. Together, these chapters provide an overview and context of the world of business communication.

In the next six chapters, various aspects of business communication are considered. In separate chapters, the subjects of listening, language, nonverbal communication, barriers in business communication, conflict management, and visual and graphic communication are discussed.

In the next five chapters a variety of oral business-communication contexts are presented and discussed. In many situations, there is a blend of oral and written effectiveness likely to result in success. Where possible, these communication blends are examined. Oral contexts include interviewing, getting a job, meetings, conferences, and committees, oral reports, and persuasive presentations.

The final three chapters of the book examine written communication. Writing principles are discussed first. Because of their importance, business letters are discussed next. The final chapter considers business reports and memoranda.

Each chapter is self-contained. Although the book is arranged in what appears to be a natural order for teaching the material, the instructor can use the material in any order, since there is no progressive or sequential building of material. This self-contained feature, which is intentional, adds to the flexibility and adaptability of the book.

*Understanding Business Communication* is a book, first and foremost, for the student. Wherever possible, I have avoided technical language and complex theoretical explanation. Business communicators need simple, uncomplicated suggestions offered in an unembellished style. Just as clarity, simplicity, and directness should be key guidelines in all business communication, I have tried to use the same in my own writing.

Richard L. Weaver, II

# Acknowledgments

My own communication background is the product of numerous people. Although they are not responsible for my weaknesses, their efforts continue to touch my life in rich and meaningful ways. Professors Kenneth E. Andersen, Henry R. Austin, Herbert W. Hildebrandt, Howard H. Martin, Edgar E. Willis, and the late William M. Sattler were major influences at the University of Michigan.

At Indiana University, Professors J. Jeffery Auer, Gail W. Compton, Robert G. Gunderson, Robert C. Jeffrey, Richard L. Johannesen, Raymond Smith, and Donald W. Zacharias played significant roles.

At the University of Massachusetts, Professors Vincent M. Bevilacqua, Jane Blankenship, Kenneth L. Brown, Richard L. Conville, Vernon E. Cronen, Ronald J. Matlon, William K. Price, Ronald F. Reid, Malcolm O. Sillars, Hermann G. and Sara L. Stelzner, and the late Karl R. Wallace made deep and lasting contributions.

Professors Ronald E. Cambra, Lauren E. Ekroth, David D. Hudson, Donald W. Klopf, Michael R. Neer, Kazuo Nishiyama, Wayne H. Oxford, and Clay Warren, at the University of Hawaii–Manoa, had an enlivening and invigorating effect causing much reassessment and reappraisal—a challenging, demanding reawakening.

The deepest, most recent effects come from those with whom I have the closest association now. Thank you to Professors Donald K. Enholm, Carl B. Holmberg, Nelson R. Ober, Raymond K. Tucker, James R. Wilcox, Dorothy K. Williamson-Ige, and Leslie J. Young, members of the Interpersonal and Public Communication Program Area of the School of Speech Communication at Bowling Green State University.

Finally, a big thank you to all those associated with the Midwest Basic Course Directors' Conference. It is from such people that I have come to realize the rich pleasure and success that effective communication can offer. These are people who make one proud to be a professional.

Several people have made major contributions to the development and production of this book. Prentice-Hall speech editor Steve Dalphin, and his assistants Debbie Ford and Edie de Coteau, have provided guidance and deadlines. Marjorie Borden, production editor, moved the book through its final stages of development. Gloria Gregor and Mary Lou Wilmarth, production assistants on the author's side, deserve more appreciation than I am capable of showing for their continuing support, numerous contributions, and unfailing faith and affection.

No single person, set of individuals, or setting dominates in the formation of my communication background. This book has grown as a result of my total experience; and when I look back over that experience, I can honestly say that I have grown.

# 1

# Communication in Business

When you look at or think about "business," what do you see? What crosses your mind? Do you see customers buying products? Do you picture stores being supplied with products? Do you envision people sitting in offices tabulating data that record the flow of these products? Do you think about the people who manufacture products? How about those who design them? Does your view include the managers and supervisors who oversee the various business processes? Or, when you look at business, do you think about those executives who control various divisions of the company? Or those who run the whole company? How about the investors in the company? Or the executive board? If you think of any of these aspects, you are indeed thinking about business, because business is not any one of them; it is *all* of them.

Business is a complex web of activities that by its very nature encompasses a wide range and variety of different processes and functions. (See Figure 1–1.) These different processes and functions operate, then, for a common purpose—that of the business as a whole. And to maintain that common purpose and direction between the various elements of any business, *communication* is necessary. *Communication* is the purposeful sharing of information through symbols—words or other types of messages. When other people have in *their* heads the idea I have in *my* head—the idea I

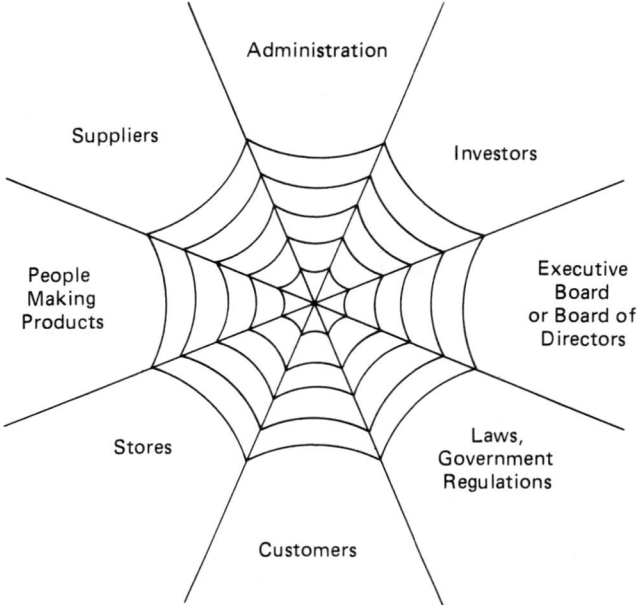

**FIGURE 1–1.** The Web of Business. All aspects of business are related to each other.

communicated to them—I have communicated. Business and communication are inseparable.

This book is about the communication that occurs in business contexts. The basic, underlying thesis is that effective communication skills—writing, speaking, reading, and listening—are absolutely essential to effective business. If you write a letter, compose a report, or orally communicate an idea to another person, you want results: You want to influence things as well as other human beings. You want your efforts to produce appropriate actions. This is not simply a personal, selfish goal. Without effective communication between the various, seemingly different, elements of the whole business, the effectiveness of the entire business can be negatively affected. Without communication there can be no sustained pattern of coordinated or unified action; that is, the business as a whole is less likely to move forward together—as a group of people with similar goals and unified purposes. Communication, then, is the bridge between the elements.

This chapter examines a systems approach to business, indicates how communication contributes to the system, mentions some of the various levels and forms of communication in business, and finally, shows how effective communication in business can pay off.

## A SYSTEMS APPROACH

A *system* is simply an organization of a regularly interacting or interdependent group of parts that together form a unified whole. It is this whole—this goal-oriented group of people—that I will refer to as the business or organization. A change in any part of a business is likely to have an effect on other parts of the whole just like the effect that touching any part of a spider's web is likely to have on other parts of the web. It is important, then, to view business as comprised of related parts.

To use a systems approach as a basis for understanding business communication simply means that one must look at communication not only from the standpoint of its own inherent strength, or even the effectiveness of how a message is communicated to another person, but also how messages affect the entire business.

A marketing specialist may make an important decision while sitting at a desk in an office that appears removed from the nerve center of a business. And yet that decision, as it vibrates one support structure of the business web, is likely to affect advertising, production, distribution, sales, collections, budgeting, as well as consumer relations. A business is a communication network: intricate, complex, and multifaceted.

## COMMUNICATION AND THE SYSTEM

Communication is *the* ingredient that makes business possible. Business functions could not be carried out without it. Managers direct through communication. "Those orders need to be out today." Coordination of areas or units as well as personnel is handled through communication. "Check with inventory to make sure the parts are in." At all levels, administrators staff, plan, and control through communication. No action is taken in an organization without communication leading to it.

It has been estimated that between 40 to 60 percent of the work time in a typical manufacturing plant involves some phase of communication. While it is true that some employees spend more of their time communicating than others, the higher up the organizational structure an employee progresses, the more communicating he or she is likely to engage in. Executives, for example, may spend as much as 75 to 95 percent of their time communicating.

And yet, despite how much people in business communicate, despite the emphasis placed on it in any business structure, and despite the need for effective, accurate, clear communication, most businesses are unhappy with the kind of communication that exists. One writer on communication management expressed the problem this way:

Communication is both the core and the bottleneck of management. It is the cement which holds organizations together, as well as the gap between vital hierarchical elements.[1]

In addition to its contribution to the system as a whole, communication satisfies certain specific functions that have not been directly discussed. Communication often serves one or more of the following functions: (1) planning, (2) organizing, (3) motivating, and (4) controlling. Each will be discussed with the purpose of showing the specific and unique role that communication occupies.

### Planning

*Planning* means determining goals and efficient methods and approaches for reaching those goals. To plan helps assure that actions taken will be orderly—systematic. It helps lay the foundation for orderly communication.

### Organizing

Once goals have been identified and means to reach those goals have been clearly delineated, then *organization* is necessary to build upon that base. Organizing involves the integration of resources: drawing together in some systematic manner the personnel, materials, equipment, and processes with the business's goals.

Imagine for a moment what it would be like if you were responsible for organizing even *one* aspect of a company's operations around a new goal that the company has decided to pursue. Questions you might need to answer before setting out to organize your branch or area might include:

1. What is (should be) the company's role?
2. What is (should be) the company's scope?
3. What have been the company's past goals? How does this one fit in?
4. What are the company's current goals? How does this one apply?
5. What are the company's future goals? How does this one fit in?
6. What are the various structural units of this company? How is each likely to be affected? How is each likely to affect the other?
7. What are the company's operating methods? How are these likely to impinge on the current goal?
8. Who authorizes the pursuit of this goal? Who will take responsibility for following through with the organizing—the implementation?

Such information is necessary. Only when questions like these are properly answered can an organizing process begin. Answers to *all* these questions may not be required; however, they provide an orientation to organizing procedures. The more information you have, the better the outcome is likely to be. It is only when a satisfactory organizing function has been secured, that messages between the various elements or units will contain correct information and be properly routed. The answers to questions like these can only be gained through accurate, precise, and detailed communication.

Just as organizing draws together and unifies resources to implement goals, it also unifies words into sentences, sentences into paragraphs, and paragraphs into messages to better satisfy the communicator's purposes. Organizing one facilitates the organizing of the other. All are part of a systems analysis of business.

### Motivating

Once resources have been unified through organizing, all the ideas and emotions must be transformed into appropriate actions. This is accomplished through *motivation*. It may involve getting employees to see how they will benefit when the company benefits. This may require communication that guides, encourages, and corrects.

Motivating others involves trust and honesty. It involves cooperation and reliability; creativity and productivity. You want employees to apply all their skills and abilities to what has been planned and organized.

Essentially, motivating employees involves positive reinforcement. "The excellent companies," say Thomas J. Peters and Robert H. Waterman, Jr., in their best selling book, *In Search of Excellence*, "seem not only to know the value of positive reinforcement but how to manage it as well."[2]

Peters and Waterman suggest that positive reinforcement be *specific*, incorporating as much information content as possible. It should have *immediacy*, like paying on-the-spot bonuses. It should take account of *achievability;* that is, any positive reinforcement system must reward both the small wins and the large ones. It must include a fair amount of *intangible* feedback in the form of attention from top management, a form of reinforcement that is the most powerful of all. Finally, it must be *unpredictable* and *intermittent;* it loses its impact when it comes to be expected. Small rewards, especially when unexpected, are often more effective than large ones.[3]

In the employees' eyes, it is positive reinforcement that results in high morale. Of a list of ten items that contribute to high morale, including such features as feeling "in" on things, sympathetic understanding of personal problems, job security, good wages, and interesting work, researchers Paul Hersey and Kenneth Blanchard rank "full appreciation for work done" as the number one item.[4]

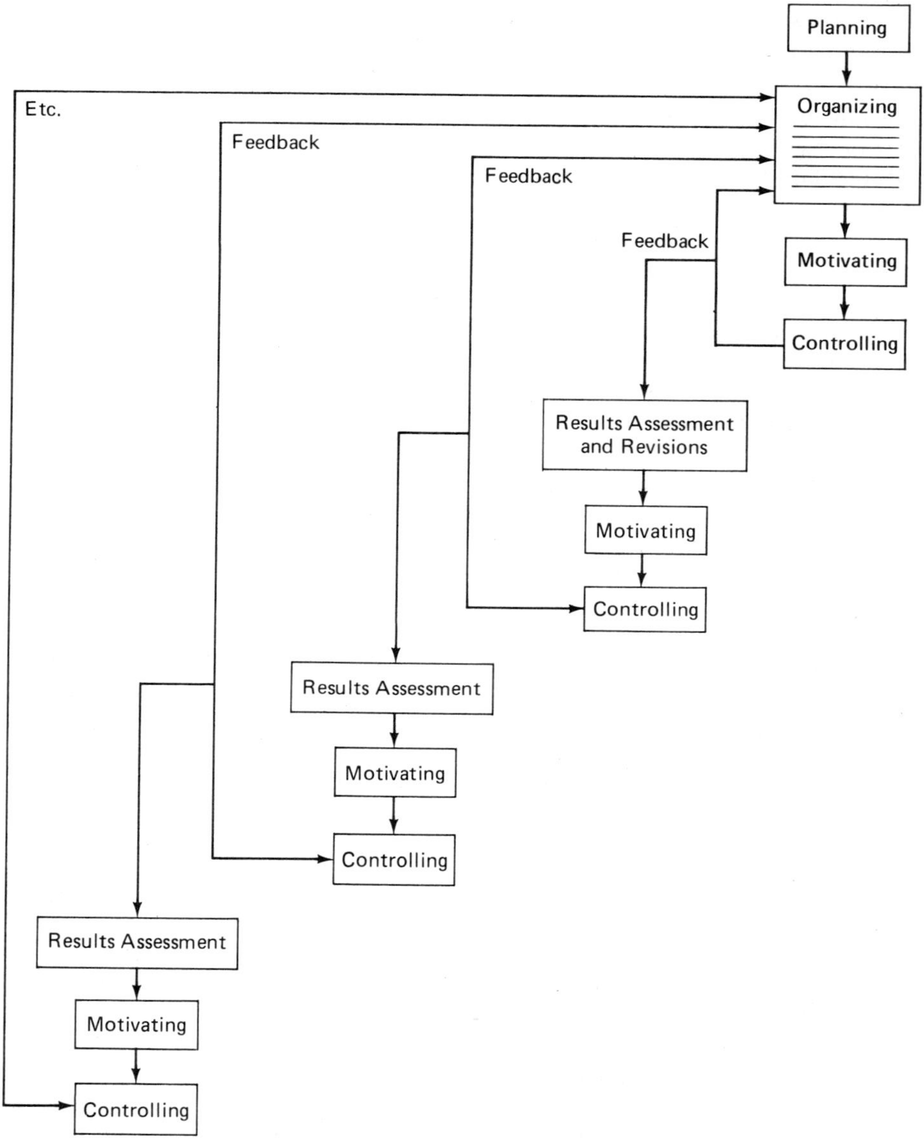

**FIGURE 1–2.** Feedback is used to relate the controlling stage back to the original organizing stage. In each case, a new evaluation occurs with new revisions, which begins a new process of motivating and controlling.

### Controlling

Action involves supervision, for this is one way to remind your associates of the goals that are shared. This may need to be a constant reminder, or, perhaps, a constant matter of clearly explaining how various functions serve to satisfy the central company goal.

*Controlling* involves appraisal. One involved in supervision determines and communicates relative success and failure to the extent company or union policy permits. Performances are often measured against standards set up during the organizing phase. Deviations from company goals may be brought back into line and new goals and standards are then determined.

At all stages as work proceeds, results are assessed. From the feedback one receives—or the reactions one gets to one's communications—one adjusts and revises ongoing communications. Thus, controlling relates employee performance to standards; it is the art of using feedback to influence future human behavior. (See Figure 1–2.)

## LEVELS OF COMMUNICATION

How does communication fit into the organization as a whole? The essential question is: How does communication occur in a business? When planning, organizing, motivating, and controlling is in process, how is communication carried on among the various levels in an organization? To answer this requires a look at downward, upward, horizontal, and diagonal communication.

### Downward Communication

Within any business structure, communication should occur between managers and employees. If the communication flows from managers to employees, this is known as *downward communication*. (See Figure 1–3.)

When top managers in a company decide to cut back production, and thus release 150 employees, they must communicate this decision to those lower in the business hierarchy. Planning has already taken place since the goal—cutting back production—is clear. Middle managers might be responsible for organizing the plan to determine which divisions will be directly affected and what resources will concurrently be reduced or curtailed. They may then convey this information to line managers who may inform the workers who will be laid off. At all points in this example of *downward* communication, different vehicles for conveying the message may be used.

In small companies, much of this information is conveyed via word of mouth. It is simply a matter of people seeing one another and talking

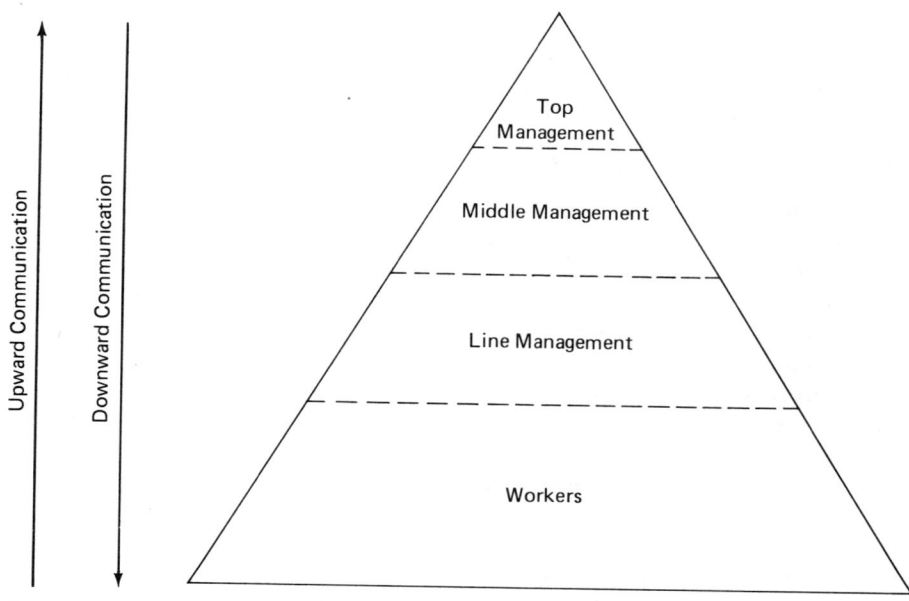

**FIGURE 1–3.** Upward and downward communication is determined by the status or rank that people hold in a business hierarchy. A supervisor has higher rank than do workers; thus, in communicating with them, he or she is engaging in downward communication. When the supervisor communicates with a middle manager—say, a division head—he or she is engaging in upward communication.

directly with them. But as businesses increase in size, other forms of communication are used because: (1) it is sometimes impossible to see everyone concerned in person, (2) oral communication is sometimes a time-consuming process, and (3) the communication must be spelled out very accurately and in some detail. One of the differences between oral and written communication is that the written word allows one to think through exactly how the communication should be worded, and what details should be included. Oral communication is more spontaneous and allows more chance for error.

Downward communication often occurs in written form. There are several reasons for this. The first is that it allows the writer to think through what needs to be said. Another positive aspect of a written communication is that it can become a matter of record. It can be filed and referred to again. A worker who receives a written communication can study it, post it, and refer back to it.

Whether a communication is complex or simple may also determine whether or not it should be written. Complex messages—those with various parts or subpoints—should be written out. Moreover, if there is a significant time delay before implementing the message, it should also be written out.

A strong case can be made for oral communication reinforced in writing. The oral communication process adds a dimension of humanness—warmth, sincerity, and concern—which can serve as a strong motivating force for the understanding, acceptance, and implementation of a written communication.

Several possibilities exist for the use of written communications within business. These include interoffice memos, bulletin boards, company publications, letters, video programs, and public address systems. All these forms facilitate downward communication.

*Memos*—interoffice memoranda—are a business's most often used form of written communication. They are like letters except they are usually briefer and exclude the formality of letters. No "Dear Mr. Smith" or "Sincerely, Bill Jones" is included. (See Figure 1–4.) The "Re" in a memorandum is the accepted form of writing "with regard to."

When a vice-president wants to inform a division manager to cut back productivity, he or she does not write the division manager a letter; that individual sends a memo through the company's mail system.

Memos are used to correspond with employees in different departments and divisions, or for managers to communicate with others in the company hierarchy. They are usually not used to communicate with people outside the company.

**FIGURE 1–4.** This memo is designed simply to make Mr. Smith aware of a problem. With more alertness or particular sensitivity, perhaps, fewer workers are likely to be injured.

```
                        M E M O R A N D U M

                                                    March 23, 1984

    TO:  Mr. Smith
    FR:  Bill Jones
    RE:  Worker Safety

        It has come to my attention that there have been several
    instances of employees in your division being injured.  Please
    keep an eye on various safety precautions in your area, and
    report any infringements directly to me.
```

*Bulletin-board messages* can be used when an announcement is to be made to all employees of a company. Memos may be too expensive because of the large numbers of employees or the time it takes to prepare the memo. The placement of the bulletin board, then, becomes important as does the amount of information on it.

If a bulletin board is placed near areas where employees find themselves waiting—near elevators, food and coffee lines, or drinking fountains—it is more likely to be seen. Since a cluttered board may cause any one message on it to appear insignificant or to be overlooked, it should be kept clear of old or irrelevant messages. If it is protected by lock and key, then when an important announcement appears it is likely to be seen as important, timely, and official—major concerns when dealing with bulletin-board announcements.

*Company publications* are another form of downward communication. *Newsletters* and *magazines* can be used to keep middle managers, line managers, and employees aware of information, activities, and events that bear on company operations.

In medium or large-sized companies, newsletters serve as an important link between top management and middle or lower managers. Such newsletters should be sent regularly, should be factual and concise, and should encourage feedback.

Magazines, on the other hand, should be directed at a larger market: employees. They usually include information that is of interest to employees such as promotions, replacements, retirements, marriages, deaths, and transfers. Other items that might be included would be recreational activities, local events, and worker profiles. But magazines must also come to grips with major issues if they are to be effective. These include:

1. What key issues are confronting the company?
2. Is the company profitable? How profitable?
3. Did the company win any important contracts?
4. How successful is the recent advertising campaign?
5. How successful is a recent product offering?
6. How well is the company competing in the marketplace?
7. What are the current issues involved in salary negotiations?
8. What is being done regarding current working conditions?
9. What are the workers' complaints? What is being done about them?

These are the kind of topics workers are interested in. They do not want or need to be told over and over what a nice, happy family the company is, nor be fed insipid company propaganda that serves little more than filler and is perceived as pablum.

*Letters* sent directly to an employee's home can also have significant impact. Since an employee's spouse has a vital interest in the well-being of his or her partner, the spouse can have a major impact on the employee's attitude. To send a letter to an employee's home is likely to get an issue discussed in that environment and to give it important visibility.

*Video programs* have been set up by a variety of firms (Bell Telephone, John Hancock, Travelers Insurance, to name a few), for the purpose of providing employees with both sides of a story—the one they read, hear, or see via the commercial media, and the one the company endorses. A video program, too, can keep workers informed of current events that affect the company and product development that is in progress. It can also be used to inform workers of current campaigns whether they be community or consumer related.

*Public-address systems,* usually used for paging employees or for emergency announcements, can also be used to keep workers informed of timely events and current negotiations or developments. By keeping employees informed, the possibility of negative or irrelevant information being circulated is lessened.

To summarize this section, research has identified five types of downward communication that are carried out by any one of the above means:

1. Job instructions—how to do specific tasks
2. Job rationale—how tasks relate to other organizational tasks
3. Procedures and practices—messages that convey company policies, rules, regulations, or benefits
4. Feedback—messages that appraise how well individuals are performing their jobs
5. Indoctrination of goals—messages designed to motivate employees by indicating the overall goal of the company and how they relate to that goal[5]

### Upward Communication

*Upward communication* is often necessary to keep business executives aware of what is happening at all levels of their company. Although discouraged in some companies, upward communication can be a form of *feedback* that business executives use to assess employee reactions to their downward communication. In addition to providing feedback, upward communication also indicates the receptivity of the environment for downward communication, facilitates acceptance of decisions by encouraging subordinate participation in the decision-making process, and encourages the submission of valuable ideas.[6]

Many Japanese companies deal with upward and downward communication by relying to a great extent upon an *egalitarian* distribution of power.[7] They truly believe in human equality with respect to social, political, and economic rights and privileges, and they accomplish this through the creation of workers' councils, systems of employee influence, and distributed centers of power.[8] Everyone in the organization participates in an egalitarian setting. William Ouchi speaks of this process in this way:

> This participative process is one of the mechanisms that provides for the broad dissemination of information and of values within the organization. . . .[9]

Even though decision making and information dissemination in many Japanese firms may be a collective, participatory function, it should be clear that the ultimate responsibility for decision resides in one individual. "It is doubtful," adds Ouchi, "that Westerners could ever tolerate the collective form of responsibility that characterizes Japanese organizations."[10]

Although downward communication is easy to initiate and control, this is *not* true in upward communication. American workers are often reluctant to express their views to superiors. Thus, channels for upward communication must be opened and maintained.

*Memos,* once again, are an effective form of upward communication. A line manager may inform a middle manager of exactly how many employees in the division would be cut. A warehouse manager may inform a traffic manager about how much stock will have to be stored or returned. A vice-president in charge of employee relations might receive the names of those who must be informed.

*Reports,* however, are the most often used form of upward communication. A report is a formal account or statement. It usually results from an investigation and sometimes includes conclusions and recommendations. Reports flow upward from all segments of a business:

| | |
|---|---|
| sales reports | shipping reports |
| production reports | wage-and-salary reports |
| quality-control reports | insurance reports |
| inventory reports | financial reports |

As a report moves upward in a business, it is gradually condensed. At lower levels, details make a big difference and must be included. At higher levels, it is impossible—because of time—to wade through all the details. That is why top managers generally deal with *exception reports*—reports that treat aspects of the business that are exceptions to normal business operating procedures. If sales are down on one product—below previously established norms—they want to know why.

*Grievance systems* within companies also facilitate upward communication. Employees need some way of communicating their complaints to upper-level managers. And upper-level managers must be aware of and sensitive to such complaints. Often, such complaints can be resolved before they become major disputes.

In unionized companies, complaints usually go to supervisors. If complaints cannot be resolved at that level, or if the supervisor is part of the problem, they traditionally go to a union representative. The union steward talks with the personnel department, and if the problem still cannot be resolved, an arbitrator is called in whose decision is binding on both management and employees.

*Suggestion systems* have been set up by many companies designed to open the channels for upward communication. These systems enable employees to communicate their thoughts directly to top management. When many layers of management exist, employees are reluctant to make suggestions for fear that someone at a higher level will not only steal but take credit for his or her idea.

Successful suggestion systems require prompt attention to all suggestions by top management, who must explain not only why certain suggestions cannot be used but also find ways to reward beneficial ideas. One means of reward would be through the newsletters, magazines, or bulletin-board announcements. Another coordinate method might be financial reward. A third, and effective method, might be a simple pat on the back—witnessed, of course, by the employee's peers.

*Attitude surveys* are another method of getting at information that should—but may not—travel upward. Attitude surveys are designed to evoke employee feelings:

1. How do you feel about working conditions?
2. How do you feel about company policies and procedures?
3. How do you feel about the company in general?
4. How do you feel about the morale of your co-workers?

When the personnel department administers such surveys, it is important that employees are not specifically identified. Results are unlikely to be honest if employees fear reprisals, and candid answers to questions are necessary if conclusions are to be reached regarding the answers to the survey.

*Exit interviews* can get at the same information as attitude surveys, but in a different manner. Members of the personnel department conduct interviews at the time employees are ready to leave a company—to get *their* side of the story.

What kinds of things can be determined? Much the same as from attitude surveys. Are other companies offering higher salaries? Is a particular manager causing problems? Are employees feeling threatened, depressed, or unmotivated?

Sometimes this information cannot be acquired in exit interviews. That is, employees may not want to be honest for fear of jeopardizing a

14   *Communication in Business*

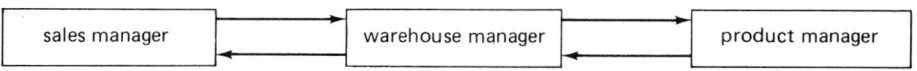

**FIGURE 1–5.** An example of horizontal communication.

positive reference for their next job. It may be prudent to send employees who have left a *questionnaire* that gets at the same information. If such a questionnaire is received after employees are already secure in their new position, they might be more willing to state their feelings about the company as well as their precise reasons for leaving.

Of course, there are weaknesses in using questionnaires. Questions may be asked that cannot be answered without a detailed explanation. The questionnaire may be filled in hurriedly rather than thoughtfully, and may not be a true index of behavior. Finally, a large part of the sample may fail to respond.

Upward communication should include information about what subordinates are doing, what problems are still unsolved, what suggestions have been made for improvement, and how subordinates think and feel about their jobs, associates, and the company.[11] Such information is indispensable for effective planning, decision making, and motivation.

### Horizontal Communication

*Horizontal communication* involves communication that exists between employees who are on the same organizational level as each other, but not necessarily in the same department or area. (See Figure 1–5.)

If a sales manager wants immediate information regarding inventory of a particular product, he or she might pick up the telephone and talk directly with the warehouse manager. If the warehouse manager had a low inventory of that product but thought it could be secured soon, the manager might call the product manager to find out when new supplies would be arriving. All this could represent horizontal communication.

Research has identified several reasons for communicating horizontally. People communicate horizontally in order to

1. *Coordinate tasks.* How are employees contributing to the system's goals?
2. *Solve problems.* How are employees meeting the current set of guidelines?
3. *Share information.* How might your employees make use of this new data? (in a discussion between department heads)
4. *Resolve conflicts.* Are there some ways we can resolve the conflicts that seem to be occurring?[12]

### Diagonal Communication

*Diagonal communication* would be represented when an employee in one division goes to the manager of another division of an equal level. For example, instead of the sales manager going to the warehouse manager, a

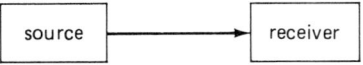

**FIGURE 1-6.** One-way communication.

sales representative went instead. This would represent diagonal communication. The same reasons cited for communicating horizontally would also be reasons for communicating diagonally.

In some businesses, horizontal and diagonal communication is discouraged because administrators insist that all communications must "go through regular channels." But experience shows that allowance for horizontal and diagonal communication increases efficiency. As levels of management become more involved, efficiency declines as does the actual speed at which information is passed and processed and at which decisions are made.

## OTHER FORMS OF COMMUNICATION

Most of the forms of communication discussed under the heading "Levels of Communication"—memos, reports, publications, letters, and so forth—are examples of one-way communication. (See Figure 1-6.)

*Feedback* in one-way communication situations, if it occurs, is usually delayed. Several days can pass before a reply or reaction is forthcoming. When you are face-to-face with the receiver of your intended message, however, feedback is instantaneous. Moreover, not only are you the source, but also the other person becomes the source immediately when he or she begins to speak; thus, source and receiver become interchangeable as the speaker–listener roles are reversed. (See Figure 1-7.)

Businesses are structured to encourage such *two-way* communication. Not only are telephones usually accessible to everyone, but committee meetings are scheduled, employees are counseled, social events are

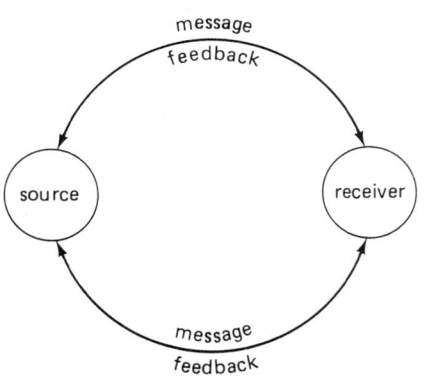

**FIGURE 1-7.** In this diagram, note the interchangeability of source and receiver as represented by the double "message–feedback" arrows.

planned, and managers make themselves available to all employees. Computers, too, facilitate two-way communication; source and receiver are brought closer together. The flow of information is faster as the *information float*—"the amount of time information spends in the communication channel" (between source and receiver) is collapsed.[13]

### Telephone

A telephone has the advantages of speed, efficiency, and relatively low cost. There are close to 40 million business telephones in the United States today, and the total number of calls (both business and personal) exceeds 640 million each day—an average of three calls for every man, woman, and child in the United States.[14]

When you telephone other people, you should value their time. But you must be concise without being curt. Plan ahead when using the telephone, keeping in mind these points:

1. What is the purpose of the call?
2. What information do you want to get or give?
3. Is this likely to be a good time to call?
4. What are the key questions to which you need answers?
5. Be sure to identify yourself immediately.

### Business Meetings

Most businesses have numerous committees that operate most of the time. From executive committees all the way down to worker–grievance committees, they are often a permanent part of the organization. And when a new idea or proposal needs to be investigated, often a new committee may be quickly formed, only to be disbanded when its work is completed.

Although committee meetings are time-consuming, they provide opportunities for effective communication. Questions and answers are exchanged, points are clarified, and participants have the opportunity to assess each others' verbal and nonverbal behavior—one weakness of the telephone, where only verbal behavior is revealed. Face-to-face communication is usually more effective because of the additional cues—especially the nonverbal ones—available to us.

### Employee Counseling

An important part of communication as it relates to the business system is the "controlling" stage. Employee counseling is a means to ensure that the "controlling" function is formally served. This involves periodic consultation between employees and their immediate superiors. Sales managers have periodic consultation with the sales staff. Personnel directors might call in departmental employees to discuss their progress on certain recently assigned projects—or, perhaps, to discuss their work in general. Employee counseling is generally confined to work-related subjects, unless, of course, employees have personal problems that negatively affect their productivity. In contrast, many Japanese firms develop holistic relationships with employees. They involve themselves more in the private lives of employees by sponsoring bowling leagues, picnics, and other family outings.[15]

### Social Events

Although some may view regularly scheduled social events as frivolous and unnecessary, activities such as company picnics, golf tournaments, and holiday parties help keep employee morale high.

In addition, social events encourage upward and downward communication among employees at all levels. Events that are well planned and controlled facilitate healthy communication. In such social climates, employees who would normally hesitate to approach a company official—and vice versa—are likely to do so more easily and comfortably.

### Managerial Visibility

The best way for managers to reveal openness and receptivity to employee ideas is for the managers and other company executives to mingle with employees. This makes it easy for employees to relate to the officials. It is also easy to converse with a manager or executive who has stopped by your work place to chat.

Those executives who profess an open-door policy probably see very few people. Not only is it sometimes difficult to get up the nerve to actually go in to see them, but it is also the fact that you are interrupting—imposing—on that person's time. Other reasons why employees fail to go see a company official—despite an often expressed open-door policy—are:

1. Lack of confidence
2. Believing the problem or concern is too minor to trouble that person with
3. Believing the other person is too busy
4. Not being sure how to express one's thoughts
5. Thinking how it will look in other people's eyes
6. Being embarrassed by the conspicuous nature of the whole thing

### Electronic Communication

Mailing a letter to someone may take several days; a report may take the same length of time; even a memorandum may take several hours to get from one desk to another. If you send any of these electronically it may take a couple of *seconds*. The amount of time it takes is called *information float*. If your response takes an hour rather than a week, we have accelerated the speed of life and commerce by reducing the information float.[16]

By shortening the time it takes to do business, however, we risk several problems:

1. First, we may need to check to ascertain that the message is, indeed, valid. (It was sent by the person to whom, you have attributed it, and it is accurate, as sent.)
   a. Electronic messages can be tampered with; thus, source and accuracy are important criteria to check.
   b. A check may determine that a message was sent off in haste—without thought, proper verification, or adequate substantiation. Electronic message transfer is instantaneous!

2. We may jump to conclusions—generalizing based on weak evidence. Our tendency may be to respond too quickly.
   a. We may need to qualify our answers with "maybe," "sometimes," or "perhaps"—being tentative—rather than coming on too strong. Being tentative allows us to cover ourselves so that we have something to fall back on if our response is proven wrong or, perhaps, is an overreaction.
   b. We need to be patient. We must give ourselves a chance to study situations in order to make thoughtful, considered responses.

3. We may hide behind our electronic response; that is, we may hide our true feelings about the message.
   a. Computers may allow us to transfer our words without the feelings attached to them.
   b. We may use this type of response to avoid openness—direct contact or even confrontation with others.

4. We may risk making a decision without knowing how others *really* feel. They, too, may be hiding behind their computers. Knowing how they feel may cause us to respond differently.
   a. We may need to seek out the source of electronic messages, face them, and talk directly with them. This would give us far more clues to their real feelings on issues.
   b. We may need to ask the sources of such messages how others may be affected by the message or the possible outcomes that may result from the information. Ramifications could, for example, vibrate the whole organizational web. Sitting at your own computer console can make you feel isolated from the central, decision-making core of an organization; thus, you may feel as if a few random (but choice!) pecks at a keyboard will make little difference; and yet find out those pecks become ripples—then waves—then maybe tidal waves in their effect.

### Rumors

As another form of communication, the company *grapevine* must be mentioned. If one were to track the movement of *rumors* through any business, one would often find a specific and elaborate network of communication channels that are both well established and well known. Bill in personnel learns from an executive secretary during coffee break that all employees are to receive a Christmas bonus. Bill passes this information to members of his grapevine, two members of the personnel department and one member of security. Sam, the fellow in security, communicates the good news to members of his grapevine—two other people in security and three at the warehouse. And each of these people pass the information to others.

Before the announcement is posted on the cafeteria bulletin board, practically everyone is aware of it. Company grapevines operate on rumors, but because of the potential for error, one must be cautious of depending on rumors for evaluations or decisions. Since rumors are passed orally, they reflect all the weaknesses of oral communication outlined earlier.

### External Communications

All the forms and levels of communication previously discussed take place within the business organization. But businesses communicate with individuals and groups outside (external to) the business as well. It is as if the business were the hub of the wheel, the various forms of communication the spokes, and individuals and groups parts of the rim. (See Figure 1–8.)

Numerous forms of communication make up the spokes of the wheel: letters, telegrams, quarterly and annual reports, bills, payments, and news releases. The form is dependent on the number of people with whom you wish to communicate and the nature of the message to be conveyed. Advertising would be another facet of external communication.

## EFFECTIVE COMMUNICATION—THE PAYOFF

What difference does it make? I can talk about the system, the various levels within the system, and the forms that communication takes—but so what? Why does it make a difference?

There are, of course, a number of reasons for concern and a number of different areas in which payoffs can be realized.[17]

### Employees

Today, employees want to be fully informed about company policies and programs. They want to participate more in the determination of policies and issues that affect them. New lines of communication must be established to maintain this information flow between managers and their employees. As attitudes and needs of employees change, communication

**FIGURE 1-8.**

channels must be available so that the changes can be both expressed and accommodated.

### Growth

Problems in communication increase as the size of an organization increases. With expansions, mergers, consolidations, amalgamations, and multinational developments, no longer can a manager of a factory call all his or her employees together for a meeting. Top executives today have little or no contact with the vast numbers of employees working in a business.

To maintain commonness of purpose and orderly behavior, effective communication is necessary. As business expands internationally and multinationally, language and culture barriers offer additional obstacles that must be overcome.

### Complexity

Businesses are no longer faced solely with internal problems. The different types of situations that must be faced are varied and they include:

Increasingly complex and expensive technology
International competition
Problems of environment and pollution
Effects of government regulations
Effects of foreign government policies and regulations

As business becomes more demanding, the need for coordination becomes more critical. And it is through effective communication that successful synchronization occurs. It is like leading an orchestra; to get the members to play the same song, they need the same music. Communication is the music.

As businesses grow more complex, employees become little more than cogs in giant machines. Morale declines. Managers and supervisors have the additional burden of seeing to it that employees are challenged and are able to find an identity within such enterprises.

### Information Explosion

Rapid improvements in data processing have resulted in an increased amount of available data. As a result, business communication systems must accommodate the explosion. Not only must the data be retrieved, but it must also be quickly and efficiently distributed to those who need it.

### Increased Competition

Accurate and rapid communication is necessary, too, if business is to compete successfully on a widespread, international scale. Competitive pressures are by no means limited to the domestic market. These pressures must result in greater efficiency in both manufacturing and marketing. Effective communication must be the means for business to receive necessary information, process it, and respond to it. Haphazard and delayed communications can create shock waves from which businesses may not be able to recover.

### Improvement in Quality

No longer can business operate as if removed from the population it serves. More and more it has become an integral part of that society as business critics have become incessantly more vociferous. Communication provides the way for businesses to explain what they are doing to guard the safety of consumers, conserve resources, and eliminate social problems. Without such communication they risk censure, litigation, and regulation.

**Regulation**

With the increased regulation of business has come an increased need for communication to relate enormous amounts of raw data, to convey detailed reports, to substantiate advertising claims, and to verify tests and results. Communication, too, must be used to show what has been done, is being done, and what is being planned for the future. The result of successful communication here is likely to be businesses that are more responsible to the needs and desires of society and businesses that are allowed to practice self-regulation and self-discipline.

*SUMMARY*

In this chapter we have looked at a systems approach to communication. To examine a system means that one must look at all the regularly interacting or interdependent parts as a unified whole. The purpose of looking at it as a system is to understand that change in any part is likely to have an effect on other parts.

When you relate communication to the system, you realize it is that ingredient that allows coordination of the various parts. Communication serves four functions within the system: (1) planning, (2) organizing, (3) motivating, and (4) controlling.

In any business, levels exist between top management and the worker or employee at the bottom of the ladder. No matter how many levels exist, when communication occurs from management to employee it is called "downward" communication; from employee to management it is called "upward." If the communication moves between people of the same level it is called "horizontal," and if between an employee of one level to a manager at the same level, but in a different division, it is "diagonal."

Within the context of "levels of communication," different forms of communication are used to maintain contact and convey information. Some that were discussed include: memos, bulletin-board messages, company publications such as newsletters and magazines, letters, video programs, public-address systems, reports, grievance systems, suggestion systems, attitude surveys, and exit interviews.

Other forms of business communication that were mentioned include the telephone, business meetings, employee counseling, social events, managerial visibility and electronic communication. In each of these, the value of two-way, face-to-face interaction was stressed. Rumors and external communications were mentioned as other forms that are important to regular business functioning.

Finally, it was demonstrated how effective communication in business can pay off. If communication is, indeed, effective, it is likely to have a significant effect on employees, on company growth, complexity, improvement in quality and, too, on the communication of regulations.

The purpose of Chapter 1 has been to provide the systems framework into which other chapters and units of this book can be placed. To study business—any business—is a complex process. To study communication is also complex. When one superimposes one upon the other, the results reveal even greater complexity and, thus, complications. It is the purpose of this book to try to simplify and explain these complexities and complications.

## NOTES

[1] Frank R. Hunsicker, "How to Approach Communication Difficulties," *Personnel Journal, 51* (1972), 680.

[2] Abridged and adapted from pp. 70–71 in *In Search of Excellence: Lessons from America's Best-Run Companies,* by Thomas J. Peters and Robert H. Waterman, Jr. Copyright © 1982 by Thomas J. Peters and Robert H. Waterman, Jr. By permission of Harper & Row, Publishers, Inc.

[3] *Ibid.,* pp. 70–71.

[4] Paul Hersey and Kenneth H. Blanchard, *Management of Organizational Behavior: Utilizing Human Resources,* 4th ed. (Englewood Cliffs, N.J.: Prentice-Hall, 1982), p. 47

[5] See Gerald M. Goldhaber, *Organizational Communication* (Dubuque, Iowa: Wm. C. Brown, 1974), pp. 114–15. Goldhaber cites Daniel Katz and Robert Kahn, *The Social Psychology of Organizations* (New York: John Wiley, 1966).

[6] Earl Planty and William Machaver, "Upward Communications: A Project in Executive Development," *Personnel, 28* (1952), 304–18.

[7] William G. Ouchi, *Theory Z: How American Business Can Meet the Japanese Challenge* (Reading, Mass.: Addison-Wesley, 1981), p. 114.

[8] *Ibid.,* pp. 114–15.

[9] *Ibid.,* p. 78.

[10] Ibid., pp. 78–79.

[11] Planty and Machaver, pp. 304–18.

[12] See R. L. Simpson, "Vertical and Horizontal Communication in Formal Organizations," *Administrative Science Quarterly, 4* (1959), 188–96; J. L. Massie, "Automatic Horizontal Communication in Management," *Academy of Management Journal, 3* (1960), 87–91; and Eugene Walton, "Communicating Down the Line: How They Really Get the Word," *Personnel, 36* (1959), 78–82.

[13] John Naisbitt, *Megatrends: Ten New Directions Transforming Our Lives* (New York: Warner Books, 1984), p. 15.

[14] Facts and figures provided by the Public Relations Department, American Telephone and Telegraph Company, 1975.

[15] Ouchi, *Theory Z,* pp. 127–28.

[16] Naisbitt, p. 15.

[17] See S. Bernard Rosenblatt, T. Richard Cheatham, and James T. Watt, *Communication in Business* (Englewood Cliffs, N.J.: Prentice-Hall, 1977), pp. 15–17.

# 2

# Communication Process and Principles

You may be thinking—after reading Chapter 1—that there is no question that communication and business *are* related, but "What does that have to do with me?" After all, you have been communicating all your life, and it is unlikely that one course or one textbook is going to make much difference. If that is your attitude, you may be correct. If people do not want to grow, develop, and change, it is unlikely that a course or a book will make much difference.

You may think, too, that if you were specifically told what to do to improve your communication, that you would improve it. ("Give me the rules and gimmicks I need to influence others, and I'll be on my way.") The problem here is that communication is a human behavior, and, as such, it is quite complex. And as it is placed into human situations—such as business—the complexity is increased. So many factors influence the success or failure of any communication situation that it is better to discuss broad principles and theories than specific instances and examples. Often, it turns out, specific instances and examples are exceptions to the rule! It is more likely you will experience success—no matter what situation you are in—if you understand the overall process and the broad principles that apply to most situations. Good practice—no matter the area of concern—is built on sound theory.

The process of communication and some of the basic principles are discussed in this chapter. I will begin by providing an overview of the entire process, then develop several different perspectives, theories, and points of view that bear directly on the communication process. First, I want to discuss some of the basic axioms of communication—propositions that are regarded as fundamental truths in the field of communication. Second, I want to offer Abraham Maslow's "need hierarchy" as a basis for understanding some aspects of human motivation. Third, I will mention Douglas McGregor's theories as further insight into motivation. Fourth, I will look at the self—the intrapersonal process—as it bears on communication. Finally, as the last perspective that bears on the communication process, I want to present the social context itself and the influence it may have.

I will close this chapter on the communication process by discussing several aspects of interpersonal communication: self-disclosure, feedback, listening, the clarity of expression, coping with angry feelings, and metacommunication. The purpose is to establish a base that can be referred back to and elaborated upon throughout the book.

Please realize as we examine the communication process that what is being said applies to both oral *and* written communication, not one or the other. Although I will be focusing more (in this chapter) on two-way communication, when you shuttle a memo or a letter off to another person in what appears to be a single (one-way) line of direction, it is likely that a great deal of two-way communication occurred (as you will discover) in the composition of that memo or letter.

## THE COMMUNICATION PROCESS: AN OVERVIEW

Normally when we think of "communicating" with other people, we think of either talking to them or sending them a memo. And, as shown in Chapter 1, much of a business person's day is spent doing just that. Studies indicate that, depending upon one's position within a company, the actual time spent communicating with other people, either orally or in writing, ranges from 50 percent to 95 percent of one's working day.

But it is unlikely that we give the actual act of communicating much more thought than that, unless, of course if breaks down, and we find ourselves remarking:

> "I wonder why that job isn't getting done—I asked Jim to do it two days ago."
> "Those letters are still going out on our old letterhead; I thought everyone was to be using the new one."
> "Leonard is still wearing those gaudy ties! It's difficult to listen to him when you are trying to figure out the symbols on his silly ties."

## Creating Meaning

The essential point is that meaning does not exist in words or acts. *Meaning* is that which is intended to be—or is—conveyed, signified, or understood by acts or language. Meaning exists in one's mind. When there is something I want to say to another person, I have a meaning in my head (intended meaning). I use words that represent (denote or signify) my meaning to try to evoke or create (convey) the same meaning in the other person's head (understanding of my meaning). The meaning is not transferred—it is created anew in the other person's mind as a result of word stimulation: my words designed to evoke a meaning similar to mine.

Understanding this principle will help you understand much of the material in this book. It also underscores the idea that no two people are alike. That is, it is an absolute impossibility to cause someone else to create the same exact meaning you have. When people wonder why communication is so complex, this is the place to begin in explaining its complexity: People don't think alike; people don't feel alike; and people don't act alike.

Thus, we have the first important insight into communication. It involves creating meaning.

## Transferring Information

The purpose of communicating is to pass along information. This is accomplished through the use of symbols. A *symbol* is simply something that stands for or suggests something else. Words are one form of symbols. In using a word or group of words, I am trying to represent the meanings *I* have for that word or group of words. If I want you "to complete the project" and I convey those words to you, I have an idea of the symbolic value of those words:

> "complete" means brought to a final end or *fully* carried out
> "project" means the *major* project we have been working on for the past six months.

It is my hope that when I say "I want you to complete the project," you have the same symbolic values for the words, and the information is properly transferred—with accuracy.

Nonverbal cues are also symbols. For example, if you perceive from my tone of voice (a nonverbal cue), my lack of forcefulness, and my body posture and position (rather slouched and unassertive), that I did not really mean what I said, the project might not be completed. If, instead, you perceive a strong command, delivered directly and forcefully with an alert body position, you might perceive its importance and move at once to complete the project.

The second insight in communication, then, involves the use of communication to transfer information. The "insight" occurs when we realize that this transfer results from the use of symbols that may be verbal *or* nonverbal.

### Involving Stimuli

It would make the communication process much simpler and less complicated if it did not potentially involve thousands of stimuli. There exists no catalogue of all the potential stimuli, and even if one did exist, it would be incomplete. Potential stimuli that might be involved in any act of communication cannot be listed; they cannot be defined for us. *We* are the only ones who can determine which are the important stimuli and which are not. I am watching two people communicate. When they are finished I say to one of them:

"Did you notice that look? That's the same look Dan always gets when he has no intention of doing what you ask him."

The other person might reply,

"No, I didn't notice any special look. I just thought he was kind of getting tired of being reminded."

A "look," a smile, a wink, or a frown—each becomes a stimulus—a message—when a person assigns meaning to it. Literally anything can become a stimulus.

The final insight offered here is that communication involves thousands of potential stimuli. Considering our varied backgrounds and experiences and the various contexts in which we encounter both words and nonverbal cues, namely symbols, it is amazing that we are able to communicate at all!

## COMMUNICATION AS TRANSACTION

An understanding of the *transactional* nature of communication builds on the insights offered above. To understand the process of communication, we must understand that it is transactional, that meanings are in people's minds, and that as we communicate with another person, our minds are at work creating meanings drawing upon some of those thousands of potential stimuli. These meanings may have to do with what is being said, but they may also have very little to do with what is being said as well!

To try to understand "communication as transaction," role-play a situation (mentally) with me right now: Pretend that you and I are communicating with each other. Let's illustrate our communication with each other in this way. (See Figure 2–1.) We are face to face. Notice that I have drawn a line around us. This line represents our specific event. Remember that how each of us perceives this specific event will be different. But what aspects of the event we choose to include in the total perception of the event directly results from our active participation or involvement in it. That is, we think about and respond to things that we see as pertinent and exclude from our thinking things that are not pertinent. What we choose to include will be those selections we make from the thousands of potential stimuli that could be included.

Not only do we form an impression of the event, but we also form an impression of the other person. I choose from the infinite number of cues you give; from those, I construct an image in my mind of who you are. You realize, of course, that I do not know you, and I will never know you. Even if we become friends, I still do not really know you—although the image I have of you will be altered as I gain more information.

Thus, it should be clear that we do not really communicate with another person at all; what we communicate with is our image—the one we have constructed—of that other person. That is why other people's impressions of us are so important; those "impressions" they have of us are, essentially, their "us," and that is what they use when they communicate with "us."

Let me now add a couple of more dimensions to our model of communication. (See Figure 2–2.)

First, the arrows represent the message-feedback, give-and-take discussed in Chapter 1. They also illustrate that either you *or* I could be a source or a receiver at any time.

Second, and more important for our current discussion, the shaded, overlapping area between us represents our shared meaning. This area involves our vocabulary, perhaps our culture and values, maybe our similar upbringing. But the larger our shaded area, the more we share (or have in

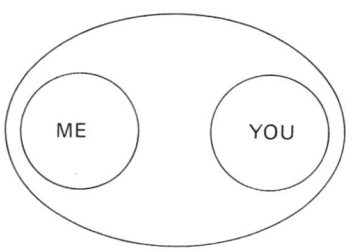

**FIGURE 2–1.** Communication as transaction—a beginning illustration.

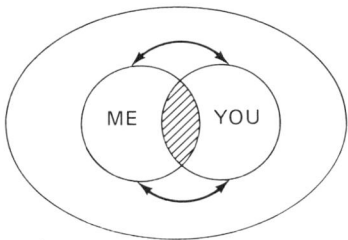

**FIGURE 2-2.** Communication as transaction.

common), and the more likely it will be that we will be able to understand each other when we communicate. No guarantees—just greater possibilities!

What are the implications of a transactional view of communication? There are several, and all are important if we want to be successful communicators.

1. Communication is *not* an act—not something that someone does *to* someone else. It is *not* an interaction either, where one person acts, then the other person acts, and so on.
2. Communication involves integration: the drawing together of what we think, imagine, and feel. Just as the concrete situation becomes part of the message, so does the other person. Thus, integration implies relationship.
3. Communication depends on what we create from the myriad of symbols that we process and respond to. We each do our own "sense making." We make claims about what we think exists or doesn't exist, what might or could exist, or even should exist. We set up for ourselves what we think we see, hear, touch, taste, and smell.
4. When we string words together into what seems to us to be a meaningful, logical order, or when we try to make sense of a situation, *our* meaning, logic, or sense is only one way of looking at the situation. It may not (indeed, often, need not or does not) have any relationship to other views of the "identical" situation.

## AXIOMS OF COMMUNICATION

As a direct and natural outgrowth of a transactional view of communication, certain axioms of communication become clear. Like the indisputable laws of nature, these principles and axioms are basic and fundamental. They not only reinforce the transactional perspective but, they also support it as the most reasonable viewpoint.[1]

### Not Communicating Is Impossible

There is no such thing as noncommunication. When a manager receives a report, reads the first paragraph and begins shaking his or her head, despite the fact that the manager does not shake it for anyone's benefit but one's own, the manager *is* communicating. If that communicating is unintentionally perceived by others, the person *has* communicated.

So much of communication occurs without intention, without a word being uttered. The contribution of nonverbal cues to any communication situation cannot be emphasized enough; they *are* important.

### Communication Conveys Information and Defines Relationships

At the same time you are transferring information (content) via a memo, you are also defining (or reflecting) a relationship. A supervisor sends a memo to a subordinate that says, "We are falling behind schedule. Please exert all possible efforts to meet deadlines." The information, or content level, seems to be clear. In this instance the nature and tone of the message—its directness and force—also clearly define the relationship of the supervisor to the subordinate. It leaves little doubt as to his or her position or role in the company's organizational hierarchy.

Messages say or imply, "This is how I see you," as well as saying, "This is how I see myself," and "This is how I see our relationship." How the relationship is defined may affect how a message is received: "Well that S.O.B.—he has no right talking to me like that!" Such a comment is a reflection on how someone else, perhaps, incorrectly, perceived a relationship. It may also affect the amount, kind, and rapidity of the action taken.

### Communication Is Punctuated into Sequences

This occurs both orally and in writing. In written communication we use commas, periods, and exclamation marks. In oral communication we use pauses, head nods, and other nonverbal cues. But the purpose is the same: Initiative, dominance, and dependency are revealed by the way language is punctuated. A memo that states: "See me at once!" makes this clear, just as *how* one handles an oral disagreement over an excessive telephone bill might also clarify the use of verbal punctuation.

### Communication Involves Verbal and Nonverbal Communication

Although this has been repeated several times, its importance cannot be understated. The verbal form of communication (words) is used primarily to communicate messages. This is sometimes referred to as *digital* communication, because it involves discrete (individually distinct or separate) units—namely, words.

Nonverbal communication (such as tone of voice, facial gestures, posture, and distance) is often referred to as *analogic* communication, because it does not involve the exact units but, rather, analogues to those words—feelings and attitudes that reveal similarities to what is being expressed verbally.

### Communication Involves Relationships That Can Be Symmetrical or Complementary

A *symmetrical relationship*—where equality is maintained in terms of behavior—is most likely to occur when communication is transacted on a horizontal level. *Complementary relationships*—when one person's behavior complements that of the other—occurs when communication is upward, downward, or diagonal. One person fills in things or provides things the other does not or cannot. The emphasis is on differences. The more that differences between the parties are maximized, the more complementary a relationship becomes. For example, a supervisor who may be taller and more attractive than you, but who is also older, dresses well, knows more, and occupies a more prestigious office than you, may tend to make the complementary relationship that exists between the two of you even more obvious or pronounced. In many relationships, people shift in and out of these roles at various times. This is not as true within the business hierarchy, where roles and relationships are often organizationally prescribed.

How do the axioms just described relate to the transactional nature of communication? In each case the principle involved may affect the communication that occurs in the setting and may affect our perception of both the situation and the other person. They lead, then, to a consideration of the primary variable that affects the outcome of any communication situation in which we are involved: our perception of the other person.

## MASLOW'S NEED HIERARCHY

How we perceive another person will have a direct effect on how we interact with that person. Part of our success in dealing with others comes from an understanding of how people behave. That is, we must answer the question, "What is it that makes people act the way they do?" Admittedly, no discussion of human behavior can be complete; books have been devoted to the topic, and yet there is much left to discover. But Abraham Maslow offers us one perspective that has not only withstood the test of time but also appears to be sensible and reasonable. To prove the validity of this viewpoint, ask yourself during the brief discussion that follows: "Does this sound like an adequate explanation of the way *I* behave?"

Maslow, a psychologist, suggested that the fulfillment of basic needs is fundamental to the motivation of human beings.[2] He constructed a "need hierarchy" to identify and order these basic needs according to their strengths. (See Figure 2–3.)

**FIGURE 2-3.** Maslow's Need Hierarchy.

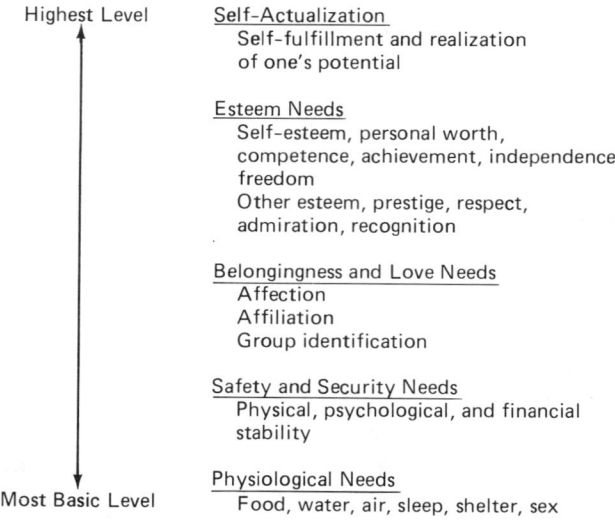

Data (for diagram) based on Hierarchy of Needs in "A Theory of Human Motivation" in Abraham H. Maslow, *Motivation and Personality*, Second ed. Copyright © 1970 by Abraham H. Maslow. By permission of Harper & Row, Inc.

*Physiological needs* are at the bottom of the hierarchy because they are the most basic, and they are what we require to sustain life—air, food, water, sleep, sex, clothing, and shelter. Until these basic needs are at least minimally satisfied, we have trouble turning our attention to any needs that occur higher in the hierarchy. In a job situation, the fulfillment of basic needs would depend upon the employee's salary and his or her personal life.

When physiological needs are satisfied, the next level of needs—*safety and security*—would become predominant. Security needs include our desire to be free from danger. We want a smooth-functioning, ordered world in which we can be comfortable and at ease. Security and safety needs would include both job security and proper working conditions. It might also include a satisfactory retirement plan as well as financial security. Having a home in a good, low-crime neighborhood might also satisfy security and safety needs.

Once physiological and security needs are satisfied, *belongingness and love* become the dominant needs. Maslow suggests that people need to belong, to be accepted, liked, and respected by friends. Some people can satisfy this need to belong within their family; others need the family as well as clubs and associations composed primarily of work associates. Still others fulfill this need through religious organizations—churches and synagogues. Others join every group that is available. The interpersonal relations one has with his or her subordinates, peers, and supervisors, as well as the status one has in the business, serve to fulfill this need.

Once an individual has satisfied belongingness and love needs, *esteem* needs become relevant. These operate on two levels: self-esteem and other esteem. Self-esteem fills our need to have a sense of personal worth and competence. Also, we need to feel as if we are achieving something. Feelings of independence and freedom in what we do contribute to our self-esteem.

Other esteem is another motive that causes employees to excel; employees seek prestige, respect, admiration, and recognition. They want to be considered a valuable member of the team. Just as members of families need reinforcement with respect to their importance within the family unit, recognition in business comes from advancement, testimonial dinners, and public compliments.

The final step on Maslow's hierarchy and the most difficult to satisfy is *self-actualization*. When all the other needs are at least partially satisfied, Maslow predicts a drive toward self-fulfillment—people attempting to become what they are capable of becoming. People will do what they think is important simply to receive satisfaction from the act itself. They seek self-actualization by assuming responsibility and by achieving. In many cases they find it through the possibilities for growth that are within a business or profession. In some instances they gain self-realization and fulfillment through the work itself.

Maslow's need hierarchy has been neither proved nor disproved. It seems to be true, however, that once lower-level needs are satisfied, they decrease in importance. Moreover, several studies indicate that lower-level workers are less satisfied with and more concerned about basic needs, whereas managers express more concern for higher-order needs—especially achievement, esteem, and self-actualization.[3]

Clayton Alderfer compressed Maslow's five need categories into three core needs and termed the result an *E.R.G. theory.*[4] Alderfer's *existence* (E) needs are comparable to Maslow's physiological and safety needs. His *relatedness* (R) needs involve relationships with other people and are similar to the safety, social, and several self-esteem needs of Maslow. Alderfer's *growth* (G) needs involve creative or personal growth and include Maslow's self-actualization and several self-esteem needs. Alderfer assumes all three needs are simultaneously active, but he suggests that individuals progress to higher-order needs once lower-order needs have been satisfied.

There are other motivation theories, too.[5] The point is not to provide a comprehensive overview. The point is that once we understand why people are motivated to do what they do, our interaction with them will be grounded on a better content base—knowing something about human nature. It is clear that human needs are part of the human-communication process. For example, a supervisor who wants to establish a positive interpersonal-relations climate with subordinates (an affiliation or acceptance need) may find this difficult to do if workers feel that they are underpaid (a physiological need), or that the working conditions are inadequate or inappropriate (a security need). No matter how much the supervisor improved his or her communication skills, that person would be undermined by a problem of needs.

Another aspect of Maslow's need hierarchy has to do with worker satisfaction. If we accept Maslow's need levels, then we should agree that a business environment that assists employees in the satisfaction of their needs would be desirable. A satisfied worker is more productive than an unsatisfied one. Thus, an understanding and application of such behavioral knowledge benefits not only the individual but also interpersonal relationships and the organization as a whole. It should be clear, too, that needs are also a function of age, culture, education, and a number of other variables not often considered in the management of organizations.

## McGREGOR'S THEORY X AND THEORY Y

In general people want to be part of things; they want to be recognized; they want to belong; they want respect. However, this has not always been the view held by business management. Indeed, business managers in the past believed that people are only concerned about putting in time and collecting their pay—the lowest need because of its basic, fundamental nature. Accepting this philosophy would likely mean that managers would feel obligated to tell employees what to do, how to do it, and when to do it. The manager would exert strong control.

### Theory X

Maslow's work and the existence of this traditional view of how people behave were, in part, responsible for Douglas McGregor's development of a theory of human behavior in organizations.[6] McGregor believed that traditional organizations could be characterized by centralized decision making, clear hierarchical structure, and strong control of employees. These features assumed certain things about human behavior, and from these assumptions an entire philosophy of organizational behavior was derived. McGregor labeled this approach *Theory X*. It assumes that people are basically lazy; they dislike work and avoid it if possible. Thus, they have to be driven and often coerced with threats of punishment to work toward the goals of the group. Since they lack creativity, they must be told what to do.

People also avoid responsibility; therefore, they must be directed and controlled. Since people want security above all, they must be given external rewards such as higher pay and titles to motivate them. The central philosophy of organizational behavior that summarizes this orientation is direction and control through the exercise of authority.

The Theory X viewpoint was partially revealed in a comment made by Mark Dempsy, a young American manager in a Japanese television manufacturing plant in San Diego. Commenting on the cultural gap between the Japanese and Americans, Dempsy said, "They [the Japanese] do not realize that some of us [Americans] live for the weekend, while lots of them live for the week—just so they can begin to work again."[7]

Managers who subscribe to this philosophy would likely reveal it in their communication behavior. That is, messages would flow from them downward. These downward communications would be limited to informative messages and announcements of decisions. Decision making would be concentrated in their hands, and, perhaps, a few others toward the top of the organizational hierarchy. Upward communication would be limited to suggestion boxes, the grapevine, and other informal systems that would allow certain employees to report to the manager on the behavior of other employees. Little interaction would be encouraged or would take place among employees, although the grapevine would prosper as a means of supplementing inadequate messages from management. Because of inadequate upward communication, decision making will often be based on partial or inadequate information, which creates distrust, fear, and lack of understanding in employees. Morale becomes depleted and production impeded.

### Theory Y

McGregor also postulated what he perceived to be the emerging, more modern, view of human behavior in organizations. The *Theory Y* philosophy is derived from Maslow's higher needs (see Figure 2–3): affiliation, esteem, and self-actualization. It assumes that people like work, that it is natural and fulfilling to accomplish tasks. Further, it assumes that self-direction and self-discipline play a role in determining behavior. People do not use their full potential. Self-achievement comes from assuming some degree of responsibility and from being able to view the outcome of a task. Many people, McGregor argues, can find sufficient reward in achievement. So, when encouraged properly, many people iron out solutions to their problems and seek greater self-control and self-direction.

The best example of Theory Y behavior in action is, perhaps, Japanese industry. "For many Japanese employees," one observer noted, "especially those of the nation's larger companies, life at the plant stresses the virtues of self-discipline and diligence."[8] These virtues are reinforced through involvement of Japanese employees in the life of the company: Trust is developed between labor and management, employees are guaranteed employment, decisions are made by consensus, companies invest heavily in research and development, employee suggestions are adopted, promotions come from within, employees are treated to vast quantities of personal attention, and workers are expected to make quality control their top priority.[9]

Expressing the high priority the Japanese place on communication between top management and the rest of the organization, one Japanese executive expressed it best when he said, "You simply could not or would not make any important decision without first achieving a consensus within your corporation."[10]

Managers who subscribe to a Theory Y philosophy would reveal it in their communication behavior. Messages would travel up, down, and across in that organization. Decision making would be spread throughout the entire company and input would be sought from members at all levels. Feedback would be encouraged; thus, no supplemental upward system would be required. Confidence and trust would characterize the frequent, honest interaction that occurred between employees. The needs of employees would be satisfied, too, by the flow of downward messages. Decisions would be characterized by accuracy and quality because they would be based upon information from all levels of the organization.

Basic to an understanding of McGregor's theories, then, is the view that people cannot become mature if their experiences throughout life remain immature. Given the proper environment—a Theory Y orientation—people will have the opportunity to be treated as mature and will develop maturity.

According to McGregor, management should view Theory X and Theory Y as end points of a continuum. The two theories should be blended together depending on the situation and the personnel. One of the qualities of a good manager would be his or her ability to perceive the needs of a given situation and personality and make use of the proper blend. McGregor agrees that managers should shift from one philosophy to another as the situation warrants.[11]

One note needs to be added on *Theory Z*. William Ouchi coined the term *Theory Z management.* He claims this to be the secret of Japanese success. It represents a special way of managing people—"a style that focuses on a strong company philosophy, a distinct corporate culture, long-range staff development, and consensus decision making."[12] Ouchi argues that such a management style results in "lower turnover, increased job commitment, and dramatically higher productivity."[13]

## THE INTRAPERSONAL PROCESS

The discussion thus far would make it appear that our perception of other people is dependent on their needs (how they are motivated), or on how we view human behavior. Although both may be factors, there is another aspect to be considered and that is the view we have of ourselves. *Intrapersonal communication* is communication within an individual. As a "process," I want to examine more than our ability to talk with ourselves; I want to look at the view we have of ourselves—our self-concept—and the relation this has to our communication behavior with others.

When we look at the intrapersonal process, we are looking at stimuli and responses that are exclusively *within* us. We make decisions and evaluations based on the flow of information inside us. When theorists say that communication is *multilevel,* they are referring both to the first level (within us) and to that which is easier to examine, namely, communication between us and others, or *interpersonal* communication, a second level.

Another level is *metacommunication,* which is communication about communication—discussion of the process of communication and *how* messages are transacted.

Group communication public communication, mass communication (television, radio, newspaper, and magazines) and the communication that occurs between people of different cultures could be considered other levels. In discussions about communication it is important to specify the level being discussed.

Intrapersonal communication is an important component of the transactional-communication process. Why? Because our view of ourself determines how we view others and how we view the world. It determines how we filter messages that come to us from outside us. If we have a negative self-concept, it is possible that we also view others negatively. For example, people with severe feelings of inferiority will put other people down: "What do *they* know?" "Who does he think *he* is, anyway?" "She's so full of hot air, she floats!" They do this to elevate themselves—to make themselves feel better. Sometimes, too, they project their own weaknesses on others: "Bill has trouble getting along with others." "Jim can't get *anything* done right." "Linda is always more concerned about trivia than she is about things that matter."

Now, place these ideas into the context established earlier about constructing images of other people with whom we communicate. When our mind is already slightly left of center, the images we construct of others tend to be slightly skewed as well. It's similar to those individuals who see everyone else as an antagonist. "You have to fight to stay alive," is their motto. Nobody can break through to them because no matter how you approach them the result is the same: "Keep off my back. I don't need your kind of help!"

You must have a strong, positive, self-concept to have healthy, satisfying, ongoing interpersonal relationships with other people. When, over a period of time, you find yourself having difficulty conversing with others, admitting that you are wrong, expressing your feelings, accepting constructive criticism from others, or voicing ideas that are different from those of other people, it may be that you have a poor self-concept.

Although it is not the purpose of this chapter to prescribe remedial behaviors, it is true that a negative self-concept can be a major communication block. Growth and development in your self-concept must include thinking better of yourself—looking at yourself and liking what you see well enough so that you can accept it, thinking better of others, realizing that you have a stake in others and that there is a mutual need, beginning to accept change as well as modifications in your personality, profiting from our errors, recognizing the importance of other people and the importance of their welfare, and viewing your situation as one in which you have the ability to become better than you already are.[14]

The point of this discussion about intrapersonal communication is simply that the locus of responsibility for effectiveness in communication does *not* fall solely on the shoulders of the other person to listen, understand, and respond appropriately. We must not only look at, but within, ourselves, for *we* are a major factor in the communication process. With respect to the intrapersonal process, we have three major goals: (1) to be aware of the process and its potential effect, (2) to be honest with ourselves as we monitor our own behavior, and (3) to grow, change, and develop as necessary to increase effectiveness at the intrapersonal level.

## THE SOCIAL CONTEXT

We behave differently in different contexts. The behavior that is appropriate when we talk to a subordinate may not be appropriate when we talk to our boss. When we look at the social context as a communication variable, we are looking at all those things that make up the situation besides the people themselves. The time of day, the weather, and the locale are all important factors that help determine the kind and nature of the communication that takes place.

When we communicate, too, we should not lose sight of the fact that our communication is part of an historical context. That is, we must at least be aware of all the communication that has preceded our particular message. If, for example, you suddenly decide without warning to use a new procedure for changing a company policy, a typical reaction to such a change might be, "That's strange, she's never done *that* before; I wonder what's gotten into her!" The reaction is to the medium and not the message.

For instance, let's say that Cheryl—your supervisor—had always preceded new innovations in your work routine with a memo of explanation and a follow-up meeting of employees to answer questions and resolve implementation problems. Suddenly, and without explanation, Cheryl initiates a new innovation by telling Bill to let everyone know about the change. Bill becomes the channel or medium, and you find yourself asking,

"Why Bill? Why did Cheryl suddenly change her ways?" These questions reveal a lack of concern—or at least a diminished concern—for the message and a new concern for the medium. The historical context has been changed.

The social context also includes what is right for *this* company or for *this* group of individuals. Patterns of behavior begin to emerge in a company (already operating in most companies) that offer new employees *norms*—proper, accepted ways of acting and behaving. To violate norms may cause a communication breakdown. To take a new idea to a vice-president, over the head of an area supervisor, may violate a norm and hinder or halt communication between the employee and the supervisor. The way memos are processed, the way grievances are handled, and who says what to whom and when are various aspects of the social context. As much as you may know about the way communication relates to a business, and as much as you know about human behavior, you may not be at liberty to exercise your wisdom because of either explicit (clearly expressed) or implicit (unexpressed) social norms.

*Culture* is another aspect of social context. What is appropriate in one culture may be taboo or offensive in another one. Could you imagine beginning and ending your work day at a company by singing the company song? How about beginning your work shift with warm-up calisthenics? How about being invited as a new worker to bring your parents and relatives to a welcoming ceremony conducted by the president of your new company? These are not unusual practices in Japan. Even in those Japanese firms operating in America, management has not forced certain policies on American workers: Workers were not forced to wear lemon-colored smocks on the assembly line at a Sony firm, nor was a general exercise program forced on American workers when managers saw it was not wanted. In another American firm, a Japanese vice-president mastered Spanish so that he could talk with his many Hispanic workers.[15]

Not to recognize the social context is likely to offend and alienate others. Just as the self and others are essential to communication situations, so is a social context. It includes *everything* that is not included when you discuss the people involved.

## INTERPERSONAL PROCESSES

The best communication is face to face and two-way. Feedback is immediate. Both communicators have access to the full range of the other person's presence and behaviors. But just because it is most effective does not mean it is best *for all situations,* as discussed previously. In the following section, some important *interpersonal* processes will be discussed. No claim is being made that these are the *only* processes.

### Self-disclosure

The more I know about you, and the more you know about me, the more effective and efficient our communication is likely to be. If I am able to convey information about my private world to you, in language that you clearly understand, then you will get to know me. But you can know me only if I let you, only if I *want* you to know me. If my desire to have you know me is great enough, I will find ways for communicating myself to you.[16]

What is the reward for my revealing myself to you? There are several. The first is *trust*. When I let you know something about my private world, you are given some assurance of the reliability of my character, ability, strength, and truthfulness, just as I demonstrate that I have confidence in you. When I say, "You know, I really don't like this assignment, and I sure will be glad when it's over!" you gain insight into my private world.

The second reward is more *self-disclosure*. Just as trust begets more trust, self-disclosure begets more self-disclosure. If you want to find out about someone else's private world, one sure way is to open up communication channels whereby full and free self-disclosure can occur. Thus, the second reward might be labeled "more information."

A third reward will follow, and that is *good will*. In cases where full, free, self-disclosure is allowed to occur, an aura of good will prevails. Those who share in the process express kindly feelings of approval and support for each other. They begin to show more concern for each other and exert more effort of a benevolent nature toward those others.

While self-disclosure is generally positive and effective, there are times when it should not be pursued. You would, for example, want to hide your reactions to a situation if another person proves to be untrustworthy. Moreover, if past experience reveals that an individual will either misinterpret or overreact to your self-disclosure, you may want to keep silent. In addition, if the other person has experienced some problems lately and your self-disclosure would be too much for the individual to handle now, you might choose to forego self-disclosure. In still another situation, you might allow others to come to a realization by themselves—without your intervention. The point is, self-disclosure requires good judgment.

### Feedback

Means must be provided in the process of communication whereby we may correct misperceptions and faulty responses to what we think we are communicating. Without some means to monitor our performance, to compare our intended and actual communication, and to use this information to guide our future action, there is little allowance for either immediate or long-range growth. When an autocratic organizational structure exists that allows for a minimal (and that forced!) amount of upward communication, repeated breakdowns are likely to occur.

But *feedback* need not be confined solely to this openness and sensitivity to the reactions of other people. This is *external* feedback. Feedback can also be *internal*—provided by ourselves.[17] This is intrapersonal communication. As we prepare to communicate with another person we engage in internal feedback: "I wonder if she will accept this?" "Maybe I should say this fast and get it over with." "I don't think he cares about this, but I'm going to say it anyway."

As we speak, we monitor the other person's reactions: "He isn't listening," "She really *is* concerned," "He is getting angrier by the minute." Then, as we near the end of what we want to say, we anticipate the response from the other person. We expect certain behavior, an expectation triggered by our conception of the moment combined with our past experiences.

Quite often we will even correct what we intend to say before we say it on the basis of what we think will be the response of the other person. In a one-way situation, we may add more supporting information or a complete explanation to a memo if we think the receiver of the memo may not understand it, or, perhaps, will respond negatively without it.

The point of this discussion of feedback is that we can be our own most intelligent listener and responder. We should not allow information to emanate from our mouth or pen that has not first passed through thorough scrutiny by our own internal feedback system.

### Listening

Listening is much more complicated than the physical process of hearing. We hear with our ears. Listening is an intellectual and emotional process. That is, listening integrates physical, emotional, and intellectual inputs in a search for meaning and for understanding. There are several important aspects of effective listening.

The "third ear" has been designated as that area where true listening occurs. When you listen to another person speak, you should not listen to the words alone. We do that with our ears. You must, instead, listen to the meanings behind the words. You must listen to what the other person says between sentences and without words—what he or she expresses soundlessly. What the speaker feels and thinks adds a "halo" effect that changes both the tone and color of the words stated. That is, we tend to generalize at times from a person's thoughts and feelings. Based on the thoughts and feelings we perceive, we may make an overly favorable evaluation of that person's whole personality—a halo effect.

Effective listening is not passive. It must be active. Although we can hear passively, if we are to listen, we must have a reason or purpose for listening, suspend our judgment as we let the other person speak, resist distractions, wait before responding, then paraphrase (use our own words to rephrase) the content and the feeling of what the other person said.

Use the difference between speech speed and thought speed. People speak at a rate of approximately 125 to 140 words a minute. They think at close to 400 to 600 words a minute. That is why when listening to another person, your mind often runs far ahead of what is actually being said at the moment. Rather than allow your mind to race ahead, to digress, or to concentrate on other things, you should try to anticipate what the other person is going to say, mentally summarize what that person has been saying, weigh the speaker's evidence by mentally questioning it, and listen between the lines for changes in tone, volume, face expression, hands, or body.[18]

*Clarity of expression.* Effective listening is difficult, but just as difficult is trying to say what you mean. We also assume that because we said it, the other person understood it; even when we have been careless and unclear, if we have said it, our assumption is that the same meaning will be evoked in the other person's mind. This is the assumption that breaks down the clarity of expression: "If it's clear to me, it must be clear to you." It is also one of the most difficult barriers to successful human communication.

Here are three brief guidelines that help improve the clarity of expression:

1. Have a clear picture in your mind of what you are trying to express.
2. Be able to clarify and elaborate on what you want to say. That is, be redundant. Some people say that in any large organization, only triple redundancy will assure that something is correct, understood, or done.
3. Be receptive to the feedback that you get and use it to further guide your efforts at communication.

*Coping with anger.* Feelings of high emotional intensity are normal. To be angry is a natural part of being human. But suppressing that anger is *not* natural. Even though we fear that another person may respond in the same way, or that when we express anger, discord will be created, or that others will become upset with us, we should also realize that harboring anger is unhealthy. Often, our stomachs keep count, and over a period of time an ulcer or other physical ailments will appear. At other times, we retain the anger until all of a sudden we can contain it no longer, and it erupts in one great emotional avalanche. Such emotional discharges represent failure to cope with anger.

But what do we do about it? First we should realize that the expression of feelings of high emotional intensity is important in building good relationships with others. Second, we must realize that people need to express their feelings, for it is the expression of such feelings that we influence, reshape, and change others, as well as ourselves, and affirm ourselves as well.

To have healthy communication, we must begin by being aware of our emotions.[19] What is the emotion we are feeling? Then we need to admit the emotion—take a look at it and find out how strong it is. We need to take responsibility for the emotion as well; it's like taking charge of our life. Next we need to investigate our emotions: How did the anger arise? Where did it come from? Report the emotion. Do not interpret or judge; just present the facts. In the heat of an argument, for example, you might say, "Hold it a minute! I'm getting too worked up." Finally, integrate your emotions with your intellect; having listened to your emotions, questioned them, and reported them, let your mind (intellect) determine what is the correct thing to do. Just remember that if you want to have healthy communication, emotions cannot be repressed.[20]

When you are confronted in a highly emotional situation, first make sure you understand what is being said. Deal with the other person using plain, understandable language. Reveal sincerity and concern; remember, even if *you* do not consider the issue or situation important, the other person does. If you are confused, gain clarification. Take time to reflect, exploring the confrontation nondefensively. If the other person gets upset or angry, try not to respond in kind. Rather, try to show that you care and that you understand. An open, sincere, and honest dealing with situations of high emotional excitement helps resolve such situations. If there are things you can do in this situation that will help decrease or remove the emotion, explain them clearly. If a conflict continues, continue to talk—don't clam up or try to avoid the conflict. Conflict is treated in Chapter 7, and specific means for managing it are outlined there. Just remember that the expression of emotion can be helpful and healthy. The attitude you have toward it and toward the other person will have a significant effect on the outcome.

### Metacommunication

We have defined metacommunication as communication about communication. To engage in metacommunication is a process of monitoring the process. It allows us to look at what we are doing as communicators and to talk about how we are communicating:

Are we sensitive to the feedback?
Have we accurately paraphrased another's message?
Are our feelings so strong that we are unable to be objective?
Can we express what we want to say more clearly or precisely?

Metacommunication allows us to look back over all of the ingredients discussed in this chapter and ask the crucial questions: Are we aware of how the principle, concept, or point of view is operative? Are we making use of what we know to respond to the phenomena appropriately?

## SUMMARY

This chapter offered a brief look at the communication process and some of the principles involved. It began with an overview of the process and went on to discuss meaning, and where meaning lies, and then the transactional nature of communication.

In the next sections, several areas of importance to communication were examined: axioms of communication, Maslow's need hierarchy, McGregor's Theory X and Theory Y, the intrapersonal process, and the social context into which communication must be placed.

The chapter ended with a discussion of some of the most important interpersonal processes: self-disclosure, feedback, listening, the clarity of expression, coping with anger, and metacommunication.

It should be clear from this chapter that communication is, first, a dynamic and ongoing phenomenon. Second, because it helps people get what they want, it is functional and purposeful. Third, it is social in that it enables us to interact with others and lets others reach us. Fourth, it is the vehicle we use to compare our view of the world with the views of others. Finally, it should now be clear that communication is complex. In discussing Maslow, it was said that air, hunger, thirst, sleep, sex, clothing, and shelter made up our strongest, most basic needs. It should be clear that communication is also basic to our survival.

It is people who make communication complex. Their attitudes, ideas, and orientations are complex and unpredictable. For this reason, the study of communication is not an exact science. But to know more about it requires the study of other aspects of human behavior such as attitudes, motivation, personality, and learning. But as one quickly realizes, no matter what the area of human behavior pursued, there are few absolutes.

## NOTES

[1] Paul Watzlawick, Janet Beavin, and Don D. Jackson, *Pragmatics of Human Communication: A Study of Interactional Patterns, Pathologies, and Paradoxes* (New York: Norton, 1967), pp. 48–54.

[2] Abraham H. Maslow, *Motivation and Personality*, 2nd ed. (New York: Harper & Row, 1970), Chapter 4, "A Theory of Human Motivation," pp. 35–58.

[3] Edward E. Lawler, III, and J. Lloyd Suttle, "A Casual Correlation Test of Need Hierarchy Concept," *Organizational Behavior and Human Performance*, 7 (1972), 265–87.

[4] Clayton P. Alderfer, "An Empirical Test of a New Theory of Human Needs," *Organizational Behavior and Human Performance*, 4 (1969), 142–75.

[5] See F. Herzberg, "One More Time: How Do You Motivate Employees?" *Harvard Business Review*, 6 (1968), 53–63; Vroom, V. H., *Work and Motivation* (New York: John Wiley,

1964); Harry Levinson, "Assinine Attitudes Toward Motivation," *Harvard Business Review, 11* (1973), 70–76; Craig C. Pinder, "Concerning the Application of Human Motivation Theories in Organizational Settings," *Academy of Management Review, 2* (1977), 384–97.

[6]See Douglas McGregor, *The Human Side of Enterprise* (New York: McGraw-Hill, 1960).

[7]"Consensus in San Diego," *Time, 117* (March 30, 1981), 58.

[8]Christopher Byron, "How Japan Does It," *Time, 117* (March 30, 1981), 57–59.

[9]*Ibid*, p. 57–59.

[10]Toshihiko Yamashita, president of Matsushita Electric Industrial Co., as quoted in "A Daily 'Samurai Duel,' " *Time, 117* (March 30, 1981), 63.

[11]Douglas McGregor, *Professional Manager* (New York: McGraw-Hill, 1967).

[12]William G. Ouchi, *Theory Z: How American Business Can Meet the Japanese Challenge* (Reading, Mass.: Addison-Wesley, 1981). From the dust jacket.

[13]*Ibid.*

[14]See Richard L. Weaver, II, *Understanding Interpersonal Communication*, 3rd ed. (Glenview, Ill.: Scott, Foresman, 1984), Chapter 2, "Getting in Touch: The Self and Self-Disclosure," pp. 41–73.

[15]"Consensus in San Diego," 58.

[16]Sidney M. Jourard, *The Transparent Self* (New York: Van Nostrand Reinhold, 1964), pp. 3, 5–6.

[17]See Wendell Johnson, *Your Most Enchanted Listener* (New York: Harper & Row, 1956), p. 174.

[18]Ralph G. Nichols, "Listening Is a 10-Part Skill," in *Speech/Communication: A Reader*, 2nd ed., ed. Richard L. Weaver, II (San Diego, Calif.: Collegiate Publishing, 1979), p. 273.

[19]The information in this discussion comes from John Powell, "Dealing With Our Emotions," in Weaver, *Speech/Communication*, pp. 79–82.

[20]For a full chapter on interpersonal conflict, see Weaver, *Understanding Interpersonal Communication*, Chapter 8, "Overcoming Barriers: Coping With Conflict," pp. 214–35. Also Joseph A. DeVito, *Communication: Concepts and Processes*, 3rd ed. (Englewood Cliffs, N.J.: Prentice–Hall, 1981), pp. 153–65.

# 3

# Listening

You feel you have just received a lucky break; you have just been given the very job you thought would make your dreams come true. Here you are, first week on the job: new faces, new duties, new expectations, and new environment. Your first task is to gain a clear understanding about everything you can. At each opportunity, you ask questions: "What does she do?" "Who is she responsible to?" "What is the form used to report these figures?" "Who is expected to do that?" "And how does this work?" *And you listen.* To gain information, to lay a base for your own thinking, to learn more, to gain an advantage, and to be an effective communicator, you listen as well as you possibly can.

This chapter will discuss the importance of listening. From the example above, you can see how listening can make an important difference in your life. The section on the nature of listening will examine some of the myths about and some of the barriers to effective listening. We will also look at the relationship of listening and feedback, and we will examine several response styles to guide your feedback. The final section of the chapter will offer specific suggestions for improving listening.

## IMPORTANCE OF LISTENING

When I presented a seminar on conflict management to a group of business people, I had them gather into groups to discuss ways to handle conflict. In every one of the five groups, effective listening was listed as one of the top three tools people have for dealing with conflict situations. But just as it provides the base for constructive discussion—people listening to each other's ideas and positions—so, too, is it a basic tool for all communication situations. Listening could even be labeled a survival strategy, for it is a vital part of human interaction.

That should be strong enough to justify its importance. But if not, let's think about it selfishly first, then as a gift for another person.

In business, rarely is the kind of information we need for day-to-day work published. What are we to do? How does our work relate to and interact with that of others? What is expected of us? What is going on in the company? How do we fit in? This was, essentially, the opening illustration. Information is transmitted orally as a result of our questions, informal conversations, interviews, and meetings. The better we listen, the more information we gain. And information is power.

By accumulating information, we learn. In her book on listening, Madelyn Burley-Allen states, "We spend 70 percent of our waking hours in verbal communication."[1] Of that amount of time, she says that 40 percent is spent listening. Listening is an important method of learning. This learning leads to our growing understanding of what life is all about.

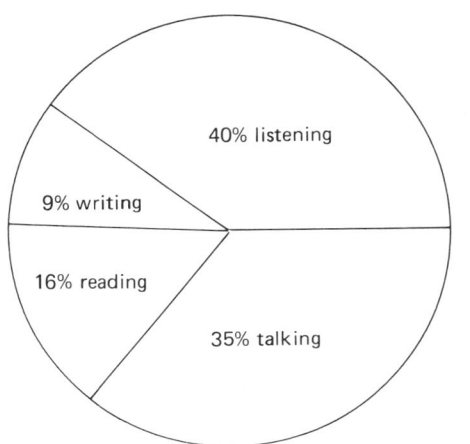

**FIGURE 3-1.**

Madelyn Burley-Allen, *Listening: The Forgotten Skill* (New York: John Wiley, 1982), p. 2. These figures are reaffirmed by Donald E. Bird, "Teaching Listening Comprehension," *Journal of Communication, 3* (1953), 127. Bird's figures are 45%, listening; 25%, talking; 15%, reading; 18%, writing.

Let me extend the illustration presented first in this chapter. What if after two weeks on the job, your supervisor came to you and said, "Okay, you have had an opportunity to survey what's going on here; how would you improve our operation?" The information you have attained through listening now becomes a base for your critical thinking: You think one process could be streamlined; you have observed some unnecessary duplication of effort; you believe one more person would make this procedure more efficient, and so on.

In much the same way, our critical thinking allows us to gain advantages. You were prepared to respond when your supervisor asked, "What would you do?" In informal conversations, interviews, and meetings, often it is the well-informed people who have an "edge." They can step in and make suggestions or provide recommendations because they have laid a foundation.

Listening is a useful method, too, for comparing our views of our world with others' views. Sounds abstract? Think of yourself on that new job. Your boss has helped you get oriented; he or she has answered some of your questions and has appeared ready to support whatever you suggest. Before you make those suggestions for streamlining and increasing efficiency just mentioned, wouldn't you want to know something more about your boss? So you listen for reactions from others. Maybe, out of curiosity, you mention something about the boss to others—and you listen. Their responses may be a key to how you present your new-found information to your boss. Much of our thinking is based on comparisons—comparing how we feel with how we think others feel.

For ourselves, we can use listening to gain information, as a base for critical thinking, to gain advantages, and for comparison. But it is important also as we relate with others. It is a vital part of human interaction because of its role in the communication process. When you see diagrams of the communication process, you do not see one-way arrows from sources to receiver (see Figure 3–2), unless the writer is depicting public-speaking situations. Even then, such a diagram omits acknowledgment of feedback—messages flowing back from receivers to the source. Most communication situations need reciprocity or give-and-take (see Figure 3–3.). Effective communication situations are a constant back-and-forth process.

But the importance of listening extends beyond this. Not only is it part of human interaction, but there is also a human need to be listened to. Just imagine what a day would be like for you if nobody listened to you—all

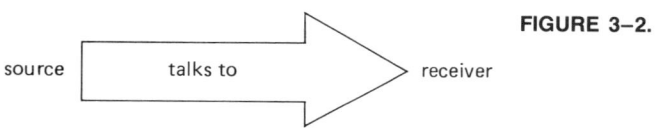

**FIGURE 3–2.**

**FIGURE 3–3.**

day! In their book *Born to Win,* Muriel James and Dorothy Jongeward declare: "Listening is one of the finest strokes one person can give another."[2] A stroke is any form of recognition or attention. Listening is warm, supportive, and friendly.

Finally, it is courteous to listen to others. It reveals respect. It lets them know we value them as human beings. And it suggests that we are willing to consider their ideas, suggestions, or positions.

## NATURE OF LISTENING

To illustrate the nature of listening, I will present some of the common myths about the process. Once we understand the nature of the process, then we need to know why it is difficult. In the second part of this section, we will discuss some of the barriers to effective listening.

### Myths About Listening

At the beginning of his book *Listening Behavior,* Larry Barker presents an eleven-item "Listening Quiz"[3] (see Figure 3–4). Each item in the quiz has students responding to one of the myths of listening. In the following section, some of the more important myths Barker addresses are discussed.

*The more intelligent you are, the better you will listen.* For a moment, think back to the most recent time you listened. Why did you listen? To find out where your roommate was going, when dinner was, what pages to read for the next class period? From situation to situation, and from person to person, people listen for different reasons. Are some reasons better than others? Nonsense. More intelligent people have neither better reasons nor better hearing. They may listen *differently*—because they think differently—but not better.

*Speaking is more important than listening.* With respect to the percentage of time spent listening, listening is actually more important than speaking! See Figure 3–1 again. But imagine what speaking would be like without listening. First, what purpose would it serve? Second, imagine how aimless it would become without guidance from listeners.

## 50  *Listening*

Answer, to the best of your ability, the following true–false questions regarding the listening process. After you have completed the quiz, turn to page 62 to check your answers.

**FIGURE 3–4.** Listening Quiz.*

---

T___  F___  1. Listening is largely a matter of intelligence.

T___  F___  2. Speaking is a more important part of the communication process than listening.

T___  F___  3. Listening requires little energy; it is "easy."

T___  F___  4. Listening is an automatic, involuntary reflex.

T___  F___  5. Speakers can command listening to occur within an audience.

T___  F___  6. Hearing ability significantly determines listening ability.

T___  F___  7. The speaker is totally responsible for the success of communication.

T___  F___  8. People listen every day. This practice eliminates the need for listening training.

T___  F___  9. Competence in listening develops naturally.

T___  F___  10. When you learned to read, you simultaneously learned to listen.

T___  F___  11. Listening is only a matter of understanding the speaker's words.

---

*Larry L. Barker, *Listening Behavior* (Englewood Cliffs, N.J.: Prentice-Hall), p. xiii.

***Listening is easy.*** One reason for this myth is the confusion between hearing—which *is* easy—and listening—which is not. Hearing is the physical process our ears accomplish. Listening is a three-part process that combines the physical with the mental and emotional. See Figure 3–5.

A second reason for this myth is that many people think they are listening when they are not. Since the average person speaks at the rate of 125 to 140 words a minute and the average thought speed ranges from 400 to 600 words a minute, our minds move much faster than the words we hear spoken. Without concentration and effort, our minds quickly wander from another's message—listening ceases.

*Listening is automatic.* Just because you understand the language does not mean you can listen. Have you ever come back from an important meeting that you and a friend attended? Your friend turns to you and says, "I have absolutely no idea what went on there." Was it the language? No—it could have been any number of problems. (See Figure 3–6.) Notice the amount and kind of interference that can occur during the process. It requires effort on our part; but effort alone is not a guarantee of good listening.

*Competence in listening develops naturally.* The problem with this myth is that we think that effective listening is associated with maturity or greater experience. Often we establish listening habits early in life; rather than change them, we use our habitual response styles over and over. We depend on them. This is likely to entrench poor listening habits rather than foster growth, change, or development. To listen well requires training; thus, competence in listening is learned.

Listening training is an ongoing process. Once you have some practical ways to improve, then you must apply them over and over. But the first step is a desire to change, or to improve. Whether you are a good listener and think you are poor, or poor and think you are good, listening training is likely to make you better at it than you are.

**FIGURE 3–5.** The Listening Process.

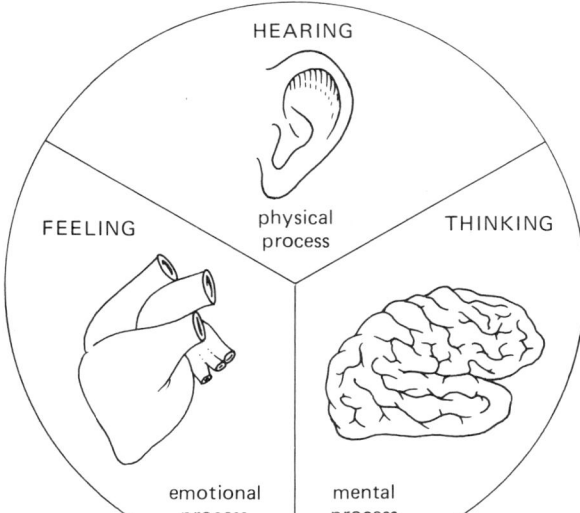

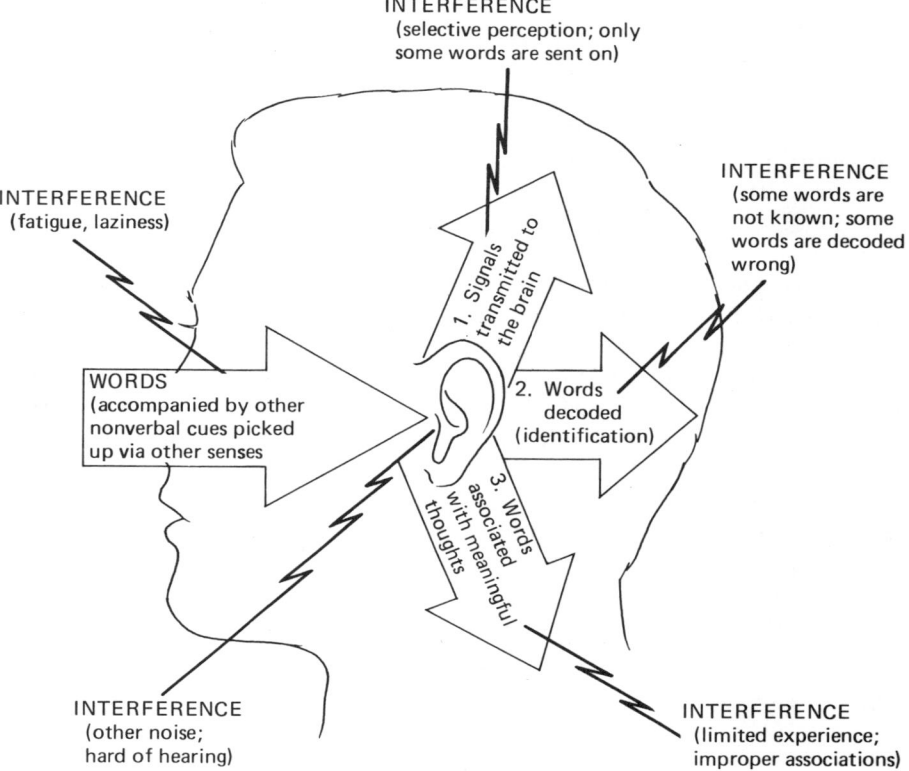

**FIGURE 3-6.** Listening Problems.

### Barriers to Listening

Listening itself is a two-way process. We often think of it as *one* part of two-way communication, but the source of messages has an equal share in helping receivers, just as receivers must also help. It is easy to believe that if the other person does not hold my attention, it is not my fault. Listening often requires tremendous energy just to find something in what the other person is saying that will be of interest—that will keep you listening. There is no question, however, that speakers can ease this burden. As we examine the three major categories of barriers—message problems, mind problems, and people problems—remember to look at each of these categories from both sides: source *and* receiver.

*Message problems* are those that relate to any portion of the content—verbal or nonverbal. Have you ever almost fallen asleep during someone's overly long story? Have you yawned as someone explained a complicated or unfamiliar procedure? In such situations, listeners are given a difficult task, but it is likely they could succeed if they would not give up too easily.

Speakers could make it easier on listeners if they would shorten and simplify their message. Details should be reduced, vocabulary tailored, and ambiguity eliminated. In addition, if speakers can add variety and energy to their presentation, attention is likely to increase.

*Mind problems* have to do with the mental state or background knowledge of either source or receiver. Listeners who are preoccupied with other things are unlikely to listen well. They would be closed-minded as well. The same is true if they are antagonistic, overly critical, or just do not want to listen. Have you ever tried to listen to someone whom you cannot tolerate? Have you ever found yourself picking apart another person's grammar, evidence, organization, style, or manner of dress? Have you ever just not been in the proper mood to listen?

Background knowledge is a mind problem because listeners may not have enough experience—or the right kind of experience—to understand a message. If they cannot associate meanings with the symbols (words and nonverbal cues) they receive, they cannot make meaning out of the message.

*People problems* are those that have to do with your *self* or the other's *self* as these selves come together. You undoubtedly know people who are overly concerned about themselves, preoccupied with their appearance or with the impression they are making. These people lose track of the other's message.

**FIGURE 3–7.** Barriers to Listening.

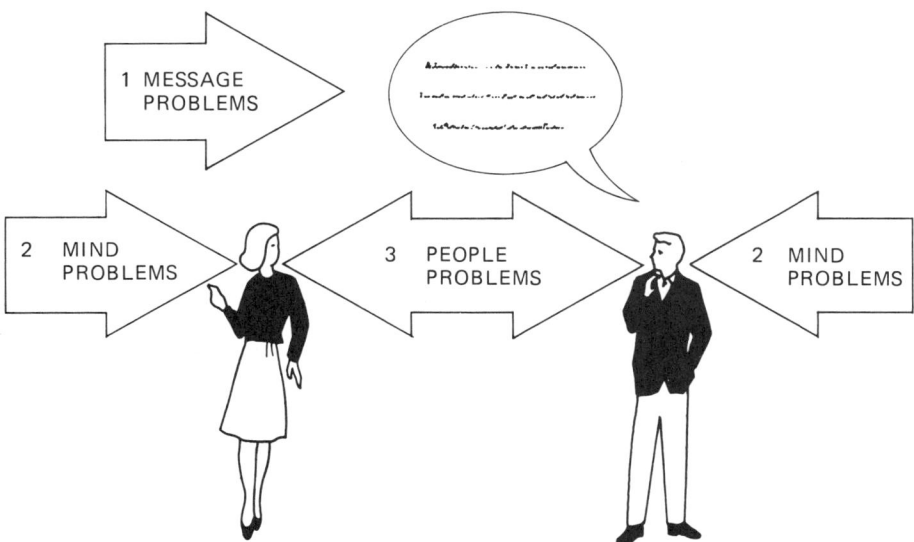

A related people problem occurs if we become preoccupied with the other person. Have you ever found yourself so emotionally involved with another person that you could not listen to him or her? Maybe you could listen, but you could not be objective about it. Becoming preoccupied with someone's closeness, physical appearance, or other features is a people problem as well.

## LISTENING AND FEEDBACK

If you want to test the relationship between listening and feedback, some time when you are listening to another person, stop all obvious feedback. No head nods, "yuhs," "uh-huhs," or other responses of any kind—just a rather blank look. What is likely to happen? The other person will, if he or she is sensitive, request some feedback from you. You aren't likely to get away with it for long.

Another test would have you increase the positive feedback. Smile, nod your head in agreement, and add vocalized responses. Often this will increase the other person's energy, make his or her language stronger, or add intensity to the message. Listening and feedback are close neighbors. And from these examples alone you can see how both can either detract or add to an interaction. An attentive listener can stimulate better communication.

Listening can be conducted in such a way as to foster relationships, promote mutual growth and understanding, and increase information flow. Five response syles have emerged from the field of counseling. John Jones and William Pfeiffer published them as part of a "Helping Relationship Inventory" designed to assess people's preferences for these styles.[4] The five response styles are *evaluative, interpretive, supportive, probing,* and *understanding*. As noted in Figure 3–8, they move from those fostering closed communication in which the other person becomes highly involved, to extremely open communication, where the other person is less involved. This will be explained in the following sections.

### Evaluative Response Style

The major characteristic that distinguishes this style is the tendency to make a judgment regarding the goodness, appropriateness, effectiveness, or rightness of another's idea, behavior, or comment. For example, a work associate comes to you and says, "I can't get along with her. Everything I say is wrong. I'm sure she hates me." An evaluative response could take many forms. You might say, "Hey, it's okay; everyone is having trouble with her," Or you could say, "You're not really having trouble; you just

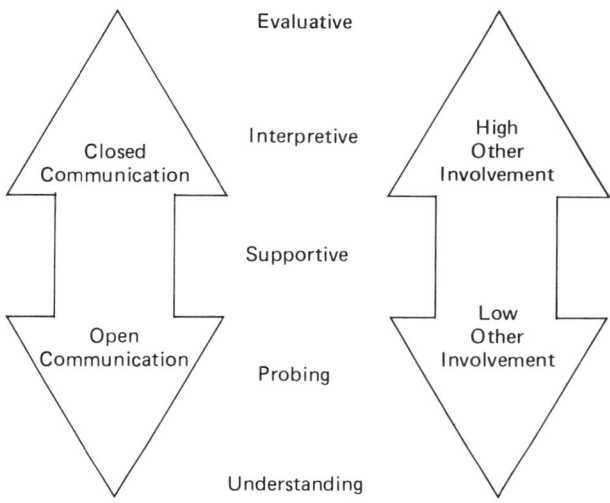

**FIGURE 3-8.** Response Styles

interpret it <u>wrong</u>. I'm sure she doesn't see it the same way." The *evaluative* terms in both cases are underlined.

An evaluative response style closes the door on communication because it offers the answer to the problem. You had the "answer" the other was looking for. And notice how involved you became; it was as if you knew the facts, considered the case, offered the only appropriate response, and closed the door. I am not suggesting that this is the only scenario, but this is why this response style has the potential for being so negative.

### Interpretive Response Style

In this case the distinguishing characteristic is the desire to teach or to impart meaning. A co-worker says to you, "You know, I don't think I can get this report done over the weekend." Using the interpretive response style, you might say, "All of us have an equal responsibility to this project. We're all busy. Sometimes we must make sacrifices—setting aside our own plans for the good of the whole." Notice that in using this response style, you have implied what the other person might think or do. This can be blatant or subtle. Those who habitually use this style sound like teachers or moralists.

### Supportive Response Style

Using this response style, you would try to reassure the other person or reduce the intensity of his or her feeling. A friend says to you, "I hate my job with a passion." Using a supportive response style, you might say,

"Yes, I know what you mean. We all go through these times, don't we? Fortunately, they pass pretty quickly." The intent is to pacify—to indicate that the friend need not feel the way he or she does. But notice that some of the weaknesses of the evaluative response are still present in both the interpretive and supportive response styles: You have made a judgment. Your co-worker's plans for the weekend are not as important as the report; your friend's feelings are not too important—they will pass. And in both cases, you have implied how the other person should feel.

### Probing Response Style

The purpose of this response style is to gather further information or provoke discussion. If someone said to you, "I just can't get here on time," you might probe this response with the question, "Are you having trouble getting up in the morning?" This response style could be any of those above, depending on how it is worded: "Do you know that the boss doesn't like latecomers?" is evaluative; "Have you thought about setting your clock earlier and doing some of your chores before going to bed?" is interpretive. "Did you know that I had the same problem when I first started here?" is supportive. These are probing responses because they are questions designed to draw out the other person.

### Understanding Response Style

The underlying purpose of this style is to gain understanding. You want to find out what the other person is saying, how he or she feels, how he or she sees things, or how something strikes him or her. The key to using this approach is paraphrasing what the other person has said. A colleague tells you, for example, "I am not getting along with our manager at all." Using an understanding response, you might reply, "You mean, you and Sharon are not seeing eye-to-eye . . . ?" Your response will automatically draw out your colleague, and it will allow him or her to expand the response. In this case the communication is highly open, and by providing the understanding response, you stay less involved than in the preceding styles. You open up the communication situation for the other person to continue talking.

The reason why the understanding response style is preferred is that it creates a positive, free communication climate. Information flow is increased. It helps others talk out, and sometimes even solve, their problems. In many cases, all others need is a chance to express themselves—to get their problems off their chest. As a supervisor, the understanding response style helps you get the information you need to deal with problem situations.

### Value of Feedback

Why should we concern ourselves with responding? Response styles are one form of feedback, and feedback is invaluable to effective communication. It can indicate sensitivity, supportiveness, open-mindedness, and helpfulness.[5] Beyond these benefits, it can make future communication more effective. That is, it helps provide the base for ongoing, effective communication.

But feedback can also help us—not just the other person. We need feedback to help us adjust our next message. It provides the information we need to keep ourself on course. If we do not get enough of it, sometimes we may even need to ask for it: "Do you know what I'm saying?" "Do you understand?" "Can you see where I'm coming from?"

The point of feedback is that messages mean different things to different people. As you cooperate by providing others feedback, and as others cooperate with you, it helps ensure that messages will be more accurate and useful. No amount of feedback, or any method of which we are currently aware, will guarantee 100 percent accuracy or usefulness, but feedback remains the best technique we have.

## IMPROVING LISTENING

It does not matter what the situation; if you are involved in oral communication, listening effectively will have a significant impact on the success or outcome of the situation. On-the-job situations include interviews, problem-solving discussion sessions, and meetings. Add to these the daily contacts you have with co-workers and supervisors and the amount of time spent on the telephone. To improve our listening will increase the amount of information we have on which to base decisions or actions. Whatever suggestions that could be offered, they have to begin by ceasing your own speech. You cannot listen effectively or completely while you are talking. There are some skills that can be used when listening; each of these can be practiced in your everyday conversations with others. These include patience, empathy, motivation, involvement, self-awareness, and capitalizing on thought speed.

### Be Patient

One reason many people do not listen well is because they do not want to take the time to listen. Some would rather talk; some want to move on to other things; some are so preoccupied with their own thoughts they cannot concentrate or focus well enough to listen. Patience requires both time and energy.

*Don't interrupt.* Unless your purpose is to clarify, let the other person complete his or her ideas before you respond. So much confusion and conflict occurs simply because we cannot wait until others complete their thoughts.

*Suspend your judgment.* Hold off making any evaluation until you have enough facts or information. Use your time probing and trying to discover the facts.

*Create a supportive atmosphere.* Relax. Do not rush others; try to put them at ease. They are more likely to express themselves fully and honestly with someone with whom they feel comfortable.

**Reveal Empathy**

Another reason people do not listen well is because they either cannot or will not participate in the other person's feelings and ideas. Charles Kelly, a writer on "Empathic Listening," says that "empathic listening occurs when the person participates in the spirit or feeling of his environment as a communication receiver."[6] Kelly warns us that this does *not* mean that the listener is uncritical or always in agreement with what he or she hears. The reason for revealing empathy is "to become fully and accurately aware of what is going on."[7]

*Try to understand the other person.* What are the attitudes, beliefs, emotions, experiences, or knowledge that would prompt this response? Try to discover the intent of the other person. Why is he or she saying these things?

*Keep from criticizing the other person.* Many people are predisposed to be disagreeable. When you think your ideas are right, or you think the other person could not hold a "proper" idea, it is easy to be critical. And yet, such a critical attitude interferes with effective listening.

*Focus on the purpose of the message.* Try to find the proper context for the message. Rather than agree or disagree with it, try to understand the message in the context of everything you know about the speaker and the situation that prompted the message.

**Be Motivated**

Listening effectively is *not* easy. It is not a passive process; it involves vigorous, productive activity. As you read the suggestions that follow, notice how each one involves energy and commitment. One of the reasons why many people do not listen well is that they do not try very hard; they think it is a natural, automatic reflex action.

*Make a commitment to listen.* In many cases, good listening is simply a question of "mental set." That is, like everything else, if you want to listen badly enough, you will; if you don't, you won't. Thus, the way you enter a situation may determine what you get out of it.

*Get physically and mentally ready to listen.* Be alert. Alert listeners sit up, lean forward slightly, and reveal interest. Mentally, they put aside personal worries, fears, or pleasant reverie; they get rid of distractions.[8]

*Concentrate.* Our attention span goes in spurts and seldom lasts long. To overcome wandering attention requires active concentration: trying to direct our mind toward a common objective.[9]

## Be Involved

Good listeners are actively involved in the communication situation. They take part in what is going on. Involvement means both physical and psychological engagement.

*Look at the other person.* The best way you have to reveal involvement is through eye contact. Turn your full attention toward the other person with respect to body position, and look sincere and interested. Smile and respond appropriately.

*Remember that communication is two-way.* A successful outcome to this communication situation requires active participation. Ask questions if things are still unclear after the other person has finished. Try to clarify intended meanings. Provide appropriate feedback and other reactions as needed.

## Be Self-aware

One of the best ways you have to improve your listening ability is to monitor your own behavior. Notice what you do and the effects you are having on the other person. Most effective communicators know how to increase their effectiveness; they replace bad habits with good ones because they are sensitive to what they do.

*React to the ideas.* It is easy to allow ourselves to be distracted by a person's attractiveness, way of dress, or manner of presentation. Good ideas seldom have anything to do with these features. Resist the temptation to be distracted from the ideas. Rather than saying, "How could anyone listen to a character like this?", force yourself to respond, "What does he or she know that I need to know?"

*Keep an open mind.* One of the biggest barriers in listening is our tendency to formulate a reply or answer before the other person is finished talking. This occurs in controversial situations. When we want to disagree and disprove, we stop listening. But it also occurs when our intent is to protect and build our self-esteem: to speak "only about what *we* want to talk about, and not giving a hoot in hell about what the other person wants to talk about."[10]

*Avoid antagonizing.* One sure way to cause others to conceal their ideas, emotions, or attitudes is to say or do things that provoke them. We may tease, jab, or become sarcastic. These behaviors tend to cause tension or frustration. Notice the effect of your behavior on the other person; when something you do tends to antagonize, back off, soften the blow, or apologize.

### Capitalize on Thought Speed[11]

Realize that people speak slowly, but they think much more quickly. Thus, when people talk to us, we have plenty of time to spare; we think much faster than they speak.

*Anticipate what will be talked about.* Try to forecast mentally where the message is leading and the important points to be made. Try to see trends and themes by summarizing what has been said and anticipating the future direction.

*Weigh the speaker's evidence.* As people speak to you, try to determine the base for their ideas. Just because ideas are spoken does not make them true. Are the facts accurate? What is their source? Is the source credible? Are you getting the full picture? Remember that there are many ways of looking at any idea or problem.

*Listen between the lines.* Notice, for example, what is not being said. Listen for changes in tone, volume, and inflection. Look, too, for meaning in facial expressions, eye contact, gestures, and other body movement.[12]

### SUMMARY

The first section of this chapter established the importance of listening. Not only is listening a vital part of human interaction, but the better we listen the more informed we are—and information is power. It provides a base for critical thinking. Listening also allows us to compare how we feel with how others feel. In addition, it provides one means for establishing warm, supportive, friendly communication situations. Finally, as a courteous behavior, listening suggests to others that we consider their ideas, suggestions, or positions important.

In the section titled "Nature of Listening," some of the common *myths* of listening were discussed. The more intelligent you are, the better you will listen; speaking is more important than listening; it is easy to do; it is automatic; and competence in listening develops naturally. Remember, these are myths—as such, they are untrue.

Barriers to listening were divided into message problems such as the need for short, simple messages. Variety and energy in a message heighten attention. The second category for barriers were mind problems—the mental state or background knowledge of communicators. Being preoccupied, antagonistic, or overly critical causes listening problems. People problems, the final problem area, concerns, distractions or barriers that result from our concern over appearance, presentation, and emotional involvement.

In the section "Listening and Feedback," the five listening and response styles were discussed. These include the evaluative, interpretive, supportive, probing, and understanding response styles. The evaluative style reflects closed communication and high other-involvement, whereas the ideal style—the understanding response—fosters more open communication with low other-involvement.

To improve your listening you can practice being patient, revealing empathy, being motivated, being involved, being self-aware, and capitalizing on thought speed. Within each of these categories, several specific and direct suggestions were made that can foster growth and change.

Listening skills are taught, not caught. Because you engage in listening so much in your daily life, you can teach yourself to listen better. Taking the time and trouble to do so will be rewarding. If you care about yourself as a person, and if you care about others as humans, you will feel more enriched when you are able to listen well. It will be one of the greatest payoffs that you have in the human relationships you establish at work.

## NOTES

[1] Madelyn Burley-Allen, *Listening: The Forgotten Skill* (New York: John Wiley, 1982).

[2] Muriel James and Dorothy Jongeward, *Born to Win: Transactional Analysis with Gestalt Experiments* (Reading, Mass.: Addison-Wesley, 1971), p. 48.

[3] Larry L. Barker, *Listening Behavior* (Englewood Cliffs, N.J.: Prentice-Hall, 1971), p. xiii.

[4] John E. Jones and J. William Pfeiffer, "Helping Relationship Inventory," *The 1973 Annual Handbook for Group Facilitators* (San Diego, Calif.: University Associates, 1973), p. 70. These five categories have been attributed to E. H. Porter, *An Introduction to Therapeutic Counseling* (Boston: Houghton Mifflin, 1950).

[5] Joseph A. DeVito, *The Interpersonal Book*, 3rd ed. (New York: Harper & Row, 1983), pp. 298–300.
[6] Charles M. Kelly, "Empathic Listening," in *Speech Communication: A Reader*, 2nd ed., ed. Richard L. Weaver, II (San Diego, Calif.: Collegiate Publishing, 1979), p. 165.
[7] Ibid., p. 165.
[8] Ibid., p. 172.
[9] Ibid., p. 172.
[10] Edmond G. Addeo and Robert E. Burger, *EgoSpeak: Why No One Listens to You* (New York: Bantam, 1973), p. xiii.
[11] Ralph G. Nichols, "Listening Is A 10-Part Skill," *Nation's Business*, 45 (July 1957), 56–60. In Richard L. Weaver, II, *Speech/Communication: A Reader*, 2nd ed. (San Diego, Calif.: Collegiate Publishing, 1979), pp. 272–74.
[12] Ibid., pp. 266–74. Also see Kelly, pp. 171–73.

(The answers to the true-false quiz on listening (Figure 3–4) are all false.)

# 4

# Language Needs

When we communicate with others, whether orally or in writing, we use symbols: *words*. We live in a symbolic environment, one filled with words. Just as breathing is essential to life, so are symbols essential to working and living with other human beings. Symbols provide the base by which we communicate. More people work at producing words than at producing anything else.[1]

Our purpose when we communicate with another person is to create in his or her mind the idea that is in our mind. Since we cannot directly implant our idea in another's mind, we must use symbols—words—to evoke or stimulate meaning. Along with our use of words, we also hope that the meaning we have for the symbol is the same as the meaning the other person has for the word. Only in that way is the other person caused to think the way we want him or her to think.

So often when we get into trouble, someone will say, "Oh, that's just a matter of words," or "Let's not quibble over the words." Such a view implies that words are not important or may not be worth consideration by serious-minded people. Yet words play a very important part in our lives. Because of the way they affect us, and how often they affect us, they are a subject worthy of serious study. What's more, there are techniques that can help us write and speak more effectively.

Whether you are aware of it or not, your age, education, intelligence, emotional state, attitudes, values, and beliefs are revealed in the words you select to communicate your ideas. That is why an understanding of language can be so important. It helps assure you that the language you choose is conveying the exact impression you want. It puts *you* in charge of your language rather than to allow your language carelessly and haphazardly to reflect you.

Your language, then, is an advertisement to others about the product it represents: *you*. Just as in advertising where you want your dollar investment to be cost-effective, you want to be able to make just the right choices so that the end results—the belief you want held, the information you want conveyed, or the action you want taken—will be effectuated. There is no need to say more than what it takes to get the job done, and if you say less, you can be assured that it probably won't get done.

If we look at the material in this chapter in this manner, it is likely to have more impact. We can all improve our uses of language. And since our language is so important, as it often determines the impression we make, then any investment in improvement should result in rich dividends.

This chapter presents an overview of language, then looks specifically at those areas where greatest improvement can occur. Characteristics of language such as clarity, simplicity, sincerity, emphasis, and triteness will be examined. In each case, specific suggestions designed to improve your use of language will be offered. The approach taken in this chapter is not applicable to either oral *or* written communication; it applies to both. Thus, the examples used will refer to both oral and written communication as well.

## AN OVERVIEW OF LANGUAGE

One reason why many people either spend little time studying or trying to improve their language is that it is taken for granted. Thus, the way our language works is not very well understood by most people. To apply the suggestions offered in this chapter is likely to cause you to stand out among your peers.

### Stereotyping

I already mentioned how our language can affect others' impressions of us. Before going on, let me indicate how dramatic that reaction can be. One author has provided some of the stereotypes (fixed impressions) that can occur because of the language we use:[2]

1. People who use correct grammar are frequently educated and knowledgeable, more cultured, respectful of the language they use, and somewhat intolerant of those who abuse or misuse the English language.

2. People who speak ungrammatically, unless the job they have or the one for which they are applying requires little or no written or oral communication, generally do not advance.
3. People with large vocabularies are thought to be well educated, possess social graces, and be intelligent, knowledgeable, and highly credible.
4. People with small vocabularies are perceived to have a limited education, experience difficulty expressing themselves, and have lower-paying jobs.
5. People who use obscene language usually have filthy minds and an anemic source of word power. They are vulgar, crass, impolite, and unpleasant company.

The author suggests, too, that the above statements "cannot apply to everyone, and should be treated as irresponsible generalizations. The danger they pose," he adds, "is a result of that 'little bit of truth' they all possess being distorted by those who use them."[3]

**Language and You**

Language affects others—and it also affects us. First, realize that, generally, we understand that for which we have language. If we see something for which we have no language, we may ignore it, forget about it, or store it until later when we *do* acquire understanding of it—or language for it. The better our ability in using words, and the broader our experiences with them (vocabulary), the more we will tend to understand.

If you have ever toured a factory, you have undoubtedly seen machines performing functions you cannot explain. But that does not mean you do not see them nor store the information regarding their presence or their action. At some point, perhaps, a tour guide then explains how a product moves through the various phases of production. Suddenly, the light goes on and you can now understand those machines you saw and their purpose. ("Oh, then the product is processed from raw material, dried, and cooked in that last room.") You now have language for something not understood at first viewing.

Second, how we define reality—what something is, or what is going on—is a function of the way we put experience into words.[4] Then we respond to those words as the experience itself. That is, it is our label—or the meaning we ascribe to the symbol—rather than the experience itself that generates understanding. I know, for example, how a particular grain is converted from raw material, dried, and cooked. My understanding of the process may have little to do with reality—how it actually happens—but I can explain it to you so that it not only makes sense but also sounds right! When someone mentions this process, it is *my* reality I revert to for understanding, until, of course, I am either educated or re-educated as to what actually occurs. This is when a closer relationship between *my* reality (in my head) and external reality (what physically exists) is created.

Notice, once again, how this idea relates to the transactional approach to communication developed in Chapter 2. The words I use to construct the images in my mind cause me to react and respond in certain ways. Those images—constructed from language—*are* my reality; my *only* reality!

When you label a situation as "drastic," "desperate," "outrageous," "wasteful," or "unreasonable"—to use extreme terms for effect—not only might you be affecting someone else's view of the situation, but you might very well be affecting your own, as in the following dialogue:

SHE: I hurried up to your office as quickly as I could after I got your memo. You said our reply to them must be "instantaneous."

HE: Yes, I thought we had a week to respond, but as it turns out we only have a couple of days.

SHE: "Instantaneous," huh? You know, we might be better off if we could fire off a reply to them this afternoon. Do you have their phone number?

Caught up in his own use of the word "instantaneous," this fellow was being persuaded by a label he chose to attach to the situation. It is, of course, difficult to determine how often self-persuasion takes place, but it is clear that the kind of words chosen to define or describe a situation creates an image, and that image can affect anyone exposed to it, including the original user.

### Saying What You Mean

It is not easy to say what you mean. How often do you hear someone say, "What I really mean to say is . . ." or "What I'm trying to say is . . .". Knowing precisely what you want to say is one thing, but being able to evoke accurately that same meaning in another person is quite another. We must learn to weave our words into meaningful units of thought. And that means learning to manipulate the words—choosing, assembling, and presenting them—so that they represent the exact meaning we wish to convey, or as close to the exact meaning as we can get. After all, that is all we can hope for.

But people do not think in words; they think in pictures. That is why we have talked about "constructing images." Words stimulate mental pictures.[5] Thus, when we speak or write, we must think about generating images so that our receivers can conjure up the appropriate sights and sounds. Even sensory perceptions—odors, tastes, and touch—can become part of this imagery if the proper words are used. These mental pictures help make communication clearer.

## Connotative and Denotative Meanings

It is perhaps overstated that to communicate effectively is no easy task. Let me introduce one other area that causes problems. The *connotative meaning* of a word lies in the mind of the person using that word. That is, he or she has an idea of what that word means based on his or her understanding of the other person, the context itself, and his or her own background, experiences, and familiarity with, and use of, that word. When we use words that have connotative meanings, we add an evaluative or subjective dimension to them. For example, when someone refers to your boss as "tight," "cheap," "frugal," "thrifty," or "wise," what does that mean? Each of these symbols is likely to evoke a specific emotional reaction with reference to your boss—from a wide range of possible reactions. Meaning will exist because we know our boss and we know those words, and when the shoe fits (especially in situations we are very close to) we not only put it on, but we're also likely to lace it up to the knee—figuratively speaking, of course.

*Denotative meanings,* on the other hand, are derived from the dictionary. A denotative meaning is *the* specific meaning that serves to point at or identify a thing or characteristic. Denotative meanings are objective rather than subjective. With these meanings there is a closer relationship between the word and the thing it represents. If we say "chair," "desk," or "window," there is greater chance that a similar meaning for these words will be evoked in a receiver's mind than if we said "rush," "opportunity," or "fringe benefit," where there is more room for interpretation.

To use denotative words, however, does not solve communication problems with respect to the use of language. Of the 2,000 most common words, according to one source—excluding scientific and technical terms—the 500 most frequently used words have more than 14,000 dictionary definitions! That is an average of twenty-eight definitions for each of the 500 most frequently used words![6] Denotative language, obviously, comes nowhere near solving problems in verbal communication; but you do not have to wonder why we have so many problems either!

Is it useful to know this distinction? Because connotative words tend to reflect our own individual perceptions and values more than denotative words, we must try to select words that accurately and precisely represent the situation. If we watch our language closely, we will be less likely to use words carelessly or thoughtlessly.

## Know Your Receivers

Interpretations are placed on words as a result of a person's background, culture, environment, education, experience, and age. Thus, the more we know about who will be receiving our communication, the more likely we will be successful in communicating with them.

How do you find out about them? Solid, well-founded knowledge does not happen instantaneously. It won't be long, however, before we will simply be able to tap out a few letters on a computer and have in front of us at least some basic demographic (vital statistics) information. Even then, we must add to that information.

1. In talking to them, listen for verbal cues that will reveal their background.
2. In written communications, read between the lines to interpret the words properly.
3. Watch for their use of vocabulary, accents in oral communication, idioms and slang words, and grammar.
4. Speaking and writing effectiveness reveals much about a person's personality, life-style, experience, background, and age.
5. Ask other company personnel about them.

We might take a hint from an effective salesman I know. He meticulously keeps records of the people with whom he has regular contact. The above aspects and other business characteristics can be condensed to 3 x 5 cards and filed alphabetically by the person's name. The rewards will be better public relations, increased dollar sales, and self-satisfaction. These are direct benefits of improved communication skills that result from knowing who is receiving your messages. Courtesy in your communications with others involves your genuine awareness of your receiver's needs, purposes, attention span, and time.

## CHARACTERISTICS OF LANGUAGE

"He (or she) speaks my language" is a colloquial way of saying that a writer or speaker communicates clearly and concisely. In a highly specialized society, most educated people speak two languages—the general language of their society and the very specialized language of their business or profession. The specialized vocabulary of businesses and professions is called *jargon*. This is obvious when a physician clearly communicates the nature of your illness to you and then writes a barely decipherable (the handwriting is really irrelevant!) message to the pharmacist regarding your prescription. It becomes even more obvious if the physician chooses to speak to you in jargon, and you must ask, "what do you mean by that?" Specialists talk with specialists in the finely honed, carefully tuned jargon of that profession. (See Figure 4–1.)

There is no doubt that we must know our receivers and adjust our language accordingly. But there are some characteristics of language that

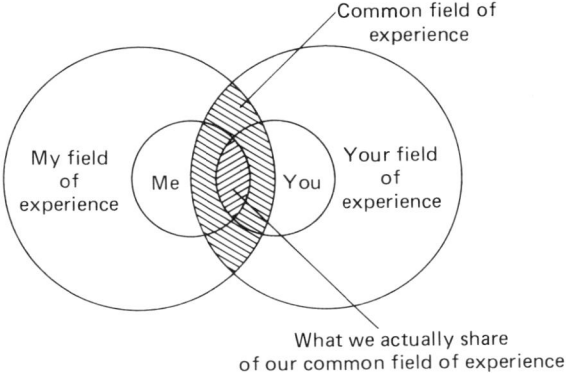

**FIGURE 4–1.** Here, the transactional perspective is illustrated to include the fields of experience of both parties. The more two people communicate, the larger the common field of experience; and the larger the common field of experience, the more both parties have to draw upon as they continue communicating.

must be present no matter who our receivers are and what their level of expertise is. This section will discuss five important characteristics; in each case suggestions for increasing your effectiveness with respect to the specific characteristic will be offered. The characteristics are: clarity, simplicity, sincerity, emphasis, and triteness.

### Clarity

One characteristic often associated with profound thinkers is their ability to explain complex ideas in clear, simple language. In contrast, the shallow mind tries to make simple things appear complex. The young employee uses the technical vocabulary of his or her college years to try to impress superiors; others pad memos and reports unnecessarily to convey intensive work and profound thought. In either case, the characteristic of *clarity* is not served.

*Clarity* simply means using language that is easily understood. We must free our language from restrictions and unnecessary limitations. What are the major factors that cause lack of clarity? Average sentence length would be one. We tend to understand shorter sentences more easily than longer ones, and simple sentences more easily than complex or compound ones. Using unfamiliar words is another factor. Of all the words available, normal, everyday conversations are made up of very few words. Of the words used most frequently, how many do we use and how often? As we deviate from everyday word usage, it can be expected that clarity will diminish too.

Moreover, passive constructions are harder to understand than are active ones. Thus, a sentence like "The order was taken by Sara" is not as easily processed as "Sara took the order." Negative sentences, too, are more difficult than affirmative ones. Along with this, double negatives present real problems. Another source of problems are *embedded* sentences, when one full sentence is embedded in another: "Ms. Elkins, whom my boss left with that lady who always carries the black notebook under her arm, never returned from lunch."

Beyond the suggestions already offered, a few others might also help:

1. Use your knowledge of yourself and other people to guide your choice of words.
2. Always state what *you* mean when you use an unfamiliar term in an unfamiliar way.
3. Select words that will make your receiver understand, identify, compare, contrast, remember, or apply what your message represents. This will help satisfy your receiver's logical needs.
4. Select words that will help make receiver experience feelings of seeing, hearing, tasting, touching, smelling, enjoying, or profiting from what your message conveys. This will help satisfy your receiver's psychological needs. This has to do with constructing mental images. For example:

   Feel yourself writing with the new XL Flow-on, designed with your writing comfort and engineered with your hand in mind. Write confidently on any surface. Feel your XL Flow-on respond effortlessly, eagerly, and dependably. Notice the smoothness. And notice, too, that the point never fades or mars. Ahhh, the freshness of a new thought, captured by the XL Flow-on. Wherever you go, rely on your XL. And enjoy writing again.

5. In using a comparison, state it fully. "Our new product is better" is not as strong as "Our new product is better than the one it replaces."
6. Use consistent grammar. "Unless business meetings are planned, it wastes time and money" should read, "Unless business meetings are planned, *they* waste time and money." A more common error is "Everyone involved in the project should realize that they. . . . "Everyone" requires a singular pronoun: "Everyone involved in the project should realize that he or she is an important link."
7. Make certain that pronoun antecedents are clear: "When Mrs. Sawyer and Ms. Flynn discussed the outcome, she said it had to be in tomorrow." Who said it had to be in tomorrow? From the sentence, it is impossible to know the pronoun referent for "she." Is it Mrs. Sawyer or Ms. Flynn?
8. Avoid sentence fragments. In informal writing and in speaking, fragmentary sentences are common. They are also used occasionally in textbook writing for emphasis, surprise, or variety. Business writers should not present dependent clauses as if those clauses are complete sentences: "These procedures have been the same since the inception of this company. Although they can be modified as needed," This would be clearer if written, "Although these products can be modified, they have been the same since. . . ."
9. Use connectors such as *and, or,* and *but,* only as required to complete a thought. "Two samples need to be sent to Stein and to Nevels and an addi-

tional set to Levitz no later than Saturday" is clearer when stated, "By Saturday, send two samples apiece to Stein, Nevels, and Levitz."
10. Finally, make certain all words needed for understanding your message are included. "Send an invoice to Hiram, Inc." might become, "Send an invoice to Hiram, Inc., at once." Or, "Sign the enclosed card" might become, "Sign and return the enclosed card."

**Simplicity**

When a simple approach is advocated, it should not be taken to mean *simpleminded*. Simpleminded means unsophisticated and foolish. A message that is plain, uncomplicated, and free from unnecessary elaboration or display is likely to be understood better than one that is not.

Some people use many words to conceal either their ignorance or lack of information. Simplicity does not mean sacrificing content. You cannot omit data that a receiver needs. Simplicity means the statement of complete, relevant information in as few words as necessary. In behavioral research, the concept is known as *parsimony:* the ability to find the simplest explanation for a behavior or set of behaviors.

In writing and speaking, simplicity comes, in part, from omitting needless words. We say "at all times" for "always"; "at the present time" or "at this point in time" for "now"; "despite the fact that" for "although" or "despite"; "due to the fact that" or "for the simple reason that" for "because" or "since." We also say "enclosed herewith for your information" for "enclosed is"; "in the event that" for "if"; "in the near future" for "soon"; "in the recent past" for "recently"; "until such a time as" for "until"; and "we would ask that you" for "please." Word thrift is important.

Simplicity also comes from using short words rather than long ones. For example, how much easier it is to say, "Last year the company lost money," than "Over the duration of the preceding year, the company operated at a financial deficit," or "Final action was taken after the reporting date," or "Definitive action was effected subsequent to the terminal deadline." A heavy proportion of long words tends to confuse the receiver. Not only are long words often the more difficult ones, but they also give the appearance of being difficult. A receiver's mental filters receive them that way and that is all that matters. Any business communicator would be wise to use long words with caution; when they are necessary, make certain they are known to the receiver.

Some suggestions to increase your simplicity in using language would include:

1. Keep your sentences short. With the possible exception of sentences of six or so words used for emphasis or variety, strive for sentences of an average sentence length of sixteen to eighteen words.[7]
2. Continually and carefully explore and evaluate the various ways to express your thoughts.

3. When you can replace a sentence or fragment with a shorter phrase or fragment, do it. Over time, the savings will add up.
4. Eliminate words that have no meaning. You may have to recast a sentence to do so, but the resulting simplicity will be worth it. For example, opening phrases such as "It can be noted that," "In addition to," "It is essential that," or "During the time that," can often be eliminated and you can begin at once with the essential content.
5. Find direct ways—rather than roundabout ways—to say things. "The committee is involved in the task of reviewing. . ." is a roundabout way of saying "The committee is reviewing. . ." or "The vice-president should take appropriate action to determine if the facilities. . . ."
6. Avoid repetition. The exceptions to this rule would be repetition used for special effect or for emphasis. ("In my opinion, I think the new proposal. . ." for "I think the new proposal," or "The most important essentials should not be overlooked," for "The essentials. . . .")

Economy of words saves time and money. The result is less dictation, transcription, and typing; shorter reading time and less filing; fewer supplies, less postage, telephone and telegraph services, and less demand, too, for interview and conference resources. Thus, both your time and that of other people is saved. Those are the kinds of saving bonuses that promotions and other rewards are made of.

### Sincerity

People must believe you. To convince others who receive communications that you mean what you say, your efforts must be courteous, friendly, and well intended. That is, your communications must reveal the quality of *sincerity* and must be marked by honesty and genuineness.

Building a reputation for sincerity is similar to building trust between two people. It takes time. It is not easy, and it depends on many different variables. But no matter how long it takes, it can be destroyed in an instant. Then, the rebuilding process becomes tedious and difficult. People are willing to extend the benefit of the doubt to you when they do not know you very well; they will believe you even though they may be skeptical. But break that trust, thus proving the merit of their skepticism, and you may find that restoring original faith is a long process.

How is insincerity detected? *By showing certainty* when it is clear that certainty is hardly possible. If you are dealing with the future, use tentative words that show that certainty cannot be expressed: "If" is a tentative word and reflects probabilities rather than surety. "I know you will exert every effort to help us" reveals the all-knowing phrase "I know" as if I am omniscient and can see all. "We are sure you will agree" has the same effect.

Use *adjectives and adverbs* sparingly. Hyperbole—exaggeration—reveals insincerity and magnifies your subjectivity. It may lead a receiver to question the factual information that supports a statement. Objective language, on the other hand, stays with the facts.

**Subjective:** Attendance was overwhelming.
**Objective:** Twenty-five people showed up; we expected less than ten because of the weather.

Adverbs can also be misleading:

This handsomely designed. . . .
A remarkably unique discovery. . . .

The problem is that the adverbs often do not have the same meaning for the receiver as they have for the sender.

Use *superlatives* sparingly. A superlative is an exaggerated expression that suggests something of the utmost degree. They cause a receiver to question the sincerity of a thought. When you use superlatives such as "best," "most," "only," "largest," "smallest," "least," and "latest," realize that the truth of your statement is likely to be questioned.

Some superlatives are necessary and useful. When you refer to the "latest directive," "the oldest employee," "the highest bid," or the "lowest rate," these superlatives can be verified and thus do not arouse resentment.

Instead of using superlatives, supply your receiver with sufficient information. Then let him or her arrive at the conclusion that this one is "best." This approach is effective because it not only allows receivers to think for themselves but also causes the impression to be deeply imbedded—and thus remembered—because the receiver came to it alone, or essentially alone.

*Euphemisms* can also reveal insincerity. A euphemism involves the substitution of an agreeable or inoffensive word or expression for one that may offend or suggest something unpleasant. Sometimes euphemisms are used to disguise unpleasant realities such as death: "Walter passed on"; or a person's firing: "Yes, Jane was given her walking papers," or "She was let go," "released," or "a victim of reorganization." It is the sarcastic euphemism that should be avoided:

Adelle is our domestic economist.
Delbert is our sanitary engineer.

These uses attempt to make the work more sophisticated than it is. "Del is a staff member here" or "Del is our custodian" are both more direct and to the point; however, "staff member" still runs the risk of having the wrong connotation. Euphemisms often become worn out and more objectionable than the words they are designed to replace. The "disadvantaged" are still poor, a "patriarch" is still elderly, and people who have "gone to their eternal reward" are still dead.

Euphemisms must be used carefully. Those that have pleasant associations are helpful in advertising and selling, especially when the products being advertised—soap, shampoo, toothpaste, detergents, and soft drinks—have essentially similar functions and ingredients. Euphemisms associate such products with pleasant experiences, but when they are too extreme they come across as obviously false.

Remembering the effects that highly connotative words can have, speakers and writers must choose their words carefully. Euphemistic words can trigger connotations of which speakers and writers were originally unaware. They should check to make certain the words have positive rather than negative connotations if sincerity is their goal.

Finally, insincerity can be revealed through expressions that suggest *surprise*. For example, "Your letter came as a great shock" sounds unrealistic. Additionally, the phrase "I cannot understand why you have not responded" suggests, by the use of "cannot understand," that any reason you offer is invalid. Words must be chosen carefully.

How, then, do you gain sincerity? There are a number of ways.

1. Believe in what you are doing. If you really believe that the techniques and approaches you are using are correct, courteous, honest, and sensitive, they are likely to come across as sincere.
2. Be honest. Dishonesty requires great effort and consistency.
3. Avoid overdoing good will. What feelings are aroused when a letter of greeting includes the statement: "We are extremely pleased to be able to help you, and we want you to know that your satisfaction means more than anything to us"?
4. Avoid exaggeration. Do not overstate the facts. Any kind of excessiveness may bring your sincerity into question.

**Emphasis**

In communicating with others, not all information you have to share is equally important. Certain information needs to be stressed—*emphasized*. Emphasis is simply the force or intensity given to an idea to give it special impressiveness. Emphasis is generally achieved by using the following methods: position, space, sentence structure, or other mechanical means. But these are only the most common ones. Often, emphasis occurs as a result of surprise. Someone does something out of the ordinary. And when we are touched in this way or caught off guard, that idea that touched us or caught us is emphasized. One man explained to people that he spells his first name ("Dann") with two "n's" to cause others to remember it. Another example: one young actor spelled his name "Kenn" to attract the attention of directors. This technique of *emphasis* worked, in both cases.

*Position.* An idea will carry more emphasis if it is located at the beginning or the end of a communication. Location at the beginning is called *primacy* (the state of being first) and positioning at the end is called *recency* (the state of being most recent—last—in the receiver's mind). Thus, how you begin a communication and how you end it become very important. Paying particular attention to the way communications are organized can have a direct effect on what the receiver takes away and remembers from the message.

*Space.* It probably goes without saying that how much you say about something determines the emphases you give it as well. The more you dwell on an idea the more emphasis it is given. In putting ideas of equal worth together, make certain you spend equal amounts of time developing each idea.

*Sentence structure.* Short, simple sentences call attention to their content. Long, involved ones do not. Place information you consider important in shorter, simple sentences; this way it does not have to compete for the receiver's attention. Even in longer constructions, the independent clauses are likely to hold one's attention better than the dependent clauses.

*Mechanical means.* In writing, numerous mechanical means can be used to give words emphasis. We underscore words, use "quotation marks," set words in *italics* or SOLID CAPITALS. Lines, arrows, and diagrams also call attention to particular parts. Adding color, special type, and drawings does the same.

In speaking we may say, "Now get this" or "This is important" or "Pay attention to this" before we make a point. After making an important point, we might add, "Note that" or ask a question, "Do you know what that means?" We might repeat a point so that listeners are sure to hear it. A change in rate (how fast one speaks) may be emphatic just as speaking slowly may be effective. Pauses and gestures can also be used to emphasize important points.

Winston Churchill observed: "If you have an important point to make, don't try to be subtle or clever. Use a pile driver. Hit the point once. Then come back and hit it again. Then hit it a third time—a tremendous whack."

How points are stressed is often vital to how they are received. We need to use different kinds of emphasis depending on the form of communication (oral or written), the point being made, or the intended receiver. One should keep in mind, though, that emphasis can be overdone. Ideas that are overemphasized, or emphasis that is overused, also can have a negative effect.

**Triteness**

Trite language is that which has grown stale from excessive use. Trite expressions are also called hackneyed words, clichés, stereotyped expressions, deadwood, or whiskered words. They are often longer than necessary and have become stiff, formal, and relatively meaningless because of overuse.

Why do we use trite language? The major reason is that it is easier. To rely on a cliché does not require much thought. To open a letter with "Enclosed please find" is a natural, comfortable cliché that could be replaced with "Enclosed is." We end speeches with "In conclusion I would just like to say that. . . ." We could more easily say, "To summarize."

To list all the currently used clichés would require a volume by itself, and would be incomplete when finished. People have their own hackneyed expressions that they come to rely on—sometimes simply slight derivations of the more popular ones. Moreover, clichés are often fadlike in their popularity. They rise and fall as rapidly as television sitcoms.

Trite expressions such as "on the other hand," "all things being equal," "as luck would have it," and "with human nature being what it is" simply clog communication by obscuring meaning and boring receivers.[8] True, they cannot always be avoided, but if guarded against, often they can be replaced with straightforward language. Indiscriminately tacking on the suffix-*wise* to form such words as saleswise, prestigewise, and customerwise shows how triteness can spread. How much better would it be to use well-established words! Being original is difficult and it takes longer. But that kind of originality often distinguishes the "fresh thinker" from the "dusty droner." When your language is littered with worn-out phrases borrowed from others, what stops receivers from assuming that the ideas being described are not shopworn and threadbare as well?

To rid yourself of trite language requires two things:

1. Become sensitive to your language. Find out how many trite expressions you use.
2. Search out simple and precise words to substitute for this trite language. Leave out trite expressions entirely if they make no contribution to the content of your message.

*Slang* can also be considered trite. Slang is language peculiar to a particular group. It is usually nonstandard language that is in transition—changing. The type of slang we use verbally advertises our level of sophistication. Can you imagine a doctor coming out of a patient's room and telling the family that the patient has just "kicked the bucket"?

The more common the job, situation, or individual, the more likely slang is to be heard. Moreover, slang will occur in certain situations where there is common consent by the parties involved. Sometimes, too, because of the relative effectiveness, aptness, or uniqueness of a particular word, it is elevated to legitimate status in our language and can be used without reservation or fear. But one is safer avoiding the use of slang. In most cases, the negative ramifications far outweigh the positive benefits.

## SUMMARY

Our language conveys our personal image. Often we do not select our language based on what will communicate most clearly. Too often we make selections on what we think will impress our receivers the most. Lawyers should sound like lawyers; doctors like doctors; college professors like college professors; and business people like business people. Our language is part of our personal communication style.

In this chapter, an overview of the language process was first presented. The ideas of language stereotyping, the relationship of language to you the user, the difficulty of saying what one means, the distinctions between connotative and denotative language, and the importance of knowing your receivers were discussed.

From there, certain characteristics of language like clarity, simplicity, sincerity, emphasis, and triteness were developed. Throughout these sections, practical suggestions for growth and improvement were offered. All of these suggestions are based on one essential thing: your willingness to monitor your own language usage. Since language is a personal matter, and since your language habits have developed over many years, change will not occur without careful observation and serious effort. To develop language that will cause people to react to you the way you want them to, you must first get a clear picture of your present language style.

There is no question that people speak differently. This difference has a direct effect upon how other people perceive them. Certain language usage renders some people more believable than others. Some people who *are* bosses, do not sound like bosses; and other people who are *not* bosses, sound like they are. But the essential idea of this chapter was that your language usage is *not* like your fingerprints—it can change. And what's more, it *can* make a difference.

## NOTES

[1] Joseph P. Dagher, *Technical Communication: A Practical Guide* (Englewood Cliffs, N.J.: Prentice-Hall, 1978), p. 146.

[2] Abné M. Eisenberg, *Job Talk: Communicating Effectively on the Job* (New York: Macmillan, 1979). Republished as *Communicating Effectively At Work* (Prospect Heights, Ill.: Waveland Press, 1983), p. 43.

[3] Ibid., pp. 43–44.

[4] Harry Hoijer, *Language in Culture* (Chicago: The University of Chicago Press, 1954), p. 93.

[5] See Richard L. Weaver, II, Howard W. Cotrell, and Thomas A. Michel, "Imaging: A Technique for Effective Lecturing," *Journal of Mental Imagery* (in press).

[6] Dale A. Level, Jr., and William P. Galle, Jr., *Business Communications: Theory and Practice* (Dallas, Tex: Business Publications, 1980), p. 23.

[7] Raymond Lesikar, *Business Communication: Theory and Application,* 4th ed. (Homewood, Ill.: Richard D. Irwin, 1980), p. 104.

[8] For lengthy lists of trite words and phrases see Donald J. Leonard, *Shurter's Communication in Business,* 4th ed. (New York: McGraw-Hill, 1979), pp. 30–34; also William C. Himstreet and Wayne Murlin Baty, *Business Communications: Principles and Methods,* 5th ed. (Boston: Kent Publishing, 1977), pp. 23–30.

# 5

# Nonverbal Communication

It is 4:30 p.m. when the phone rings. The manager wants to see you at once. You put the phone down quickly and rush off, indicating to one of your associates by pointing upward and saying, "I'm going upstairs for a meeting," and shrugging your shoulders and looking bewildered to show that you do not know why. When you get to the elevator, it just happens to be open. You put your hand out to hold the door—looking relieved, but still in a hurry. There are two people already in the elevator; you nod to them, acknowledging their presence. They smile and move to each corner. You move to the back—dead center between them. No one talks. All eyes are on the floor numbers. You get off at the third floor and go through the second door on the left. The secretary nods and points the way. You head down a long corridor to the manager's office. As you step onto the plush carpeting and look at her, you realize from her stern gaze that something is wrong. She holds the look for what seems an eternity. You already know what she is going to say. Is a statement even necessary? What else could it be at 4:30 on Friday at the end of the first week of the new month? Last month's sales figures are in, and they don't look good! You pause, then shake your head to show that you understand, mimicking her concern.

Notice the value and importance of nonverbal communication in this example. It is powerful and often determines the meaning behind verbal communication. At other times, it *is* the message.

In this chapter the nature of nonverbal communication will be discussed briefly, and the functions that it serves will be outlined. In the final section, various types of nonverbal communication will be examined.

## WHAT IS THE NATURE OF NONVERBAL COMMUNICATION?

Just as the term *communication* has been subject to a variety of interpretations, so is the term *nonverbal*. The issue in defining what is nonverbal seems to be whether or not "the events that are traditionally studied under the heading *nonverbal* are literally nonverbal."[1] The point is that verbal and nonverbal communication are so intimately and subtly woven together that it is difficult to separate them.

Further confusion arises when it comes to separating the signal or nonverbal event from the interpretation of the signal. Does nonverbal communication refer to the signal or to the interpretation? Generally, people refer to the signal produced, not to the attribution or attachment of meaning.[2] When you think about it, the attachment of meaning—categorizing, labeling, explaining, and clarifying—is often a verbal process. Just because the words are not expressed aloud does not mean they do not occur.

In this book, *nonverbal communication* refers to the exchange of messages primarily through nonlinguistic (nonword) means.[3] Specifically, this will refer to signals transmitted by voice, appearance, face and eyes, touch, the body, personal space and distance, silence and time, and environment.

## WHAT FUNCTIONS DOES NONVERBAL COMMUNICATION SERVE?

If you go back and examine the nonverbal communication in the example at the opening of this chapter, you will detect all of the functions demonstrated in that short space. Nonverbal communication complements verbal messages. It substitutes for them, and it accents them as well.[4] Nonverbal communication can also serve a regulating and an expressing function.

### Complementing

When nonverbal communication *complements* verbal communication it adds to the meaning of the verbal communication. Putting the phone down quickly and rushing off complemented the importance of the verbal message, "I'm going upstairs for a meeting." If the verbal message is further complemented by tone of voice, facial expression, and gestures (pointing upward), the importance of the meeting is further reinforced. Nonverbal communication contributes further insights and information. Can you imagine what colleagues within hearing distance would think if, after slamming down the phone, you said, "I am *not* going upstairs to see her; if she wants to talk to me, she can just come down here!"

Nonverbal communication can also *contradict* the verbal communication. How often have you been forced to wear a false smile, to act like you enjoyed what you thought was dull, or demonstrated that you were in a good mood when you felt lousy? Contradictions, if detected, create confusion. And when the verbal and nonverbal disagree, most people believe the nonverbal; it is habitual and, more often than not, instinctual. Thus, the nonverbal is less likely to be fabricated.

### Substituting

When nonverbal communication is used in place of verbal communication, *substituting* occurs. In the opening example, you substituted nonverbal for verbal when you nodded to the two people in the elevator rather than saying "Hi, how are you?" They did the same when they smiled. It could be interpreted as substituting when you all adjusted your positions in the elevator. You didn't have to explain the process of adjusting positions. The secretary on the third floor substituted when she nodded and pointed the way to the manager's office instead of saying, "She's waiting for you at the end of the hall; you may go right in."

### Accenting

When the manager revealed a stern look, she *accented* her mood. Holding the look further accented the severity of the situation. Accenting emphasizes a point. When you paused, then shook your head, you were accenting your own understanding. After an argument with someone you love, you might reach out and touch the person or even hold or kiss him or her, accenting your love.

### Regulating

When nonverbal communication *regulates*, it coordinates the dialogue between people. Your nonverbal nod in the elevator prompted the smile from the others. The manager's willingness to hold her stern look prompted your shaking your head—and even mimicking her concern. Notice sometime when you are talking with others the nonverbal cues that regulate communication: What do you or others do, for example, to let the other person know he or she can talk? Do you drop your vocal tone, nod your head, pause, or gesture? There are probably numerous nonverbal cues that you use to regulate communication about which you are almost totally unaware.

**Expressing**

When nonverbal communication is used in *expressing*, it makes known our opinions or feelings. Expressing is one of the important functions because it is often a key to how we relate with others. Moods, attitudes, and emotions are sometimes best revealed nonverbally. A subordinate may be reluctant to approach a manager who looks sullen, depressed, sad, or mad. Because of the expressing function, in the preceding meeting with the manager, you chose to say nothing, initiating the nonverbal mood.

Expressing is not always within our conscious control. Nonverbal expression of emotions is often involuntary. We convey annoyance in our tone of voice. A brief scowl or squint of an eye may reveal disagreement. If you were disagreeing with an idea a colleague offered, his or her emotional tone might be the clue to defensiveness or insecurity. Think of all the additional information you can get by being sensitive to nonverbal communication.

Complementing, substituting, accenting, regulating, and expressing are the most important functions nonverbal communication serves. Notice in the examples how these functions overlap each other. Nonverbal cues can serve many of the functions at the same time. For different people, the same cue can be interpreted in different ways. All, however, make an important contribution to the way we create meaning.

## WHAT ARE THE TYPES OF NONVERBAL COMMUNICATION?

One writer on nonverbal communication, Albert Mehrabian, identified three dimensions of human feelings and attitudes communicated more effectively through nonverbal cues: like–dislike, potency or status (power), and responsiveness.[5] In business situations it is useful to know the effects that nonverbal cues can have. In each case these dimensions become crucial to business-related interactions; thus, the control we exert over the cues that determine these dimensions becomes important.

What is important to understand, however, is that everything you do as you interact with others is a form of communication. You are always telling others something whether you mean to or not. It is impossible to categorize or list all nonverbal elements: that is, to list all elements outside the words themselves from which you can make meaning.

This section will look at some of the most important areas of nonverbal communication—those areas that are most obvious or most likely to make a difference when communicating with others. Voice, appearance, face and eyes, touch, the body, personal space and distance, time, and environment will be discussed.

### Voice

You have been asked into your manager's office. Pretend that this time it is the manager herself on the phone saying, "I'd like to see you in my office." Immediately you begin to seek cues that would reveal the possible content of your manager's potential message, but more importantly, you try to determine the severity of the meeting. "Is something wrong?" "Is she upset?" "Does she mean 'instantly,' or do I have a few minutes?" Cues regarding content are likely to come from your past environment: projects you have worked on, former conversations with the manager, or endeavors that have been discussed as future possibilities. But cues regarding importance, severity, and immediacy are likely to come from the manager's voice—the way she communicated her invitation into her office. These vocal cues that we look for have been referred to as *vocalics*—aspects of the voice such as pitch, volume, quality, and rate. The way these vocal cues are used in a message situation, as they accompany a verbal message, is referred to as *paralanguage:* how a message is said.

It is likely that the manager deliberately manipulated her voice to communicate the importance, severity, or immediacy of the situation, just as we do when we command another person to "type the letter," "turn off the lights," or "close the door." Vocal cues frequently play a role in determining responses in human communication situations.

But vocal cues do not simply concern how something is said. Often they *are* what is said. What is said may be an attitude, "I think this is important" or it may convey a relationship, "I am superior to you." What is said could be an emotion, some background information, how the conversation is to be managed, some aspect of a person's personality or physical features. In some situations, vocal cues carry more information than in others.[6]

As a business person actively involved with a wide variety of other people, it is important to recognize the role vocal stereotypes play in determining the responses of other people. Not only do others use them to judge a person's occupation, race, and body type, but also to judge personality attributes such as a person's sociability and degree of introversion or extroversion. Undoubtedly, there are many other qualities evaluated, and the evaluators use well-learned and securely entrenched stereotypes on which to base their guesses.

The guesses that are made may have little relationship to the person to whom they are attached. They may be totally inaccurate for that matter, but they will influence the interaction. Those areas where accuracy is likely to be greatest include age and status.[7]

Judgments of another person's emotions from vocal cues alone have been more consistently accurate. People are able to judge our emotions and feelings based on wordless vocal messages. One of the problems in this area is that you are likely to express the same emotion in a different way on another day, in a different situation, or because you were responding to some new stimuli. New circumstances call for, in many cases, a whole new set of response patterns.

The voice is an important variable in the effect we have on others. Although we are unlikely to have a strong negative effect on how much of our message listeners comprehend if we have moderately weak vocal behaviors (pitch, volume, quality, and rate), it is likely that we can increase a listener's comprehension by using variety. Avoiding monotony in any situation is likely to have positive benefits as well.[8] Thus, if we have an important message to convey, we want to convey it with a degree of expressiveness. That is, changes in pitch, volume, or rate should reflect our sincerity and enthusiasm. Important messages delivered in a dull or unenergetic manner can be misinterpreted.

If you are actively engaging in persuading others, the voice can have a powerful effect. People are perceived as persuasive through their use of more intonation, higher rate, more volume, and less halting speech. It is likely, too, that how credible a person you are will be determined, in part, through your vocal cues. And how trustworthy, dynamic, likable, and competent you appear plays an important role in some situations.[9] Once again, you want to control your expressiveness. A strong, pleasant voice is the greatest asset you can have. People with disagreeable voice qualities are not considered good. Self-limiting behaviors such as high pitch, strident tone, nasality, and low volume contribute to feelings of inferiority and the impression of inferiority in those with whom we relate. Energy, enthusiasm, and power come from voice control.

The voice, then, can communicate a great deal of information about another person. But it is how the voice combines with other verbal and nonverbal cues that should be of concern. To take the voice out of context fails to recognize it as an interactive part of the whole picture, and it is the picture of the whole that creates the final image.

### Appearance

An exercise used in some communication classes has a student sitting in the middle of a circle with all the other students in the class giving their first impressions of that student one at a time.[10] Students are amazed, oftentimes, at the role that appearance plays in these impressions. One student said, "If I had worn other clothes, it is likely that their impressions would have been completely different." No doubt this is true.

In his book *Dress for Success,* John T. Molloy cites the results of an informal experiment he ran to prove that people who look successful and well educated tend to receive preferential treatment. Men were sent out twice, once in "lower-middle-class" business suits and again in "upper-middle-class" suits. In what he labeled "push tests," he determined which men were allowed to go ahead through a revolving door. The results seem obvious. Men in "upper garments" were allowed to go ahead: those in "lower garments" were pushed aside.[11] But the principle is important: Appearance makes a difference.

Women send clear status messages too. A woman carrying a briefcase conveys a clear business message. So that they are not confused with secretaries, such women are advised by experts to carry briefcases not only to business meetings but also to cocktail lounges, restaurants, and when traveling. A woman interested in building a career must avoid looking cute or sexy; therefore, slit skirts, low-cut dresses, and heavy makeup are strictly forbidden.[12]

There is no question that fashion—appearance—plays a major role in business. The number of books on the subject alone attests to this fact. And the suggestion that appears most reasonable from all that is written is to dress conservatively. "Everything in moderation" might be the appropriate aphorism. Conservative dress has two distinct advantages. First, following current trends too closely will cause clothes to be out of style each new fashion season. Extreme styles call attention to one's appearance and with changing styles make the style even more noticeable. Second, conservative dress saves money; moderate fashions can be phased out over a longer period of time. The main point regarding conservative dress, however, may be overlooked. It is *you* or *your message* that you want noticed, not your clothes.

But fashion and style must not be overemphasized. The way clothes look and fit is important too. Clothes should be pressed and clean to convey the impression that you are a neat, responsible person concerned about personal hygiene. Of course, personal grooming such as neatly combed hair, clean fingernails, and overall cleanliness is part of this impression as well. Such aspects of your appearance tell other people in no uncertain terms exactly what you think of yourself. Appearance makes a statement about you.

The impression you convey or the feeling that is generated when you find that you have dressed appropriately for an occasion is also important to communication. It enhances your self-concept or self-image, and this feeling about yourself affects the way you communicate. First, it may make you feel more relaxed and comfortable to know that you are dressed properly. I am sure you know people who worry a great deal about their attire: "Am I dressed right?" "Oh, I hope others are dressed this way," they say.

Just as inappropriate attire distracts others, it may distract the person so dressed. Second, appropriate dress increases self-confidence. When we feel we fit in, we have a small success experience: "We did it!" Now we can turn our attention to the matters at hand, whether they be business or simply cocktail conversation.

Part of your appearance also has to do with your physique—another early and obvious nonverbal cue. Are you fat (endomorphic), thin (ectomorphic) or athletic (mesomorphic)? Are you short or tall? Research indicates that people associate very specific personality traits with these major physical cues; thus, these cues should be given some consideration. In most cases, our physique *is* under our control.

| **ENDOMORPHS** | **MESOMORPHS** | **ECTOMORPHS** |
| --- | --- | --- |
| sluggish | dominant | detached |
| tolerant | cheerful | introspective |
| affable | reckless | serious |
| warm | argumentative | cautious |
| affectionate | hot-tempered | meticulous |
| generous | optimistic | thoughtful |
| complacent | enthusiastic | sensitive |
| kind | confident | tactful |
| less needful of sex | efficient | shy |
| dependent | competitive | suspicious |
| relaxed | nonconformist | conscientious |
| even-tempered | independent | anxious[13] |

There is no suggestion here that if you have a particular physique that you have the corresponding personality traits. What is suggested is that if you recognize the existence of this kind of prejudice, you can confront it when necessary. There is no question that physique communicates a nonverbal message, but it is just a partial statement of who or what an individual is. It is the dust jacket of a book, perhaps, and may be totally irrelevant to the content.

One final note on appearance may be helpful here. When you are in total control of the image you want to convey—that is, when the business or organization does not impose uniforms or dress codes—it will be to your advantage to dress for the role you wish to play. It is a workable concept. If you are currently a middle-manager and you want top managers to view you as a candidate for higher positions, dress the part. If you consider "imitation is the highest form of flattery," then emulate the person or persons in whose footsteps you want to follow, or members of the group that you want to join. And remember that appearance includes your shoes, desk, car, and home. It is the overall impression that you are broadcasting.

### Face and Eyes

Like appearance, your face and eyes are some of the first cues others perceive. Facial cues are, for example, the major cues people look at to determine another person's sincerity. And they are the most expressive nonverbal source for revealing certain emotions. Face and eyes reflect attitudes as well. Some have said that next to human speech, they are *the* primary source of information.[14]

*The face.* Like physique, certain personality traits have been associated with facial cues. For example, a high forehead is associated with intelligence; thin lips with conscientiousness; thick lips on females with sexiness.[15] In studies that were conducted, people who had more extreme facial features, such as eyes that were too close or too far apart or a nose that was very big or very slender, were seen as "undesirable." Awareness of facial clues, once again, adds to the information we can rely upon.

Although much remains to be known about it, it is clear that the face conveys certain emotions well. Sadness, for example, is seen primarily in the eyes, while happiness and surprise are shown by the lower face as well as the eyes. Anger involves the lower face, brows, and forehead. Fear is revealed most clearly in the eyes.[16] Facial expressions have been shown to mirror both our intentions and our emotional state.

In daily interaction, the face (or parts of it) may be used to open and close communication channels, complement or qualify other behaviors, or even replace speech.[17] For example, a common indication of a person's desire to speak is an open mouth. This is sometimes accompanied by an intake of breath. When we want to interact with another person we often flash our eyebrows (raise them slightly) and smile. A smile may also be used to close a channel of communication.

The face also is an effective emphasizer. When we want to magnify behavior, minimize a behavior, or support a message, we often depend on the face. Just think how you add emphasis to a happy or sad message with your face. A person may tell a story and then smile slightly afterwards to indicate that it isn't true. Think about how a wink and a smile complement each other when you are flirting with someone.

But there are facial cues, too—sometimes referred to as *emblems*[18]— that have a consistent verbal translation. That is, when someone uses them, they are almost immediately recognized. For example, a person drops his or her jaw and holds his or her mouth open. This is sometimes accompanied by an open-eyed expression. Surprise? Of course. Here are others:

| | |
|---|---|
| Wrinkling nose and/or raising all or part of upper lip | Disgust |
| Furrowing your eyebrows and pulling head back slightly | Puzzlement or "I doubt that" |

| | |
|---|---|
| Widening your eyes | "Wow!" |
| Biting your lip | "I'm worried" |
| Winking | "*You* know what I mean" |
| Sticking out your tongue | Insult or disapproval |

*Eye contact.* As part of facial expression, eye contact is very important. The eyes are likely to be the most effective single form of human communication for establishing the most immediate basis for a relationship. For example, the eyes can be used to signal that the communication channel is open. In a restaurant you must catch the eye of your waiter or waitress to indicate you want something. In a classroom, students who do not want to be called on lower their eyes to signal that the communication channel is closed. In conversation, eye behavior is used to regulate the flow of communication by providing the participants with turn-taking signals.

The eyes also monitor the feedback you get in communication. The eyes convey attentiveness to messages as well as the degree of interest in it. They are an important aspect in how much information one is able to gain while communicating with others; the more observant, the more information.

As indicated previously, eye behavior is a prominent part of expressing emotions. Try, for example, expressing surprise, fear, disgust, anger, happiness, or sadness without some eye behavior. Some emotions, like surprise or fear, reveal many changes in the eye area; other emotions, like happiness and disgust, may not.

The other major aspect of eye behavior is the role it plays in interpersonal relationships. For example, a higher-status person will engage a lower-status person in eye contact more steadily and more frequently than that person would to someone of equal status or higher. In this regard, eye contact could be regarded as a form of touching. In dominant–submissive pairs, dominant people look boldly at submissive people.[19]

There are several other aspects of eye behavior in interpersonal relationships. We make more eye contact when we look at something rewarding to us—looking at an interviewer we like. We look more at those who like us—if for no other reason than to discover signs of approval or friendliness. To take this another step, we increase eye contact with people with whom we are seeking to develop more intimate relationships.[20]

## Touch

The importance of touch was emphasized in Blanchard and Johnson's *The One Minute Manager.*

Touch is very honest. People know immediately when you touch them whether you care about them, or whether you are just trying to find a new way to manipulate them.

"There is a very simple rule about touching," the manager continued. *"When you touch—don't take.* Touch the people you manage only when you are *giving* them something—reassurance, support, encouragement, whatever."[21]

The acceptable kinds of touch Blanchard and Johnson refer to involve putting an arm on another's shoulder as an indication of support and encouragement. It should be clear that status is an important part of touching behavior. A manager can put an arm on a subordinate's shoulder, but seldom can a subordinate put an arm on the boss's shoulder. One caution here involves communication between males and females. Many view touching between males and females as having sexual connotations.[22]

The other acceptable area of touching behavior is the handshake. Used in connection with Blanchard and Johnson's context—giving—it reveals liking and acceptance. Even the type of handshake we receive from others may affect how we perceive them.[23] Firm handshakes convey positive feelings when delivered by men. Whether or not a woman gives a firm or weak handshake makes no difference to men. Women prefer firm handshakes from men; they feel positively toward them. But they feel negatively toward other women who give them a firm handshake.[24]

**The Body**

The body covers a broad category of nonverbal communication. And because the body has such a large part in nonverbal communication, *congruency* becomes an important consideration. Communication is *congruent* when verbal and nonverbal cues are communicating essentially the same meaning. Dale Leathers, author of *Nonverbal Communication Systems,* observes: "When the meanings communicated verbally and nonverbally are congruent there can be little doubt that speech and body movements are related to each other in very definite patterns."[25] It is just such patterns of communication that we look for when we interpret others' behavior. The two major body cues discussed in this section are posture and gestures.

*Posture.* Studies by Albert Mehrabian of body posture indicate a relationship between posture and liking for the other person. People who like each other tend to lean forward; negative feelings are conveyed by leaning backward. It was found that women will look away from someone they intensely dislike; if they like a person, they vary the direction of face, sometimes looking at them squarely, sometimes looking away. Moreover, for women, the position of their arms and legs indicate liking: They are open when meeting people they like and closed (folding arms and crossing legs) when meeting people they dislike.[26]

Mood also is conveyed via posture. The way you stand or sit often tells whether you are happy or sad. Your posture, too, may advertise self-confidence, arrogance, shyness, friendliness, or insecurity. With so many potential meanings conveyed by posture, it is easy to see how congruency enters in. We may say that we are sure of ourselves with our words and yet blatantly advertise our insecurity with our posture. Our postures, too, tell much about our feelings for or attitudes toward those with whom we communicate.

*Gestures.* Research on gesturing is skimpy. There appears to be some relationship between how much gesturing people do and their desire to exert influence on others. Research indicates that people trying to persuade others exhibit frequent gestures and positive head nods.[27]

Monitoring our gestures is important. Many gestures are purposeless, detracting from the meaning being shared. Notice the distracting gesturing exhibited while talking to another person: He or she will pick fingernails, straighten hair, drum fingers on the desk, look out the window, shuffle papers, fix clothing, scratch, rub, chew, and do a variety of other purposeless things. When a gesture contributes to the intended meaning, it is purposeful; when it detracts, it is purposeless. But many of these gestures are done unconsciously and cannot be eliminated until you become aware of them. That is why monitoring them is so important.

**Personal Space and Distance**

Wherever we go we carry with us an invisible bubble—a "personal bubble"—of space that surrounds us. You may have noticed it when someone approached to talk with you and they infringed on your bubble of space; you backed off. The size of the bubble is simply how close another person can stand to you before you begin feeling uncomfortable and want to pull away or lean backward.

The bubble can vary from person to person just as it can vary from situation to situation. You would feel differently, for example, if your boss or teacher stood very close to you than if your spouse or close friend stood the same distance. Additionally, you might feel differently if there were only two of you in a room as opposed to having the room crowded with people, where you cannot as easily protect your bubble.

The researcher who has done the most work in this area—called *proxemics*—is Edward T. Hall. He suggests that in addition to people and situations, the kind of activity one engages in may be a determiner of the space one chooses to use. Hall has classified these bubbles into four types, and each type has a *close phase* and *far phase*.[28] See Figure 5-1.

Nonverbal Communication 91

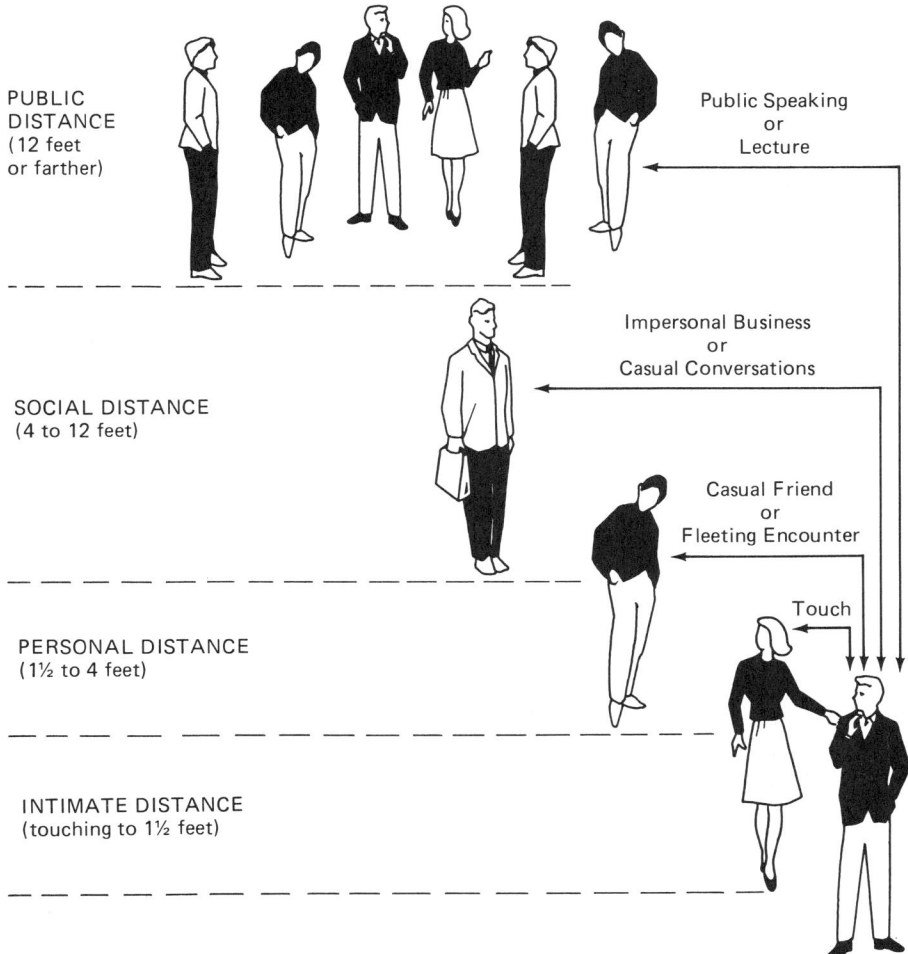

**FIGURE 5–1.**

Hall's first zone, from touching to 1½ feet apart, is labeled *intimate distance*. It is reserved for lovemaking, comforting, wrestling, and protecting. The sharing of secrets or highly personal information between people who are very close or familiar would occur in this zone.

*Personal distance*, from 1½ to 4 feet, is the second zone, and it is where people carry on conversations. But the distance is usually reserved for more than just casual friends or for fleeting encounters.

Hall's *social distance*, from 4 to 12 feet, is reserved for people conversing at a social gathering or carrying on a business transaction. Generally, at this distance, it is casual conversation or impersonal business. At this distance, people are very much aware of the other's presence, but neither one interferes with the other; thus, personal bubbles are not usually threatened at this distance.

Hall's final zone, from 12 to 25 feet or farther, is called *public distance*. People at this distance are outside the circle of involvement. This zone operates during a lecture or some other form of speaker–audience function.

### Time

Time is money, power, and status in our society.[29] Lawyers and psychiatrists are paid by the hour for their time. That time is power is demonstrated by the view that people with busy schedules are sometimes seen as more powerful. When important people donate their time to others, it indicates the power they have. When we must make an appointment to see a professor, business person, or doctor, it indicates their status. Status also is revealed when a business superior can drop in on us at any time and yet we must make an appointment to see him or her.

Probably the most fundamental values that undergird businesses are related to time: "being on time" and "saving time." Thus, time carries significant nonverbal messages. Time allowances and time consciousness can either facilitate or undermine communication. Often, this depends on whether communicators have similar time expectations.

Businesses have very specific rules regarding the use of time. Most are unpublished, but it is important for employees to know and observe them. Usually, there are different scales depending upon one's status in the organization. The higher the status, for example, the more permissible is lateness. But in most situations—especially when one is unfamiliar with the rules—punctuality is advised.

Beyond being on time or saving time, we must consider also how much time we spend on tasks, how much time we give to others, and how we divide our time among projects. One aspect of time management, for example, has to do with trying to distribute our time appropriately between various tasks we have to complete. Too often we spend excessive amounts of time on tasks we enjoy—to the exclusion of tasks we find distasteful. Incompetence, too, can be conveyed when we spend too much time on small details and not enough on the larger, more important, projects.[30]

### Environment

The broadest category of nonverbal communication has been left for last. The environment, or the world we work in, influences our interactions and communications. It permeates all that we do because it affects our psychological mood. Albert Mehrabian contends that we react emotionally to our surroundings.[31] He suggests that our emotional reaction involves three parts: (1) arousal, (2) pleasure, and (3) dominance. When you feel active, stimulated, and alert in your work place these are signs of arousal. Feeling joy, satisfaction, and happiness reflects pleasure. And dominance has to do with feeling in control and important. Dominance conveys freedom to act in a variety of ways. Because of the effect of our surroundings on our emotions, if we experience negative reactions to them, we should strive to make changes that will enhance our emotional responses and, thus, our work. The better we feel, the better our work.

How we arrange the objects in our environment will not only affect our own perceptions, but also the perceptions of others. For example, Mark Knapp suggests that others will perceive formality, warmth, privacy, familiarity, constraint, and distance. These are some of the dimensions along which a communication setting can be perceived.[32] It is wise to be familiar with environmental factors from a personal point of view—how it can affect you—and from the viewpoint of others—how they are likely to be affected. Our environment influences the communication that occurs.

### SUMMARY

Nonverbal communication is closely related to verbal communication. It refers to the exchange of messages primarily through nonlinguistic or nonword means. It is powerful and often determines the meaning behind verbal communication.

Nonverbal communication serves several functions. It *complements* verbal communication when it adds something to its meaning. It *contradicts* when it opposes verbal communication. It *substitutes* when it is used in place of verbal communication. When you highlight or reinforce verbal communication you use nonverbal to *accent*. Coordinating dialogue with another person through nonverbal cues is a *regulating* function. To make our opinions or feelings known through nonverbal communication is *expressing*.

In the section on types of nonverbal communication, the following areas were examined: voice, appearance, face and eyes, touch, the body, personal space and distance, time, and environment. Although other areas could be discussed, these are the most important, and they are the areas over which you are likely to have most control.

The more aware you are of everything going on about you as you communicate with others, the more information you will have on which to base further communication. Nonverbal communication often supplies essential information on which to make decisions and judgments. Effective communicators are sensitive to their own and others' nonverbal communication.

## NOTES

[1] Mark L. Knapp, *Essentials of Nonverbal Communication* (New York: Holt, Rinehart & Winston, 1980), pp. 2–3.
[2] Ibid., p. 3.
[3] Thomas R. Tortoriello, Stephen J. Blatt, and Sue DeWine, *Communication in the Organization: An Applied Approach* (New York: McGraw-Hill, 1978), p. 115.
[4] Loretta A. Malandro and Larry Barker, *Nonverbal Communication* (Reading, Mass.: Addison-Wesley, 1983), pp. 13–15.
[5] Albert Mehrabian, *Silent Messages: Implicit Communication of Emotions and Attitudes*, 2nd ed. (Belmont, Cal.: Wadsworth, 1981), pp. 1–55.
[6] Mark L. Knapp, *Nonverbal Communication in Human Interaction*, 2nd ed. (New York: Holt, Rinehart & Winston, 1978), p. 361.
[7] Ibid., p. 362.
[8] Ibid., p. 362.
[9] Ibid., p. 362.
[10] Richard L. Weaver, II, "Reflections: An Introduction to the Transactionist Perspective," *Today's Speech*, 23 (1975), 25–28.
[11] John T. Molloy, *Dress for Success* (New York: Warner Books, 1975), pp. 29–31.
[12] John T. Molloy, *Women's Dress for Success Book*, as cited in Susan Dellinger, and Barbara Deane, *Communicating Effectively: A Complete Guide for Better Managing* (Radnor, Pa.: Chilton, 1980), p. 67.
[13] Abné M. Eisenberg, *Job Talk: Communicating Effectively on the Job* (New York: Macmillan, 1979), p. 21. This research is reported in W. Wells and B. Siegel, "Stereotyped Somatypes," *Psychological Reports*, 8 (1961), 77–78. Another study found similar results: K. T. Strongman and C. J. Hart, "Stereotyped Reactions to Body Build," *Psychological Reports*, 23 (1968), 1175–78.
[14] Knapp, *Human Interaction*, p. 263.
[15] P. F. Secord, W. F. Dukes, and W. Bevan, "Personalities in Faces, I: An Experiment in Social Perceiving," *Genetic Psychology Monographs*, 49 (1959), 231–279.
[16] P. Ekman, W. Friesen, and P. Ellsworth, *The Face and Emotion* (New York: Pergamon Press, 1971).
[17] Knapp, *Human Interaction*, pp. 265–66.
[18] See P. Eckman and W. Friesen, *Unmasking the Face* (Englewood Cliffs, N.J.: Prentice-Hall, 1974).
[19] Knapp, *Human Interaction*, pp. 301–304.
[20] Susan Dellinger and Barbara Deane, *Communicating Effectively: A Complete Guide for Better Managing* (Radnor, Pa.: Chilton, 1980), pp. 64–65.
[21] Kenneth Blanchard, and Spencer Johnson, *The One Minute Manager* (New York: Berkley, 1982), p. 95.
[22] Lyle Sussman, and Paul D. Krivonos, *Communication for Supervisors and Managers* (Sherman Oaks, Cal.: Alfred Publishing, 1979), p. 82.
[23] Michael Houglum, Steven Mandel, and Paul D. Krivonos, "Affective Response to Handshakes" (unpublished manuscript, Department of Speech Communication, California State University: Northridge).
[24] Ibid.
[25] Dale G. Leathers, *Nonverbal Communication Systems* (Boston: Allyn & Bacon, 1976), pp. 234–35.
[26] Albert Mehrabian, "Significance of Posture and Position in the Communication of Attitude and Status Relationships," *Psychological Bulletin*, 71 (1969), 359–72.
[27] H. Rosenfeld, "Instrumental Affiliative Functions of Facial and Gestural Expressions," *Journal of Personality and Social Psychology*, 4 (1966), 65–72. Also see A. Mehrabian and M. Williams, "Nonverbal Concomitants of Perceived and Intended Persuasiveness," *Journal of Personality and Social Psychology*, 13 (1969), 37–58.
[28] "Distances and Man" condensed from *The Hidden Dimension* by Edward T. Hall. Copyright © 1966 by Edward T. Hall. Reprinted by permission of Doubleday & Co., Inc.

[29] Lawrence B. Rosenfeld and Jean M. Civikly, *With Words Unspoken: The Nonverbal Experience* (New York: Holt, Rinehart & Winston, 1976), pp. 197–98.
[30] Lawrence Peter and R. Hull, *The Peter Principle* (New York: Bantam, 1969), pp. 116–25.
[31] Albert Mehrabian, *Public Places and Private Spaces* (New York: Basic Books, 1976).
[32] Knapp, *Essentials*, pp. 54–55.

# 6

# Barriers in Business Communication

"Nobody's perfect" is the caption of a cartoon that shows two owls sitting right-side up on a tree limb and a third owl sitting on the bottom-side of the limb: upside down. "Nobody's perfect" may be one of the best explanations for much of the communication that occurs daily in the business world. And even though you read and understand the concepts and principles of proper and efficient business communication, the end result may be the same: "Nobody's perfect."

Some of the most evident signs of the "nobody's perfect" syndrome are comments you overhear, such as:

"I don't know how many times I have to tell you, Bill; it's next week, not this week. Next week, Bill!"

"I just don't understand what Mary's problem is. It seems like every other day I'm explaining the same things to her—over and over and over again."

"I can't believe it. I reminded them a couple days ago; I sent them a follow-up memo; and I talked to Jim just this morning. And here *we* are and nobody from that department is here at the meeting!"

Everyday occurrences? You bet. Breakdowns in communication? Most likely. Avoidable? To a large extent they are. Of course, as responsible, alert, and sensitive as we may be, or will become, it is unlikely that we can eliminate the breakdowns. They are not a natural part of communication, but considering the amount of communication that occurs daily, the averages tend to work against having accurate communication 100 percent of the time.

This chapter will look at several barriers to effective business communication, for there are many. I have tried to focus on those that offer us a broader view of the problem. That is, if seen from the perspective of this chapter, it is likely that many of the smaller barriers will be resolved. We will look at selective attention, selective retention, bipolar (bifurcated) thinking, and evaluative thinking.

## SELECTIVE ATTENTION

To be an effective communicator, you must be a skilled "noticer." But you must also realize that the world you see is not the real world—it is *your* world and your world *only*. And it is unlike anyone else's world. This might be easier to understand if you realize that there are essentially two kinds of reality: (1) Physical reality (that which exists) is what you see, touch, hear, taste, and smell—a tree has a physical reality just as the sweet smell of perfume; (2) Personal reality (that which exists in our minds) adds an interpretative dimension to physical reality, and because everyone views physical reality differently, this is where barriers occur. See Figure 6–1.

An argument erupts between two workers. A supervisor comes over and resolves the conflict; the solution causes one worker to have to redo a project. Everyone involved views the scene differently. The supervisor takes the position that one worker's effort more accurately reflects the supervisor's own goals; the workers each have their own perspective. You, as an outsider viewing the argument and the results, also have a perspective: At least four different personal realities are in conflict.

As can be seen in Figure 6–1, people perceive physical reality from different perspectives. To say this in a different way, we selectively perceive—or *selectively attend*. Attention is simply the process of turning our senses selectively to part of the environment. This selective observation is necessary because we cannot give attention to all stimuli; that is impossible. A very small portion of the stimuli to which we are exposed actually reaches our level of awareness. Some even say we actually perceive less than 0.01 of what goes on around us at any given time. For example, until you direct your attention to it, you are probably unaware of the pressure of your foot against the floor. Or how about your back against the chair? Although

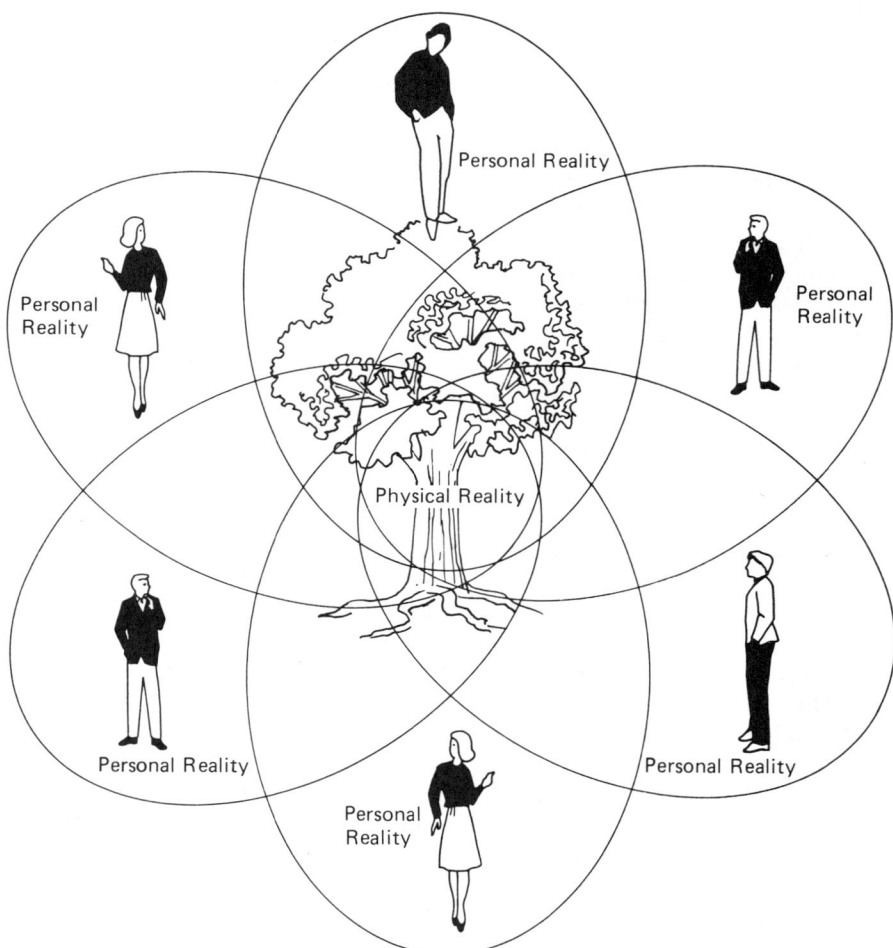

**FIGURE 6-1.** The Difference between Physical Reality and Personal Reality. Notice how people's personal realities tend to overlap. But they need not. All people have a view of physical reality, but their views, in the situation depicted, differ significantly.

these pressures were present, until you tuned in your senses to them, you were probably unaware of them. Another case in point: Your eyes are capable of handling more than 5 million bits of data per second, but your brain is only capable of interpreting about 500 bits per second.[1]

What causes us to see certain things and not others? The causes are numerous. They could be either internal or external. Internal factors include our physiological abilities, mental set, or anticipatory adjustments.

Many of these relate to our general health, anxieties, sensory capacities, attitudes, physical requirements, or even social needs. For example, if you are hungry you tend to look for food.

External factors include things associated with the source of the message, such as the source's credibility, perception of his or her competence, character, composure, sociability, and extroversion. It could also be the source's attraction, or how you perceive his or her attitude, morals, values, appearance, status, or class. How similar these are to your own—a concept called *homophily*—would also be important.

How you decide what to attend to could be a result of the background or setting. That is, we attend to certain stimuli in relation to other stimuli surrounding it. If you were looking for a piece of paper on a cluttered desk, for example, it would be more difficult to find as when the desk is clean and neat.

Other external stimuli include intensity, size, concreteness, contrast or novelty, and impressiveness. We will attend to a stimulus if it is louder, brighter, or more vivid. In the same way, we notice things that are larger, longer, or bigger. If something has a clear, distinct, and definite shape, we are also more likely to notice it. We will also notice something that has a striking quality; if it is animated, active, moving, or changing. Variety and novelty are other important features. Finally, under external factors, how impressive something is may also grasp our attention. We notice things that are repeated and are extended over a period of time. We heed the long siren, the long wait for someone, or the long pause in someone's speech.

The point is not just to realize the factors that cause your selective attention; your primary goal should be to understand that people see things differently. And it is not because the physical world changes; it is because personal realities differ.

But our selective attention does not end with the observations alone. It is what we do with the observations, for they affect our behavior. We act according to our personal reality. So do others; thus, just as our social realities may conflict, so may our behaviors. That was precisely the problem in the worker-supervisor example cited previously; worker behaviors were in conflict. The supervisor determined that the supervisor's own goals (personal reality) would be better served with one outcome rather than another and thus encouraged one set of behaviors over another.

Is awareness of differing personal realities sufficient? Probably not. We must also search for internal or external cues or signals that indicate differences—knowing, of course, that we are likely to find them. These cues or signals will help us communicate effectively because they will help us more accurately adapt our message to our audience.

Another aid to bringing personal realities together is to welcome opportunities that will help you see things as others do. Encourage people to explain their position and the various reasons or feelings behind it.

Furthermore, try to see things from the other person's point of view. In reading a letter, for example, try to visualize the writer of the letter as you read it carefully. Try to put yourself in the other person's shoes. In this way you are more likely to understand why he or she is saying or feeling these things. You get a more complete picture of the attitudes, emotions, and thoughts that undergird and reinforce the ideas.

As another way of countering the problem of selective attention, work at improving all of your skills of perception:

1. Don't jump to conclusions.
2. Be patient; give your mind time to sift through relevant information.
3. Make yourself available; try to see things as others see them.
4. Make a conscious effort to perceive accurately.
5. Establish the proper climate; openness and trust should be fostered.
6. Be willing to adjust; keep flexible.[2]

As you become a more accurate observer, a more thorough reader, and a more sensitive listener, you will become a more effective communicator. Reality is not simple; perception is not simple. When you add the multiplicity of clues involved in one to the multiplicity of factors involved in the other, the result may well be confusion—a confusion that is left for you to resolve.

Finally, in trying to counter the problems that result from selective attention, we must try to keep our attention on the communicator's message. Distraction occurs easily, especially because we think so much faster than we speak. Our mind tends to wander. To help keep our mind on the message, we need to try to anticipate what the communicator is going to say next. This involves a constant series of guesses and then comparisons and contrasts between the guesses and what was actually said. In addition, we can keep our mind on the supporting materials of the communicator. This will help us discover those ideas that merit our support as opposed to ideas that are merely assertions. It helps, too, to mentally summarize what the communicator is saying. Such summaries help both to maintain a perspective of the communicator's theme and aid us in keeping track of his or her progress.

## SELECTIVE RETENTION

How you perceive a source and what you choose to attend to will affect the accuracy of your understanding and how much of the imparted information you retain. *Selective retention* refers to our ability to preserve certain ideas in our mind—the aftereffects of experience and learning—so that later recall or recognition is possible. To see how this works in relationship to a model of the process, see Figure 6–2.

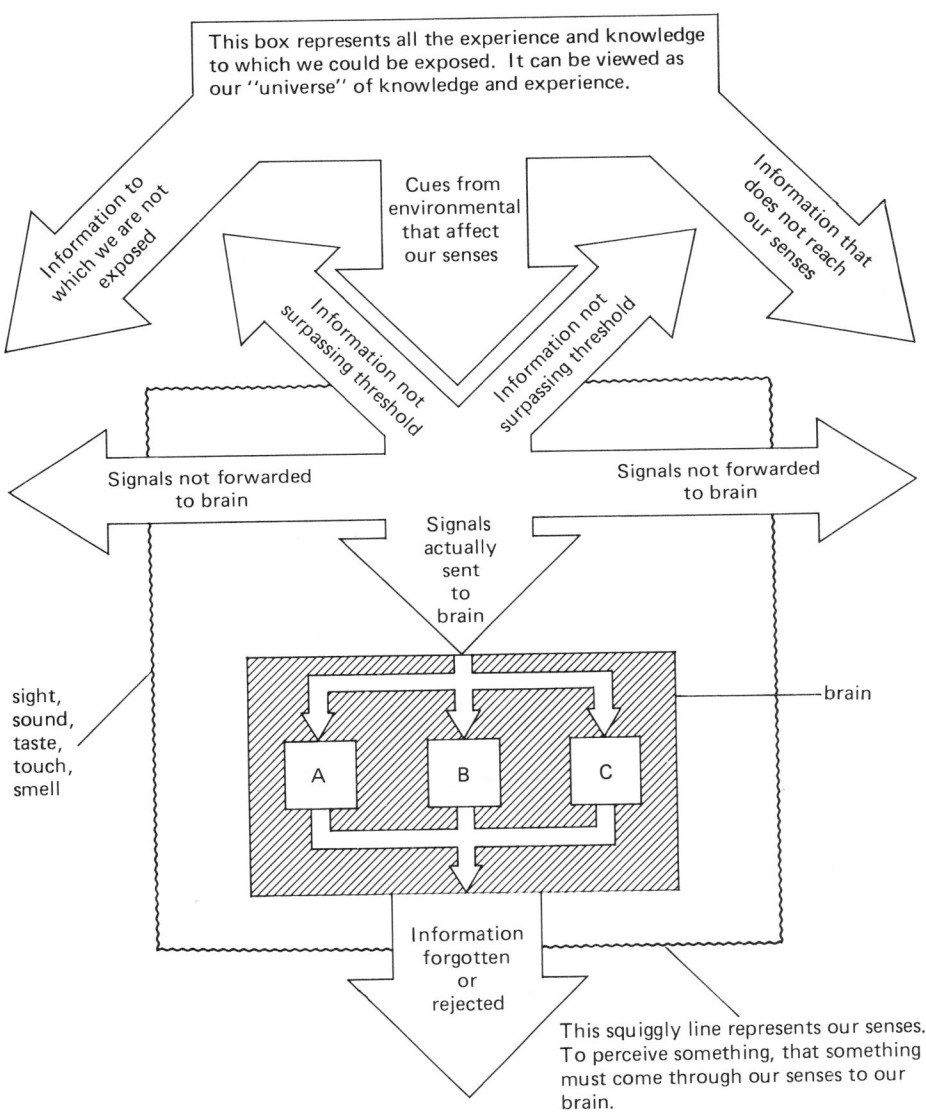

**FIGURE 6-2.** A Model of the Perception Process.

From the "universe" of experience and knowledge to which we could be exposed—a vast, almost uncalculable potential—we either consciously draw (selectively perceive) cues and signals or are exposed to cues and signals in some manner. These cues and signals penetrate our senses. Some to which we are exposed do not meet our thresholds; that is, a sound is not loud enough, a touch is not hard enough, or a taste is not strong enough. These cues and signals, then, are not passed on to the brain.

Once a cue or signal is sent on to the brain (the shaded black box in Fig. 6–2), there are three possibilities. The cue or signal is matched with prior experience and knowledge, interpretation is made, and a meaning is discovered. This occurs in Box A. This meaning is current and usable and helps determine our behavior. We clearly understand the cues and symbols because we have words, experiences, or knowledge that we can use for interpretation.

In Box B, the cues and symbols are received, interpreted, and stored. We have no use for the information at present, but we understand it, and we can draw upon it as needed. For example, we come to work one morning, and our secretary reminds us of an eleven o'clock appointment with Mr. Sackwitz. We have no use for the information at present, so it goes into Box B. Of course, information moves back and forth between the boxes. Information about our appointment with Mr. Sackwitz may go right into Box A as we pull a file and make some notes, then move it to Box B as we complete this task and turn our attention to other matters.

Box C is unique; it is essentially a storage bin. Into it goes information (cues and signals) for which we have no current words, experiences, or knowledge. That is, we have no present means for interpreting the cues and signals, but we retain them. Sometimes, as a result of new vocabulary, new experiences, or new knowledge, we can draw material from Box C and put it in Box A or Box B. For example, one day when you came to work you noticed a new "something" on someone's desk. No big deal. You did not have time to inquire about it; and because it did not directly affect you, you really did not care. Later on during the week, one of your colleagues was explaining some new electronic system of communication that was being tried at your company. Suddenly, from Box C, you dredge up this observation, and you now (because it is appropriate) decide to ask, "Does that system have anything to do with that box that I saw on Lou's desk the other day?"

The perception-process model also recognizes that information is forgotten or otherwise not retained. From all the "boxes" information slips. Some information gets old. Some gets contradicted by new information. And some is lost simply because of the enormous amount to which we are exposed and the limited capacity of our brains.

Now you begin to see how "selectivity" occurs. It is amazing at how many junctures information may not "get through." Even the neurons that send the information from our senses to our brain may not send the information forward. If the impulse is not strong enough to trip a synapse, the impulse lies dormant. The point, however, is not how the system works as much as it is how what is finally retained for current or future use is selected. The selection process is complex and intricate—as well as fast. Consider that most of this filtering and "decision making" occurs within seven-tenths of a second.

## BIPOLAR THINKING

Just as the system we use to perceive the world is complex, the world we view is complex as well. Through our intricate system of selective attention and selective retention, we try to create order through simplification. Interpretation is easiest when the information being interpreted is simplified.

But when information is made too simple, it can cause inaccuracy or distortion. This is what happens in *bipolar thinking*. It interferes with effective communication because it reduces complex phenomena to simple, either-or, good-or-bad, black-or-white dimensions. But the world is not that simple. *Bipolar thinking*, then, is characterized by this two-value orientation where something is divided into two diametrically opposed views.

We do this as we deal with other people. We fit them into categories and use the category as a basis for explaining their behavior. It is much easier to dismiss a person totally for a character trait of which we disapprove than to consider the divergent facets of every person. Thus, we may view a person with a messy desk as "unorganized," a person who comes to work late as "lazy" or "irresponsible," or a person who doesn't share our view of the world as "bad" or "wrong."

It is not difficult to trace the cause for our two-value orientation. Our society promotes it. Heroes are portrayed as "good," villains as "bad." People are "American" or "un-American," saved or damned, wholesome or degenerate.

For us to force people into such categories as honest-dishonest, liberal-conservative, for us or "agin" us, clean or dirty, responsible or irresponsible, sane or insane ignores the various degrees between the two extremes. A boss may appear "for" us as we are provided incentives and promotions, but that same boss should be allowed decisions that may not seem to support us as fully and yet not be labeled "agin" us. Such labels become stifling, restrictive, and limiting.

The world is not simple enough to allow for our reduction of events, things, or people to a two-value system. We must learn to become tolerant. Others do not have to accept our ideas exactly as presented. Considering how meanings are likely to differ, we should be surprised when they do accept our ideas exactly as presented! One's refusal to accept our ideas should not merit outright rejection: a result of bipolar thinking. Countless problems result when employees consider questions on a policy as outright rejection of that policy. It is like the student who perceived every mark on her graded essay as a sign of rejection: a serious problem that lowered her grade. What she failed to see was a teacher interested in helping her become a better writer.

To improve ourselves, we need feedback—not just good feedback, but constructive feedback of *all* types:

1. Solicit it. Ask others what they think, how they feel about it, or what they would do.
2. Get involved with others. The more meaningful relationships you have, the more feedback you are likely to get.
3. Be open, aware, and alert. Try to broaden your horizons. The more you see, hear, feel, taste, and touch, the more information you have on which to base your decisions.
4. Be flexible. Realize that your view is only *one* view of the situation. When you know there could be as many other views as there are people to hold those views, you become more willing to adapt and respond.

Often, in our two-value orientation, we stifle feedback that is not positive, or that comes from what we consider to be a source "who is not for me, but against me." We become inhibited, confined, and controlled by our bipolar thinking. The world is not simple enough—nor are most issues—to be divided into two dimensions. I knew someone who was fond of saying, "There are only two kinds of people in the world—the quick and the dead." The best kind of thinking and decision making result from a foundation grounded on synthesis: the combining of diverse parts, elements, or conceptions into a coherent idea or decision. We draw together the parts to form a whole.

## EVALUATIVE THINKING

Probably the most common response we make when trying to help another person is an *evaluative* one. Evaluative thinking involves placing a judgment of relative goodness, appropriateness, effectiveness, or rightness on what the communicator is thinking or doing. Carl Rogers was responsible for labeling this behavior as "the tendency to evaluate."[3]

Evaluative responses communicate a judgmental, corrective, suggestive, or moralizing attitude or intent.[4] This response implies what the other person ought or might do to solve a problem. When such advice is timely and relevant, it can help a person. Most often, however, it builds a communication barrier, for it not only keeps you from being helpful but also may even prevent any type of closer relationship from developing.

Why is this? First, an evaluative reaction can be threatening, and when people feel threatened they are likely to become defensive. Defensiveness may cause a person to close-mindedly reject any advice, to resist any influence, to stop exploring a problem altogether, and to become indecisive. This defensiveness occurs because people do not like to be placed in an inferior position. When people become evaluative, they place themselves in a superior position to that of the other person. Think about it: When you have a problem, you do not want to be made to feel inferior—by anyone.

Second, an evaluative reaction can reveal lack of concern. It is a convenient way to reveal false involvement with another person's problems or concerns. Someone having difficulty in a relationship with another can be dismissed with a comment like, "It would be *best* [the evaluative word] just never to see him again." Just like that, you have generalized about the other person's problem and also demonstrated that you do not want to take the time to fully understand it. To avoid being evaluative, avoid phrases like "It would be best. . . ." Or other phrases that begin: "The best thing to do. . . ," "What *I* would do if I were you. . . . ," "One good way to. . . ," "You might consider. . . ," "You should. . . ," "Don't you think. . . ," or "Why don't you. . . ."[5]

But there are positive kinds of responses you can make that will substitute for an evaluative phrase and gain positive results as well. One of these is the *probing* question. If it is your desire to get additional information or to develop or discuss a point further, then the probing question is an important skill. An *open* question, which encourages another person to answer at greater length and in more detail, will elicit more information than a closed question, which usually asks for only a simple yes or no, or other single-word, answer. For example, an open question that would draw out another person with respect to a project he or she is working on might be, "How do you feel about the project?" A closed question would be, "Do you like the project?"

In substituting for an evaluative response, however, "why" questions should be avoided. Being asked "why" you did something or "why" you feel something can, like the evaluative response, cause others to become defensive. They immediately feel compelled to justify their actions. "Why" questions are often used to indicate disapproval ("Why did you raise your voice to her?" "Why did you write that letter in the first place?" These imply, "You shouldn't have raised your voice" and "You shouldn't have written that letter.") Often you can get the same information by asking "what," "where," "when," "how," or "who" questions. These will draw out other people and cause them to be more specific, precise, and revealing.[6]

Perhaps the best way, however, to substitute for an evaluative response is to use a *paraphrasing* or *understanding* one. (This was discussed in Chapter 3.) To paraphrase is to restate an idea or feeling in your own words. Such a response has the additional advantages of determining whether or not you have understood the other person's thoughts and feelings, assuring the sender that you, indeed, have understood, and, whether you have understood or not, it lets the sender know that you are trying to understand. Also, it forces us to listen more accurately, makes others feel like they are being listened to, and helps stop "egospeak."

The value of the paraphrasing or understanding response is that it reveals empathy—the ability mentally to place yourself in the position of the other person. A listener who responds with empathy tries to understand the other person's thoughts and feelings, not just the words being said. It is revealed in the listener's ability to share in the meaning, spirit, or feeling of what the communicator has said.[7]

Our natural tendency is to judge, evaluate, and approve, but these become barriers to communication because of how they are viewed and responded to by others. The best way to prevent such barriers is simply to avoid evaluative thinking. This is a realistic and useful suggestion. The best approach one can take instead of evaluation is paraphrasing. Probing, supportive, and interpretive are other alternative response styles (covered in Chapter 3). Since these approaches tend to be both supportive and constructive, we should practice them.

## ADDITIONAL BARRIERS

Selective attention, selective retention, bipolar thinking, and evaluative thinking are behind many of the problems that result in communication breakdowns. But they are not the only ones.[8] Words or nonverbal cues may mean different things to people and may thus cause a problem.

When a message source and a receiver attribute different meanings to the same words or use different words though intending the same meanings, *bypassing* occurs. It isn't surprising when you consider that many words have several different meanings; some over 100. In addition, people have their own meanings for some words. This may be especially true with respect to jargon. You hear a specialized word or phrase used for the first time; you are too embarrassed to ask what it means (after all, you should know!). Then it is used in an instruction to you. You think you know its meaning from the context you heard so you go with that meaning. Then the bypassing occurs: Different meanings were attributed to the word, and as a result you did the wrong thing.

*Lack of understanding* may be another barrier. This is not necessarily a case of misunderstanding; this is just not understanding at all. It would be as if someone wrote a letter to you in a language you could not read. When you do not know the code, a barrier results.

Another barrier might be the existence of *noise*. Although noise may be of many types, the most common are: (1) physical, and (2) psychological. *Physical noise* is the most obvious. You are talking to a secretary when a construction jackhammer starts up out on the street. You are telling people in your car pool when you will pick them up and a jet flies overhead, drowning out your instructions.

*Psychological noise* is not as obvious and is more difficult to detect or plan for. With physical noise you can pause a moment, close a window, or move away from the noise. Psychological noise occurs in our head. How do you close a head or move away from it? Pausing is unlikely to make it go away! But psychological noise is likely to be a more serious and devastating communication barrier. For example, you have just put away all your things so that you can leave work immediately for a golf appointment. The boss comes in and explains what he wants you to do tomorrow. Do you listen well? Maybe. But probably not as well as you would if the time of day and the golf appointment were not affecting your concentration.

Psychological noise is an even greater barrier if we are biased or prejudiced against the source of the communication. When nonverbal cues such as appearance, odor, or body position (a person who stands too close when he or she talks to you) distract from the intended message, those cues create psychological noise.

*Noise,* simply, is unwanted disturbance. There are other types besides physical and psychological, and they are usually labeled according to their origin. That which occurs within our body—such as problems we may have with our sense organs (a numb hand limits our touching ability with that hand)—is *physiological noise*. When we have difficulties with the meaning of the words used in conversations, this would be labeled *semantic noise*. If our problem had to do with the way another person put words together to form odd phrases, clauses, or sentences, this would be *syntactic noise*. If the disturbance originated with the administrative or functional structure of our place of work, it would be labeled *organizational noise*. If it originated in the neighborhood, community, state, or nation, it could be labeled *societal noise*. Noise can be a barrier at any level, but recognition of its existence is the first step toward either eliminating or at least minimizing its effect.

A final but additional barrier is *poor listening*. Because this was discussed in Chapter 3, we will only mention it briefly here. You might blame your breakdown in communication to having only attended to certain phenomena or having remembered only selected ideas, but it may be that you just did not listen properly. Sometimes this occurs because we become too analytical. Instead of trying to listen to the whole person, we are predisposed to being disagreeable, summarizing, or clarifying. We want to be sure to expose his or her faulty reasoning or lack of evidence or support. There is no attempt made at sharing in the meaning, spirit, or feeling of what the communicator is saying.

Sometimes we do not listen well because our mind is already made up. This is "My mind is made up, so don't bother me with the facts" type of thinking. We all have opinions, and there is no harm in having or expressing them. But when our opinions are so strong that we cannot listen to the ideas of others, we cut off a channel of information. We never know how our ideas or position compares with that of another, and we never really come to understand *why* the other person feels as he or she does.

Listening is also negatively affected when our egos get too wrapped up in the conversation. "I'm going to prove that person wrong," or "I'm going to have the last word on this one!" Sometimes we are busy planning our next verbal assault; sometimes we are just trying to figure out how we will fill the dead air when the person stops talking. Whatever we're doing, we're not listening.

But perhaps the biggest problem in effective listening has to do with daydreaming. Others talk so much slower than we think that while they are pouring out their hearts to us, our minds race on to more pleasant subjects or thoughts. Or we might hop from subject to subject pausing briefly to add an "Oh?" or "Uh, huh" designed to prove we are tuned in when we really are not. These vacant exercises serve no one's purpose and are a waste of time.

## OVERCOMING BARRIERS

Although some problems are likely to remain despite anything we might do, there are guidelines both senders and receivers can use to improve message accuracy. These guidelines include feedback, multiple channels, repetition, reinforcement, and simplicity.[9]

### Feedback

A receiver who gives feedback is much easier to talk to than one who does not. This can be as simple as nodding the head at points of agreement or using verbal phrases revealing your understanding. A low level of participation in the communication hinders the sender and causes, essentially, a one-way flow rather than the more complete, interactive two-way flow of information.

But senders should also be sensitive to the feedback that occurs and be willing to adjust their message accordingly. To get feedback and not use it makes the feedback meaningless. Sensitivity is not enough. Adaptation to it is also necessary.

Senders also can encourage feedback. To try to make certain their message is being understood, they can ask the receiver a question, such as: "Do you know what I mean?" This may be ample enough to secure the necessary feedback. Senders can pause and allow the other person time to respond. They can give nonverbal encouragement through head nods, voice inflection, and direct eye contact. If all this fails, they can play "devil's advocate" and implant an idea or suggestion that will provoke the other's response or reaction.

### Multiple Channels

Receivers can transmit their feedback through a variety of channels. Facial expression is one common channel. Body position might be another. A third would be use of the voice.

In much the same way, communicators can send their messages through a variety of channels. Employing the many nonverbal means mentioned earlier in Chapter 4 and 5 offers multiple-channel variety.

The point here is simply that the more expressive we are as communicators (whether we are communicating a message *or* feedback), the more likely our intended message will get through. Awareness and use of channels other than the verbal (language) one alone aids expressiveness.

### Repetition

In an important message situation it would be inappropriate to leave the proper reception of that message to chance. Because a receiver does not have an opportunity to reread the message, it is far better if the sender gives that second opportunity. To repeat a message is to say it a second time in exactly the same way. You might say to someone, "The report is due tomorrow morning," and then add at the end of the conversation, "Remember, won't you, that the report is due at 9:30 tomorrow morning?" Restatement (saying it in a different way) or asking a question at this point assures proper reception.

Of course, like any guideline, repetition can be overused. It is wise to repeat an idea minimally. Once is usually sufficient; however, triple redundancy may be better assurance of receipt. The point is, *any* technique loses its effectiveness if overused.

### Reinforcement

If you as a sender can reinforce your message with action, that will also increase accuracy. For example, after telling an employee how to prepare a report, you could show him or her one prepared according to the proper format. If you were advocating a new policy, to show that you are also following the policy, or that you have already reinforced the policy with other employees, would help.

### Simplicity

*Simplicity* means being natural and direct. Sometimes we get carried away in wanting to sound eloquent, sophisticated, or intelligent, and we use big words to convey this message. We may become excessively complex or intricate and, thus, risk misunderstanding or confusion.

The more important a message is, and the more important it is that it is correctly received, the more important simple, everyday, commonly used and understood language is.

Along with simple language, also try to code the message in a simple manner. That is, try to avoid complex or compound sentences. Use conversational style as opposed to a written one. A written style is often more stilted and more difficult to understand. The following is a written style:

> One of the most important decisions a manager must make in organizations today is that of determining effective communicative strategies to influence subordinates. . . . Managers differ in preferred style of leadership and power preference. Subordinates respond differently to different types of managerial influence and have definite preferences for certain forms of influence over others. Thus it becomes both practically and theoretically important for communication scholars concerned with organizations to determine those factors which may affect the choice of influence mode.[10]

Talking to a group of managers, a speaker and fellow manager might recast the paragraph above to read as follows:

> How do you influence your employees? Not only do *we* differ in our style and approach, employees differ in how they respond to our different styles and approaches. What we need to look at are the factors that influence our choices. Don't you think that will make a difference?

Notice the changes in this "conversational" paragraph. There are shorter sentences, fewer different words, words with fewer syllables, and even a contraction. It is more colloquial with simpler words and two direct questions. It contains more personal pronouns such as *you, we* and *our.* Words are repeated more. In other conversational examples, you may find more qualifying statements such as *if, however, but,* and *except;* more absolute terms such as *none, all, every, always,* and *never;* and more qualifying terms such as *apparently, it seems,* or *appears,* and *to me.*[11] Every oral communication does not include all these characteristics; however, most of them contribute to simplicity, naturalness, directness, and ease of understanding.

### SUMMARY

When you think about it, there are probably as many different barriers in business communication as there are participants, messages, and situations. This chapter has focused on the major problem areas, and the purpose has been to offer a broader—as opposed to a more specific—examination of communication barriers.

The first section on selective attention discussed the process of turning our senses selectively to part of the environment. There are differences between physical reality and our own personal reality just as there are differences between the personal realities of different people. The internal and external causes for these differences were mentioned. To help compensate for this problem, we need to work to improve all of our skills of perception.

In the section on selective retention, it was shown how retention occurs and the various factors that reduce our overall retention ability. That is, there are factors that cause selectivity to occur; some of these we have no control over. It is a complex, intricate, and rapid process.

Bipolar thinking, discussed in the third section, is a simplifying process. It reduces complex phenomena into either-or, good-or-bad, black-or-white dimensions. Our society encourages this two-value orientation. To compensate for it, we must show tolerance of others and of messages and situations.

Evaluative thinking involves placing a judgment of relative goodness, appropriateness, effectiveness, or rightness on what another person is saying, thinking, or doing. Evaluative reactions may be threatening or may show lack of concern. To substitute for an evaluative response, one can use a probing question or an open question. "Why" questions should be avoided; a paraphrasing or understanding response could be used. Their value is that they reveal empathy.

In the final section, some additional barriers were discussed. Bypassing occurs when a message source and a receiver attribute different meanings to the same words or use different words though intending the same meaning. Lack of understanding may be another barrier. Noise can also be a barrier. The final barrier mentioned was poor listening.

To end on a positive note, the chapter discussed five guidelines for overcoming barriers: Feedback, the use of multiple channels, repetition, reinforcement, and simplicity all help to clarify messages and make them more accurate.

But despite all the effort that may be expended in overcoming barriers, conflict can still occur. In the next chapter the nature and function of conflict will be discussed, and some specific, practical methods for coping with conflict will be presented. Look at Chapter 7 as a natural outgrowth and extension of this chapter. Both are important in business and personal relationships.

### NOTES

[1] Philip. G. Zimbardo and Floyd L. Ruch, *Psychology and Life*, 9th ed. (Glenview, Ill.: Scott, Foresman, 1975), pp. 241–48.
[2] Richard L. Weaver, II, *Understanding Interpersonal Communication* (Glenview, Ill.: Scott, Foresman, 1984), pp. 91–96.
[3] Carl R. Rogers, "Barriers and Gateways to Communication," *Harvard Business Review*, 30 (1952), 46–52.

[4] David W. Johnson, *Reaching Out: Interpersonal Effectiveness and Self-Actualization*, 2nd ed. (Englewood Cliffs, N.J.: Prentice-Hall, 1981), p. 151.

[5] Ibid., p. 152.

[6] Charles M. Kelly, "Empathic Listening," in *Speech Communication: A Reader*, 2nd ed., ed. Richard L. Weaver, II (San Diego, Cal.: Collegiate Publishing, 1979), pp. 165–67.

[7] Johnson, *Reaching Out*, p. 154.

[8] James Gibson, John Ivancevich, and James Donnelly, *Organizations: Structure, Processes, Behavior* (Dallas: Business Publications, 1973), p. 183.

[9] Ibid., p. 184.

[10] Samuel C. Riccillo and Sarah Trenholm, "Predicting Managers' Choice of Influence Mode: The Effects of Interpersonal Trust and Worker Attributions on Managerial Tactics in a Simulated Organizational Setting," *The Western Journal of Speech Communication*, 47 (1983), 323–39.

[11] Charles R. Gruner, Cal M. Logue, Dwight L. Freshley, and Richard C. Huseman, *Speech Communication in Society* (Boston: Allyn & Bacon, 1972), p. 167.

# 7

# Profiting from Conflict Management

For every person who loves a good battle, there are probably a dozen others who are terrified of conflicts and avoid them at all costs. People may avoid a conflict because they are afraid of the potential results, even when they recognize that one of those results could be so positive or valuable that it would outweigh any negative repercussions. In the last chapter, communication barriers were discussed. But careful as people are to avoid or overcome those barriers, conflict can still occur.

In this chapter the values of conflict will first be presented. If we know what the profits or rewards are, perhaps that will serve as sufficient encouragement to engage in conflict, or at least change our view of it. Next, a brief comparison of the old view and the new view of conflict will be offered to indicate how times have changed, and also to show why the profits of conflict are acceptable. In the third section, it is suggested that conflict follows a predictable series of stages. This is followed by a discussion of alternative approaches to conflict. The final section of the chapter presents a step-by-step method for resolving conflict. The overall purpose of the chapter is to offer a perspective on conflict that will put it in a positive light—to make it something we will be less likely to shrink from, as opposed to engage actively in.

Conflict is neither good nor bad, but the way people choose to engage in it can be judged positive or negative depending on how it affects the participants and what the results are.

## THE PROFITS OF CONFLICT

In a relationship with another person, we can gain a greater understanding of the other person, ourselves, and the relationship through conflict. Conflict can also clarify similarities and dissimilarities. By opening, defining, and maintaining channels of communication, it can assist people in learning how to cope with future conflicts. Further, it can reveal areas where communicative effort and adaptation need to be strengthened, or areas where we need to work harder if we want a strong relationship.[1] Thus, conflict helps us learn about relationships, and when it threatens relationships, it lets us know how solid the ties are that bind that relationship together.[2]

But the profits from conflict go far beyond the values to the two participants alone. In a business setting, it is important that supervisors, leaders, managers, employees, and organization members sharpen their ability to recognize constructive effects of conflicts. Benefits must be weighed against the costs, but often, benefits are not perceived. Only the destructive, wrenching effects are seen; and they, because of their negative strength, outweigh and overshadow any positive qualities.[3]

*Conflict energizes people.* This is one of its major values. There is an inherent force, vigor, or vitality to conflict that wakes people up and gets them moving. Even if all the resulting activity is not constructive, it still may have as its overriding outcome a new level of activity.

*Conflict may result in the discovery of organizational weaknesses.* For example, an employee who must bring a problem to a supervisor may run into a conflict every time the problem is raised. The conflict, however, results not from the problem itself, but because this supervisor should not be the one dealing with this problem, and he or she knows it. A system change is made so that problems of this nature are taken to the appropriate supervisor, or a new position is created and a new supervisor appointed to accommodate these kinds of problems. The point is that conflict pointed up the needed changes in the organizational system, which were then implemented. This is known as a *functional* or *strategic* conflict since it has to do with either the way the organization functions or with strategies used in resolving issues. The resultant search for a resolution of the underlying issue, however, is the reward or value of this type of conflict.

The result of the problem the employee had in the example above may also be different. What if the employee took the problem to a supervisor, a conflict occurred, the supervisor and the employee worked out the problem, and the result was a new and perhaps lasting channel of communication? How does growth, progress, and development occur? Yes, it may have been risky for the employee to approach the supervisor; yes, it may have been risky for the supervisor to take on the new problem, or to seek its solution; but the new channel of communication that was opened may have far exceeded all the risks involved.

*Another value of conflict is catharsis.* Often, we need an outlet for pent-up tensions and frustrations. The larger and more impersonal a business becomes, the greater the need for some channel of release for the stresses and strains produced. Conflict often provides the outlet for this uneasiness. Once the air is cleared, the participants can again concentrate on their primary responsibilities. The value of the release may be so great that for some people, finding a place where nobody else is and just screaming or crying or letting it all out can also serve to clear the air. It certainly has advantages over holding it in, or letting it out in an emotional avalanche over some petty or inconsequential problem.

*Conflict may be an educational experience.* Think how much we might learn as a result of a conflict. We might become more aware and more understanding of the other person's functions and problems. "I didn't realize you were responsible for all of that," you might say. And think how much more empathetic you might be in the future with that person because you learned what you did. You might discover more about yourself and how you cope in various situations as well. Since each of us is continually experiencing and learning, we cannot always predict how we are going to face a new situation. But each new situation becomes a new past that we can build upon and use in the future. We use the past, in the present, to help predict the future.

## OLD VIEW OF CONFLICT VERSUS NEW VIEW

The idea that you might be able to profit from conflict may be new. That may be because you view conflict as "bad"—something to be avoided. Many people feel that conflict has to be eliminated or resolved. This is all part of the old view of it.[4]

In the old view, people believed that conflict was not inevitable. That is, they viewed humans as essentially good and that trust, cooperation, and goodness were inherent in us all. If these motives could be properly tapped, conflict would be less likely to rear its ugly head.

In the old view, people believed they knew the causes for conflict. "If not in the nature of the human being, then where?" you might ask. They felt, first, that it resulted from breakdowns in communication. That is, conflict came about from a lack of understanding between participants, a lack of trust, or a lack of openness. They also believed that the environment played a major role in conflict; the environment shaped our behavior. Inappropriate behavior like aggressiveness or competitiveness resulted from circumstances in the environment that could be altered.

A new view has emerged that deals with effects rather than causes.[5] It appears to be far more realistic and practical. The new view suggests that conflict is good and should be encouraged. If you accept the values, rewards, or profits outlined in the first section of this chapter, then this characteristic should come as no surprise. Of course, certain regulations should be enforced so that conflict doesn't get out of hand.

The new view also presents conflict as inevitable. It suggests that human beings, if not essentially bad, are driven by aggressive, self-seeking, competitive instincts. When people exhibit these characteristics, conflict must occur. The new view, then, pictures humans as egotistic—people more interested in themselves than in anything else.[6]

Furthermore, the new view recognizes that conflict results from a struggle for limited rewards, whether those rewards are food, status, power, or responsibility. The new view also downplays breakdowns in communication because of lack of understanding, trust, and openness.

The new view further suggests that the importance of the environment has been overplayed. There are many determinants of behavior besides the environment, including genetic and physiological causes. People can actually be programmed to act aggressively.

The overall perspective here is more important than the specific features. That is, if we realize that conflict is inevitable and desirable and should be encouraged, this places an emphasis upon management: How do we effectively manage conflict? The goal of management is not necessarily harmony and cooperation; rather, the goal of management is effective goal attainment. Eliminating conflict is neither realistic nor desirable. A climate should be maintained that supports conflict because it can result in new challenges; it can stimulate ideas and solutions to problems; it can offer a means for successfully adapting to change; it can offer a means for business or organizational survival.[7]

## THE STAGES OF CONFLICT

Conflict can best be viewed as a dynamic process.[8] It usually occurs as a sequence of episodes. This is not to suggest that it always follows these stages or that if it does not it cannot legitimately be called "conflict." To use

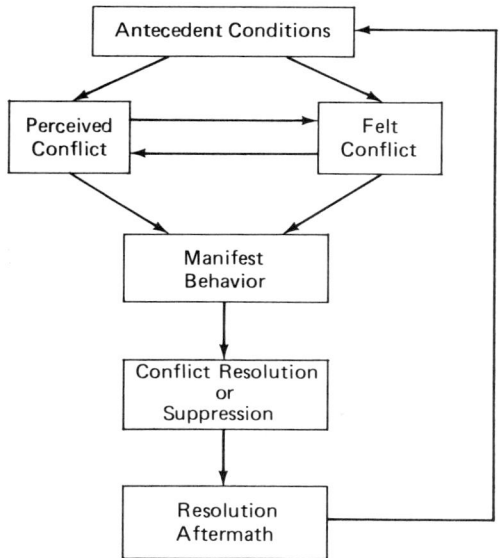

**FIGURE 7-1.**

From Alan C. Filley, *Interpersonal Conflict Resolution* (Glenview, Ill.: Scott, Foresman, 1975), p. 8. Used with permission.

a model to explain conflict will help both to describe and analyze its operation as well as some additional facets. See Figure 7-1.

### Antecedent Conditions

Antecedent conditions—preceding events or causes—are characteristics of a situation that increase the likelihood of conflict. Some of these conditions have already been pointed out, such as the struggle for limited rewards, or communication barriers, such as understanding, trust, and openness. Personal factors were also mentioned. Some people seem to be programmed to conflict! There are other factors as well.

*Unequal task dependency* may be a factor that causes conflict. For example, some people must follow exact rules or procedures to complete a task; others can complete it with a creative, unique flair. It is like the difference between the cook who can just "put things together" to get a meal and the person who must follow each recipe line by line, item by item (no substitutions, no changes) to accomplish the same goal. Conflict is generated when the rewards are distributed—whether they go to the person who followed the rules exactly or to the person who added a little extra.

An antecedent condition may also result from *different objectives and values*, such as when people see the same situation through different eyes. A boss may want to get things done immediately, with a certain sacrifice of quality, whereas you may want to take longer and achieve a higher level of quality: two people operating with different values.

*Goals may differ* in similar ways. One person may see a company as a bottom-line, productivity-oriented business, whereas another may see it as a humanistic, people-oriented company. No doubt a company can be both; however, one that stresses either to the exclusion of the other is likely to generate conflict.

A very common antecedent condition for conflict may be *role dissatisfaction*. You may not like what you have to do. Often, people will enter a company in a lower-status, lower-paying job, just to get into that company. It opens the door to opportunity. And yet, if you are doing something you do not like to do, for pay you consider unsatisfactory, your dissatisfaction may well affect your work as well as your associations with those around you. This can occur on a smaller scale if you are given a task you do not want to do, or you feel is more appropriate for someone else.

Finally, an antecedent condition may result from *ambiguities in assigning credit or blame*. A supervisor asks you to do a task then takes credit for it in front of a vice-president. Or you worked on a project with a committee and another member got the credit for the work when you put in more time and effort than anyone else. These are common conflict-arousing situations.

Obviously, there are other antecedent conditons, but these are some of the major ones. It is likely that there are as many as there are people, events, or circumstances. We create antecedent conditions; that is, they result from the meaning we construct in our mind. There may be stimuli in a situation or in another person that kindles our ire, but when it is aroused, we are the ones who cause it to rise.

**Perceived Conflict**

Just because antecedent conditons exist does not make conflict inevitable. For example, you may be able to live with a boss who has a different set of values from your own. You may be able to live with other people getting credit for things you did, knowing that one day "your day will come." You may even be able to live with the lack of trust between you and another employee or even one who is always ready to fight; you just avoid them both! Conflict is more likely to develop when conditions are perceived as threatening.

*Perceived conflict* is that which is impersonally perceived as harmful to both parties. That is, it goes on in one person's mind; it is highly individualized and subjective. Moreover, the perception—or evaluation—that results may or may not be an accurate account of existing conditions. Accuracy at this level is unimportant; what counts is that someone perceives harm.

At this level, too, conflict may or may not result. It could be ignored, or it could be stored—either to be forgotten or, perhaps, used at a later time. Often, those issues that are especially novel, highly explosive, or not susceptible to routine resolution procedures are suppressed.

### Felt Conflict

Perceived conflict is impersonal; *felt conflict* is personal. Felt conflict is usually expressed in feelings of threat, hostility, fear, or mistrust. Personalization of conflict occurs when the whole personality of an individual becomes involved. You may become preoccupied with the problem, your body tenses when you think of it, and often you begin to rehearse scenarios for confronting the other person, getting the upper hand, or resolving the problem.

Just as you can perceive conflict when none exists, you can experience feelings that create conflict when none exists. Emotions can be stimulated and feelings aroused because of a perception later proven to be incorrect. Notice in Figure 7–1 the arrows between the "perceived conflict" and "felt conflict" stages. There is constant internal interaction (intrapersonal communication) between our perceptions and our feelings. For example, think how you would feel if several of you were involved in a project and you felt you were doing the most work. You perceived that the others on the project did not like you and were letting you do the work just to show their hatred. These perceptions would have a direct effect on your feelings: "Those lazy bums" or "Those 'good-for-nothings,'" you might have muttered. You began to feel threatened, hostile, and started to mistrust the others.

To show that feelings can create conflict when none exists, what if you started doing little things to undermine the work of the others? More conflict would very likely be created. Then, later, what if you found out that all the others had understood that you were the leader or director of the project? And they believed that you had assigned yourself these additional tasks and, because of your position, were unwilling to confront you? All of this was felt conflict—conflict that was perceived and felt when none actually existed—at least in the beginning.

### Manifest Behavior

*Manifest behavior* is the action resulting from perceived or felt conflict. It is overt behavior.

We can view our overt behavior with reference to conflict situations as part of a continuum. See Figure 7–2. At the opposing ends of the continuum are the *withdrawer* and the *problem solver*. But heading off in sepa-

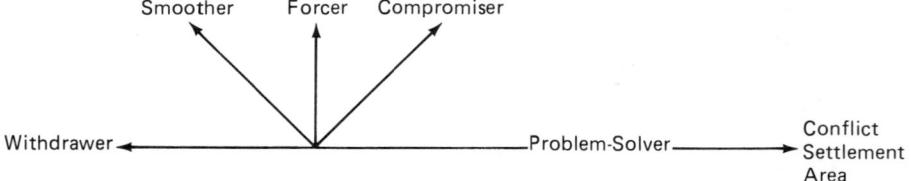

**FIGURE 7-2.**

rate directions from the same continuum are the *smoother,* the *forcer,* and the *compromiser.*

It should be clear that actual human behavior cannot be so conveniently pigeonholed. That is, just because you are predominantly a problem solver does not mean you are not a smoother or compromiser as well. The methods overlap.

In addition, we must recognize that certain situations or conditions call for certain behaviors while others call for different ones. An effective problem solver is likely to be a person sensitive to varying circumstances and willing to meet and alter behaviors as his or her perceptions change.

### Conflict Resolution or Suppression

*Conflict resolution* or *suppression* has to do with bringing the conflict to an end. This usually occurs either through the agreement of all parties or the defeat of one. How the parties feel about the settlement will depend upon the strategy used to resolve the conflict. There are three basic strategies for dealing with conflict: (1) win-lose, (2) lose-lose, and (3) win-win.

*Win-lose* strategy results when one party fails to achieve his or her objective. This may occur because of an exercise of authority or power. The win-lose strategy is an outcome of majority rule. That is, when issues are put to a vote and the majority rules, a win-lose situation results. Minority rule creates a similar outcome. When a few members are so powerful that they can get what they want either by dominating a meeting or railroading items through, the same win-lose situation results.

*Lose-lose* strategy results when neither side gets what it wants, or gets but a fraction of what it wants. The assumption often underlying this strategy is "something is better than nothing." It could be, too, a preference for avoiding conflict. There are a number of lose-lose strategies: (1) compromise, (2) suppression, (3) smoothing, (4) submission of an issue to a third party, or (5) avoidance. Since all of these, except 2 and 4, will be discussed in the section titled "Alternative Approaches to Conflict," a brief consideration of 2 and 4 follows:

Suppression is a form of avoidance. It does not necessarily become lose-lose. Usually, with suppression, no side wins and no side completely loses either. Suppression serves the purpose of concealing differences between participants. If you operate at cross-purposes with another person, you may simply avoid one another and suppress the differences when talking.[9]

Submitting something (an issue) to a third party, likewise, may not be a lose-lose strategy. For example, a third party could decide the issue in favor of one side, thus creating a win-lose situation. But normally, when a decision is submitted to a third party, a middle-ground position is created that offers something of value to both parties. This is what occurs in arbitration; there is a hearing and determination of a case by someone chosen by the parties or appointed under statutory authority. Both parties, however, have avoided further confrontation and problem solving in hopes of a favorable decision. The decision is likely to be unsatisfactory to both sides.

*Win-win* strategies focus on acceptable gains for all parties. Consensus and problem solving are the two most-often-used means of getting a win-win result. Problem solving will be discussed in the next section as an alternative strategy. Consensus is a method used to achieve a solution acceptable to all.

Consensus means general agreement. The first step in reaching a general agreement is to define the goals of both parties. It is the only way to discover how far apart the parties are at the outset. As negotiation begins, both parties focus on resolving the problem, *not* on defeating the other person. No personal battle is waged. Voting, trading, or averaging—either finding the arithmetic mean or getting a midpoint between various extremes—is avoided in seeking consensus because, as pointed out previously, these methods result in win-lose or lose-lose outcomes. Dilemmas are faced by using or gaining more facts. Discussion focuses on the facts. In seeking consensus, too, conflict is viewed as helpful as long as it does not elicit threats or defensiveness. Moreover, self-oriented behavior is avoided because it gives the impression that the other person's needs or positions are not being recognized or valued.

A win-win discussion that focused on movement into a new product market, for example, would require input from all divisions of a business. Discussion might focus on competition, the growth potential of the market, available resources and outlets for sales, and many other production and cost considerations. It would be easy for people representing any division to express self-oriented behavior. They might feel that such a move would cause greater stress on already overtaxed employees, or that they just did not want to exert the time and energy to make the move successful. Notice how such attitudes—whether appropriate or not—would very likely elicit threats and defensiveness. A strong, fact-oriented discussion could help participants resolve their personal dilemmas. With facts, consensus can be reached even in emotionally charged discussions.

### Resolution Aftermath

*Resolution aftermath* defines the consequences of the conflict. If the conflict is genuinely resolved to the satisfaction of all parties, then the aftermath is likely to be a more cooperative relationship among participants. When the air has been cleared, there is a strong, healthy, satisfying feeling that results—proof that conflict resolution, if managed properly, can have positive benefits.

But conflict resolution can also lead to future conflicts. In Figure 7–1, this is demonstrated by the arrow from "resolution aftermath" back up to "antecedent conditions." In other words, one conflict can become an antecedent conditon for another. In a win-lose situation, for example, when you have been on the losing end, you may, indeed, want to strike back, to get even, or to get what belongs to you. You may figure, too, "All right, I let you win this battle, buddy, but just you wait until next time!" As a result of this feeling of high emotional intensity, you become more sensitive to potential conflict conditions—hoping to seize upon an issue that will make you a winner.

Nobody likes being a loser, and it is for that reason, and the intensity of the feelings that often accompany losing, that a win-win strategy is important. Also, goal achievement is most important; thus, when both parties can objectively focus on goals—avoiding the subjective dependence on personalities—everyone benefits.

### ALTERNATIVE APPROACHES TO CONFLICT

Because the positions of withdrawing, smoothing, forcing, compromising, and problem solving are so important, each should be discussed in some detail. Perhaps they can be seen as parts of a conflict matrix. See Figure 7–3. As indicated in the matrix, the position one takes in approaching conflict is often one that relates to how one treats or values people in relationship to how one treats or values the task or goal. This will be demonstrated as each alternative approach is discussed.

#### Withdrawing

*Withdrawers* in a conflict situation wish to maintain neutrality at all costs. By retreating, they can relieve themselves of the necessity for dealing with situations that might arouse conflict. Withdrawers see conflict as hopeless, useless, even a punishing experience. Rather than undergo any tension or frustration, they remove themselves either mentally or physically.

Because of their dislike of conflict, withdrawers keep their dealings with other people very impersonal. Besides revealing a low concern for other people, they also reveal a low concern for the task. Because organiza-

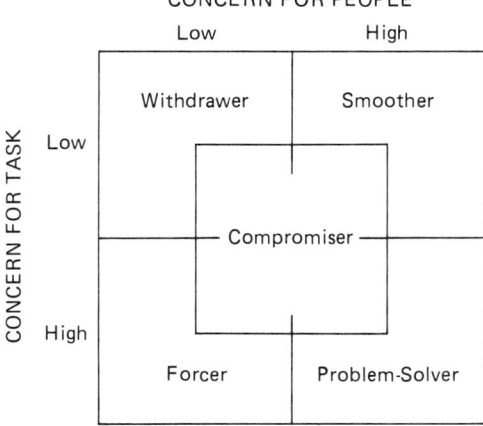

**FIGURE 7-3.** Conflict Matrix.

tions are dependent on communication—that is, communication is what helps gets things done—then it would seem reasonable that a person who withdraws from contact with others will likely affect organization tasks and goals in a similarly negative manner.

### Smoothing

*Smoothers* are just the opposite of withdrawers with respect to people. Smoothers place a high priority on maintaining relationships with others, and they are less concerned about the achievement of either their own or company goals.

The overall feeling of smoothers is that anger is bad and confrontation destructive. They believe that differences between people only serve to drive them apart; thus, they feel, it is better to ignore differences than to risk open combat by being oversensitive. Often, smoothers will give in to the other person when they find the other person's views are in conflict with their own. Acceptance by others is an important value.

### Forcing

*Forcers* seek to meet their own goals at all costs. There is little concern here for the needs or acceptance of others. Forcers will even show willingness to sacrifice individuals in a group if they refuse to go along with their desires.

Forcers believe that differences are to be expected among people, but the conflict that occurs as a result of these differences is suppressed because of authority—the obedience approach. Conflict is simply a nuisance that occurs because others do not see the correctness of the forcer's position.

Forcers believe in the effectiveness of persuasion. Their persuasion is backed up by power and force. Such win-lose power struggles are fought out, but they are decided by the highest common boss or third-party arbitration. They are firm believers that right will prevail and is the central issue in conflict.

### Compromising

*Compromisers* seek to find a position that allows all sides to win. Differences must be treated in light of the common good. Compromisers are bargainers; they try to find that middle ground.

In negotiating settlements, compromisers believe everyone should have an opportunity to air his or her views and feelings. Resolutions require a mixture of skill and persuasive ability coupled with flexibility. They may resort to voting or the invocation of rules as ways to avoid direct confrontation on issues.

Compromisers occupy the middle square in Figure 7–3 because of their flexibility and because, as a result of their work, no one wins and no one loses. Here is the classic lose-lose situation where a "workable" solution may be obtained, but no one is particularly happy with the outcome.

### Problem Solving

*Problem solvers* are ideal types because they have a high concern for both people and for the task. They seek to satisfy their own goals as well as the goals of others. They view conflict as natural and helpful.

Problem solvers are helpful in organizations because they realize that everyone's position needs to be aired and the varying points of view must then be objectively evaluated against facts, emotions, reservations, and doubts. The alternative positions are worked through in a mature, responsible, concerned manner.

Most effective problem solvers will not sacrifice anyone for the good of the group. They view differences as neither good nor bad, but simply as a symptom of tensions in relationships. Conflict requires confrontation and objective problem solving. This is the only means for successfully reaching the "conflict settlement area" (see Figure 7–2) in a positive, mutually agreeable, way.

## A METHOD FOR RESOLVING CONFLICT

Now you may say, "I either am or want to become a problem solver." But being a problem solver really does not provide a methodology for resolving conflict; rather, it offers an attitude or perspective. In this concluding section, a specific methodology for resolving conflict is suggested.[10] The methodology includes (1) setting the stage, (2) defining the problem, (3) seeking causes and positions, (4) finding alternatives, (5) reaching an agreement, and (6) implementing the result.[11]

### Setting the Stage

Conflict is best dealt with in an atmosphere conducive to negotiation, open communication, and trust. Often, such an atmosphere cannot be hastily constructed. That is, if a rather hostile, combatant environment exists, it is almost impossible—at least on the spur of the moment—to turn this around to deal with an immediate conflict situation. Atmosphere is something that has roots or history. The way a situation "feels" may result from the personalities of those in charge, the arrangement of furniture, or previous conflict occurrences.

A proper setting where conflict can occur would likely be some place private. It would be a place where listening can occur without distractions or interruptions. It would be a place where confidentiality could be maintained. It would be a place, too, where honest, open communication can be conducted on fairly neutral grounds. Although neutrality cannot always be achieved—especially as in the case of a conflict with a boss who is part-owner of the company—it should be sought to the degree possible. At least both parties should feel comfortable in the location.

As part of setting the stage, keep the problem separate from the people. True, you will be dealing with human beings who have strong emotions, deeply held values, specific backgrounds, and unique viewpoints, and they must be dealt with sensitively. People problems will be major factors in resolving conflicts. But they must be treated separately from the substance. That is, you must deal with others as human beings and consider the problem on its own merits. A diagram of how this can be done is contained in Figure 7-4. How to approach the problem as a common or joint task is the subject of the remaining sections of this chapter.

### Defining the Problem

Here, the parties to the conflict must seek a *common definition*. A common definition is one that recognizes the problem as a mutual one—not a win-lose situation. To accept one definition over another may give one participant an advantage, if not a direct advantage, perhaps a perceived (mental) one by one party or the other.

The definition should be specific and concrete. This avoids having to deal with a general, diffuse, or abstract situation. This also avoids confusion. With a common definition it is more likely that the final solution will tie back into the exact problem agreed upon.

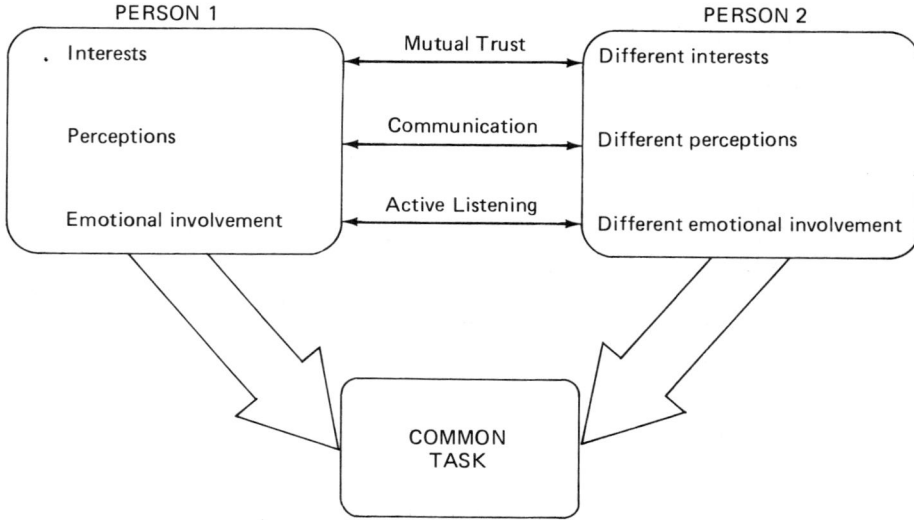

**FIGURE 7-4.**

Gaining a common definition will be easier if the problem is defined not in terms of positions but in terms of needs. For example, two people are arguing over having a window in their work space opened or closed. Each position is clear: One wants it open; the other wants it closed. The supervisor enters and hears the arguing. She asks one worker, "Why do you want the window open?"

"To let in some fresh air," he says.

She asks the other, "Why do you want it closed?" "To avoid a draft," comes the reply. After thinking for a moment, she goes into the next room and opens a window. This allows fresh air without the draft.[12]

To ensure the definition is complete, all feelings and actions of both parties must be brought out. Full, relevant disclosure at this point will help guarantee completeness.

### Seeking Causes and Interests

It is assumed at this stage that all of the parties involved have agreed to cooperate. Without cooperation, it is unlikely that a common definition could have been agreed upon, but even more unlikely that the negotiation could proceed beyond that stage.

Disagreements and differences must be aired. Seeking the causes for the problem may be helpful since that may provide some history or evolution; this will also help assure that participants are not just treating the symptoms—which could result in superficial treatment rather than in-depth solutions.

Areas of agreement and areas that are unacceptable should be clearly outlined. Again, this lays the foundation for resolution because boundaries, restrictions, and various limits can be established at this point.

What some people in conflict forget is that behind all the opposition lie some compatible interests as well as conflicting ones.[13] We tend to assume, in conflict, that we, and everything we stand for, are under attack. Think about almost any conflict an employee might have with a supervisor. What compatible interests do they have? They both want stability; they both want the business to survive; they are both interested in a good relationship with each other.[14]

Roger Fisher and William Ury, in their book *Getting to Yes*, offer their readers eleven different ways to identify interests:

1. Ask "Why?"—put yourself in their shoes.
2. Ask "Why not?" Think about their choice. Why are they *not* willing to accept your decision?
3. Realize that each side has multiple interests.
4. Recognize that the most powerful interests are basic human needs such as security, economic well-being, a sense of belonging, recognition, and control over one's life.
5. Talk about interests: communicate.
6. Make your interests come alive by being specific, serious, and by establishing their legitimacy—that they are just and are neither spurious nor false.
7. Acknowledge others' interests as part of the problem: Pay heed to the interests of others.
8. Put the problem before your answer. People are more likely to listen to your interests and reasons if they come first, followed by your conclusion or proposal.
9. Look forward, not back; talk about where you want to go not from where you have come.
10. Be concrete but flexible. Be open to fresh ideas.
11. Be hard on the problem, soft on the people. Be a strong advocate of your interests, but while attacking the problem, listen, show respect, treat others with courtesy, express appreciation, and emphasize concern. Show them you are attacking the problem, not them.[15]

### Finding Alternatives

Possible solutions should be suggested by both parties. The best situation would be to generate multiple solutions without evaluation. Much like "brainstorming," both parties should spontaneously and vigorously develop solutions—workable or not. One party might even "hitchhike" on ideas presented by the other; that is, one party suggests an idea and the other takes that same idea even further or finds a similar idea as a result of the first suggestion.

During brainstorming, no one should criticize in any way. The focus should be on the quantity of ideas produced. Allow your imagination to flow freely. Approach the problem from every conceivable angle. Only after brainstorming do you want to put an asterisk by the most important ideas, revise them as needed, combine any that can be combined, and evaluate them. The goal here is to come up with a solution that will be as painless as possible for all sides.

### Reaching an Agreement

This is the stage in which the real negotiation occurs and where all of a person's problem-solving ability is brought into play. The agreement is usually a synthesis of a variety of the alternatives offered in the previous stage. It is a drawing together or a composite.

To reach agreement, both parties must lay out various costs and gains. These costs and gains may have to be changed as a formal, final solution is reached and a joint position achieved.

Once you seem to be close to agreement, several methods can be used to test for it. The problem is that one party may assume agreement, and yet it may not be there. Feedback channels should be kept open; seek and encourage it. If confusion is suspected, ask the other party for clarification. Record agreements when they occur so that they can be checked and reviewed. To continually assure that agreement is being maintained, restate positions periodically. This can be done using the paraphrasing (understanding) response style as discussion proceeds—each party to the conflict restating the position of the previous speaker to that person's satisfaction before stating his or her own. Before moving to the next stage, both parties could summarize and gain commitment from the other.

### Implementing the Result

This entire procedure of conflict resolution is unnecessary, even a waste of time, if the result is not actually put into practice. It will be useful if both individuals can explain how they will act differently as a result of the new agreement. How (or to what extent) has cooperation been restored? How will mutual goals be achieved?

It is useful, too, if parties can arrange some future meeting for reassessment. There should be a method for evaluating the solution or for making certain that everything is operating as agreed upon. If the problem is an obvious one and the results regularly perceived or viewed, this stage may not be as necessary.

The value of some evaluation or reassessment helps assure that the resolution aftermath will continue to result in cooperation, or at least the perception of cooperation. It helps reduce the likelihood, then, that this conflict will be an antecedent condition for the next one.

## SUMMARY

Conflict is a normal outcome when people interact. And since businesses and organizations are built on interaction, conflict is a normal, natural part of businesses and organizations.

In this chapter, the profits of conflict were first presented. How conflict energizes people, reveals organizational weaknesses, opens new and perhaps lasting channels of communication, provides catharsis, or becomes an educational experience were all discussed. Conflict should be viewed as positive and useful.

The view of conflict as positive and useful is relatively new. The old and new views were contrasted in the second section of the chapter. The new view suggests not only that conflict is good and should be encouraged, but also that it is inevitable. It portrays human beings as driven by aggressive, self-seeking, and competitive instincts. It also acknowledges that conflicts result from a struggle for limited rewards, not just from breakdowns in communication. The new view places its emphasis on conflict management.

Managing conflict, however, is easier if it is viewed as a dynamic process that occurs as a sequence of episodes. The stages that conflict seems to follow include antecedent conditions, perceived conflict, felt conflict, manifest behavior, conflict resolution or suppression, and the resolution aftermath.

Managing conflict is easier, too, if various approaches to resolving conflict are recognized. Often, the roles of withdrawer, smoother, forcer, compromiser, and problem solver are not clear and distinct. These roles may overlap, and they may be combined in a variety of ways. Problem solving was presented as a rather ideal approach.

But to be a problem solver does not provide a specific method to resolve conflict. The final section of this chapter outlined a step-by-step method that included setting the stage, defining the problem, seeking causes and positions, finding alternatives, reaching an agreement, and implementing the result.

It is unlikely that conflict participants will resolve their conflict by following this step-by-step method in the exact order suggested. But effective conflict resolution is unlikely to occur in a haphazard or happenstance manner. That is the point. The more understanding of conflict and the more foresight and planning that occurs, the more likely the results will be positive and beneficial for all concerned.

## NOTES

[1] Mark L. Knapp, *Interpersonal Communication and Human Relationships* (Boston: Allyn & Bacon, 1984), p. 215.

[2] Ibid., p. 215.

[3] J. Templeton, "For Corporate Vigor, Plan a Fight Today," *Sales Management, 102* (1969), 32–36. As cited in Jerry W. Koehler, Karl W. E. Anatol, and Ronald L. Applbaum, *Organizational Communication: Behavioral Perspectives,* 2nd ed. (New York: Holt, Rinehart & Winston, 1981), p. 306. Used with permission.

[4] Material in this section has been adapted from Charles R. Milton, *Human Behavior in Organizations: Three Levels of Behavior* (Englewood Cliffs, N.J.: Prentice-Hall, 1981), pp. 428–29.

[5] See Donald Nightingale, "Conflict and Conflict Resolution," in George Strauss, ed., *Organizational Behavior: Research and Issues* (Madison: Industrial Relations Research Association, University of Wisconsin, 1974), pp. 141–63.

[6] Ibid., pp. 141–63.

[7] Milton, *Human Behavior,* pp. 428–29.

[8] From Alan C. Filley, *Interpersonal Conflict Resolution.* Copyright © 1974 by Scott, Foresman and Co. Reprinted by permission.

[9] See Stephen P. Robbins, *Managing Organizational Conflict* (Englewood Cliffs, N.J.: Prentice-Hall, 1974), pp. 69–70. As cited in Milton, *Human Behavior,* p. 437.

[10] This is an adaptation of the step-by-step methodology suggested in David W. Johnson, *Reaching Out: Interpersonal Effectiveness and Self-Actualization,* 2nd ed. (Englewood Cliffs, N.J.: Prentice-Hall, 1981, Chapter 11, "Confrontation and Negotiation," pp. 229–44.

[11] Also see Richard L. Weaver, II, *Understanding Interpersonal Communication,* 3rd ed. (Glenview, Ill.: Scott, Foresman, 1984), Chapter 8, "Overcoming Barriers: Coping with Conflict," pp. 214–35.

[12] Adapted from *Getting to Yes* by Roger Fisher and William Ury. Copyright © 1981 by Roger Fisher and William Ury. Reprinted by permission of Houghton Mifflin Co.

[13] Ibid., p. 43.

[14] Ibid., p. 44.

[15] Ibid.

# 8

# Visual and Graphic Communication

Confucius said, "A picture is worth a thousand words." Whether he actually said a thousand words or ten thousand is beside the point. The truth of this phrase is proven time and again as we sit in meetings listening to presenters describing something we would probably understand instantly if we could only see it. A visual aid is an instructional device (as a chart, map, or model) that appeals chiefly to vision. (I do not want to exclude audio or audio-visual aids; most comments in this chapter also apply to audio and audio-visual aids.) Lack of visual aids can be a barrier to clear understanding. In report writing, visual aids are called "graphic aids."

Because of the significance of visual and graphic communication in business communication, a whole chapter of this book is devoted to it. This includes both written and oral presentations. In this chapter, the values of visual communication will be outlined first. In the second section, some pointers on using visual and graphic aids will be discussed. If one were to prepare a convenient checklist to assure the best use of visual or graphic aids, the headings in this section would make a useful, practical list.

In the third section, attention will be focused specifically on written reports and then various types of graphic aids that can be used in written reports. The final sections focus on oral reports and various types of visual aids.

Whether or not to use a visual or graphic aid depends on many different factors, including the speaker's or writer's ability, accessibility to the aid desired, the audience for whom the aid will be used, the message itself (and whether it will benefit from reinforcement), as well as the situation as a whole and how appropriate an aid would be. There is no way for this author to decide these things for the reader; the final decision must be yours. But I *can* make you aware of their value and methods for using them. In that way, the decision of whether or not to use them should be easier.

## VALUES OF VISUAL AIDS

Essentially, there are three major values that can be gained from using visual aids. They are not unlike those values we expect to gain as a result of any communication with another person: understanding, retention, and interest.

### Understanding

*Understanding* is the most obvious value. By using a visual aid we have increased the number of senses we are depending on to evoke meaning in another person. Normally we depend on sound if the communication is oral; thus, the aid adds the visual or sight dimension. In writing, it broadens the channel of sight by presenting the information in a new or different way; thus, the aid adds redundancy—saying essentially the same thing in a different way. This is true also in the oral channel; using sight as well is redundant. And redundancy is a useful learning aid.

But visual aids can enhance understanding in other ways too. They can gain attention if effectively presented; understanding is more likely to occur if the receiver is actively attending. Visual aids can also save time. In a well-done presentation, the aid will cause attention to be focused specifically and directly. Since superfluous material will have been removed, this increases the likelihood that receivers will not only see but understand what remains: the essentials. Visual aids, in most cases, have this simplifying effect: they reduce things to their barest essentials. Also, they can represent something that cannot easily be explained orally, like a process or the internal working of a machine. Thus, visual aids assist the receiver in interpretation.

### Retention

In addition to facilitating understanding, visual aids also contribute to retention, the receiver's ability to recall our ideas. First, we are more likely to remember an idea because we have received it either through more than one sense (sound and sight) or in more than one way through the same sense (a chart in a written report accompanied by an explanation of that chart). So, a redundant message is more likely to be recalled.

We also tend to recall that which has an impact on us. If the visual aid is practical and has an effective appearance, it is likely to make an impression. We often remember the advertisements on television or in magazines that have made an impression on us: "Oh, I like this one," you might say as an effective, familiar advertisement appears.

In tests that have compared the same oral communications with and without visual aids, it has been proven that listeners recall more when visual aids are used. In one test, those exposed to visual aids recalled up to 55 percent more immediately after the presentation and even more in delayed testing.[1]

**Interest**

Visual aids not only increase understanding and retention, but they also heighten listener interest. They add interest primarily by adding variety. Considering the amount of communication we receive, most of it becomes rather dull, monotonous, or routine over a period of time. How many people write or speak with a flair that immediately grasps and holds our attention? Out of all those you hear or read? I suspect the answer is "few." That is precisely why visual aids can enhance interest; they add a dimension not normally present in everyday communication.

In addition, the visual aid provides a clear mental impression. A listener enjoys being able to picture a situation or an idea. It is like mental closure: the drawing together of disparate elements to complete an image. But it can also be simply a renewal of one's interest in an idea or even of the moment, such as what is being revealed when we say, "Ah, something new, different, or unusual to which I can turn my attention. Great!"

Finally, a visual aid can interest receivers by arousing curiosity. We are all naturally curious. ("What point is being made here?" "I wonder what figure [chart or graph] will appear next?" "How will the speaker [or writer] introduce that one?")

Visual aids satisfy important values in written and oral communication, but how effectively they serve these values will depend, in part, on how they are used.

**USING VISUAL AIDS**

Just as the values discussed in the previous section apply both to written and oral communication, so do the following techniques apply to the use of visual and graphic aids. In this section, foresight, reinforcement, placement, explanation, and construction will be examined.

## Foresight

You must exhibit care in your use of visual and graphic aids just as you must at all points in making a presentation. Care here is a bit different in that a visual or graphic aid is usually a supplement. That is, it can or cannot be used. And it would be too bad if its use distracted from the intended message more than it aided or supplemented it.

Keep in mind your fundamental reason for communicating. Will the aids you intend to use promote and support that reason? You should never arbitrarily select five or nine illustrations to include. Rather, you must ask, "How many illustrations will it take to convey my message effectively and efficiently? It is a matter of cost-effectiveness. Preparing good visual and graphic aids takes time, and that amount of time may be better spent in perfecting the verbal message: the language of your presentation. But once a decision has been reached as to how many aids are needed (and this may not be known until one has worked through the material in a precise and detailed manner), then each aid must be planned for a specific communication need. Do they add to clarity? Do they allow you to present many data in a small space? Each aid must help present the information, but more importantly, each must help further the speaker's goal. Does the aid contribute to moving the receiver forward in his or her understanding or belief?

## Reinforcement

If you were discussing the productivity of your company and you wanted to indicate that productivity had risen 10 percent from 1965 to 1970, 15 percent from 1970 to 1975, and 25 percent from 1975 to 1980, this data could be illustrated on a graph. The line on that graph may provide a mental image of the increase that is both better and stronger than what could be provided by the words alone. See Figure 8-1.

There are people, too, who are not as word-oriented as others. Because meaning lies in people and not in words, presenting data in graphic form helps reinforce meanings. This also helps receivers compare and contrast data. Charts, graphs, and tables must be viewed as reinforcement tools: as supplement or backup forces, rather than first or front-line equipment.

Reinforcement has one additional dimension. The dictionary defines "reinforce" this way: "to strengthen by additional assistance, material, or support."[2] This definition places the aid as reinforcer in a subordinate role. It must, in any presentation, remain the servant and not the master. An aid is a means to an end, not an end in itself. This can be kept in mind if we remember that it is an *aid*—an aid only. It can be kept in mind, too, if we introduce the aid before using or showing it and not allow the aid to lead

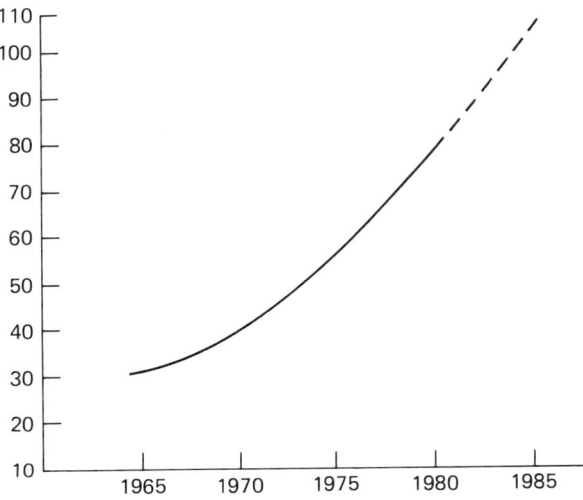

**FIGURE 8-1.**

us. It gains its strength as it provides a fresh *addition* through *support*—all subservient functions.

### Placement

As reinforcement tools, the location of an aid in a presentation is extremely important. They must appear in the right place, at the proper angle, and displayed only when they are relevant to the point being made.

Further, you should call the reader's or listener's attention to the aid's location. This sounds like it could be awkward or mechanical, but it needn't be. If you are reading along and suddenly you encounter a graph, a table, or chart, you must pause to determine the purpose of the visual aid. This is true in oral communication as well. This delay is a distraction; it reduces effectiveness.

This does not mean that the writer or speaker should make a production number out of the introduction. "As you can see in the accompanying diagram . . . ," may be sufficient, or simply, "Here we see. . . ." The point is that a relationship between the text and the aid must be made, and the best place to do this is just before the aid is revealed. This reader or listener preparation aids understanding.

Another problem associated with placement may occur when you have charts, graphs, or tables that you wish to include but which do not tell a specific part of the presentational story. They are included to tell the whole story (to give the full picture) or for future reference. Moreover, if they are long and complex, they may not serve the presenter's purpose to

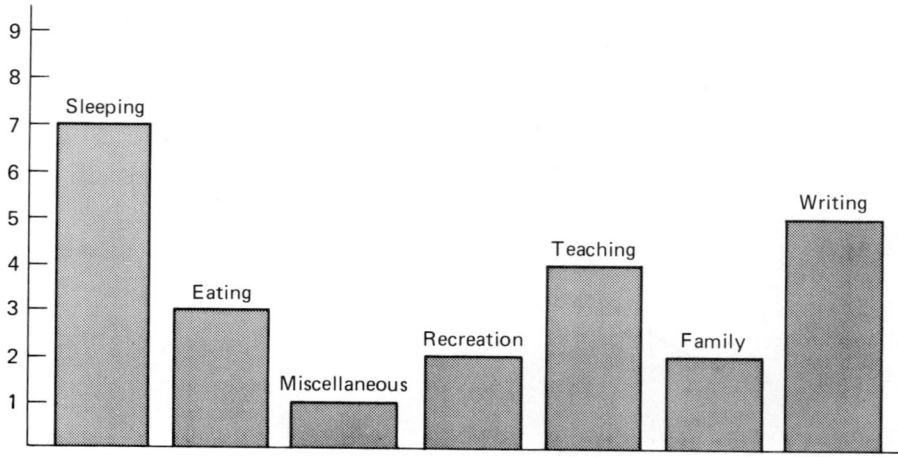

**FIGURE 8–2.**[3]

be placed within the text, for this could spoil the flow of material. In these cases, the aids may be placed at the end of the report with a short note or referral in the text, such as: "as shown in Table 3."

In an oral presentation, use of visual aids is slightly different. You use only those aids that directly promote and support your ideas and that can be used during the speech. There are no appendices or additional tables, in most cases. If there must be, these can be supplied to audience members as a handout or booklet at the end of the speech.

Partially because of informational overload, demands on time, efficiency and certainly for other reasons as well, there is a move toward providing material in a free-flowing, fast-moving manner unobstructed with highly technical material.

Effective reports must catch observers' attention. Charts, graphs, and tables are simplified, numbers are rounded off, and material is constructed for high visual impact. In this way, too, complicated explanations are unnecessary because, in many cases, the visuals speak for themselves. This approach tends to satisfy self-centered people with short attention spans who need to be presented dramatic information that does not require heavy, in-depth thought. In many cases, this is how people have been conditioned to respond because of advertising, television programming, and the continual assault on their senses by people who demand their attention—others who have already learned to use visual material of high impact!

Because of increasing demands on their time, many top executives prefer this style as well. It presents facts quickly and easily. This job is best done by short summary reports supported by clear, concise, visual or graphic aids.

### Explanation

It would be so easy if we could say, "Notice that factor as it is shown in Table 2," and leave it at that. Or how about saying simply, "Table 7 is on page 8," or "You will find that chart in the supplementary material I handed out before this talk." We cannot. If you do not want a reader or listener to look at or understand a chart, graph, or table, this will do it.

Never assume that your listeners or readers will study or pursue important information on their own, that is, information *you* consider important. In most cases they won't. In addition, if they do study or read on their own, you cannot assume that the message they get (the meaning they make) will be the same one you intended.

To increase the impact of a visual or graphic aid in a communication, an explanation is necessary. How much of an explanation depends on the need. If the information is especially complex, more explanation may be necessary. Remember that you prepared or planned the visual aid and you are close to the information it portrays. Just because it is clear to you does not mean it will be clear to others. Even the simplest of messages can be misunderstood. If there is a question of whether or not to explain an aid, the best advice would be to explain it.

### Construction

There is no doubt that in planning and preparing visual or graphic aids you will encounter problems unique to a particular situation. The best way to solve these problems results from the intelligent appraisal of the situation, or consultation with others close to that situation. But there are problems of construction common to most situations when visual or graphic aids are to be used. These include size, simplicity, appearance, and color.

*Size.* One of the first decisions involving the construction of a visual or graphic aid is how large should it be. The answer to the question of size should be neither arbitrary nor based solely on convenience. Size should be at least in part, determined by the contents of the aid. A highly complex model may need considerable size to spread the information out and to make the relationship of model parts clear and distinct. A simple bar graph with only three bars may require much less space.

Other considerations that may help you decide on what size to make the visual or graphic aid include how much it contributes to the overall understanding of the subject, how easily it can be understood, and how distortion can best be minimized. Recognize that whenever numbers are converted to charts, graphs, and tables, some distortion occurs. There is a direct relationship between the amount of distortion and the level of understanding: The less the distortion, the greater the level of audience understanding.

In a written report, extremely complex or technical data may need more space than a normal page can supply. Long presentations can be carefully inserted and folded within the report, but ease in opening them must be an important consideration in their use.

In an oral presentation, size may also be determined by the location of the speech as well as the number of people in the audience. Everyone must be able to see the visual aid. In some cases, it might be best to have the aid reduced in size and duplicated so that all audience members can have a copy in front of them as it is being discussed. This procedure, however, raises other problems such as ease of distribution or having audience members exposed to the material well before it is discussed—especially if it is passed out before the speech.

*Simplicity.* Although this characteristic has been touched on before, here it is emphasized as part of the construction process. Aids must be kept simple. As the complexity of the aid increases, audience understanding (or interest in it) will decrease: an inverse ratio.

All right, you say, but what if the material I want to impart *is* complicated? First reduce it to its simplest elements. If it is still complex, then it should be divided into phases, steps, or exposures so that each can be added to the next in sequential fashion—building on its predecessor. The result, or whole picture, results from an accumulative effect.

Whether you like it or not, people will read their own meaning into whatever you present. The more information you give them, the more stimuli they have to create meanings. Even the longer they look at a stimulus, the more time they have to read meanings into it. Thus, simplicity of presentation controls some of this interpretation—to the extent that is possible.

*Appearance.* Anything of yours that is to be seen by others should have a neat, professional appearance. It is like the employee who turned in material to his boss, and when it was returned with evaluative comments on it was heard to say, "I didn't know he was really going to look at it!" No matter the stage of development, it is wise to consider anything going out with your name attached to be proper material for evaluation. This helps you maintain constant attention to professional appearance.

Appearance may involve the overall layout. And the layout will be affected by the amount of information being illustrated. Too many lines, too narrow or confined borders, or the use of a variety of perspectives may confuse the reader or viewer and cause confusion.

But confusion is just one result of poor appearance. More seriously, poor appearance may affect source credibility. A sloppy, careless approach is likely to produce the same effect that you would have if you received a business letter full of smudges, strikeovers, white-outs, and uneven margins. Even if the message is important or deemed (by you) to be of high quality, flaws produce a negative impression. They may well reflect on both your propriety (your ability to know what is proper) and your competence.

A professional appearance does not require skilled artistry, however. What it requires, instead, is some attention to factors such as neatness, legibility, balance, and harmony. If attention to these elude your ability (or desire) then it may be worth your while to seek aid of others who can help. Propriety and competence are too important to sacrifice.

*Color.* Color increases the physical attractiveness of a visual aid. It may increase the readability of a chart or graph by allowing the reader or viewer to see comparisons and distinctions. In a graph, a red line could represent one product line, a blue line another, and so on. The reader or viewer can then compare statistics like this on one graph. If color is not available, dots, hyphens, or crossed lines could be used, even though the effect may not be as striking.

The major problem in using color is choosing ones that do not "read" well. Pastel colors or yellow may not project, or you may get two colors, like black and blue (assuming you will allow me to call "black" a color), which may not be seen as different when printed or when seen from the back of the room.

## GRAPHIC AIDS IN WRITTEN REPORTS

Graphic aids can help the writer present quantitative data (figures and statistics) or describe a technical process or procedure. The most common types of graphic aids include tables, graphs, and pictograms. Variations and combinations of these are possible.

### Tables

A table is an advantage when you want to present quantitative data systematically in rows and columns. In a table, the titles of the rows (horizontal) are called "stubs," and the titles of the columns (vertical) are called "captions." To increase reader understanding, it is important that stubs and captions be accurate and concise.

The real advantage of a table is that a large amount of data can be presented in a small area. It is efficient. Even though it would take many sentences to cover all the data conveyed in most tables, remember that a table does not speak for itself. It requires explanation. See Table 8–1.

**TABLE 8–1**   Distribution of Each Dollar of Sales Income

| | |
|---|---|
| Material cost . . . . . . . | $ .13 |
| Labor cost . . . . . . . . . | .49 |
| Marketing cost . . . . . | .31 |
| Profit . . . . . . . . . . . . . | .05 |
| Taxes . . . . . . . . . . . . | .02 |

### Graphs

There are many kinds of graphs: line, bar, and circle are some examples. In each case, a series of points, a line, a curve, or an area represents the variation of one variable (a quantity that may assume any one set of values) in comparison with one or more other variables. The advantage of a graph is this quick comparison.

A *line graph* will plot the quantities as points on a scale. The points will then be connected to form a line. See Figure 8–3.

A *bar graph* can also be used to present business data. It can present data either horizontally or vertically. Figure 8–2 offers an example of a vertical bar graph. Figure 8–4 is a horizontal bar graph. It compares the simple magnitudes by the lengths of equal-width bars.

**FIGURE 8–3.**   Melrampco Incorporated Sales Growth (in thousands of dollars) 1978–1984.

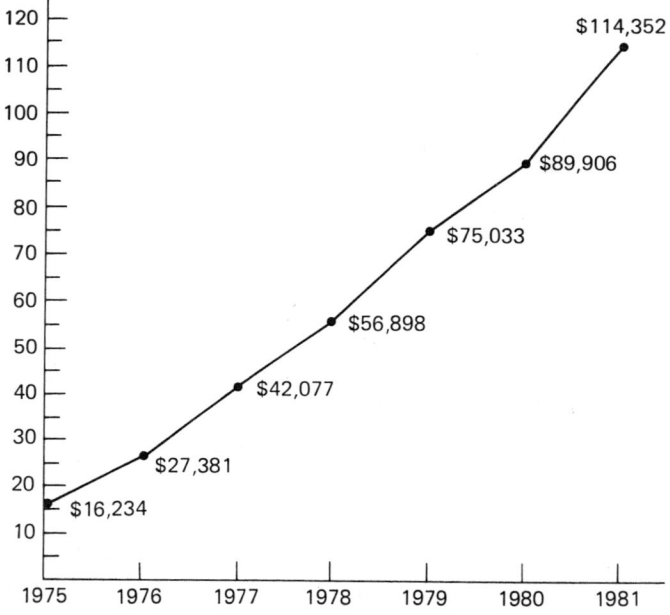

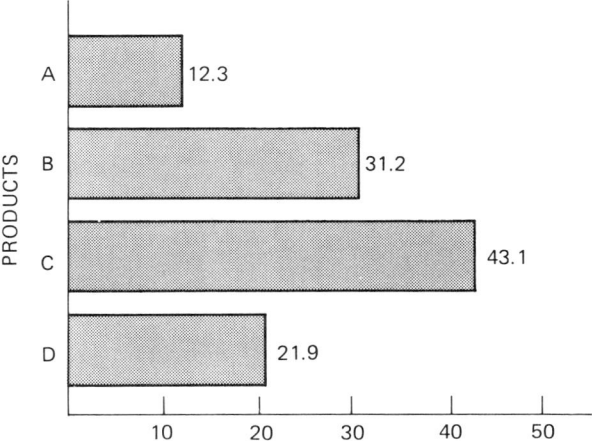

**FIGURE 8–4.** Sales in Thousands of Units—A Horizontal Bar Graph.

A *circle graph*, sometimes called a *pie graph*, is yet another way to depict business data. It is easy to construct if you compute the total amount you want to depict. Now divide each segment's quantity by the total to get the percentage of the total each segment represents. Multiply this percentage by 360°. Add up the sums to make certain they total 360°. Use a protractor to plot the segments.

### Pictograms

A pictogram is simply a bar chart that uses pictures rather than bars to convey the information. A company, for example, might use stacks of coins instead of bars to represent dollar growth or sales. See Figure 8–6.

**FIGURE 8–5.** A Circle (or Pie) Graph.

Sales in 1980 for three products were:
1. 28,500
2. 24,750
3. 21,750

TOTAL in sales was: $75,000

1. 28,500 divided by 75,000 = 0.38
2. 24,750 divided by 75,000 = 0.33
3. 21,750 divided by 75,000 = <u>0.29</u>
                            1.00 = total

1. 0.38 × 360 = 136.8°
2. 0.33 × 360 = 118.8°
3. 0.29 × 360 = <u>104.4°</u>
                    360° = total

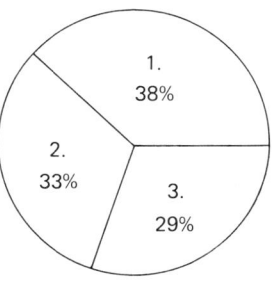

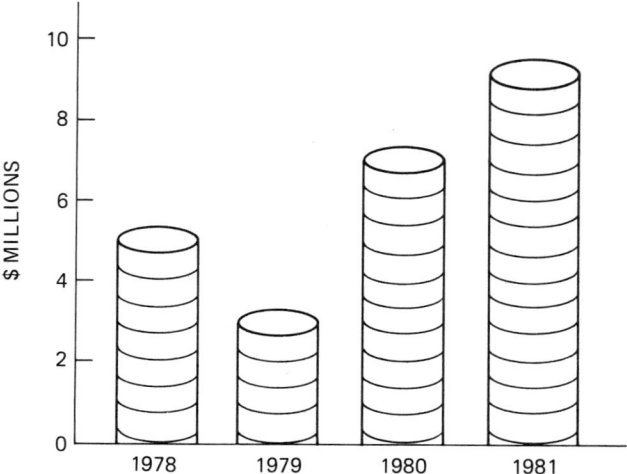

**FIGURE 8–6.** Growth in Sales.

### Other Aids

Those aids already mentioned are by far the most popular. But there are others: Photographs, drawings, maps, pictures, and diagrams are some of these. Actually, any form of graphic design is acceptable as long as it communicates the true story. The possibilities are limitless.

## VISUAL AIDS IN ORAL REPORTS

Any of the previous kinds of graphic aids can be adapted for use as a visual aid in an oral report. As a supplement to an oral report, they would be presented on a chalkboard, on a chart, or on an overhead, slide, or movie projector. But in the oral situation, the speaker has one handicap: Viewers cannot go back and pick up information missed, nor can they devote extra time and study to material that is complex. In using visual aids, speakers must make certain they are relatively simple. An audience burdened with too much information or too much detail may not understand, may become confused, or may lose interest altogether.

In oral presentations, it is best not to pass visual aids around during the report. The point here is that audience attention should be focused on the speaker. Passing objects around invites chaos. A speaker describing safety problems in the work area had taken snapshots of each of the problem areas. To impress his audience with the severity of the situation, he handed one stack of snapshots to the left and another stack to the right. During his report, people were looking at the pictures, whispering, turning, picking up pictures from the floor—everything but listening to him.

It is all right to give listeners handouts if the handouts are all alike and not to be passed around. One speaker, for example, made photocopies of her chart, instead of making a large one, and handed these out. The additional advantage was that audience members carried away the information from her report for future reference.

### Chalkboards

Providing the quantity of information is not extensive and providing the room in which you will be speaking is not too large, using the chalkboard to present data can be effective. But there are some precautions that need to be followed. For example, a presenter should try to place the information on the board before the presentation. Not having used a chalkboard before, some people find that writing on a board takes far longer than anticipated. It can eat up a presenter's valuable time.

Moreover, people forget to write clearly enough or big enough. When you write large enough, you will often find that not nearly as much information can be squeezed onto a chalkboard as thought. In addition, if you have never written with chalk, you will find you must write harder than you may think to produce a clear, legible impression, especially one that can be read from the back of a room. And if you hold the chalk perpendicular to the board rather than at about a 30° angle to it, you may also get a spine-tingling squeal when you write—or the chalk may bounce over the board. Practice beforehand to find the proper pressure and angle.

Another precaution has to do with your own body position when you use the chalkboard. Too often presenters talk to the board and not to the audience. Directing your attention toward the audience is not easy, but it is important. Also, when you look at the board be certain to raise your voice so everyone in the audience can hear.

Be certain to keep any information you write covered in some way before needed. A portable chalkboard that revolves is excellent for this purpose since it can be written on, then revolved when needed. Information shown prior to or after it is needed simply increases the possibility of distraction. And we must be at war with distraction—like erasing completely. It is distracting when a person leaves lines and parts of words when erasing a chalkboard. Take a moment more to be careful and complete.

A speaker who chooses to use the chalkboard should realize that it lacks some of the professional appearance that many in business prefer. Also, it cannot be preserved for future speeches; this may mean time wasted in recreating the material several times.

### Charts

A chart can be prepared beforehand and can more easily be kept out of sight of the audience. Moreover, charts have an advantage because they can be used more than once. It is important that drawings and letters be dark and that colors be bold. Light colors cannot be seen from a distance.

Speakers should face their audience when discussing charts. Occasional glances at the chart are permitted, but speaking to it—rather than the audience—should be avoided. Speakers should make certain all audience members can see the chart, especially those seated to their far left or far right. They must avoid standing between the chart and the people being addressed. It is helpful if the chart can be supported by a stand, by the chalkboard tray, or by tape or thumbtacks, and if speakers can use a pointer when describing the chart.

Some rooms are equipped for chart usage, some are not. It is wise to check beforehand to determine available facilities. Some speakers have found flip charts convenient. A flip chart is simply an easel that can hold numerous charts secured at the top. When finished using one chart, it is flipped to the back side of the easel out of sight and a new chart is revealed. A speaker whose report is to be heavily illustrated with charts, graphs, and tables may best utilize a flip chart because of its convenience and ease of use. Some speakers use a blank page in between each chart to be used so that they can flip from chart to blank page while explaining material in between the various diagrams. Indexing of charts is important; speakers should not have to search for the appropriate material while audiences watch—impatiently.

### Overhead Projector

The overhead projector projects onto a screen information contained on a transparency. Transparencies can be made from most documents simply by running the document with a blank transparency through a multilith machine. Felt-tip pens can be used to add color to transparencies.

Since overhead projectors can be operated from the front of the room, speakers can operate them while facing and talking to the audience. This gives speakers great control of their material and its presentation. To add to the control factor, speakers can use a wax pencil or felt-tip marker and add to the transparency while talking. A pointer can also be used to show an exact location, or a specific piece of data being referred to. Transparencies can also be stored and used again.

However, there are several disadvantages to using an overhead projector. The first is that for the best reception, they must be displayed in dark or semidark rooms. This may interfere with speaker-audience rapport. It can also be distracting if lights must be continually turned on and off.

The second disadvantage is that it sometimes requires a special machine to produce high-quality transparencies. Of course, they can be made by hand, too, by tracing drawings or by making original drawings. Access to this machine may not be easy, or preparation time may not be available.

Additionally, with a large number of transparencies, it is easy to get them out of sequence.

One precaution is suggested in using overhead projectors: Know how to operate the machine before getting up in front of an audience. How does the machine turn on? How is it focused? How far from the screen should it be? Which way is the transparency mounted? These are some of the common problems experienced. Remember to leave on the machine until the cooling fan stops running. The projector bulb may be ruined otherwise, and projector bulbs have a habit of burning out at inopportune times. Therefore, have a replacement bulb available, and know how to install it.

### Slide Projectors

Slides are suitable when your presentation requires the use of many visual aids. This is even truer if those visual aids include photographs. The use of slides gives you flexibility because you can improve a speech or adapt it to different audiences by adding, deleting, or rearranging the slides.

Slides are versatile. In one oral report, a speaker provided the title of the presentation, an outline of it, as well as periodic summaries of content, with models, drawings, and photographed examples all with slides. The speaker even provided an abbreviated bibliography by showing slides of the actual books referred to during the presentation.

The major problem with slides, besides having to show them in darkened or semidarkened rooms, is that preparing professional-looking slides requires expertise, expense, and effort. But when available, an effective slide presentation can be a dynamic and attractive feature.

### Opaque Projectors

When you have pictures, sections from magazines or books to show, the opaque projector is a convenient tool. The problem some speakers have is trying to keep the pictures and articles and book sections organized.

One major audience frustration is speaker disorganization. Watching speakers search for a misplaced visual aid or an out-of-place picture is both annoying and distracting. When audience members' level of annoyance reaches a certain peak—when they feel their time is being wasted—they may discredit the speaker or the ideas being shared. Warning: Be prepared and organized. Do a complete run-through using all visuals and all other speech accessories.

### Movie Projectors

There are many sources for films. Some companies maintain their own libraries. If you will be talking before groups on a regular basis, it would be wise to learn how to use a movie projector.

Any movie chosen for use before an audience should be previewed. Further, an effective introduction into it makes its use even more impressive. For example, what are the key points audience members should look for? How does the film tie into the main point of your presentation?

It is easy to let a film take over your presentation. Films command audience attention easily. Thus, it could be that a speaker is upstaged (has his or her "show" stolen) by a film. To help avoid this possibility, speakers should select the best film, show it at the most appropriate time, use sound judgment in introducing it, speak while it is playing, and make comments about it afterwards.

Precautions regarding use are the same as when using any mechanical or electrical device. Malfunctions occur. Avoid last-minute problems by checking out the equipment before using it, and even mounting the film well in advance of the presentation.

## SUMMARY

High technology—the use of and dependence upon computers—has helped underscore the importance of visual and graphic communication. Computers produce high-impact graphics with ease. Businesses have encouraged their use when they are appropriate, because of their effectiveness, and they back up this encouragement by providing equipment and photographic and graphic art services to those responsible for making technical presentations. In some cases, businesses depend on outside resources, but more and more they have their own inside production facilities.

The first section outlined the values of visual aids. When business people talk or write using numbers they are likely to lose the attention of their audience unless they accompany their remarks with visual aids. They can aid audience understanding, retention, and interest. In addition, they can help to simplify complex information. But whether or not they satisfy these values depends on their use.

To use visual aids effectively requires foresight and planning. One must always keep in mind his or her fundamental reason for communicating. Does the visual aid contribute to this? Additionally, reinforcement, placement, explanation, and construction were discussed. Regarding the construction of an effective visual or graphic aid, the elements of size, simplicity, appearance, and color were examined.

In the section on graphic aids in written reports, the most common types of graphic aids were mentioned: tables, graphs, and pictograms. Other possible aids include photographs, drawings, maps, pictures, and diagrams. Any form of graphic aid is acceptable as long as it communicates the true story.

Visual aids in oral reports, the final section, presented information on the use of the chalkboard, chart, overhead, slide, and movie projector. But in the visual arena, since a viewer cannot go back and pick up information missed, the visual aid must be kept simple. Audience members burdened with too much information or too much detail may not understand, may become confused, or may lose interest.

No matter what type of visual aid is chosen, all audience members should be able to see it. It should not break the speaker-audience rapport. It should be simple, clear, colorful, and interesting. It must be appropriate to the intellectual capabilities of the audience, and it should be removed from sight after use.

Whether the presentation is written or oral, words and pictures work together; the aids used and the words chosen require careful coordination and integration. It is ineffective to carefully design an aid then provide virtually no introduction to or explanation of it. Osmosis is not an effective communication tool. Visual and graphic aids are an indispensible part of many technical presentations. The purpose of this chapter has been to help you use them to maximum advantage.

## NOTES

[1] Roger P. Wilcox, *Oral Reporting in Business and Industry* (Englewood Cliffs, N.J.: Prentice-Hall, 1967), p. 148.

[2] *Webster's New Collegiate Dictionary* (Springfield, Mass.: G.&C. Merriam Company, 1977), p. 975.

[3] I simply divided a 24-hour day into how I spend my time, or better still, how I would like to spend my time. There is no purpose to this graph or to its presence in this place; however, it makes the point that a chart or a graph can be a distraction without any introduction or purpose.

# 9

# The Interview

In business, there is no more frequently used communication format than the interview. Often, the initial job or employment interview initiates our contact and involvement with a company. Once employed, we are informed of our progress, problems, and promise through interviews. Within the interview itself we receive praise or discipline, give or receive information, complain or are counseled, or we solve or discover problems. Even in leaving a company, many people engage in an exit interview that allows them to reflect on their achievements and disappointments, their triumphs and defeats. Interviewing is a vital part of organizational behavior because organizations must encourage the exchange of information and because people often interact in twos or threes.

Add to the interviewing done in business that which occurs between doctor and patient, lawyer and client, teacher and student, police and their public, journalists and their sources, and you begin to see how pervasive it is. In each case, there is a predetermined and serious purpose; usually planning is involved, and oral interaction occurs between the two parties.[1] That is what interviewing is all about. The word interview is derived from the French *entrevoir*, which means "to see one another," or "meet."

In this chapter the various purposes of interviewing will be briefly discussed, and the numerous types of interviews will be presented. The role and responsibility of interviewer and interviewee will be developed in separate sections. Because of the value of listening in interviews, this will be considered in a separate section too. Since questions and answers make up the bulk of interview work, the art of questioning also will be discussed. The final section offers suggestions on structuring the interview for efficiency and effectiveness.

## PURPOSES OF INTERVIEWS

Before an interviewee is ever asked a question, interviewers must know the purpose of the interview: What goal do I hope to achieve in this interview? If the question cannot be answered or if the answer is vague, the interviewer should not conduct the interview or should take time to clarify the purpose.

Have you ever walked out of an interview as an interviewee and not understood what took place? Have you ever received conflicting messages or had doubts about what took place? No interviewee should end up harboring such confusion. Interviewers have the responsibility of making purposes clear. Otherwise valuable time and energy may be wasted, unnecessary work may be done, or the interview can become a basis or cause for future conflict.

Basically, interview purposes can be divided into three types: (1) to secure information, (2) to give information, or (3) to influence behavior.[2] I have avoided a discussion of interviews engaged in for the mere pleasure of communicating. Often, these are unstructured and casual encounters important to the informal information channels of a business and to relationship development and maintenance. But because of their informal nature, they do not fit our definition of an interview as an interaction that is both planned and contains a predetermined and serious purpose.

When interviewers are trying to *secure information,* they are attempting to discover interviewees' level of knowledge, skills, attitudes, and feelings. As you will discover in the next section on types of interviews, securing information becomes a primary focus in employment interviews, polling (where attitudes and opinions are sought), and in exit interviews. Once information is secured, it is then summarized and categorized. After the data is organized, it can be used to develop standards, determine trends, identify problem areas, or propose changes. Thus, an interview can be undertaken for the sole purpose of securing information.

*Giving information* through interviewers helps to convey company policies and procedures, give explanations and evidence for evaluations, identify information that will be helpful to interviewees or that will affect their relationship with the company. In the next section it will become clear that giving information is appropriate in employment, appraisal, training, and counseling interviews. Just as interviews can be undertaken solely to secure information, they can also be engaged in just to give information.

The purposes of securing and giving information indicate the two-way process of interviewing. Sometimes interview time is divided equally between these purposes. For example, an interviewer in an employment interview might explain hiring procedures, company policy, differences in job categories, salaries, or advancement programs while interviewees might discuss personal goals, strengths, or needs. Securing and giving information become equally important, too, in transfer and promotion interviews as well as in complaint and grievance interviews.

*Influencing behavior* is a purpose that should follow securing and giving information. When disciplining, reprimanding, or counseling, it is important that the proper foundation of information be established first. The purpose of influencing behavior is to suggest changes or to modify the behavior of the interviewee. This will become clearer as types of interviews are discussed. An interview can be initiated just for the purpose of influencing behavior, but this more commonly is tied to one of the interview types.

The point of discussing purposes is to encourage interviewers to think about their goals. If they handle the interview improperly, it can become a source for distortions and inaccuracies. It can also impede the flow of communication. Ultimately, it can subvert the very purpose it was intended to achieve.

## TYPES OF INTERVIEWS

Interviewer purposes are likely to be directly influenced by the type of interview they are planning to conduct.[3] Human behavior being what it is, it is unlikely that an interview will be conducted where no influence is exerted. That is, there is likely to be some mix of information and influence in most interview situations; however, it should be just as clear that some interviews are likely to stress one with respect to ultimate purpose more than another or, perhaps, both. The significance of interviews in a business becomes clearer when the wide variety of purposes they serve are examined. In this section, the following types will be discussed: (1) selection interviews, (2) appraisal interviews, (3) disciplinary interviews, (4) counseling interviews, and (5) exit interviews. There are numerous other types such as induction interviews and sales interviews and in some cases different labels are used. But these five constitute the most common types.

### Selection Interviews

Some authors refer to these as *employment* interviews. Some years back it was estimated that about 15 million selection interviews were conducted each year.[4] Early interviews in the employment process are sometimes referred to as *screening* interviews, and these are used to eliminate applicants who do not meet the qualifications for a job. An applicant who survives the screening interview is usually invited for a second interview. Depending on how many applicants have applied and how many are to be hired, second-level interviews usually include a tour of the company, introductions to or interviews with company executives, and, perhaps, the job offer.

But the traditional process outlined is not the one always followed or always recommended. One author even suggests that:

> ... it is perfectly possible for you to get a job without ever being trained in interview techniques, ever getting together a resume, or knowing the art of salary negotiation....[5]

The view held by that author and others[6] places the individual seeking employment in the driver's seat. That is, individuals should view themselves as creative resources with ideas and skills that they can contribute to an organization and, in turn, who can gain by being involved with a company. To come to such an understanding requires that individuals decide what it is they want to do, turn their skills into careers, find out where they want to do what they have decided, and what will get them a job. Then they must make contact with those they identify as the ones with the power to hire and show them how these skills will help them with their problems.[7]

The selection interview is truly a situation of securing and giving information. First, the interviewer wants to secure sufficient knowledge about the interviewee to determine whether or not a job offer would be appropriate. Second, the interviewer also wants to give information to the interviewee about the company and the position.

The selection interview should serve a third purpose as well. It should promote good will for the organization. It is a form of advertisement, and those interviewed, whether hired or not, are likely to form impressions about the company based on these first impressions. The interviewer should realize that creating a favorable impression will promote positive word-of-mouth advertising for future job applicants and for products and services the company offers.

The selection interview will be discussed in some detail in Chapter 10, "Getting A Job."

### Appraisal Interviews

The *appraisal interview*, sometimes called a *performance interview*, is the second major type of interview conducted in organizations. It is because all organizations are concerned with productivity that there is a need to evaluate the quality and quantity of employee work. Thus, work appraisal interviews are part of every organization's evaluative process. Usually, this evaluation occurs periodically.

The typical appraisal interview involves employees being called into their supervisor's office about once a year to be told how the organization perceives their work over that time. In some cases, the employee and supervisor simply chat informally. Productive appraisal interviews focus on positive *and* negative feedback, are reciprocal exchanges, and end with suggestions of ways employee performance and job satisfaction can be improved.

In other cases, the appraisal process is more formal. Supervisors must answer specific questions on employees' work performance: Did they perform their job competently? Are they a candidate for promotion? Have they been responsive to supervision? Did they make a contribution to the productivity of their unit? Have they contributed workable ideas and plans to their unit? Often, supervisors must also respond to their employees' work in groups: Have they been looked to for leadership? Do they get along with their peers? Do they demonstrate good work habits? Do they operate as a contributing part of the team? Can they be looked to for expertise? Finally, supervisors may be asked for an overall evaluation: What are the employee's greatest strengths? What are the areas that need improvement? In many cases these responses are written for the employee to see, and the employee's response is solicited.[8]

Success in appraisal interviewing requires that the interviewer focus on job improvement and that a proper problem-solving climate be created. Because evaluation of any kind can be threatening, interviewers must be careful not to use this event to surprise interviewees with irrelevant, unnecessary, or unexpected information. Job improvement is unlikely to occur as a result of these circumstances.

To emphasize problem solving, the interviewer must focus on employee behavior that needs improvement. The interview should not become personal. If punishment and reprimand are avoided, too, a problem-solving atmosphere is more likely to be sustained.

Once again, the appraisal interview depends on both securing and giving information. But influencing behavior may also be important. It is important that a base of information be established first, before the interview proceeds to the influencing stage. If employee job performance has been outstanding, it may only be necessary to motivate the employee to continue.

Because of the potential impact of an appraisal interview on the supervisor, the organization, and the subordinate, the amount of information available throughout the process is important. Pre-interview material and communication will help prevent surprise. Post-interview follow-up will help assure that the appraisal aftermath (just like conflict aftermath) is positive and supportive.

## Disciplinary Interviews

Clearly related to the appraisal interview, but much less enjoyable or appreciated, is the *disciplinary interview*. Supervisors are often faced with matters that must be confronted and corrected. Whether it be employee absenteeism or tardiness, reduced or lack of productivity, unethical or tasteless behavior, such activity cannot be allowed to continue.

The nature of the interview creates a rather rigid format. In most cases the interview is initiated by the employer. It is also controlled by the employer. But initiation and control should not limit communication.

Although the control factor in a disciplinary interview is often high, partially because of the threat involved and the accompanying high level of anxiety on the part of the employee, two-way communication must be maintained and feelings must be shared. Workers must be allowed, even encouraged, to offer insights as well as to respond to all accusations. Further, they must know the outcome of the interview and how it will affect them. If a new procedure will be implemented, they must also know what they can anticipate.

The disciplinary interview represents a situation in which the influence of behavior is at a maximum. But influence is likely to best occur in a situation where a solid information base is established. A worker must have specific information: when, what, where, and how? Once the evidence is offered and acknowledgment is provided in an atmosphere that emphasizes information giving, then influence can take place.

The same interview format, although worker initiated and controlled, is the *grievance* interview in which employees are allowed to voice their discontent. Such interviews are usually prompted because of weak employee interactions, poor working conditions, inadequate salaries, or unfair treatment. But whatever the reason, major or minor, this form of upward communication must be encouraged.

Supervisors faced with a grievance must be open and receptive. A strong listening environment should be found where few distractions will occur. This situation must be taken seriously. Defensiveness or evaluation must be avoided as information is conveyed. Interviewers should ask questions and probe to discover specifics and details. Also, some commitment needs to be made toward resolving the grievance, even if this is simply a willingness to consider it with care. Productive, harmonious climates are created and maintained when superiors can encourage and listen to employee grievances.

Supervisors may have less difficulty handling the grievance interview if they realize that besides serving as an arena for employee complaints, it can point up legitimate problems or weaknesses in the organization. In addition, it provides a useful outlet for subordinates' frustrations. It is a cathartic mechanism and can reduce tensions. In most cases the subordinate is in the position of receiving information. Whether it moves to the level of influencing behavior depends upon the nature of the grievance, how it is presented, and how it is received.

### Counseling Interviews

*Counseling interviews* are directed toward personal considerations. That is one of the major differences between this type of interview and others; most others focus on task-related matters. The exact nature of this type, because personal needs or concerns may vary dramatically, is less specific than others.

Although supervisors may feel that counseling is not within their realm of responsibility, most engage in it at some time or other.[9] The reason is that most organizations find it impossible to separate a worker's professional life from his or her personal life. Personal problems often have a direct effect on life at work whether they be domestic, alcohol or drug problems, mental problems, stress-related problems, fear of retirement, or problems that occur when a worker's life interfaces with the community.[10]

The counseling interview is an excellent example of an information-receiving situation on the part of the supervisor, who must serve as listener, not as advisor. While the interviewee assumes much of the control in the interview, the supervisor must create a climate of trust, empathy, encouragement, and nonevaluation so that causes of problems can be identified and useful solutions can be sought.

### Exit Interviews

An *exit interview* occurs when an employee is leaving a company. Most other types take place either at the beginning or throughout the working lives of employees. There are three basic reasons to conduct exit interviews: (1) to find out why employees are leaving, (2) to show appreciation for employees' work, and (3) to foster good will between the employee and the organization.

As it turns out, however, exit interviews tend not to work very well. Research has indicated, for example, that employees are not always candid in their exit interviews.[11] Conflict with the management, for example, is usually not mentioned in exit interviews as a reason for leaving. And seldom mentioned is long-term job dissatisfaction, unhappiness with job content, and displeasure with advancement procedures. Reasons for leaving given in exit interviews tend to be related to such factors as higher earnings and the desire to live in another part of the country.

The exit interview may be one that includes both information securing and giving, but from the management point of view, information securing is probably most important. However, an employee may approach the interview with some suspicion: How will this information be used? Will it affect my recommendations? Why can't I just leave the company on a positive note?

To allay suspicions and to create a climate in which information can be shared, interviewers must explain the purpose of the interview. In addition, they must assure the employee of their sincerity and trustworthiness. Employees must be told that honest responses will not affect their futures or any of the people they are leaving behind.

One way to avoid the exit interview and to discover some of the same information—if an organization chooses to dispense with any show of appreciation or attempt at good will—would be to use a mailed questionnaire and a follow-up interview several months after the employee leaves. Employees, then, secure in their new positions and with less fear of reprisal, may be more honest in their answers.

## ROLE AND RESPONSIBILITY OF THE INTERVIEWER

Although the interviewer has the dominant role in the interview, the interview is an interaction and the relationship that develops is a key part of the interview. But no interaction or relationship will develop if the interviewer does not want it to. That is, the attitude of the interviewer is not only an important factor but one of the determining factors.

This section will discuss some of the elements under interviewer control. Many of these will be specifically shaped or focused by the type of interview being planned, but all of the elements pertain to all of the types previously discussed. Interviewer attitude will be examined first. Climate, orientation, frame of reference, objectivity, and tone follow.

### Attitude

Perhaps the most important factor that will determine interview success will be interviewer *attitude*. It is so important that it may well govern the other factors as well. Attitude involves the mental position interviewers take going into an interview. It can be affected by interviewers' knowledge, skills, personality characteristics, as well as their feelings and emotions.

Much of this attitude will be positive if interviewers view each interview situation as unique and each interviewee as an individual. In that way a freshness and vigor can be brought to each situation. The problem is that many interviewers do a great deal of interviewing, but when one interview starts to look like another, and a certain callousness sets in, the interview is doomed to failure. You begin to realize the influence of interviewers and their attitudes.

### Climate

The attitudes of both interviewer and interviewee are likely to be affected by the *climate* of the interview. Thus, creating a positive, constructive climate is of major importance. By climate is meant both the prevailing temper and environmental conditions.

*Temper* refers to the mental set of both parties. It is not different from attitudes (discussed above) but it must be clear that these attitudes can affect the climate that surrounds an interview. Extreme, yet realistic, examples would be the hostility that might be present in a disciplinary interview or the defensiveness that might surround a grievance interview. Often, however, the temper is not that obvious. It is like the feeling you have when leaving an interview where "Everything clicked," or the opposite, "Things just didn't seem to flow well."

The physical nature of the surroundings, too, may determine the success of the interview. Location, for example, should be both convenient and private. Distractions must be minimal; for this reason many interviewers do not use their own offices.

Location variables also include the elements of furnishings, distance, and barriers. Comfortable chairs in a pleasant room with attractive surroundings create an informal, relaxed climate where a great deal of disclosure can take place. The distance interviewers choose to sit from interviewees will be determined by how well the parties know each other and the level of formality interviewers wish to maintain. See Figure 9–1. More formality can be attained, too, if interviewers place a barrier between themselves and interviewees. A desk serves as a common barrier. But even the

**FIGURE 9–1.**

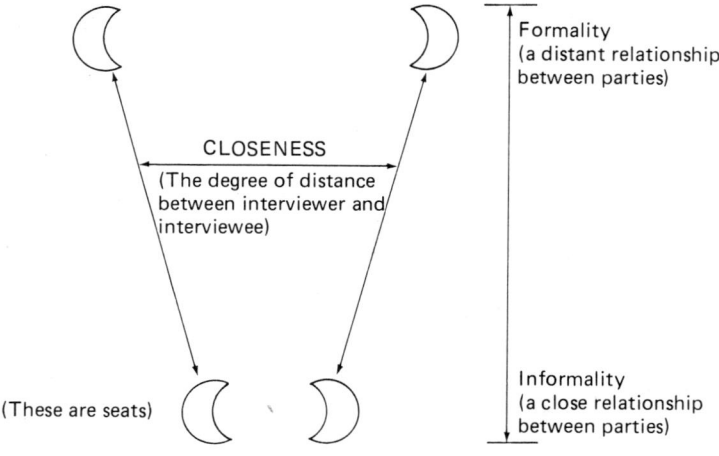

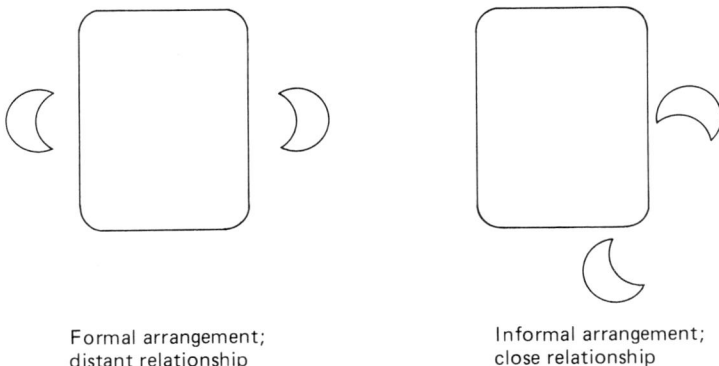

Formal arrangement; distant relationship

Informal arrangement; close relationship encouraged

**FIGURE 9–2.**

seating arrangement behind a desk can be altered if interviewers, rather than sitting behind the desk, prefer a corner or angle arrangement. See Figure 9–2.

The type of interview and the relationship between the individuals will determine the climate. Most interviews are carried on at a distance of two to five feet. The important thing to remember is that all aspects of the climate should support the "psychological temper" desired by the interviewer.

### Orientation

Already discussed in this chapter was the need and importance of information to the success of the interview. This section reinforces that and suggests that it is the job of interviewers to supply it. To *orient*, interviewers must acquaint interviewees with existing conditions. For example, interviewees should know the purpose of the interview and how it will proceed. Who will give information first? What is expected of the interviewees?

Orientation serves three purposes. First, it helps to organize the time available for the interview. Usually time is scarce. Second, it provides some guidelines, however general, for procedure. What can be expected? How will things proceed? Third, it helps reduce the element of surprise, thus easing any unnecessary tension or anxiety that might be associated with the situation.

### Frame of Reference

Effective communication requires a common *frame of reference,* or *viewpoint*. But when a common frame of reference is referred to, this means that interviewers try to use language that will be understood by inter-

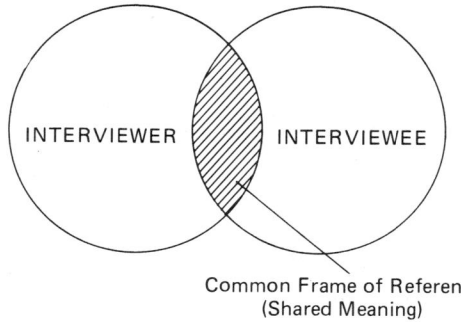

FIGURE 9-3. The larger the shaded area, the greater the likelihood of effective communication.

viewees as well as reference to situations or occurrences that are mutually shared. This refers to Chapter 2, where the transactional process was described. See Figure 9-3. The larger the area of shared background, experience, and language, the greater the likelihood of effective communication.

**Objectivity**

Because interviewers often initiate the interview, plan it, prepare for it, and guide it, these processes give them a great deal of control or dominance. "Control" can easily go to interviewers' heads; that is, it can be taken advantage of. Given an element of control, some people get carried away. It is easy to feel, "My view is the proper one. Now, if I can only get so-and-so to see it my way."

*Objectivity* is a minimum essential for effective interviewing. To be objective means trying to maintain a view of the world apart from one's own personal reflections and feelings. This can be accomplished, in part, if interviewers stress facts in their interviews without distortion by personal feelings and prejudices. True, this cannot be done entirely, but if interviewers are aware that their biases become one of the most troublesome problems in interviewing, at least this awareness is a beginning.

Another method for maintaining objectivity includes suspending judgment. Interviewers must wait until all the evidence is in before rendering an evaluation. This means, of course, allowing interviewees a full and free opportunity to present their side. To suspend judgment requires effective listening. The importance of listening in an interview cannot be undervalued. Because of its importance, it will be given a separate section in this chapter.

Being open-minded is yet another method for maintaining objectivity. Tearing off blinders is not an easy task, but the rewards for open-mindedness can be rich, satisfying, and worthwhile. Whether it be suspending judgment, listening, open-mindedness, or other methods, interviewers conscious of the need for objectivity are more likely to be just and fair in their interviews.

## Tone

*Tone* is an overall quality that reflects the general character of the interview. All of the preceding variables contribute to tone. In this section tone will refer to some of the more obvious verbal and nonverbal characteristics. For example, the way the interview is opened and the eye contact interviewers use may have a direct effect on interview tone.

"First impressions are important." This is neither the first nor the last time you have heard that phrase. But the opening of an interview *is* important, for it helps establish interview tone. It is here that interviewers can establish rapport with interviewees. This, too, is when they can encourage them to take an active part. Empathy, sensitivity, warmth, and responsiveness can be demonstrated at the outset of the interview. Often, these characteristics can be revealed through small talk, informal conversation, even humor. There is much value in these seemingly unimportant processes. Besides establishing rapport, they can also reduce tension and defensiveness.

*Eye contact* can serve the same purposes. When interviewers make eye contact with interviewees they establish a direct link with them. This link conveys several immediate impressions. First, it says, "I care about you," or "I am concerned about you." Second, it makes the process a human one. So often, especially in large corporations, employees feel like a mere cog in a large machine. An interview can be no more than an exercise, a further confirmation that "no one really cares." Thus, eye contact humanizes the process. Third, it establishes control. It is a signal to interviewees that the communication channel is open. In a sense, it almost establishes an obligation to interact. Fourth, it may convey a great deal of information about the interviewers' emotions. Interviewers can convey surprise, fear, disgust, anger, happiness, or sadness via the eyes.[12]

Eye contact can also communicate information about the nature of the interpersonal relationship.[13] It can reflect the different status of the participants, reveal how rewarding or favorable one party views the other, convey how positive or negative interviewers or interviewees feel, and even suggest further interest and involvement. Because of the many purposes eye contact can serve, it is clear that it can be a major factor in determining interview tone.

## ROLE AND RESPONSIBILITY OF THE INTERVIEWEE

By "interviewer" I mean "one who interviews" and by "interviewee" I mean "the one being interviewed." Because interviewers have the dominant role in interviews, the role and responsibility of the interviewee is sometimes overlooked.[14] But interviewees can do a number of things to assist an interview. They do not, and should not, sit passively and watch the interview unfold. If, indeed, the interview is an interaction or a relationship, their participation and involvement are necessary.

Chapter 10 of this book, "Getting A Job," will focus, in part, on the employment (screening and selection) interviews. At that point an outline of appropriate interviewer and interviewee activities and behaviors will be offered. Here, a brief review of procedures appropriate to most interview situations will be presented. These include preparation, enthusiasm, honesty, responsiveness, and confidence.[15]

**Preparation**

*Preparation* simply means being in a state of readiness. Having information, facts, and opinions available helps prepare us. Being alert and sensitive to conditions that surround us also helps us be prepared. Most interviewees simply do not realize that despite the dominance of or control by interviewers, they (interviewees) still control the content of the interview. Interviewees, in a sense, are sales people, and the product they are selling is themselves.

Alert, aware, active interviewees need not allow interviewers to stray wildly, searching for relevant questions. They can, instead, gently lead interviewers toward their own strengths: areas of competence and knowledge, effort, contribution, and general positive point of view. But this is unlikely to occur if they are not prepared.

**Enthusiasm**

Emerson observed, "Nothing great has ever been done without enthusiasm." *Enthusiasm* is the excitement or inspiration interviewees can manifest. It is important because of the impression it can leave on the interviewer and for the effect it can have on your own outlook. If you are enthusiastic, this spirit will animate your whole body, and interviewers will see it in your face, voice, and actions. It helps make you an attractive and convincing sales person.

The point here is that when interviewees take part in an interview, it isn't enough that they say they are interested, or even that they look and think "interested." Actions are what reveal interest.

There are several ways to project enthusiasm. One is to try to make the other person enthusiastic. Can you ask him or her a question? For example, try to hitchhike (build) on something that he or she said. You could say, "I didn't know you were interested in _____; did you see that article in last night's paper on it?" Can you project genuine interest in something he or she is doing? For instance, you could say that you attended a meeting, watched a TV program, or heard a speech that you know pertains to a topic in which the interviewer has genuine interest.

There are a few precautions that should be noted, however. First, you do not want to distract from the purpose of the interview. A casual aside is all right; but it should not appear as if you are purposely changing the topic. Moreover, you do not want to appear as if you are trying to take over the interview. Some interviewers may perceive your questions as a ploy.

Look at the interview as a unique experience, even a challenge. Things are monotonous, dull, or boring because we make them so. Go into interviews with a positive state of mind. How do you reflect a positive mental attitude?

1. Relax.
2. See the other person as a friend.
3. Smile.
4. Feel positive about yourself.
5. Feel confident in the actions you have taken.
6. Look at the interview as a learning experience.
7. Prepare yourself to listen.
8. Be flexible.
9. Be alert and attentive.
10. Reveal empathy and sensitivity.

Be willing to take a chance—to do something that might set you, or this interview, apart from others. Most anything that could be described here would not very likely be spontaneous and natural for you. It might appear contrived, rehearsed, awkward, and clumsy. In one interview, the interviewee noticed a picture of the interviewer's family and asked about a son who was the same age as the interviewee's own. In another, the interviewee referred to the results of a study that she remembered from a book sitting open on the interviewer's desk. These were both spontaneous, unplanned responses. To take gambles, you must be so enthusiastic about the potential rewards that you are even willing to risk what initially may look like certain failure.

### Honesty

*Honesty* means fairness and straightforwardness of conduct. It consists of three elements: truth, consistency, and candor.[16]

*Truth* means sincerity in action, character, and utterance. One can achieve truth by sticking to the facts, by relying on his or her own body of real things and events. There comes a time in many interview situations when we want to exaggerate our accomplishments. We say we make more than we do, that we have done more than we have, or that we have said something we would like to have said. Sir Walter Scott wrote, "O, what a tangled web we weave, when first we practice to deceive." Paraphrased, this means—when in doubt, tell the truth. When we do not, we have the potential of losing credibility as the intricate, and sometimes confusing, network of lies and deceits entangles and, finally, ensnares us. Why take the risk?

Exaggeration is not just an expansion of the truth; it is a lie. And when you lie, it will haunt you the rest of your days. The liar forever fears discovery, and well he or she should, for when discovered, a lie can destroy the liar's credibility forever. Credibility that can sometimes take years to establish, can be destroyed in a second.

*Consistency* reveals an agreement or harmony of the parts or features of the interview as they relate together and are perceived as a whole. In other words, interviewees should reveal no inconsistency. Inconsistencies are viewed much as lies are.

Perhaps the best method for assuring a consistent presentation is knowing yourself well. Often, the people conducting interviews are trained and skillful. If they detect inconsistencies between their information and yours, they are likely to ask the same questions again in different ways to test your observations. Thinking through your facts or views beforehand will help you maintain consistency.

When you hedge on an answer to show yourself in the best light, or if you have misrepresented something, you have to be careful that each time the issue is raised, you say the same thing. Once you vary, you may be rejected, your credibility may be questioned or destroyed, or you may be asked to justify the variance.

*Candor* reflects interviewees' forthrightness. It is a certain unreserved, honest, and sincere expression. Interviewees must be willing to be candid. Doubts and concerns that are allowed to linger become antecedent conditions for conflict.

To bring doubts and concerns into the open allows them to be discussed. Sometimes they can be shown to be unfounded. Or, they can be shown to have foundation, but at least you are given some substantial information on which to make future decisions. Either way, expressing doubts and concerns has benefits.

**Responsiveness**

*Responsiveness* refers to interviewees' willingness to take an active oral part in the interview. It is possible, at times, to go through an entire interview responding simply "yes" and "no." But interviewees should demonstrate the ability to speak up and to express their own ideas.

Engage in the small talk that often precedes the formal part of the interview. This will relax you and make you feel more comfortable. Interviewers ask questions to gain information, but they are often also interested in how you convey the information. Don't be reluctant to talk. Answer questions accurately and tactfully, but be brief and to the point as well. Try to keep the atmosphere as natural as possible. And if you do not have answers, admit it. Nobody knows—or is supposed to know—everything. Interviewers, in most cases, respond better to candor than to those who presume to "know it all."

But speaking up and being expressive does not mean filling every gap in the conversation with words. The best advice to interviewees is to relax. Pretend, if you must, that this is a conversation where both parties must hold up their end of the conversation. Just as in any conversation, both participants should have a fairly equal chance to contribute. But in an interview, interviewers should be given an opportunity to guide the discussion. Interviewees should be sensitive to their wishes, watching for feedback as they proceed. Is the interviewer losing interest? Does he or she want me to comment further on this topic? Have I answered the question? A comment like, "Oh, I'm sorry, Mr. Manners, I never get tired of talking about pluckets; maybe you have some other questions," can win interviewees points because it demonstrates alertness as well as tact and empathy.

**Confidence**

*Confidence* is revealed when interviewees convey faith in their own skills, powers, or circumstances. It is belief in themselves. And even if they do not, they should make interviewers believe that they do. The best route to gaining this self-confidence, of course, is preparation. If the interview is planned and announced, and preparation time is provided, interviewees can take several steps to prepare (providing the interview topic is announced):

1. Ask yourself questions; probe your knowledge.
2. Ask questions of colleagues and others who have resource material.
3. Be aware of the situation; be alert and responsive.
4. Take notes

When you know a great deal about the subject being discussed (maybe even more than the interviewer), you will feel this confidence.

Nervousness can undermine confidence; however, remember that interviewers expect a certain amount of nervousness. It is human. The other side of this same coin is that most signs of nervousness, like a dry mouth or shaky knees, are not usually perceived by other people. The best way to control nervousness is, again, by thorough preparation, but then, after all this, trust yourself. Let your whole creative being do its work in an open, unrestrained way. Trust yourself to say and do the right things. If we could just let go, to stop trying so hard, or to not care so much, then we could act creatively and spontaneously. Then it would become more likely that we would really be ourselves.

Confidence is often revealed to interviewers as a result of an overall positive feeling. Interviewees should try to be positive. Despite frustrations and annoyances, do not dwell on the negative. Negative comments imply not only that you have experienced difficulty with others, but also that others have had difficulty in their relationships with you. Although you want to be candid, as pointed out before, this should not become a situation where you dwell on the negative. Since both communication and relationships are essential aspects of business, try to demonstrate in interviews your ability to relate well to people.

## LISTENING

Listening was discussed in Chapter 3, but it deserves attention, too, in a chapter devoted to interviewing. With the exception of some periods of silence, someone is listening 50 percent of the time in the interview.

What many people do not realize is that listening requires energy and concentration. When you are actively listening, your heart action is faster, blood circulates more quickly, and there is even a slight rise in body temperature.[17] Thus, if one participant is tired or not in a good frame of mind, this is likely to affect his or her ability to listen.

Careful, accurate listening must be practiced. If you think that it is natural and everyone does it, you are wrong. Most people are poor listeners. We ignore, misunderstand, or forget close to 75 percent of what we hear, and this is because most people do not know how to listen.[18] The more we try to listen effectively in our everyday conversations with others, the more likely we are to become better listeners. Practice will not make perfect, but practice will prepare us for better interview participation.

So what can you do? First, be willing to ask questions to make certain your ideas are getting through. Questions help clear up misunderstandings, and they open channels for feedback. (For example, "Now let me make sure I understand, is this what you mean . . . ?")

Second, paraphrase the other person's ideas before stating your own. This simply means rewording his or her thoughts or feelings—the content of his or her message—so that it conveys understanding. For example, if the interviewee has just said, "What we are going to have to do is to make our deadlines on Wednesdays rather than Fridays," you could paraphrase to help guarantee accuracy by saying first, before adding your own reaction, "You want to move up our weekly deadlines from Fridays to Wednesdays?" Paraphrasing is a nonjudgmental process.

Third, be open-minded. Try to make certain you are clear about the other person's ideas and feelings before pushing through your own ideas. For instance, you might say, "You think we can increase productivity, then, if we stagger our breaks?" This might draw out further clarification from the interviewee and allow you to think through your own ideas more thoroughly before responding: "Do you think this may have some effect on worker morale?" If you already know what you are going to think or feel, regardless of what the other person says, your mind is closed, and there is little reason for an interview. You might just as well send the other person a memo outlining your position and tell him or her what to do. Open-mindedness prevents immediate rejection, keeps self-interest at a minimum, allows potential acceptance of the other's ideas, and opens up channels for further communication just as a "welcome mat" and a friendly handshake encourage a visitor to enter your house.[19]

Effective listeners pay attention, stay awake and alert, are courteous, and ask questions. In addition, you can enter interviews with the idea of trying to understand and not just to criticize and evaluate. This, too, will help listening. Most interviewing will benefit from this approach. When you function as a critic you will be predisposed to evaluating what is said in terms of good or bad, right or wrong, agree or disagree. Instead of trying to understand, you criticize. The suggestion here is to try to understand the message first, then you can engage in summarizing it, drawing conclusions from it, or agreeing and disagreeing with it. To listen well, allow your evaluation to follow your understanding.[20]

## QUESTIONING

Successful interviews depend a great deal on the techniques of questioning. Interviewer skill in this area results in information gain, interviewee understanding, successful influence as far as attitude or behavior change, or problems solved. Regardless of interviewers' purposes, questioning plays a central role. The type of interview to be used will help determine the nature of the questions. The kinds of questions interviewers can choose from include open, closed, mirror, and probing.[21]

### Open Questions

*Open questions* are useful when interviewers are attempting to draw out interviewees. They are called "open" because of the freedom they give the interviewee in answering. Some examples of open questions might be:

"What is your view of our benefit program?"
"Tell me what you've done the past few months."
"How do you think your unit could increase its productivity?"

The advantages of open questions are that interviewers can assess interviewees' ability to communicate as well as to organize their ideas. They often provide some knowledge about how interviewees think, how observant they are, and, too, how responsive.

There are disadvantages to open questions, however. The main one is that they take time to answer. The interviewers must have considerable time to allow interviewees to respond. Also, a skillful interviewee can guide the interview to areas that reflect his or her strengths; that is, there is less interviewer control. In addition, and partly as a result of decreased control, interviews dependent on open questions may meander from topic to topic, reflecting lack of purpose and organization.

### Closed Questions

*Closed questions,* useful when interviewers want specific responses, limit interviewees' response flexibility considerably. They are called "closed" because they are restrictive in nature. Some examples might be:

"How many hours have you invested in this project?"
"What did that venture cost?"
"When was the last time you talked to Jim Staples?"

Closed questions may also be bipolar. That is, they may restrict interviewees to only two choices such as yes/no, like/dislike, approve/disapprove, or high/low. Such questions are highly restrictive and do not account for people who may be undecided, have no opinion, or do not know the answer. Moreover, they do not allow for degrees of agreement or shades of disagreement. You cannot be mildly opposed to such a question. Questions requiring bipolar responses should be reexamined to check for false assumptions and poor wording. Many of these may not be planned and are phrased this way because of habit (it's easier) or carelessness. Bipolar questions are useful because they can be helpful in obtaining a clear-cut answer; however, the restrictions noted above also should be considered when using them. Some examples follow. They are neither good nor bad; that must be determined by the context in which they are used.

Do you approve of our new contract?
Do you think your unit should take on this project or not?
Has your productivity this year been high or low?

There are some advantages to using closed questions. First, it saves time. Responses are short; thus, interviewers can move on to other questions quickly and efficiently. Control, then, remains in the hands of the interviewer. Also, interviewers can get at specific pieces of information. Because of this, answers to closed questions can be replicated, coded, tabulated, and analyzed more easily than responses to open questions. If numerous, similar interviews are being conducted—as when a survey is being done—this would be important. Closed questions may be less threatening, too, because they do not require justifications or explanations.

Disadvantages of closed questions are numerous. Interviewers may not get enough information, thus follow-up questions might be necessary. Often, you get only an answer and no reason why interviewees feel the way they do. It takes some of the humanness—the feeling or emotional level—out of interviewing. Bipolar questions are weak because they force interviewees to adopt a specific position, perhaps a position on a topic they know little about. Finally, closed questions can inhibit open communication. Because of their restrictiveness, and because they can be delivered in rapid-fire progression, they may reveal that interviewers have little interest in the other person.

### Mirror Questions

*Mirror questions* are used to draw out interviewees or to make certain that what you heard was correct. They got their name because they "mirror," in the form of restatement, the exact content of an interviewee's message. Some examples of mirror questions might be:

"Did I understand you to say that breaks are being shortened?"
"You said that unit productivity has increased?"

Mirror questions serve to elicit more information from the other person. When a response is incomplete, superficial, vague, suggestive, irrelevant, or inaccurate, a mirror question allows elaboration with no threat. It is a simple, effective procedure. It can also serve as a way to summarize a series of questions or answers. For example, "Okay, Sue, let me see if I have this right, you want me to . . . then. . . ."

The only disadvantage of a mirror question is that it may make the user look strange when it is first asked. That is, because it encompasses content already covered, it may appear that the questioner is being needlessly redundant or inquisitive. In the same manner, it can reflect disbelief or entrapment. Mirror questions must be phrased carefully.

### Probing Questions

A *probing question* is used by interviewers to explore more fully responses that appear to be incomplete. It is a follow-up or secondary type of question. Sometimes it can be used when interviewees are having difficulty putting thoughts into words. Some examples might be:

"Why do you feel this way?"
"Could you elaborate on what you mean by that?"
"Tell me a little more about your thinking on this new procedure."

Probing questions have the advantage of getting further development of specific viewpoints or ideas. They can be specific and pointed. Interviewers can guide the interview to subjects of specific interest to them.

Weaknesses here are the same as those for mirror questions because, often, interviewers are probing areas already covered. Thus, interviewers must be careful in how they are asked so as not to reveal disbelief or entrapment.

### Questioning: A Summary

Interviews are not comprised of just one type of question. A mixture of questions is the normal format. A mixture makes the interview more interesting and enjoyable because of the variety it offers.

But no matter what type of questions are asked, those asking them must be cautious when it comes to their answers, or when it comes to no answers at all! What is your immediate response when someone does not respond to a question you ask? You either repeat it, or you rephrase it and ask it again, right? In an interview, no response to a question may reflect a number of things.[22] Interviewees may be unsure about how much information or detail the interviewer wants or the kind of answer she desires. They may not understand the question or have the information requested. They might also feel the question is irrelevant, or they might be unable to express their feelings on it.

Reasons why interviewees may not be able to express their feelings include emotional trauma, lack of training, language barriers, low intelligence, or societal traditions and practices. These problems may be responsible for different frames of reference between interviewers and interviewees. What if interviewees felt that interviewers would not understand even if they answered? Perhaps they feel the topic is too technical, personal, or foreign. Sensitivity, alertness, feedback, flexibility, and responsiveness to the other's needs are important characteristics that questioners need to manifest if interviewing is to be successful.

## STRUCTURING THE INTERVIEW

Now that questions are planned, an overall structure should be considered. There are three modes used in structuring interviews: structured, casual, or focused.[23]

## Structured Interviews

There are many ways to structure an interview.[24] *Structure* is the degree to which an interview is arranged according to a definite pattern of organization. The degree of structure will also reflect the amount of control interviewers have in the interview. See Figure 9–4.

The choice of how to structure the interview depends upon its purpose, the type of interview, who is being interviewed, when and where, and the relationship between interviewer and interviewee. It could also be affected by the degree of training of interviewers or their experience. Those who have less training or are less experienced might be inclined to use a highly structured format to maintain strict control. This might be safer for them. But just as likely, because of lack of training or experience, the interviewee could end up controlling the interview!

*Highly structured interviews* are those in which interviewers know exactly where they want to go and what they want to accomplish. They maintain full control, having planned every step in advance. Poll takers often use this form. Because the wording and sequencing of questions is planned in advance, just as are various answer options and even the opening and closing of the interview, novice interviewers find this format easy to handle.

*Moderately structured interviews* are similar to highly structured ones in that the questions are all planned and sequenced, but answer options are not included. Interviewees supply their own answers. Interviewers require little experience to use this format.

Disadvantages of the highly and moderately structured interviews include the restrictions caused by preplanning and sequencing. No probing of answers occurs, nor can questions be explained. Thus, these formats allow no adjustment to the needs of respondents or circumstances.

*Minimally structured interviews* do not depend on a schedule of questions as those above. Using this format, interviewers work with a list of topics they want to address. They form the questions on the spot, adapting

FIGURE 9–4. A continuum that represents the degrees of structure that can be found in interviews and the corresponding degree of interviewer control.

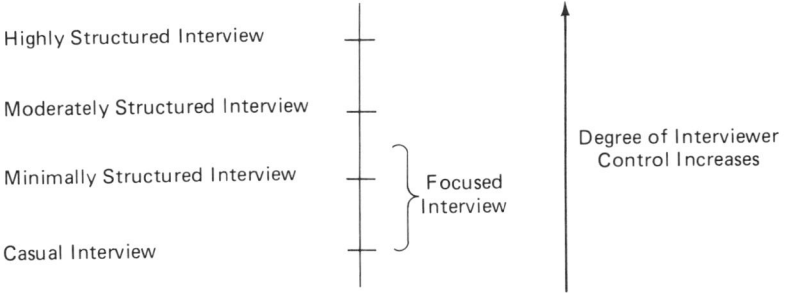

the wording to interviewees specifically. There is full allowance for rephrasing questions or for probing answers.

In *casual interviews*, interviewers can draw out interviewees. The actual result of such interviews is not known at the outset because the content emerges during the interview and determines the direction of it and how long it takes. Time must not be a constraining factor in casual interviews.

But to successfully handle this unstructured format requires skill, training, and experience. Interviewers must know the subject well, and they need to concentrate on encouraging interviewees to tell their story. To use this format effectively, interviewers need to reflect empathy, suspension of judgment, and objectivity. Listening becomes of primary importance if, indeed, a full, accurate story is to unfold. Interviewers limit their own talk to comments used to guide and encourage interviewees.

Casual interviews would not be practical for poll takers. In circumstances, however, where complaints and grievances are involved, appraisals are made, solutions are sought for problems, or where counseling is performed, the casual style is ideal. Also, when an interview is interviewee-initiated, it can be handled using this format.

*Focused interviews* are synthetic. From Figure 9–4 it should be clear that the focused interview is not a pure type but, rather, a combination of other types. The point is that most interviews are not structured or casual. This format allows for both approaches. Interviewers may want or need to ask some standard questions yet still want to allow for free interaction with interviewees.

Using this format, interviewers will plan some topics they want to cover as well as some specific questions they may want to ask. But the wording and the sequence of questions are likely to vary from interview to interview. Interviews conducted for inducting a person into a business or company, or for training, might use a focused format. Appraisal, grievance, and exit interviews are also likely to make use of this format. Its strength is its flexibility.

## SUMMARY

The interview is one of the most important interpersonal communication techniques available to the business communicator. This chapter described considerations that will enable you to be more professional in both conducting interviews and being interviewed. We can achieve our desired results without having to depend on a trial-and-error approach.

Purposes of interviewing were discussed first. Securing information, giving information, and influencing behavior were the three major purposes. Each could also define a specific interview type as well. Interviewers must determine their goal: "What do I want to achieve in this interview?" is the key question.

Interviewer purposes will be influenced by the type of interview planned. Five of the most common types are: (1) selection interviews, (2) appraisal interviews, (3) disciplinary interviews, (4) counseling interviews, and (5) exit interviews. Although there are numerous other types and even different labels for some of these, these are the most common and most often used.

As parts of the role and responsibility of interviewers, attitude, climate, orientation, frame of reference, objectivity, and tone were discussed. Many of these elements will be shaped or focused by the type of interview planned, but all of them apply to the types of interview presented in the previous section.

Preparation, enthusiasm, honesty, responsiveness, and confidence were the variables discussed as part of the role and responsibility of interviewees. The main point of this section was that interviewees should not sit by passively and simply watch the interview unfold. Active involvement is essential.

For successful interviewing, careful, accurate listening must be practiced. To listen more effectively, participants need to ask questions, paraphrase, be open-minded, and try to understand the other person. To listen well, evaluation should follow understanding.

Because interviewing depends on questioning, open, closed, mirror, and probing questions were discussed. The type of interview is likely to determine the nature of the questions. A short section on what it might mean if an interviewee does not, or is unable to, answer a question was also included.

In the final section on interview structure, three basic formats were offered: structured, casual, and focused. Within the structured mode, highly, moderately, and minimally structured formats were explained. The format with least structure was the casual one. But the most realistic would seem to be the focused interview, which combines the other two approaches.

Portions of interviews require planning and portions may need to be spontaneous. This chapter should help you analyze situations to determine various alternatives and approaches. Behind your decisions should lie some kind of rationale. This chapter should help you place interviewing in its proper perspective and make decision making easier.

### NOTES

[1] See Robert S. Goyer, W. Charles Redding, and John T. Rickey, *Interviewing Principles and Techniques: A Project Text* (Dubuque, Iowa: Kendall/Hunt, 1968).

[2] Adapted from Dale A. Level, Jr., and William P. Galle, Jr., *Business Communications:*

*Theory and Practice* (Dallas: Business Publications, 1980), pp. 244–46. © 1980 Business Publications, Inc.

[3] For further information on interview types, see Cal W. Downs, G. Paul Smeyak, and Ernest Martin, *Professional Interviewing* (New York: Harper & Row, 1980), Chapters 7–13, pp. 107–268.

[4] V. R. Taylor, "A Hard Look at the Selection Interview," *Public Personnel Review, 30* (1969), 148–53. Another author suggests that 150 million interviews occur each year. See Lynn Ulrich and Don Trumbo, "The Selection Interview Since 1949," *Psychological Bulletin, 63* (1965), 100–116.

[5] See Richard Nelson Bolles, *What Color Is Your Parachute?* (Berkeley, Cal.: Ten Speed Press, 1979), p. 156. This volume is updated annually.

[6] E. Djeddah, *Moving Up: How to Get High-Salaried Jobs* (Berkeley, Cal.: Ten Speed Press, 1971).

[7] Bolles, pp. 63–169.

[8] Gary T. Hunt, *Communication Skills in the Organization* (Englewood Cliffs, N.J.: Prentice-Hall, 1980), pp. 102–103.

[9] See H. Eilbert, "A Study of Current Counseling Practices in Industry," *The Journal of Business, 31* (1958), 28–37.

[10] For major sources of executive stress, see I. Carson, "What Are the Causes of Executive Stress?" *International Management, 27,* (1972), 14–19.

[11] J. Lefkowitz and M. L. Katz, "Validity of the Exit Interview," *Personnel Psychology, 8* (1969), 26–31; J. R. Hinrichs, "Employees Going and Coming: The Exit Interview," *Personnel, 48* (1971), 27–32; Wayne L. McNaughton, "Attitudes of Ex-employees at Intervals after Quitting," *Personnel Journal, 35* (1956), 61–63.

[12] See Mark L. Knapp, *Nonverbal Communication in Human Interaction,* 2nd ed. (New York: Holt, Rinehart & Winston, 1978), pp. 300–301.

[13] Ibid., pp. 301–304. Also see Chapter 5 of this book, "Nonverbal Communication."

[14] From *Sweaty Palms: The neglected Art of Being Interviewed,* by H. Anthony Medley, p. xii. © 1978 by Lifetime Learning Publications, Belmont, Calif. 94002, a division of Wadsworth Inc. Reprinted by permission of the publisher.

[15] Ibid.

[16] Ibid., pp. 85–95.

[17] Ralph Nichols, "Listening is a Ten-Part Skill," *Nation's Business, 45* (1957), 56–59.

[18] Donald W. Klopf and Ronald E. Cambra, *Personal and Public Speaking* (Denver: Morton Publishing, 1981), p. 45.

[19] E. F. Elson and Alberta Peck, *The Art of Speaking,* 2nd rev. ed. (Boston: Ginn, 1966), p. 101.

[20] Charles M. Kelly, "Empathic Listening," in *Speech/Communication: A Reader,* 2nd ed., Richard L. Weaver, II (San Diego: Collegiate Publishing, 1979), pp. 164–73.

[21] Adapted from Charles J. Stewart and William B. Cash, Jr., *Interviewing: Principles and Practices,* 3rd ed. (Dubuque, Iowa: Wm. C. Brown, 1982), pp. 75–102.

[22] The list in this section comes from Robert L. Kahn and Charles F. Cannell, *The Dynamics of Interviewing* (New York: John Wiley, 1964), pp. 217–20.

[23] Adapted from Dale A. Level, Jr., and William P. Galle, Jr., *Business Communications: Theory and Practice* (Dallas, Tx.: Business Publications, Inc., 1980), pp. 250–51.

[24] Klopf and Cambra, *Personal and Public Speaking,* pp. 80–81.

# 10

# Getting a Job

Communication skills are an essential element in a successful employment campaign. In some cases it represents the effective merger of a prospective employee's oral and writing skills. It may even be that the prospective employee's total communication ability is never tested more thoroughly than in this situation.[1] This means that prospective employees will have to know how to write a good presentation of themselves as well to make a good presentation orally. And that is what this chapter is all about.

Sometime in your life—and probably several times—you will be looking for a job. Effective communication skills will very likely contribute significantly (more than you may realize) to getting a job or to getting a better, more satisfying one. When you are in the job market you are involved in the process of selling a product. The research, planning, and presenting you do as you wage this employment campaign should be just as thorough and effective as if you were selling any other product—maybe even more thorough and effective. After all, this is *you* we are talking about! In this chapter, five aspects of getting a job will be considered: (1) evaluating yourself, (2) preparing a résumé, (3) getting job information, (4) applying for jobs, (5) interviewing for jobs.

## EVALUATING YOURSELF

Whenever we sell something we want to be certain that we represent the product fairly and accurately. We must analyze it to know what we are selling before we start investigating where or how to sell it. When we are dealing with ourselves, the approach is the same. When was the last time we stopped and took a good long look in the mirror and appraised what others see when they look at us? Evaluating ourselves is an important step because others are going to be evaluating us. And others will see what we show them! We control the sales situation, and if we do not present strong evidence of why we are right for a particular job, others certainly will not do it for us.

But how do we get to know ourselves? There are several methods, and each may provide different but useful information.[2] First, ask some of your friends to write down five adjectives that they believe best describe you. Do this seriously. After they have the adjectives listed, ask them to give an example that substantiates (or tells why) the adjective describes you. This will give you a beginning picture of how others think of you and the kind of image you project. This may help you with ways to describe yourself—a popular question in some job-interview situations.

A second way is to write down ten statements that begin with "I am...." Take time out and do this now. Put your statements into the following categories:

1. Physical attributes (age, height, weight, etc.)
2. Emotional attributes (shy, happy, cynical, cheerful, frustrated, etc.)
3. Mental attributes (smart, average, dumb, etc.)
4. Roles (roommate, student, leader, etc.)
5. Relationships with others (accessible to others, closed and withdrawn from others, neutral, moderate, or indifferent to others)[3]

When you examine the categories into which your "I am" statements fall, you begin to get an idea of what is important to you. It offers an approximate profile. Additional information can be gained if you put a plus (+) next to each statement to indicate characteristics you feel good about having or a minus (−) next to those you feel bad about. Numerous minuses may reveal low self-confidence. This is a crude measuring tool, to be sure, but it may contribute to self-evaluation.

The third way to find out about yourself is through further self-analysis. The attempt here is to discover positive, personality-related qualitites. What you would like are four or five adjectives that best describe you and a couple of specific examples of why they describe you. These adjectives and examples will be worth every bit of time you devote to their discovery when it comes to the interview experience. The following list of personality qualities is by no means comprehensive, but it should suggest some useful characteristics.

| | | | |
|---|---|---|---|
| accurate | creative | logical | punctual |
| alert | dependable | mature | realistic |
| ambitious | determined | mechanical | research-oriented |
| analytical | disciplined | motivated | respectful |
| assertive | earnest | objective | responsible |
| attractive | efficient | optimistic | sales type |
| bold | enthusiastic | organized | self-starting |
| brave | fair | outgoing | sensitive |
| broad-minded | flexible | patient | serious |
| capable | friendly | people-oriented | sincere |
| communicative | hard-working | perceptive | stable |
| competent | honest | perfectionistic | supervisory |
| competitive | idea-oriented | persuasive | tactful |
| confident | imaginative | pioneering | thorough |
| congenial | independent | pleasant | tolerant |
| conscientious | innovative | poised | unique |
| consistent | inspiring | practical | versatile |
| cooperative | intelligent | productive | warm |

Notice that the traits mentioned are positive ones. The point of this self-analysis is to try to create a positive image of yourself in your own mind first if you are to create a positive image of yourself in the minds of others. This is just a beginning.

The fourth way to find out about yourself is to list all of your accomplishments during your high school and college years. These could be academic, part-time jobs, or hobbies. Write about each of the accomplishments in detail. What happened? How did it come about? What was the outcome? You should have a pool of three sources of information: friends, self, and your accomplishments.

A fifth way to discover information about yourself is from a tape recording. Using a tape recorder, have a friend ask you a series of questions—any questions. They could be from the list of "Questions for the Interviewee From a Potential Employer"—just for practice. After a short while (no more than fifteen minutes) have the friend leave while you spend time with the recording:

> How did you sound?
> Did you come across as enthusiastic?
> Did you sound credible?—confident?
> Did you sound competent?—knowledgeable?
> Were you sincere?

Would this be the kind of person you could trust? Were you honest?
Would you want to employ a person who sounded like this?
Were your answers certain and definite?
Were you able to deal comfortably with selected topics?
Were you too wordy?
Did you speak clearly and distinctly, so that you could be understood?

We will refer back to this list of questions later in the chapter. For the present, just get an idea of how you sound.

One final way to find out more about yourself is through studying other people. As we monitor the behavior of others we also examine our own. If you have the chance, listen to the speech of people in the organization to which you want to belong. Notice their use of slang and vocalized pauses ("uhms" and "ahhs"). Notice any distinctions that make their language stand out. This is not a plea for total accommodation—simply doing what they do; it is, instead, a plea for increased sensitivity and awareness. Try to eliminate your own use of slang, profanity, and vocalized pauses. Adapt your language comfortably to the people with whom you speak.

Objective self-analysis is a useful process. It allows you to see patterns of behavior regarding your capabilities, desires, interests, and achievements. No one else has exactly the same personal qualities you have. The purpose of this self-analysis is to discover your strengths, to make you think specifically about the product you are selling, and to try to construct an accurate picture of the unique *you*. When you sort out your strengths, you will be able to determine your most salable qualifications. Make a concrete, accurate list of all your strengths. Place the most important ones first. These are the areas you will want to emphasize in job interviews. Then, in the remaining stages of getting a job, you can emphasize and capitalize on those strengths.

## PREPARING A RÉSUMÉ

The *résumé*[4] is a sales tool written and designed to obtain interviews with employers and to summarize your qualifications for a job. It is a concise outline highlighting personal, educational, and work experiences especially as they relate to a particular position. The résumé goes by various names—personal data sheet, summary, qualification sheet, personal profile, vita, or C.V. (current vita). Résumés are often clipped to the back of application letters, but they are written first. More about application letters in a later section.

The résumé summarizes all pertinent data about an applicant, and the application letter interprets that data. Once you have a résumé prepared, it will be easier to write the letter because you select the most outstanding facts from the résumé and show, in the letter, how these qualify you to do what an employer wants done. Thus, because the résumé includes facts on which the letter will be based, the résumé is prepared first.

*Why prepare a résumé?* Because most employers expect one. Also, it helps clarify your thinking. And even if you never show it to anyone, a résumé will help you to present yourself better because it will organize your thinking. It will benefit readers as well.

The résumé saves time for readers. The applicant's work experience can be located quickly. Facts can be learned immediately because they are in a shortened form. Headings are used in a résumé to draw the reader's attention to various categories. Moreover, phrases are used instead of full sentences, which also facilitates ease of data acquisition. Finally, since a résumé is a summary of the most impressive qualifications, the person reading it does not have to wade through a complete catalogue.

### Résumé Format

Résumés are individually prepared and have many acceptable forms. One overall and important criteria is that the format you decide upon should be attractive, designed to make a good impression. Typing should be done so that space is used economically, yet does not make the résumé look crowded. Also, headings should be obvious enough to make location easy. Several formats will be offered in this section.

The *conventional* format for résumés begins with the applicant's name, address, and telephone number and ends with the references, as follows:

1. Name, address, and telephone number
2. Job, or career objective
3. Education:
   a. Advanced schooling or training
   b. School names, locations, dates attended, degrees and certificates
   c. Major, significant or pertinent courses, academic honors, grade-point average, special skills, speeches, research, reports
4. Work experience:
   a. Employers' names, locations, dates
   b. Titles and positions held
   c. Duties, supervisors (or number supervised), accomplishments
   d. Volunteer work, research, publications
5. Activities, achievements, awards:
   a. Offices held in school and community
   b. School and community memberships
   c. Honors, publications
   d. Travel, languages, self-support
6. Personal data (optional):
   a. Birthdate
   b. Health, height, and weight

c. Marital status, dependents
   d. Military service
   e. Hobbies
   f. Date of availability
7. References

These are the sections normally included in résumés. From this list you will need to select just those parts that best fit your background and the job you seek.

With respect to the order of the parts, the résumé in Figure 10–1 is conventional, traditional. To be more modern, you should begin your résumé with the part you want to emphasize most. The first position is most emphatic. For those who have just finished college, for example, the most distinctive selling point is likely to be their education. For those who have had considerable experience, they should emphasize that experience by placing it first. If you have had little experience, list it all, part-time and full-time. For those who have had a great variety of experience, list only full-time.

There is no rule that states experiences must be reported in chronological order. It might be more effective to list first the experience most related to the desired job and end with the least related. Once again, emphasis can be gained in this way. Furthermore, no rule suggests that every job or experience must be listed. First, that might be too long. Second, that might not allow a person with a great deal of experience to tailor a résumé to a specific job by including only relevant material. A long list could also suggest that a person moved about a great deal or that he or she was unpopular at the places worked. A résumé does not have to account for every month and year since entering the world of work. Doing so might deemphasize significant experiences.

Because there are no rules governing the format, the following will serve as practical guidelines to keep in mind while preparing your résumé:

1. Keep it short. One page is usually sufficient. Remember, in most cases, readers speed-read résumés. List only the important facts.
2. Consolidate information. Try to keep similar experiences together. Use headings to guide readers.
3. Keep it factual. A well-designed résumé should make a potential employer want to learn more about you. It does not have to be thorough, but it must shape your experience to fit the job you are after.
4. Plan the format. The categories should follow the best psychological sequence. Thus, if you are interested in several fields of work, make several sets of résumés.
5. Keep it neat. Résumés should be typed or professionally crafted. They should also be clean. Use white, beige, cream-colored, or light paper, $8\frac{1}{2}$-by-11-inch good quality bond paper.

|  |  |
|---|---|
|  | CYNTHIA J. HALL |
| ADDRESS AND TELEPHONE | 1563 Kirtland Place<br>Chagrin Falls, Ohio  44022<br>(614) 555-2596 |
| OBJECTIVE | Clerical position to start.  Career objective is an accounting position. |
| EDUCATION | Ohio University, Athens, Ohio  45701<br><br>Accounting major (earned A's in all accounting courses).  Will graduate May 10, 1985, with an M.B.A.  Dean's honor list four semesters. |
| WORK EXPERIENCE | 1984-85 - National Life Insurance Company<br>          1780 Edgewood Drive<br>          Cleveland, Ohio  44144<br><br>1982-84 - Part-time work<br>          T.R. Pern Department Store<br>          1236 Main Street<br>          Athens, Ohio  45701 |
| ACTIVITIES, ACHIEVEMENTS, AWARDS | Member, National Honor Society, 1981-83<br><br>Member and Treasurer, Beta Alpha Psi Accounting Honorary **1982-83**<br><br>Marching Band, four years, 1979-83<br><br>Co-captain, Women's Tennis, 1980-81<br><br>President, senior high school class, 1979-80 |
| PERSONAL DATA | Single; perfect health; 22 years old;<br>5 feet 4 inches tall; 112 pounds<br>Aggressive; willing to travel and relocate |
| REFERENCES | Available upon request from:<br><br>    Ohio University Placement Office<br>    Student Services Building<br>    Ohio University<br>    Athens, Ohio  45701 |

**FIGURE 10-1.** A Conventional, Traditional Résumé

WILLIAM A. SAUNDERS
414 West 46th Street
Phoenix, Arizona 85031
(602) 247-3510

| | | |
|---|---|---|
| career objectives | Desire position as data-processing manager, a position that will enable me to use my knowledge of sophisticated computer systems. | |
| practical computer experience | Data-processing Manager<br>June 1980 - present | Hillside Hospital<br>3312 Crescent Drive<br>Phoenix, Arizona 85005 |
| | Managed the activities of eight employees: three computer operators and five key-punch operators.<br>Determined data requirements (format and timing), designed forms, and planned file layouts and program specifications.<br>Wrote, revised, and tested programs. | |
| | Computer Operator<br>May 1976 - December 1979 | Electronics Unlimited<br>156 Broadway Avenue<br>Tempe, Arizona 85281 |
| | Ran scheduled jobs, checked validity of output, distributed printouts, and maintained a log of computer utilization. | |
| related education | Business Administration Major<br>September 1978 - May 1980 | Arizona State University<br>Tempe, Arizona 85281 |
| | Emphasis on computers and economics.<br>G.P.A. in major 3.8 (on a 4.0 scale)<br>Member Beta Gamma Sigma (honorary business fraternity) | |
| | General Business Major<br>September 1976 - June 1978 | Phoenix College<br>Phoenix, Arizona 85013 |
| | Emphasis on data processing.<br>Dean's honor list every semester. | |
| personal | Single; excellent health; 5' 9½", 150 pounds<br>Born: September 28, 1960<br>Hobbies include all sports; avid jogger | |
| references | Available upon request. | |

**FIGURE 10-2.** A Contemporary Résumé

Figure 10–1 presents a traditional résumé that follows exactly the six-part outline described previously. Parts have not been rearranged for psychological effectiveness or for emphasis.

A wide variety of possible formats are available for résumés. Figure 10–2 offers another possibility.

Things you should *not* put on your résumé, and things about which an employer cannot ask you, have been detailed in various court rulings. They include your race, religion, age, weight, sex, marital status, present living situation, children's ages, childcare arrangements while you are at work, plans to have more children, relationship with your ex-husband or ex-wife, criminal record, military background (name of service, type of discharge) or living accomodations (whether you own or rent a home).[5] If you are in the process of compiling a résumé and you want several sources that will help you, the following are recommended:

JUVENAL L. ANGEL, *The Complete Résumé Book and Job-Getters' Guide* (New York: Pocket Books, 1980).

CARL R. BOLL, *Executive Jobs Unlimited,* Updated Edition (New York: Macmillan, 1979), pp 13–32.

ELI DJEDDAH, *Moving Up: How to Get High-Salaried Jobs* (Berkeley, Calif.: Ten Speed Press, 1978), pp 10–26.

MELVIN W. DONAHO AND JOHN L. MEYER, *How to Get the Job You Want: A Guide to Résumés, Interviews, and Job-Hunting Strategy* (Englewood Cliffs, N.J.: Prentice-Hall, 1976), pp 44–66.

LOIS J. EINHORN, PATRICIA HAYES BRADLEY, AND JOHN E. BAIRD, JR., *Effective Employment Interviewing: Unlocking Human Potential* (Glenview, Ill.: Scott, Foresman, 1982), pp 42–58.

RICHARD LATHROP, *Don't Use a Résumé: Use a Qualifications Brief* (Berkeley, Calif.: Ten Speed Press, 1980).

―――――, *Who's Hiring Who?* (Berkeley, Calif.: Ten Speed Press, 1977).

HERTA A. MURPHY AND CHARLES E. PECK, *Effective Business Communications,* 3rd ed. (New York: McGraw-Hill, 1980), pp 406–24.

## GETTING JOB INFORMATION

This is an essential step in securing a job. Imagine yourself going out to buy a new car. Would you buy the first one shown to you? Of course not. Because of the importance of the purchase—the investment it represents—you would take your time. You would survey the market. What are the competitive products? What are the strengths and weaknesses of the products available? A career choice is far more important than buying a new automobile; thus, more time and effort are required to assess employment opportunities. How do you get job information?

The sooner the survey begins, the more useful the information may be. If begun soon enough, survey results could actually help you select courses appropriate for jobs pursued. More important, perhaps, with the survey under way early, when you are ready to seek employment you will know what is available and you will be prepared with appropriate skills and knowledge.

To begin a search, there are basic kinds of information needed. What are the jobs or job types available? Of these, which are likely to provide increasing opportunities in the future? Are these jobs likely to become overcrowded? Is there likely to be active and rapid technological change in these jobs? Are changes taking place in the skills required for these jobs?—in the knowledge required? Where are these jobs located? Which ones are likely to be higher paying?

Answering questions like these will help job seekers gain an overview of available opportunities. The more questions that can be raised and the more answers that can be found, the more comprehensive the search and the more valuable the results will be. It is the same principle stated elsewhere in this book: the more preparation, the stronger the results are likely to be.

### Getting Information: Level One

Answers to these questions can be found in a variety of locations. The first place is the most obvious: the career planning or placement center at your own college or university. Often, faculty members also have useful information that can provide a starting point. To begin the search, then, one should begin at the local, most obvious, level—using sources immediately available.

### Getting Information: Level Two

At the second level, numerous books and periodicals are available to help in the search. In using these, the important thing is to make certain they are current. Because of supply and demand, the employment picture changes from year to year. Books that could be consulted include:

*Career Planning Handbook: A Guide to Career Fields and Opportunities.* (U.S. Civil Service Commission: U.S. Government Printing Office, Washington, D.C.).
*College Placement Annual* (Placement Council, 35 East Elizabeth St., Bethlehem, Penn.).
*Dictionary of Occupational Titles* (U.S. Department of Labor: U.S. Government Printing Office, Washington, D.C.).
*Guide to Career Education,* by Muriel Lederer (New York: Quadrangle/The New York Times Book Co.).
*Occupational Outlook Handbook* (U.S. Bureau of Labor Statistics: U.S. Government Printing Office, Washington, D.C.).

*Poor's Register of Directors and Executives: United States and Canada* (New York: Standard and Poor's Corp.).

*SRA Occupational Briefs* (Chicago: Science Research Associates).

*Thomas' Register of American Manufacturers* (New York: Thomas Publishing Co.).

*What Color Is Your Parachute? A Practical Manual for Job-Hunters and Career Changers* by Richard Nelson Bolles (Berkeley, Calif.: Ten-Speed Press), revised annually.

Research may also involve consultation of articles on possible careers. Recent articles can be found in periodical indexes such as *Applied Science and Technology, Business Periodicals, Public Affairs Information Service, Reader's Guide to Periodical Literature, Standard and Poor's Industrial Index,* and *Standard Register of Advertisers.* Occasionally, the following magazines will contain an article or even part of an issue devoted to careers: *American Journal of Sociology, Fortune, M.B.A. Magazine, Time,* and *Wall Street Journal.*

### Getting Information: Level Three

At the third level, there are a variety of people familiar with work or with firms in a chosen career area. Business librarians can be helpful. So can business people in the chosen field or firm; most people in these positions enjoy "talking shop." Chambers of commerce, company representatives, and college recruiters can supply information. In addition, employment agencies, friends, family, and working acquaintances can offer useful advice or tips. See Figure 10–3, which provides several additional sources. As these sources are approached, searchers need a good list of questions. And as the questions are answered, a clear picture of the market will emerge.

**FIGURE 10–3.** Sources of Job Information

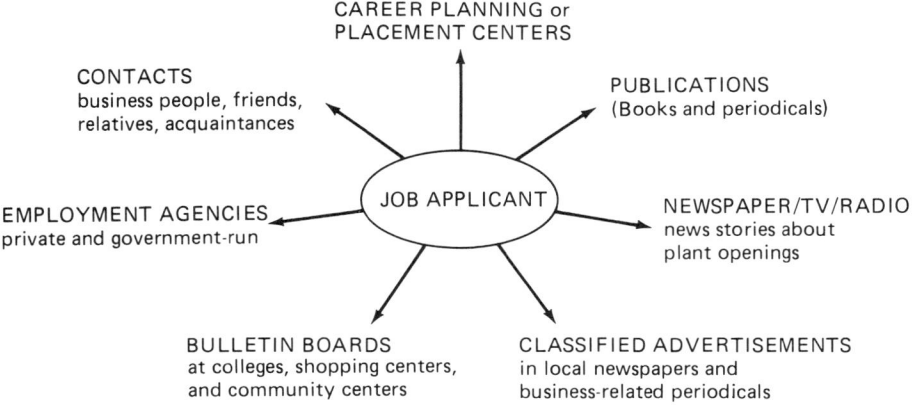

## APPLYING FOR JOBS

Once you have sufficient job information and have compared that information with your own abilities, skills, and characteristics, you are ready to apply for a job. The ultimate goal is to secure employment, but the immediate goal is to secure an interview—the means for getting your foot in the door. Once in the door, applicants can more effectively sell themselves.

An effective application letter is one way to get your foot in the door. The résumé is an essential part of applying for jobs, but a strong application letter can not only enhance the résumé but can also interpret the information in the résumé for the reader's benefit. Think of the application letter as "sales promotion"—to sell an employer on *you* as the right candidate for the job.

Few application letters are well written and appealing enough to merit interviews. Some are confusing because they do not make it clear what the applicant has to offer. Others are sloppy and inaccurate. When an applicant tries to make a good impression and fails, it makes the employer wonder about his or her overall capability.

The letter of application should be a business letter, that is, strongly persuasive. As a persuasive letter, it must make a clear and positive impression. And to do that, it must be tailored to the specific reader or job.

The letter should not repeat facts already listed in the résumé. This clutters the letter with unnecessary facts and wastes the reader's time. For example, let us assume that you have had extensive part-time experience as a cashier in a restaurant and you are applying for a job that requires experience in dealing with people. To deal with the part-time experience as a cashier would be unnecessary. Rather, it would be more valuable, useful, and persuasive to state what you have learned about people from your work as a cashier and how this would be an asset to you in working for your new employer.

In the same manner, if your whole background is composed of educational experience, you do not need to repeat it in your letter. If the job you are applying for requires education, your letter should show how your education has helped you prepare for the job. The letter explains, develops, and interprets the information in the résumé; it does not repeat it.

The most effective format for the job-application letter follows:

1. Get attention and gain interest.
2. Identify your specific preparation to do the job.

3. Give sufficient evidence of this to be convincing.
4. Ask for action.

All of this will be easier for the writer if the suggestions for "evaluating yourself" provided in the first section of this chapter are followed. The more information you have on the product, the easier it will be to write positively and clearly about it.

### Get Attention and Gain Interest

To get attention or gain interest, job applicants can use a variety of techniques. Remember, this is an important position, thus, what goes first is likely to make a strong impression. If your qualifications for the job are outstanding, they can be placed first. Using a name of someone in the organization or stating the source of the job information may get attention. Describing job requirements or using a catch phrase that leads to the presentation of your qualifications are effective openers, but are probably not as strong as beginning with your own qualifications or the name of someone the reader knows.

### Identify Specific Preparation

If you open the letter with your personal qualifications, the second paragraph can offer supporting details. If not, they should be offered as quickly as possible. It is best not to present a simple, chronological accounting of your past experiences, and it is wise to avoid overusing the personal pronoun "I." What your reader most likely wants to learn is whether or not you can do the job for which you are applying. Which phases of your experience are most related to the job you are seeking? Make this relationship for your reader.

### Offer Convincing Evidence

After making the relationship, the writer should provide convincing evidence. Just because writers state they are qualified or feel they have the necessary qualifications, readers need evidence. Once again, writers must condense the concrete experiences they supply. They should focus on one or two of the major aspects of the product; these can be highlighted and stressed.

But highlighting and stressing prominent features must not turn into bragging. There is a fine line between selling our assets and bragging. Bragging is unacceptable and may even alienate an employer. There is no clear distinction between the two—it relates to the tone with which the ideas are shared.

In citing concrete evidence, writers should also reveal knowledge of the business or firm they are planning to join. They could weave into their writing something to show they are aware of present conditions or future plans. (For example, "In addition to my formal business courses, I have taken several courses in computer programming. In one, I received special training on the same kind of computer your company depends upon.")

**Ask for Action**

The final paragraph of the letter should ask for action. If the action desired is clear before you begin, then the letter can be designed to build toward the final, desired action that can, in turn, serve as an appropriate climax to the letter. Action could include having the employer invite you for an interview, giving you some indication of interest, or filing your application for future openings. Make certain the specific action desired is mentioned. It should sound natural and original, not forced or stereotyped. A request for action must not be trite. You need to express gratitude because you are asking a favor. Moreover, because this is the end part of the letter, try to work in a final reference to your most outstanding feature or preparation for the job.

**Cautions**

There are some important cautions, too. For effectiveness, writers must avoid using a form letter, which lacks spontaneity and adaptation. Writers must not overwrite—it is easy to say too much or to write an autobiography. Readers want a short, clear presentation. If writers avoid "I," "me," and "my," they shift attention from themselves to their strengths, abilities, and qualifications for the job. These personal pronouns quickly become excessive, overused, and obtrusive. Writers should also avoid undue humbleness, begging or asking for sympathy, sounding too casual, or lecturing.

Writers must also refrain from sounding negative. Expressing dissatisfaction with one's employer or fellow employees comes across as "sour grapes." If you do it in this letter, what would lead your potential employer to believe you would not sound "sour grapes" when leaving future employment. It comes across as negative: defensive, questionable, maybe even disgusting.

**Positive Features**

The aforementioned problems can be overcome if writers concentrate on positive features. If writers can be themselves in the letter, it will not appear "canned." If their message is concise, clear, and considerate, it

November 17, 1984

Mr. Arnold Randolph, President
Randolph and Associates
3321 Main Street
Indianapolis, Indiana  48201

Dear Mr. Randolph:

The description of Sales Representative given to me by Ms. Arlene Crathwohl, one of your current sales representatives, parallels my own education and experience.

I have majored in business with emphases in economics, marketing, and computers. I identify with your motto, "Put people first." My ability to put people first won me the title "Salesperson of the Month" for Manson's Department Store.

I am looking for a sales position that will build on my economics, marketing, and computer background. I will earn my B.S. degree in May 1985 from Bowling Green State University, where I have maintained a 3.79 grade point average.

In addition to courses in economics, marketing, and computers, I took several courses in communication. I am sure that my courses in speech-communication, business communication, and business and professional speaking will contribute to my sales success. A course in organizational communication gave me a more complete picture of the role of communication in a business setting.

I will be visiting my relatives in Indianapolis between December 19 and January 15 and would like to set up an interview with you during that time. If I have not heard from you by December 19, I will call you when I get to Indianapolis.

Thank you for your consideration.

Sincerely,

*William S. Melsmyth*

William S. Melsmyth
833 S. Clough Street
Bowling Green, OH 43402
(419) 352-1877

**FIGURE 10–4.** Sample Letter of Inquiry

is unlikely to be wordy. If they personalize their message, with the reader in mind, this will tailor the letter to the reader, job, or company and will help subdue the need to use "I," "me," and "my."

If writers assume an appropriate businesslike approach, they will avoid humbleness, begging for sympathy, sounding too casual, or lecturing. Taking a smart aleck, cute, or novel approach must also be avoided. Revealing discreet (subtle) originality is the desirable quality.

To avoid sounding negative, writers should stick to positive information. Any information that may detract from writers' favorable qualifications should be excluded from application letters. Writers must emphasize the areas of job-related responsibilities in which they have past records of excellence. Only positive specific information relative to the position should be included.

## INTERVIEWING FOR JOBS

At this stage the written "sales" presentation ends and the oral one begins. This may be the most important step toward getting the desired job, for it is the most widely used tool of selection. This section provides suggestions regarding preparation for the interview, conduct of the interview, questions frequently asked, questions interviewees should ask, and negative factors to avoid.

### Preparation for Interviews

No other situation could mean more in your life than this one. And if you approach the interview situation with that frame of mind, you are likely to have prepared adequately for it. You will have evaluated yourself, done some research on the company, answered questions you will probably be asked, listed questions you want to ask, paid attention to your appearance, and checked all final details.

*Evaluate yourself.* This is the most important preparation you can do, and that is why the opening section of this chapter was devoted to it. The essential thing now is to know the job or job area you are interviewing for, its requirements, and how your strengths and weaknesses compare with those requirements. Remember to take to the interview at least two copies of your résumé—just in case your interviewer does not have a copy of it available.

*Research the company.* One certain way to please and impress interviewers is to demonstrate extensive knowledge of the company's organization and operations. Excellent resources are available for this. Libraries carry *Thomas' Register, Dunn and Bradstreet, Moody's Industrials,* and *Standard*

& *Poor's*, leading financial publications that will give you an idea of the financial condition of the company. School placement offices, employees of the company, company suppliers, customers, competitors, as well as annual reports of the company are also useful for gaining other kinds of information.

But what should you find out? Applicants should know the age of the company and the location of its plants and outlets. What are the types of products and services it offers? What has been the company's growth during the past few years? What are the prospects for the future? Showing interest in the company as well as knowledge that you have gained through your own initiative will make a favorable impression.

*Answer questions you will be asked.* Some general areas for preparation can get you started. You are likely to be asked about your short-term and long-term occupational goals, your major strengths and weaknesses, and whether you work better with others or alone. You should also know why you would want to work for this employer. Another question you are likely to be asked has to do with how you spend your time. These are not easy, and they deserve careful thought. Avoid cliché answers. Fifty frequently asked questions are listed near the end of this chapter.

*List questions you want to ask.* You need to be concerned about your future growth; thus, formal or informal training provided by the company after employment becomes important. What is the company's policy regarding moving you (or you and your family) to a new location? Another concern should be your promotion and advancement; questions regarding the company's management system, average age of executives, promotion system (whether it is from within or without), and why the person you are replacing left the firm should be high on your priority list. Usually near the end of an interview, interviewees can show concern over fringe benefits and salary.

*Pay attention to your appearance.* How you look is important. Perhaps the best overall suggestion is to be conservative: nothing in excess. Wear conservative clothes appropriate for the office. Clean your shoes. Wear lotions and perfumes sparingly. Any accessories should complement your suit or dress. Hair and fingernails must be clean, hairstyle appropriate, and breath fresh. Overall neatness projects an attitude of personal concern, responsibility, preciseness, and organization. When the interviewee wears the best clothing he or she can afford, it projects an image of quality and success.

*Check final details.* Know exactly where the interview is to be held and how to get there. Arrive ten to twenty minutes early; this allows room for possible last-minute foul-ups—traffic, trains blocking streets, lack of available parking, misdirections—and for filling out required forms and applications. Being late, for whatever reason, is inexcusable. Promptness is important.

Check to make certain you have appropriate information and can record any new information you may discover. Have the full name and address of the company, the interviewer's name and current title, and how to pronounce the name properly. Also, have a working pen and a spare, plus a small notebook immediately available. Do not hesitate to jot down names of people and their titles as you discover them; they will come in handy later. Have any supporting information you may need with you. Will you be asked for samples of your work? Transcripts of grades? Additional recommendations? These could be carried in a briefcase.

### Conduct of Interview

One of the first things that is likely to happen when you show up for an interview is that you will be asked to fill out an application. This usually asks for the same kinds of things as those on your résumé; thus, having a copy of your résumé with you (and a pen) will help you. Read the form carefully and completely before filling it out. More is being evaluated here than the information recorded for company files. Be careful. You are likely to be judged on your ability to follow directions, thoroughness in completing a task, and neatness in your responses.

*Nonverbal impressions.* In any interview situation, more is going on than what you may realize. The impression you make will be dependent on every aspect of your behavior: dress, manners, grooming, how you sit (posture), composure (how relaxed, comfortable, and confident you appear), as well as your behavior in the interview. See Figure 10–5. Interviewees must remember that everything they do from the first time they are seen until they leave will be observed and may be important.

*First impressions.* When you first see the interviewer, smile and greet him or her pleasantly, and by name if you know it. From that point on, interviewees should take their cues from the interviewer. If he or she offers to shake hands, it should be done firmly. Negative impressions are created when interviewees set out to crush the interviewer's hand or, conversely, offer a limp handshake. Interviewees should remain standing until invited to sit; in a small room where the interviewer is already seated, one should sit down immediately and should maintain fairly constant and direct eye contact with (without staring at) the interviewer.

*Making the best impressions.* Interviewees should show interest in the interview by sitting and looking alert, and by asking relevant questions.

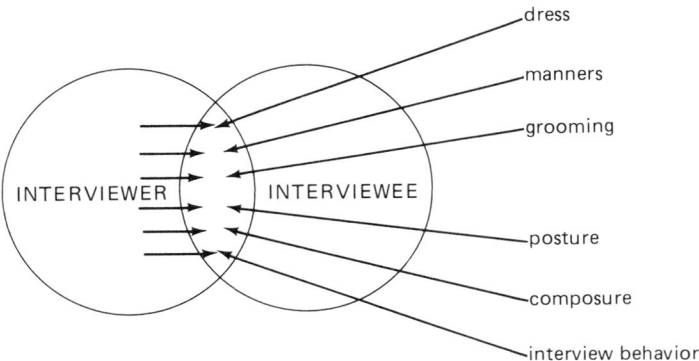

**FIGURE 10-5.**

They can demonstrate respect and courteousness by refraining from chewing gum and smoking (unless invited to do so by the interviewer) and by not taking notes during the interview. Record pertinent notes immediately after the interview.

Throughout the interview, interviewees must be themselves. If they try to put on airs, they are likely to be less at ease, less comfortable, and on less familiar ground. Sincerity and honesty are important at all times. Exaggeration or fabrication are likely to be discovered and if discovered are likely to affect their qualifications for the job.

Although the interview must be a two-way process in which both members question, listen, and respond to discover important, relevant, and needed information, interviewees must concentrate on being good listeners. Interviewers want the best person for a job, but they are trained to be sensitive, effective listeners and observers even though some may not be. Interviewees, on the other hand, want to get the best job suitable to their capabilities, but they are neither trained for nor charged with the responsibility to listen. Listening allows them to be ready to reply to questions; helps them seem interested, active, and involved; may provide valuable cues about interviewer attitudes, values, or impressions. Remember, it is not always what is being said that is important.

Be positive. Interviewees must avoid conveying any negative attitudes or feelings. Such feelings can be related through a slighting reference to a former employer or professor, as discussed earlier. If you cannot say something nice about a person, do not say anything at all. Moreover, avoid negative words such as "can't," "won't," "unable," "hate," "no," "failure," "incompetent," or "stupid." Avoid phrases such as "you know" and "stuff like that." Competence and dependability come from the use of positive words and expressions. Even if they think the interview is going badly, applicants should not allow their discouragement or rejection to show.

Sometimes interviewers purposely appear disinterested to test interviewees' reaction, self-confidence, and ability to respond.

*Be positive.* Maybe this is easier said than done. What does a positive person sound like? Refer back to the questions raised in the section on "Evaluating Yourself." These are the questions you used to evaluate the tape recording of your voice. Make certain that you come across enthusiastic, credible, confident, competent, knowledgeable, sincere, trustworthy, and definite. You must speak comfortably, clearly, and distinctly. Avoid wordiness. If your recording did not reflect these traits, allow them to be goals—and begin now to reach those goals.

*Final impressions.* Interviewees need to be alert to signs from the interviewer that the interview is about to end. That is one reason why listening and nonverbal sensitivity are so important. They may want or need some kind of commitment as to what will follow. When will the interviewer let them know the decision? And when the interview is over, make sure you thank the interviewer. Again, all behavior is likely to be observed, so interviewees must accept the cues and not drag out the interview. They must help bring it all to a natural, comfortable, positive conclusion.

*Follow-up Impressions.* Throughout the job-hunting process, seekers must realize that it is the whole impression, no single part of it necessarily, that wins the job. And when the interview is over, impression formation need not end. *Post interview letters* are an absolutely essential piece of job-hunting etiquette. Regardless of how successful or disappointing the interview may have been, a follow-up letter indicates courtesy. Applicants who are too lazy to make this simple effort are doing themselves irreparable damage, either for the immediate job at hand or for future benefits—which they may be too shortsighted to see.

On the surface, these letters are "thank you" notes, expressing your appreciation for the time and attention you received. But their real function, in most cases, is to enhance your candidacy. They show that you are genuinely interested in the job or company; they reveal determination; and they serve as a reminder to the employer. But applicants must realize, too, that follow-up letters allow employers more understanding of them.

Follow-up letters, then, must be carefully composed selling messages. The ideal letter should:

1. Thank the interviewer for his or her time and attention.
2. Reiterate your most positive attributes. Outline just those qualifications you know he or she values and appreciates.
3. Counter any negative impressions that may have been damaging. There is no need for further negatives, for defensiveness, or for reintroducing negatives the interviewer may have ignored. Do not dwell on those that cannot be overcome in terse sentences.

4. Introduce positive news. Give your reader some positive job-related information not revealed during the interview, like special attributes, attitudes, training, experience, or insights. Being aware that you will be writing a follow-up letter, these "discoveries" can be jotted down as they occur to you after the interview. See Figure 10–6.

**FIGURE 10–6.** Sample Follow-up Letter

---

Dear Mr. Clark:

Your interview with me yesterday was both enjoyable and informative. Thank you for your courtesies and for the interest you took in my qualifications as a sales representative for your firm.

During our conversation you mentioned that the ideal person for the job would have at least two years of practical experience beyond college. There is no doubt that such practical experience provides one with a mature outlook and a knack for working with other people. Fortunately, these qualities were developed in me during my college years.

Because of my business concentration, an extra year was added to my college curriculum. I switched majors late in my undergraduate career. But while in school, my activities included a number of leadership positions and numerous opportunities to work with others. As president of the Business Sales Club, membership during my term increased 20%. While I was sales manager for Business As A Career, sales of advertisements in the college paper increased 25%. As team captain of the tennis and intermural touch-football team, I had many opportunities to work with others.

In my work with my fraternity and on college committees (five during my undergraduate years), I also gained a great deal of experience in working with others. These jobs and activities have provided knowledge, experience, and judgment equivalent to the two years of business experience your firm wants its sales representatives to have.

Because of my background, experience, and desire, I believe that I can become one of your top sales representatives. Allow me the opportunity to prove it.

Sincerely,

_____

Custom-tailor your letter for your reader. Be aware, too, that these letters may be routed to several different people. Avoid composing a form letter. Try to mention points of common interest. If you can include clippings to support important points discussed, this also personalizes the letter. Mentioning a relevant piece of current company or business news serves the same purpose. Avoid repeating information the employer already possesses.

The sooner your letter is in the mail, the more likely your interviewer will still remember your name and face. Before posting the letter, check it over. Are you using the person's correct name and title? Is your language fresh? Does it communicate both your personality and your enthusiasm? Is your reader likely to take your candidacy more seriously after reading your letter? Have you checked over your letter for errors in spelling, grammar, and punctuation? Finally, is it neatly typed?

**Frequently Asked Questions**

The purpose of this section is to give potential interviewees an idea of the exact kinds of questions they can expect. Remember that interviewers range broadly not only in what they ask but also in how they ask questions. Some prefer being direct and straightforward; others pose hypothetical cases and ask interviewees for their reaction. In some instances the cases are taken from actual situations. Some interviewers mix these approaches.

The following questions will serve as useful guidelines. To feel confident, prepare specific answers to each one. The list was prepared by Frank S. Endicott, placement director at Northwestern University, from questions asked by employers of college seniors. These are fifty most frequently asked questions.[6]

1. What are your long-range and short-range goals and objectives, when and why did you establish these goals, and how are you preparing yourself to achieve them?
2. What specific goals, other than those related to your occupation, have you established for yourself for the next ten years?
3. What do you see yourself doing five years from now?
4. What do you *really* want to do in life?
5. What are your long-range career objectives?
6. How do you plan to achieve your career goals?
7. What are the most important rewards you expect in your business career?
8. What do you expect to be earning five years from now?
9. Why did you choose the career for which you are preparing?
10. Which is more important to you, the money or the type of job?
11. What do you consider to be your greatest strengths and weaknesses?
12. How would you describe yourself?

13. How do you think a friend or professor who knows you well would describe you?
14. What motivates you to put forth your greatest effort?
15. How has your college experience prepared you for a business career?
16. Why should I hire you?
17. What qualifications do you have that make you think that you will be successful in business?
18. How do you determine or evaluate success?
19. What do you think it takes to be successful in a company like ours?
20. In what ways do you think you can make a contribution to our company?
21. What qualities should a successful manager possess?
22. Describe the relationship that should exist between a supervisor and those reporting to him or her?
23. What two or three accomplishments have given you the most satisfaction? Why?
24. Describe your most rewarding college experience.
25. If you were hiring a graduate for this position, what qualities would you look for?
26. Why did you select your college or university?
27. What led you to choose your field or major study?
28. What college subjects did you like best? Why?
29. What college subjects did you like least? Why?
30. If you could do so, how would you plan your academic study differently? Why?
31. What changes would you make in your college or university? Why?
32. Do you have plans for continued study? An advanced degree?
33. Do you think that your grades are a good indication of your academic achievement?
34. What have you learned from participation in extracurricular activities?
35. In what kind of work environment are you most comfortable?
36. How do you work under pressure?
37. In what part-time or summer jobs have you been most interested? Why?
38. How would you describe the ideal job for you following graduation?
39. Why did you decide to seek a position with this company?
40. What do you know about our company?
41. What two or three things are most important to you in your job?
42. Are you seeking employment in a company of a certain size? Why?
43. What criteria are you using to evaluate the company for which you hope to work?
44. Do you have a geographical preference? Why?
45. Will you relocate? Does relocation bother you?
46. Are you willing to travel?
47. Are you willing to spend at least six months as a trainee?
48. Why do you think you might like to live in the community in which our company is located?

49. What major problem have you encountered and how did you deal with it?
50. What have you learned from your mistakes?

Federal laws do not expressly prohibit interviewers from asking questions about your race, color, religion, or national origin. The Equal Employment Opportunity Commission (EEOC), however, has issued a statement that it regards such inquiries with "extreme disfavor." State laws are more specific. Each state has laws that relate to employment practices. They forbid employment bias based on race, color, sex, age, religion, national origin, or ancestry. The point interviewers and interviewees need to remember is that all questions should be job related.

### Questions Interviewees Should Ask

One of the single most neglected areas of interviewing is that area which should concern the job seeker the most: "Is this really the job for me?" Interviewees who tell their interviewers that they have no questions are making a classic error that can result in losing a job offer or becoming entrapped in a job they never wanted in the first place.

The following questions will serve four vital functions for the interviewee. First, they enhance interviewees' candidacy because they are reflective of serious, probing people. Second, good questions may indicate to interviewers that interviewees are ready for positions of greater responsibility. More important, however, effective questioning by interviewees will help interviewers remember them and, perhaps, select them out of a sea of qualified applicants. Finally, and most important, these questions will help interviewees through the difficult decision process. Is this job suitable? Should I accept the job offer if given?

1. Why do you want someone for this job?
2. Why isn't this job being filled by someone within the company?
3. Can you draw me an organization chart so I can see just where I fit in?
4. How many people held this job in the last five years?
5. May I interview the person(s) who had this job last?
6. Was the person who held this position promoted?
7. What do you like most about your company? Least?
8. What are your biggest problems?
9. How has this position been filled in the past?
10. What are some examples of the best results produced by people in this job?
11. How many people are you interviewing?
12. What do I have to do to be promoted?
13. What are the company's future plans and goals?
14. How does this company treat its employees?
15. Who owns the company?
16. What qualifications are you looking for in the person you need?

17. What exactly would you like to have me accomplish in this position?
18. Can you afford me?
19. How many people do I supervise?
20. How do you feel about their (people who report to me) performance?
21. How does their pay compare with what they could receive elsewhere?
22. What is the biggest single problem facing your company right now?
23. Will you be asking me to relocate out of town?
24. How soon will you decide if you want to hire me?
25. Do you have any questions about my qualifications?[7]

Not all these questions should be asked. First, that would require too much time. Second, some will be answered in your research of the company. And third, some will be answered by your interviewer without having a question asked. Listen closely. Interviewees must pick and choose those questions that are relevant and important.

## Avoiding Negative Factors

At all times, interviewees must avoid factors that detract. Dr. Endicott, in a copyrighted report published by the Northwestern University Placement Center, surveyed negative factors evaluated during the employment interview.[8] Interviewees can use this list as a guide and reminder.

1. Poor personal appearance
2. Overbearing, overaggressive, conceited, "superiority complex," "know-it-all"
3. Inability to communicate clearly—poor voice, diction, grammar
4. Lack of planning for career—no purpose and goals
5. Lack of interest and enthusiasm—passive, indifferent
6. Lack of confidence and poise—nervous, ill-at-ease
7. Failure to participate in activities
8. Overemphasis on money—interest only in best dollar offer
9. Poor scholastic record—just got by
10. Unwillingness to start at the bottom—expects too much too soon
11. Excuses—evasiveness—hedges on unfavorable factors in record
12. Lack of tact
13. Lack of maturity
14. Lack of courtesy—ill-mannered
15. Condemnation of past employers
16. Marked dislike for school work
17. Failure to look interviewer in the eye
18. Limp, fishy handshake
19. Sloppy application blank
20. Merely shopping around
21. Wants job only for short time
22. Little sense of humor

198  *Getting A Job*

23. Lack of knowledge of field of specialization
24. No interest in company or in industry
25. Unwillingness to relocate
26. Cynical
27. Low moral standards
28. Lazy
29. Inability to take criticism
30. Lack of appreciation of the value of experience
31. Late to interview without good reason
32. Never heard of company
33. Failure to express appreciation for interviewer's time
34. Asks no questions about the job
35. High-pressure type
36. Indefinite response to questions

### SUMMARY

Getting a job requires effective oral and written skills. It is—throughout—a persuasive sales presentation. To handle the process well will help you not only as you begin a career, but also at other times during your career.

The best way to begin the process is to find out about yourself. We find out about ourselves by asking friends, through self-analysis, by listing accomplishments, from analyzing a tape recording, and by studying others. Evaluating yourself allows you to see patterns of behavior regarding your capabilities, desires, interests, and achievements.

Once you understand the product of the persuasive sales presentation, you must understand one method for selling that product: the résumé—the summary of all pertinent data about the applicant. People prepare résumés because employers expect them, to clarify thinking, to present themselves better, to organize their thinking, and to benefit readers. A list of items that should be included was presented as well as practical guidelines and additional sources for information.

Next, there is a need for job information. This can be found at your own college or university, in publications, from people familiar with work, or from firms in a chosen career area. Any source is valuable if it provides information, therefore employment agencies, bulletin boards, classified advertisements, and newspapers, television, and radio must not be overlooked.

To apply for a job, a letter of application will probably be written. It must get attention and gain interest, identify specific preparation, offer convincing evidence, and ask for action. There are some cautions to observe as well as some positive features to emphasize.

At the interviewing stage, the written "sales" presentation ends and the oral one begins. Preparation for the interview includes evaluating yourself, researching the company, answering questions you will be asked, listing questions you will want to ask, paying attention to your appearance, and checking final details.

To conduct the interview, applicants should be conscious of nonverbal impressions, first impressions, making the best impression, the final impressions, and follow-up impressions. Follow-up impressions involve the use of post interview letters—an absolutely essential piece of job-hunting etiquette.

The final sections of the chapter covered questions frequently asked by potential interviewers, questions interviewees should ask, and negative factors that detract from the interview setting. These are practical sections that list valuable information designed to give interviewees specific material to build their confidence before going into the interview.

Getting a job can be a simple, quick process or a complex, time-consuming one. It depends on you! How important do you think it is? How you answer that question may say something about how far you are likely to progress in the business world or, perhaps, how far you want to progress. Because this may be the most important process you engage in, you should give it sufficient time and thought. Finally, it represents one of the best examples of how effective oral and written skills come together. Winning the job, just like being successful, requires effectiveness in both. That is what understanding business communication is all about: *success*.

## NOTES

[1] Paul Elsen, Director of Human Resources, Honeywell, Inc., as cited in Robert E. Swindle, *The Business Communicator* (Englewood Cliffs, N.J.: Prentice-Hall, 1980), p. 379.

[2] More information on self-evaluation can be found in Lois J. Einhorn, Patricia Hayes Bradley, and John E. Baird, Jr., *Effective Employment Interviewing: Unlocking Human Potential* (Glenview, Ill.: Scott, Foresman, 1982), pp. 20–32.

[3] John J. Makay and Beverly A. Gaw, *Personal and Interpersonal Communication: Dialogue with the Self and with Others* (Columbus, Ohio: Charles E. Merrill (a Bell & Howell company), 1975), pp. 27–28. Reprinted by permission of John J. Makay.

[4] The word *résumé* is French and has a diacritical marking called an acute accent ( ´ ) over each of the e's in the word. The accent marks indicate correct pronunciation: *ray'*-zoo-may. Since the word is common in English usage, the tendency is to omit these markings. Such a spelling is incorrect, but accepted.

[5] Theodore T. Pettus, *One on One: Win the Interview, Win the Job* (New York: Random House, 1981), pp. 114–15.

[6] Frank S. Endicott, *Trends in Employment of College and University Graduates in Business and Industry* (Evanston, Ill.: The Placement Service, Northwestern University, 1974), pp. 9–10. Used with his permission.

[7] Pettus, *One on One*, 138–41. Used with permission.

[8] These factors can be found in the New York Life Insurance Company's booklet, *Making the Most of Your Job Interview*, (n.d.). Dr. Frank S. Endicott is currently Professor of Education, Emeritus and Director of Placement, retired, Northwestern University.

# 11

# Meetings, Conferences, and Committees

In his book *How to Win the Meeting,* Frank Snell begins with this comment:

> The meeting is the communications switchboard of every organization. It stands at the center of almost all company decisions. More than 75 percent of executive time is spent around the meeting room table.[1]

The meeting, conference, or committee is a vital element in the organizational web. And because they are decision-making bodies, they are places of force and persuasion. The member who knows how to use this communication forum is likely to be successful. But knowing how to use this forum is not just a matter of being prepared, direct, and quick—certainly useful individual skills. The person who is successful in using this communication forum takes advantage of a number of talents and techniques that, when combined, bring success in meetings, conferences, and committees.

In the first part of this chapter, meetings, conferences, and committees are considered together as groups. A *group* consists of a number of people (usually between three and twenty) who engage in face-to-face interaction and perceive themselves to be a group.[2] But why assemble a group? That is the first question addressed. Then some of the basic characteristics, ideal conditions, methods for group problem solving, and membership and leadership functions are discussed. This material leads to a consideration of meetings, conferences and committees, in detail. The final section focuses on dealing with conflict in groups.

The modern business manager considers meetings to be major time wasters. According to *Fortune*'s list of top-ten time wasters, meetings rank third, right behind the telephone and mail. Thus, it is not uncommon to hear, "I could get a lot more accomplished here if I didn't have to spend so much time in meetings."[3]

## WHY GROUPS?

### Advantages

Many of the purposes of groups are obvious; some are not. For example, keeping people informed and promoting an exchange of ideas appear to be obvious purposes. Groups utilize the knowledge and experience of people throughout the organization. Groups can also contribute to the coordination of information between departments as well as exposing people to the problems and demands with which other areas of the organization must cope.[4]

What might not be as obvious is the value of groups in improving morale. A major reason it improves morale is that it involves workers in decisions that affect their jobs. Groups can also improve morale by improving job performance because groups increase members' exposure to other people's ideas, views, and experiences. Having reached a decision or solved a problem, the result will likely get greater support, since group members, having been part of the decision process, will be committed to it and more likely to lend their support to implementing the result. There is an allegiance to a cause that results when people have participated in the decision-making process.

### Disadvantages

Naturally, groups have disadvantages too. The biggest is that they are time-consuming. An individual working alone will, in most circumstances, arrive at a decision or a solution more quickly. This fact, I'm sure, generated the aphorism "God so loved the world that He did not send a committee." The time element is a problem in both how long it takes to prepare for a group meeting and in the time consumed in the decision-making process.[5]

Because the group process often divides the responsibility for decisions or solutions among group members, no one feels accountable for the decision. This can be a problem in the initiative necessary to implement, follow-through, or complete group results. It is "the other person will do it" syndrome.

The nature of group compromise and decision making may also cause decisions and recommendations to be watered down. It is often said that "A camel is a horse put together by a committee," indicating that the camel's humps were added in committee to satisfy (perhaps pacify) certain members. But a horse would have been more efficient and, depending on needs, more satisfactory.

There is always an implied assumption that a group will solve a problem. "If you have a problem, give it to a committee," of "If all else fails, let's form a committee." Groups are not a panacea.

A final disadvantage is the conflict or competitiveness groups can generate. Because of the feelings people have about being in the "in-group" or the "out-group," hostilities and rivalries are sometimes created. Just as teams compete, members of groups often band together to compete with other groups. It is a natural (and regularly reinforced) tendency.

**Should a Group Be Formed?**

If one weighs advantages and disadvantages, it might not be clear whether a group would be worthwhile.[6] Most people think the advantages outweigh the disadvantages. But that does not mean you automatically form a group when you have a problem. The best method is to ask yourself some questions about its overall value. For example, if you are simply providing information or instructions why not prepare a brief oral report then take questions afterwards? Is having a group discussion efficient under these circumstances?

Is discussion, that is, having people voice their opinions and questions, important to the information or instruction being provided? If the information or instructions require clarification, explanation, or elaboration, discussion might be helpful. Sometimes, information and instructions affect people or units of an organization differently, or the various effects and interactions need to be explored.

Do you have enough time to hold a group discussion? Is it the most efficient method? Will it accomplish your goals and objectives in a way that will save everyone involved energy, time, and money? You must consider the overall cost-reward ratio. That is, you must weigh the time and effort the discussion will require against the benefits that are likely to accrue. Remember that taking employees away from their regularly scheduled duties can result in a loss of money.

Finally, one should question whether the group meeting will likely result in a greater feeling of team effort or if it will facilitate individual identification with the group's purpose. Can it help bring people together, or unite them in a common purpose? Will it encourage cohesiveness? And will it bring about the evaluation and development of a proposed plan or program?

## CHARACTERISTICS OF GROUPS

There are no guarantees for success. This is true in anything you pursue, but it is especially true in the area of small-group communication because of the dramatic increase in variables that determine success when you bring together a number of individuals. Without considering the environment or the reason for meeting, just think about the mix of feelings, attitudes, and perceptions involved as the number of people in a group increases. The possibility for conflict, or simply differences, increases geometrically.

There are, however, some variables that have a direct effect on group success. Although you may find yourself in a group where these factors have already been determined, and where you can do nothing to remedy or reshape the situation, there are times when you can (or will be able to) exert some influence or control. At that point your considerations of the group size, structure, personality, norms, and cohesiveness may be important.

### Size

One survey with 1,200 respondents suggests that the average size of policy-making committees is 8.6 members.[7] Earlier in this chapter the definition of a group suggested that groups consist of from three to twenty members. But what is the ideal size? That is, what size would work best? Most experts on small-group communication suggest that a group should have no fewer than three and no more than nine members. But there is probably a better guide than counting members.

A group must be no larger than the number of individuals who, once together, feel free and willing to express their positive and negative feelings. You have probably experienced a group situation where the group was too large: You actually felt uncomfortable talking, and as a result you remained silent. Members, too, need to feel free enough to make aggressive efforts toward problem solving even at the risk of antagonizing other members of the group. And yet, the group should be small enough that individuals will demonstrate some regard for the feelings and needs of others. Finally, groups should be large enough that a loss of a member can be tolerated, and yet small enough that that loss cannot be ignored.[8]

The most obvious problem that occurs when group size is increased concerns overall group participation. First, as the group gets larger, and given the same amount of time to interact as a smaller group, the amount of time for each person to communicate is decreased. Second, as the group swells, those people who are more forceful, dominant, or aggressive begin to influence the group—as the less forceful, less dominant, and less aggressive find it easier and more comfortable not to communicate. Third, participants become less sensitive to other group members because feedback cues are not as easily noticed as groups get larger. This is especially clear when you notice the number of interactions possible as groups increase in size:[9]

| NUMBER IN GROUP | INTERACTIONS POSSIBLE |
|---|---|
| 2 | 2 |
| 3 | 9 |
| 4 | 28 |
| 5 | 75 |
| 6 | 186 |
| 7 | 441 |
| 8 | 1,056 |

**Structure**

What may happen when the size of a group changes has to do with group structure. A group in which full, free, and constant interaction occurs (see Figure 11–1) may change to one in which several members only dominate the interaction as it grows in size. It may also become entirely leader-centered in which conversation is channelled through just one person, or one person predominantly. (See Figure 11–2).

The structure may be affected, too, by the nature of the leader's role. This will be addressed in a later section on leadership functions. Suffice it

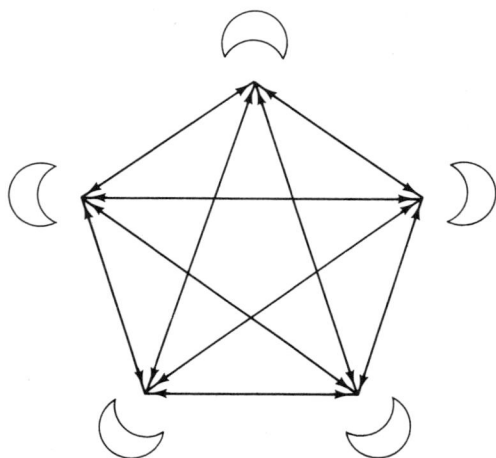

**FIGURE 11–1.** Participant-Oriented Small-Group Discussion. The arrows indicate channels of communication. Although all channels have been used in the diagram, even if some were not this would still be participant-oriented because no single person dominates the discussion.

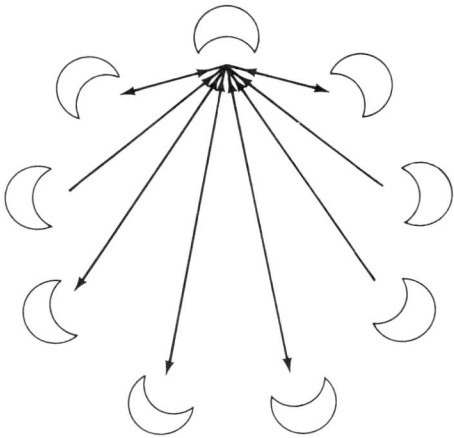

**FIGURE 11-2.** Leader-Oriented Small-group Discussion. Although a situation where every member establishes a communication channel with the leader—especially in a group as large as the one depicted here—is perhaps unrealistic, the model indicates what one-way communication looks like. The group is leader dominated.

to say that an imposed leader, elected leader, or a leader with a dominant personality may create leader-centered discussion because of the power given to that individual, the power they perceive invested in them, or the power others ascribe to the position. This does not have to occur, but often does.

A leaderless group, or one that allows members to lead as the information or circumstances dictate (functional leadership), would likely promote an open, cooperative atmosphere characterized by freedom of interaction: less control. Rigid structure sometimes limits group flexibility whereas freedom and flexibility may result in spontaneous and fulfilling interpersonal relationships. In some cases control is necessary and important, as when a manager has a policy formulated with facts and other information to back it up but needs worker input for shaping and adjustment. In other cases little control might be more beneficial as when workers are asked to hammer out a policy from scratch, which would serve to regulate information flow among them in emergency situations.

Structure may also be more formalized. It may involve the hierarchical relationships or working arrangements agreed upon by the group or imposed on the group. This hierarchy may determine leadership as well as who is to present certain ideas. These responsibilities often come with high status. Who is to record the proceedings and who is to be the listener(s) may also be determined by status.

Groups also need to know the structure governing them, how the structure was established, which aspects can be changed, and how flexible they can be. First, some groups get so carried away with their task or with deliberations that they forget that they operate under a set of rules. If they know how that structure was established, they begin to understand which aspects can be changed or even who must authorize any structural change.

This may determine their flexibility—especially when a structure becomes unworkable. For example, a group that began by allowing full and free participation—a self-imposed structure—might discover that it can't get anything accomplished. Members can change their structure by imposing more rigid rules or guidelines to accomplish their task.

**Personality**

Groups have a *personality,* that complex of characteristics that distinguishes it as a group. It usually does not reflect the personality of any single member; rather, the group's personality is a combined or conglomerate feature, sometimes even greater than or different from the sum of the individual parts. Personality is usually a function of member satisfaction, which results when the expectations of individuals are fulfilled. That is, when members feel they are getting something they want, they are likely to be happy.

In general, member satisfaction is dependent on several factors. It results when members are rewarded. Rewards come in the form of support from other members, acknowledgement of efforts, consideration of and consultation with them, and the absence of punishment. It also results when members like each other. Individuals prefer working with people they like. They also want to be in on the decision-making process. This is part of the reward system of being considered and consulted. That is, members enjoy offering, or being asked for, their facts and opinions. To have others regard our facts or opinions as important is rewarding because it makes us feel good about ourselves. We feel good about ourselves when we believe what we say to others is important and makes a difference. Group members also prefer it when all individuals are allowed to participate. That is, they prefer a format like Figure 11–1 as opposed to Figure 11–2. Members like to undertake tasks that relate to them and that they feel they can realistically accomplish. Some prefer highly regimented tasks, others loosely structured ones, but there is no doubt that the nature of the task affects member satisfaction.[10] Some people prefer problem solving in tightly structured situations. When time is of the essence, and the problem is pressing and important, a rigid structure can yield valuable results. Also, when a group meeting is relatively large in size, rigid structuring is likely to be required.

In most discussions there are times when we should have tight structure and times when we should have free discussion. Exclusive devotion to either extreme may be harmful. Being adaptive is best. For example, when an issue is presented on which strong feelings are expressed, it is probably better to forget about structure and permit full and free discussion at least for a while, maybe even for a long while. In a discussion we must figure out when orderliness or free meandering will be most appropriate.

Finally, member satisfaction results from playing high-status roles. *Status* has to do with the degree of importance members attach to roles. The idea is that some members occupy more important positions in the group and can more directly influence group outcomes. These are not always overtly acknowledged. For example, in one group all members tended to look toward the oldest member of the group for final words on a proposal or for a "go-ahead" to approve a new idea. The oldest member had a direct influence on group outcomes.

Groups with positive, satisfying personalities allow many different members to give ideas, provide direction, and encourage participation.[11] Functional leadership—where anyone can lead as the task, needs of the group, or member desire dictate—may be a factor in group personality. But this is likely to work only where all members trust each other, where none aspires to leadership above all others, and where all are enthusiastic about the task.

### Norms

A *norm* is a set of assumptions or expectations held by members of groups about the kind of behavior that is right or wrong, good or bad, appropriate or inappropriate, allowed or not allowed by the members of that group. These norms may be *implicit*. That is, they are understood and accepted and never specifically or directly stated. *Explicit* norms are more formal and are usually verbalized. An implicit group norm might be to defer to the member with the highest status, allowing him or her to begin the meeting, establish the agenda, and suggest new ideas. Explicit norms might cover personal appearance, language usage, or even who should participate in meetings. Length of lunch breaks, coffee breaks, or time allowed for meetings might be explicit norms too.

How individuals conform to norms can indicate how accepted or accepting they are. Oftentimes, there is a difference between private and public acceptance of norms. We may go along with an idea in front of others because of the public image it provides us, but privately we may reject the idea outright. But how accepted we are into the circles that count—especially by company management—may result from how well we can demonstrate our acceptance of company (formal) norms.[12]

How accepting individuals are of norms may reveal comfort. That is, if people feel they are always beating their heads against company norms (implicit or explicit), it can be an anxious and frustrating experience. It can even carry over into their personal lives. So whether or not individuals decide to adhere to such norms depends, in part, on how they value group membership or organizational affiliation. It may also reflect certain personality characteristics. Some researchers suggest that conformity to norms is more likely in people who are submissive, are low in self-confidence, lack intelligence and originality, and need social approval.[13]

## Cohesiveness

The attractiveness a group has for its members is defined as *cohesiveness*. A highly cohesive group will have a great deal of interest in staying together. Group members like to be together, but they also establish or conform to rigid norms, well-defined attitudes, and clear-cut values. Individuals feel a strong sense of belonging, and they prefer membership in such groups to membership in others.

In cohesive groups, pleasantness and morale are usually high. That is, cohesiveness contributes substantially to the socioemotional climate, but it has no effect on productivity. It neither increases nor decreases it.[14] However, it is likely that group performance will be enhanced when cohesiveness is high. That is because people perform better when the climate in which they perform is pleasing.

## IDEAL CONDITIONS

It is difficult to determine or define ideal conditions for group behavior because what is "ideal" is likely to vary with the task, leader, participants, and circumstances, in addition to variations in the five characteristics cited above: the size, structure, personality, norms, and cohesiveness of a group.

The key to finding an ideal situation (and remember, this is a goal) lies in preparation: laying the proper foundation. It lies in discovering as many of the interacting variables as possible, controlling those over which we have control, and recognizing and either dealing with or acknowledging those we do not. The ideal situation is likely to result in higher productivity, greater satisfaction, and potential personal development.

To achieve these outcomes requires that we examine management assumptions and practices. Further, we must determine the leadership behavior necessary. This will be discussed in a later section. What organizational structures are we operating under? What rules and procedures are we to (or must we) follow? Finally, what reward system is operative?[15]

We must consider, too, what the various individuals bring to the group. What are their unique backgrounds, personal systems, and their status or position? Again, some items will influence the group, some will not. Some will be controllable, others will not. The point, once again, is preparation: knowing as much as possible about possible variables.

To gain success means more, however, than simply controlling all factors that occur before a group meets. Most of the items discussed so far refer to preceding events, conditions, and causes. And there is little doubt of their significance. But success is not dependent on antecedent conditions alone. It may result from what happens in the group during group deliberations.

## GROUP PROBLEM SOLVING

Not all groups are task oriented, but in business, more are than are not. To know how to operate in problem-solving or decision-making situations will be a positive asset because the format is applicable in conflicts (as outlined previously), in personal problem-oriented situations, and in groups.

This section will outline the process of group problem solving. This process will help assure that the group purpose will be achieved. The process involves recognizing the difficulty, expressing feelings, describing the problem, developing solutions, and implementing the result.

### Recognizing the Difficulty

A requirement in group problem solving is *recognizing the difficulty*, and it must come near the beginning. First, recognizing the difficulty serves to identify where the difficulty or irritation lies. "What's the problem?" is a question that is quickly addressed. Second, it alerts members, some of whom may not even realize a problem exists, to the nature and purpose of the meeting. Third, it sets the stage. It makes certain there is a common focus. See Figure 11–3. This common focus, too, helps the group move from this common base as one (a group)—not necessarily in the same direction, but at least starting from the same point.

### Expressing Feelings

Often, when a problem area is defined people will automatically identify with one side or another, or they will want to place blame, or to find

**FIGURE 11–3.** Recognizing the difficulty establishes a common ground. It is similar to the area of shared meaning in the model of "communication as transaction" outlined in Chapter 2, except in this case three more people have been added to make it a group of five—a small group.

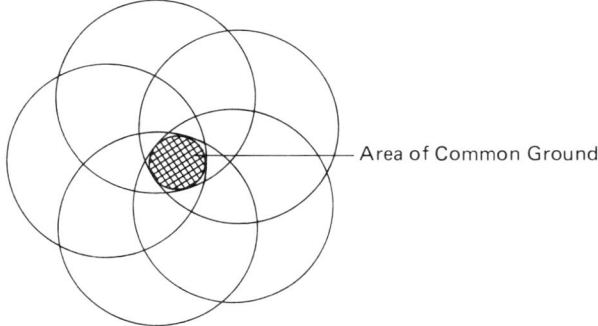
Area of Common Ground

excuses. It is sometimes amazing to watch how people respond as a problem area that affects them is defined. The way they respond results from a wide variety of factors (many of them discussed in Chapter 7, "Conflict") including their personality and relationships with others, to their credibility and status in the company. It could be almost anything.

The purpose of this stage in group problem solving is to let out some of these feelings. It allows a certain amount of cathartic release. Sometimes problems become so personally agonizing that people must be allowed to release their tensions through expression. In some cases, too, this may mean bringing hidden agendas (concealed plans) out into the open.

A group that is willing to allow time for the expression of feelings may be laying the foundation for free-flowing, open, nondefensive communication. Feelings that can be damaged and personal conflicts that can be resolved, or at least brought to the attention of the group, can be made known. When these are left unresolved they become antecedent conditions for conflict. And the problem is that often, feelings that can be damaged or personal conflicts that can be resolved, are not and will not be known until it is too late (when conflict erupts), unless allowed to surface early.

### Describing the Problem

In a problem-solving group, *describing the problem* is one of the most important stages. To engage in it involves a variety of steps. For example, description must first begin with *definition*. To define a problem means to fix its limits or boundary. We are looking at company productivity, or we think we have a problem with the task force. This, then, makes it distinct and clear. Once it is defined, it should be *worded*. "To what extent should we increase production?" "Should the number of employees assigned to this task force be cut?" Careful wording is important because often the problem, as worded, becomes a convenient referent point throughout deliberations: "I'm not sure you are speaking to the problem as we phrased it," or "That solution applies to another problem, ours is. . . ."

As part of the wording of a problem, its *limits* must also be clearly established. "To what extent should we increase production *on the alpha project?*" "Should the number of employees *assigned to the 'xenobia' task force* be cut?" There are a variety of factors that affect the limits that should be established. For example, how much time do you have to work on this problem? Some problems are so voluminous that it would be impossible to approach them because it would take years. But people must also consider the expertise of the group members. Is the problem within our scope, jurisdiction, range of authority, competence, responsibility, understanding, or concern? Some problems must be *narrowed*, members considering just a portion of it, if it is to be discussed or approached at all. Rather than do a market analysis on a national scale, for example, the problem could be narrowed to the regional or local level.

Once a topic is narrowed, another part of describing it involves *gathering data* on it. Most problems, if they are significant, cannot be addressed based on personal opinion alone. They demand careful research. Sometimes group members must be encouraged, even challenged, to discover information from reliable, credible, recent sources.

After the data are gathered, *analysis* is the next step. The interaction that a group encourages aids the analysis step. This is when data are studied to determine the relationship of the parts. Analysis involves dividing a complex problem into its component parts or essential elements. Interaction can stimulate the mind in new directions and cause one to see new relationships. Again, two heads can be better than one, and this is one area where this aphorism can be proven correct.

Often, following thorough analysis, it is discovered that the problem is too broad, or not well focused. The final step in the description stage is *reformulation*. This is when a group changes its focus slightly. Sometimes it is only through analysis that groups discover a need for reformulation, so at this point they refocus on a different dimension or aspect of the problem. Rather than do a market analysis at the present time, a company could focus, first, on the availability of resources to manufacture a product for this market. Such reformulations often result when members have asked such questions as:

1. Do we really have a problem?
2. Is it worth our time and effort to try to solve it?
3. What barriers must be overcome?
4. Is anything being done now to solve the problem?
5. What will happen if nothing is done?

### Developing Solutions

If securing an accurate, well-defined, worded, and narrowed problem constitutes one major part of group problem solving, discovering a complete, workable, and economical *solution* constitutes the other major part. Again, this stage is composed of several important steps. First, the *criteria* for an acceptable solution must be agreed upon. Criteria could even be listed. The solution must

1. Be compatible with our other product lines
2. Be agreeable to our stockholders
3. Not require us to establish new markets
4. Allow us to depend on resources we already have available.

Obviously, the group wants a solution that best solves the problem—and not just an incomplete or partial solution. In addition, it must be workable and feasible. Any group could come up with an ideal solution which when matched against reality proves unworkable or unfeasible. But that would be a waste of time.

Other important considerations include the cost of the solution—or cost of implementation—whether it would create more problems, or create disadvantages that would outweigh the advantages, and whether it could be implemented in a reasonable amount of time. Just because a solution looks good on paper does not mean it is good. It does not even mean that when all facts are considered that it can be implemented at all.

The second step in developing solutions, after establishing the criteria, is to *list* them. The best way discovered for coming up with a variety of possible solutions is the technique called *brainstorming* that was discussed in the chapter on conflict. To make this work, all group members must

1. Generate solutions
2. Encourage each other
3. Allow uninhibited freedom and creativity (wild ideas)
4. Suspend judgment and evaluation
5. Move with speed.

Usually it is best if recorders are available to write down *all* the ideas produced. Members should be encouraged to hitchhike on the ideas produced by others or "leapfrog": go one better. The wilder the ideas generated, the more likely a creative or unique solution will be discovered.

Once all solutions have been proposed, then the *evaluation* process can begin. (Evaluation must not occur during brainstorming because it is both distracting and inhibiting at that stage.) Evaluation is the process of determining the significance (influence, effect, or importance) of the solutions by careful appraisal and study. Pros and cons are weighed. Also, group members should now compare proposed solutions with the criteria they established for selecting a satisfactory solution. All solutions should be challenged and supported.

This is the time when active discussion and constructive argument must take place. Following these guidelines will help get useful results:

1. Create an "everybody wins" atmosphere; all participants should not think of themselves, or be thought of, as losers as a result of the discussion.
2. Encourage participation—the open expression of feelings, ideas, and positions. The more contributions, the better the outcome.
3. Seek critical evaluation; explore the assumptions and implications of ideas.
4. Allow all ideas to have a serious, interested hearing from everyone.
5. Keep ideas separated from the members who offer them.

6. Encourage restatement of positions, feelings, and values, especially when disagreements occur.
7. Strive to equalize status power so all ideas are listened to and evaluated on their own merits.
8. Stress teamwork.
9. Introduce controversy so all sides of issues are discussed.
10. Point out and rebuke any trickery, bargaining, manipulation, and deception.[16]

For group members, then, to *choose the most desirable solution*, the next step, all members could be asked to rank-order the solutions proposed, the ones that meet established criteria, or their favorites. At this point, solutions should be examined with an eye toward combining or synthesizing the strong elements of several of them. Creativity may not involve coming up with a brand new idea, but rather recombining old ideas in new ways.

### Implementing the Result

The final step in group problem solving is *implementing the result*. Group members must develop a plan by which the solution can be enacted. Sometimes this involves assigning particular assignments to each individual group member. Sometimes the group, as a whole, can implement the solution, whether that means informing superiors, securing public approval, or planning budgets.

Implementation, too, may involve follow-up. Sometimes it is helpful to establish ways to monitor progress, evaluate effects, or gauge reactions. Sometimes, too, this aspect is handled by other groups or other parts of the company.

Throughout the group problem-solving process, free-flowing, open communication should be maintained. This can be assured if all group members remain attentive, offer feedback, ask questions, paraphrase the remarks of others, communicate with them eye-to-eye, and, overall, try to preserve a positive, supportive mental attitude.

## MEMBERSHIP FUNCTIONS

Groups are not successful because they establish or follow an agenda. Nor are they successful because they are of the right size, have a clear structure, reveal a clear personality, agree upon norms, or show cohesiveness. Groups are successful because of people; it is the individuals who make up groups who determine their success. Sometimes it is just the members, sometimes it is an impressive leader, and sometimes it is a unique blend of both.

In this section, membership functions will be discussed. The next section considers leadership functions. Within a group, there are a variety of roles that need to be filled, and these roles help a group fulfill its task as well as maintain cohesiveness. Also, there are self-centered roles that must be avoided.[17]

**Group Task Roles**

The roles to be outlined here, when performed, help groups accomplish their task. When groups must solve problems, make decisions, exchange information, or resolve conflicts, most of these roles will contribute to that effort. Usually the roles are distributed among group members; however, effective participants are likely to fill most of them.

The point in listing these roles is twofold. First, it outlines some of the roles that facilitate group functioning. Second, it provides each of us a way to monitor our own group behavior: How many of these roles do you play? How many can you play? Do you see why effective group functioning depends on the willingness of members to play different roles?

*Initiators* get groups started and keep them going by proposing new ideas, procedures, goals, and solutions.

*Information givers* provide the substance or content of the discussion. They offer facts, examples, as well as personal experiences relevant to the task.

*Information seekers* ask for facts, opinions, and examples from others and seek for clarification. This helps make certain that relevant information is not overlooked.

*Opinion givers* offer their beliefs, attitudes, and judgments about relevant issues.

*Opinion seekers* solicit these views from others. How do others feel? What are their attitudes and convictions?

*Elaborators* help to clarify and expand the ideas of others. Often this is done through the use of examples, illustrations, and explanations.

*Integrators* tie together elements of a discussion. They clarify relationships between facts, opinions, and other comments. Without integrators, contributions sometimes appear unrelated and disjointed.

*Orienters* help keep groups on track. They remind groups of their goal, clarify purposes and positions, and help identify distractions, irrelevancies, and digressions.

*Energizers* motivate group members to reach decisions, solve problems, and become more involved. They are enthusiastic and active.

**Group Maintenance Roles**

The roles to be outlined in this section, when performed, help a group build and maintain interpersonal relationships among members.

They determine the social-emotional climate of a group. When these roles are not performed, the result may be a lack of cohesiveness in the group or even conflict. When performed, members of groups feel closer to each other, interaction occurs more smoothly, and members, generally, are happier with the outcome of the discussion.

*Encouragers* show support for the other members of the group. They provide a warm, hospitable atmosphere by praising and agreeing with group members.

*Harmonizers* help reduce conflict by aiding in mediating differences, introducing compromises, and reconciling differences.

*Tension relievers* will decrease the formality in a situation by interjecting humor. They may even suppress their own emotional reaction to help reduce the conflict of others.

*Gatekeepers* control the flow of communication in a group by opening or shutting channels. They might encourage a nontalker or cut off one who monopolizes the discussion. They help groups continue functioning.

*Followers* serve as a neutralizing element. Such roles are useful in stress situations but not advisable otherwise. A follower acquiesces to the wishes of others. Although such roles do not contribute to conflict, in most cases, they serve little purpose in aiding the progress of the group.

### Negative Roles

Members sometimes function in less than desirable ways. They put themselves and their interests before those of the group. The following roles reduce group effectiveness because they lower productivity, cohesion, and satisfaction.

*Blockers* are totally negative and prevent group progress by objecting to the ideas and suggestions of others. They are constant complainers and are always dissatisfied.

*Aggressors* are also negative and this negativism comes through as discontentedness and disapproval. Aggressors tend to distrust and dislike others, and they reveal this through criticism, jealousy, and ill-will.

*Anecdoters* get carried away in the stories and personal experiences they tell. They retard group progress by distracting members from their task.

*Recognition seekers* demand the recognition and sympathy of others. They are the boasters and braggarts.

*Dominators* try to monopolize group interaction. These are the people who are unhappy unless things are running their way.

*Confessors* involve other group members in their personal problems. They readily reveal their fears, needs, shortcomings, or whatever when they think they have someone who will listen.

*Special-interest pleaders* have loyalties and group affiliations that lie outside this immediate group, and they plead for favors and attention for that outside group.

*Clowns* are distractors. They use jokes, antics, and irrelevant comments to entertain the group. They prefer play to work and will use sarcasm and horseplay to attain their purpose.

Many people have negative tendencies. To control these tendencies will help the group focus on task and maintenance roles. Control can be exhibited by those revealing these tendencies. But since this is a bit unrealistic, group leaders and other members must reveal control. Not only should they point out the role, but they need to show how it negatively influences group work and progress.

Effective membership can be summed up by suggesting some specific guidelines. All group members should share their ideas freely, listen to others' points of view, focus only on the point under discussion, engage in constructive disagreement, be prepared, assist in both task and maintenance needs, help the leader wherever possible, and keep an open mind. These functions should be accomplished within a framework of critical thinking and ethical conduct. Members should never knowingly distort, falsify, or suppress information. The use of power, threats, and bribes, too, must be avoided.[18]

## LEADERSHIP FUNCTIONS

Leaders can be imposed on groups from outside. Group members may have no choice in the selection of a leader. A leader may emerge from the group as members look for guidance or rally around a person who seems to have the information or who seems to offer some good suggestions about the direction the group should take. Some groups elect leaders while others rely on the willing cooperation of all participants working toward a common goal. No matter how leaders are chosen, there are certain functions naturally or normally associated with their role.

Leaders often establish a format for the group.[19] This may include an agenda, meeting times, nature of the information needed, and procedures as to how the group will function. Leaders are also responsible for initiating discussion in pertinent and productive directions. Their opening comments may establish a foundation through relevant comments, or present a question to challenge the group. Leaders also keep groups moving by summarizing progress, asking new questions, and encouraging participation from everyone.

Leaders assume responsibility for keeping groups moving in the proper direction. They display a sense of organization. This may require some assertiveness as they interrupt members to keep them from lengthy digressions. Leaders are group watchdogs, sensitive to the overall needs and requirements of the group. This may involve using clarifying summaries, drawing out new viewpoints, or playing devil's advocate (championing a less accepted or approved position for the sake of argument).

When conflicts in a group become excessive or especially heated, leaders must be willing to help relieve tension. This means they should have some understanding of the nature and value of conflict (see Chapter 7, "Profiting from Conflict Management"). Open confrontation must be encouraged; however, leaders are often those who must make certain it is productive (contributing to the progress of the group). And leaders must be open-minded and fair.

Leaders also are responsible for the vitality or energy level of the group. They fill in the gaps when groups flounder with relevant questions or an analysis of group progress. They keep groups from becoming dull and dreary by keeping the flow of comments active and spontaneous. Leaders are excellent listeners who are able to respond to what is being said and meant.[20]

Finally, leaders are active participants. They do not always play the roles that participants do, but they often are just as active and involved as any other member. When they serve as leader as well as participant they are not only prepared to discuss, but are likely to present just as many ideas and opinions as others. When they have established the proper atmosphere in which functional leadership can occur, and other members do take over the leadership functions when that is appropriate, the imposed, elected, or designated leader can blend into the group and monitor progress while allowing the group to assume leadership responsibilities.

One of the best ways to illustrate graphically the relationship between leader control and decision making by group members is presented by Harold Zelko and Frank Dance.[21] See Figure 11–4. On this model, which is self-explanatory, I have placed three letters; these letters help reveal the nature of leadership style. *A* represents autocratic or authoritarian leadership, *B* represents democratic, or a shared-leadership style, and *C* represents laissez-faire leadership in which group members lead and the leader

**FIGURE 11–4.** This diagram shows the level of responsibility leaders take in decision making and the corresponding involvement or noninvolvement of members.

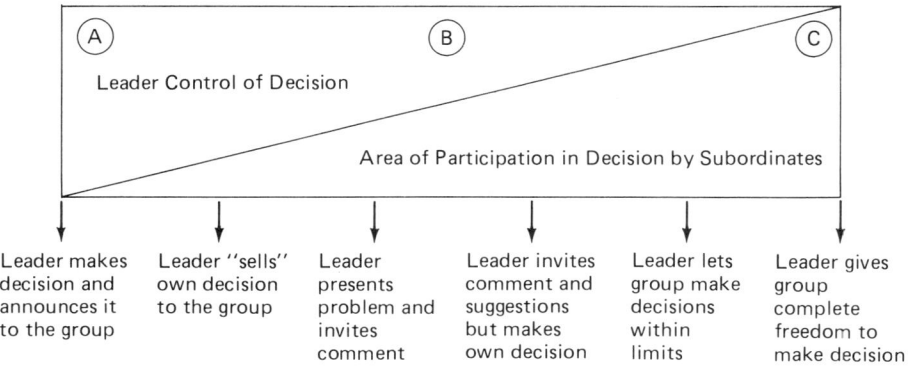

serves merely as a guide or resource person. The style of leadership that is appropriate depends on the person, problem, members, and circumstances.

## IMPROVING MEETINGS, CONFERENCES, AND COMMITTEES

Meetings, conferences, and committees are all similar in that they consist of a group of people meeting together for some purpose. A *meeting* is usually an "assembly" of people—a company or group. A *conference* is usually a representative assembly—that is, a smaller group than a meeting and representative of a larger group. A *committee* is also a body or group of people, but usually it is delegated to consider, investigate, or take action on some matter. Meetings, conferences, and committees can all become more effective if the considerations discussed previously in this chapter are considered and used when these groups gather.

### Meetings

Most meetings are run by a *presiding officer* who conducts the proceedings in a fair, impartial, and efficient manner. When presiding officers wish to engage in the discussion, they must leave or "step down" from their chair and appoint someone else to take it. They can then sit with the other members, secure the chance to speak like other members, and express their feelings on the topic as they wish. After the matter is completed, they resume control.

There are five criteria that characterize an effective meeting:

1. There is a common focus on content.
2. There is a common focus on process.
3. Someone is responsible for maintaining an open, even flow of conversation.
4. Individuals should be free from any personal attack. Ideas must be considered apart from personalities.
5. Everyone must agree on everyone else's roles and responsibilities. These should be clearly defined.[22]

Because group structure and leadership are necessary, as groups get larger the likelihood of chaos becomes greater. Thus, in large meetings, *parliamentary procedure*—the rules governing the proceedings of deliberative assemblies—should be followed to ensure fairness, equal representation, and orderly proceedings. It is not my purpose to present a list of such rules. It should be pointed out, however, when presiding officers do not understand parliamentary procedure, or when they have but meager knowledge of it, chaos can occur. It is advisable that parliamentary manuals be consulted for assistance if you are placed in charge of running a large meeting.[23]

Another required member of the large meeting is the *recording secretary*. Someone must keep accurate records of the business transacted. Recording secretaries prepare a written official record (minutes) of meetings, keep accurate records of motions, and maintain tallies of all votes taken. Usually recording secretaries are aided by members who submit written copies of the motions they make. Secretaries may also keep track of the time that a motion is debated *if* a time limit for debate is set.

When meetings become very large, a *sergeant-at-arms* may be appointed. This person's duty is to make certain no members become disorderly, and they are authorized to deal with those who do. In even larger meetings, security guards and local police may be used to help prevent trouble.

## Conferences

Conferences may be more formal than meetings and usually last longer. The formality does not result from stricter rules and procedures, but rather the planning that is needed to make it effective. A conference may last a full day, several days, even a week.

The essentials necessary for planning and leading a conference include determining objectives and considering purposes. Clear objectives build interest and help assure efficiency. Objectives may include sharing information, training, educating, problem solving, policy formulation, appointing or electing officers or administrators, or simply strengthening membership.

Another necessity in planning and leading conferences is deciding who should attend and then finding out more about those invited. In some cases a strongly homogeneous group is desired. In other cases, it may be decided that a heterogeneous group (consisting of dissimilar individuals) would ensure a more successful conference. It might be that individual differences could produce new insights or fresh perspectives. Once this decision is made, planners need to find out the conferees' level of knowledge, interest, desire to attend, skills, level of commitment, attitudes, and knowledge of or relationship with other participants.

Planners of conferences must also choose the appropriate format for the conference. Many formats are available. Some conferences begin with a general assembly; many also include committee meetings. Other possibilities include brainstorming groups, panel discussions, symposia, speeches and lectures, parliamentary debates, and forums, as well as informal learning or sharing groups.

The selected format may help determine where the conference is held. Certain sites may not offer the facilities that accommodate the chosen

```
              Business Conference on Communication Skills

Friday, October 23

      8:45 - 9:15    Registration
      9:15 - 10:00   Introductions
                     Keynote Address
     10:15 - 11:00   Panel Discussion on Interview Types and Skills
     11:15 - 12:00   Speaker -- Oral Reports
     12:00           Luncheon
      1:45 - 2:45    Executive Forum
                            Business Executives Discuss Communication
                            Needs
      3:00 - 5:00    Free Time
      5:00 - 6:00    Reception


Saturday, October 24


      8:45 - 9:00    Registration
      9:15 - 10:00   Exercises and Activities on Listening
     10:15 - 11:00   Lecture on Meeting Management
     11:15 - 12:00   Panel on Conflict Resolution
     12:00           Luncheon
      1:15 - 2:00    Desensitization Discussion and Exercises
                     on Speech Fright
      2:15 - 3:00    Guest Lecturer on Dressing for Success
      3:15           Final Assembly and Evaluation
```

**FIGURE 11-5.** A Sample Conference Agenda

format. Once a site and date are selected, the conference agenda must be planned and sent to participants. See Figure 11–5.

### Committees

A committee is a small group, but it is usually a small group with a specific task, mission, or charge. Committees are usually appointed from within an organization and, if effective, can overcome weak links or barriers in the formal communication structure of the company. The success of committees depends on the abilities of both group members and leaders.[24]

There are three kinds of committees: standing, special, and ad hoc. *Standing* committees are usually permanent parts of an organization and are assigned work to do on some regular basis. They relieve administrators of much of their work burden. Examples of standing committees include safety committees or personnel committees.

*Special* committees are designed to deal with a single and specific issue that cannot be handled within ordinary company procedures. The issue may be complex, controversial, or highly emotional. A special committee disbands after its work is done. Some examples of special committees include those assembled to deal with disciplinary action, policy review, or conflicts within the company.

*Ad hoc* committees are like special committees in that they deal with nonrecurrent, or one-time, special tasks. The difference is that ad hoc committees typically handle noncontroversial tasks. They are often smaller than special committees and do not necessarily represent the views of organization members. Members of ad hoc committees are often selected on the basis of interest or competence. Ad hoc committees may be assigned to draft a statement, inspect an item, arrange conference or convention facilities, or survey organization needs.

## DEALING WITH CONFLICT IN GROUPS

Since conflict has already been discussed, further coverage of the same material would be inappropriate. However, conflict possibilities increase proportionately with the number of people confronting each other. In addition, groups often treat sensitive or emotional issues; thus, the likelihood of conflict is increased. Effective group interaction must include successfully coping with conflict.

It is important that a win-win orientation be established and maintained. Conflict must be regulated, not eliminated. Abrasive action among group members can help to polish the final outcome. Skillful leaders must seek the free exchange of information and ideas but without unregulated conflict.

Leaders must avoid win-lose or lose-lose destructiveness. This is one of the most delicate and difficult areas of group deliberation. The key is effective communication. Members and leaders must encourage the generation of information without turning off or inhibiting members. Essential to this process are skills already discussed. The climate in the group must be supportive and constructive, and defensiveness must be avoided. Both data and feelings must be exchanged freely with the ultimate goal being mutual understanding.

## SUMMARY

Meetings, conferences, and committees are decision-making bodies. They are places of force and persuasion. Members who are prepared, direct, quick, and know how to use this communication forum are likely to be successful. This chapter lays the foundation for that knowledge and action.

In the first section, the advantages and disadvantages of groups were discussed. The value of groups in information exchange, morale improvement, and increased exposure were some of the advantages listed. Disadvantages of groups included the time factor, division of responsibility, watering down of decisions, and the possible conflict and competitiveness that can be generated. Some questions were provided that are key ones in determining if you should assemble a group.

Characteristics that are likely to affect all groups include their size, structure, personality, norms, and cohesiveness. Some of the essential elements of each were mentioned. These can serve as guidelines to help determine how groups should be formed. It is important to have as much information as you can when put in charge of group formation or deliberation. It should not be merely a chance effort. The more preplanning, the greater the likelihood of success.

In business, many groups are task oriented; thus, to know how to operate in a problem-solving or decision-making group situation is valuable. The process involves recognizing the difficulty, expressing feelings, describing the problem, developing solutions, and implementing the result. Each stage was discussed. The stages that describe the problem and develop solutions have numerous steps within them that help members achieve progress.

Groups are successful, however, because of people; the individuals who make up groups determine the group's success. In the section on membership functions, group task roles, group membership roles, and dysfunctional roles were examined. In the section that followed, leadership functions were considered. These included establishing the format, maintaining the direction, relieving tension, motivating members, and being an active participant.

Meetings, conferences, and committees were each discussed in separate sections since these are the major small groups that occur in business. A meeting is an assembly of people; a conference is usually a representative assembly of a larger group; a committee is usually delegated to consider, investigate, or take action on some matter. There are three types of committees: standing, special, and ad hoc.

The final section on dealing with conflict in groups was brief because a full chapter on conflict has already been offered. This section was a reminder first that a win-win orientation is essential. In addition, it reminded members and leaders of the need for a supportive and constructive group climate. It reinforced the need for the free exchange of both data and feelings. It also encouraged the reader to focus on the ultimate goal of group deliberation: mutual understanding.

## NOTES

[1] Frank Snell, *How to Win the Meeting* (New York: Hawthorn, 1979), p. xi.
[2] George C. Homans, *The Human Group* (New York: Harcourt Brace Jovanovich, 1950), p. 1.
[3] As cited in Susan Dellinger and Barbara Deane, *Communicating Effectively: A Complete Guide for Better Managing* (Radnor, Pa.: Chilton, 1980), p. 153.
[4] See Harold Zelko, *The Business Conference* (New York: McGraw-Hill, 1969), pp. 16, 24.
[5] Vincent DiSalvo with Craig Monroe and Benjamin Morse, *Business and Professional Communication: Basic Skills and Principles* (Columbus, Ohio: Chas. E. Merrill, 1977), p. 224.
[6] Richard C. Anderson, *Communication: The Vital Artery* (Los Gatos, Calif.: Correlon Publications, 1973), p. 29.
[7] Rollie Tillman, Jr., "Problems in Review: Committees on Trial," *Harvard Business Review*, 38 (1960), 6-8+.
[8] P. E. Slater, "Contrasting Correlates of Group Size," *Sociometry*, 21 (1958), 137–38.
[9] Robert N. Bostrom, "Patterns of Communicative Interaction in Small Groups," *Communication Monographs*, 37 (1970), 257–58.
[10] See Fred Edward Fiedler, *A Theory of Leadership Effectiveness* (New York: McGraw-Hill, 1967), p. 116.
[11] See Gary T. Hunt, *Communication Skills in the Organization* (Englewood Cliffs, N.J.: Prentice-Hall, 1980), pp. 136–37.
[12] An excellent example of how one individual coped with explicit norms is reflected in the story of John Z. DeLorean. See J. Patrick Wright, *On a Clear Day You Can See General Motors: John Z. DeLorean's Look Inside the Automotive Giant* (New York: Avon Books, 1979).
[13] Robert R. Blake and Jane S. Mouton, "Conformity, Resistance, and Conversion," in *Conformity and Deviation*, eds. I. A. Berg and B. M. Bass (New York: Harper & Row, 1961) as cited in Patricia Hayes Bradley and John E. Baird, Jr., *Communication for Business and the Professions* (Dubuque, Iowa: Wm. C. Brown, 1980), p. 158.
[14] Leonard Berkowitz, "Group Standards, Cohesiveness, and Productivity," *Human Relations*, 7 (1954), 509–19; Stanley Schachter et al, "An Experimental Study of Cohesiveness and Productivity," *Human Relations*, 4 (1951), 229–38.
[15] Charles R. Milton, *Human Behavior in Organizations: Three Levels of Behavior* (Englewood Cliffs, N.J.: Prentice-Hall, 1981), pp. 232–33.

[16]David W. Johnson and Frank P. Johnson, *Joining Together: Group Theory and Group Skills,* © 1982, pp. 256–58. Adapted by permission of Prentice-Hall, Inc., Englewood Cliffs, N.J.

[17]For a complete catalogue of roles, see Kenneth D. Benne and Paul Sheats, "Functional Roles of Group Members," *Journal of Social Issues, 4* (1948), 41–49. Used with the permission of Kenneth D. Benne. For a condensed version of this article, see Michael Burgoon, Judee K. Heston, and James McCroskey, "Communication Roles in Small Group Interaction," in Stewart Ferguson and Sherry Devereaux Ferguson, *Intercom: Readings in Organizational Communication* (Rochelle Park, N.J.: Hayden, pp. 333–36).

[18]See Allan D. Frank, *Communicating on the Job* (Glenview, Ill.: Scott, Foresman, 1982), "Successful Participation," pp. 260–62.

[19]The following functions are discussed in John J. Makay and Ronald C. Fetzer, *Business Communication Skills: A Career Focus* (New York: D. Van Nostrand, 1980), "The Question of Leadership," pp. 53–60.

[20]John Brilhart, *Effective Group Discussion,* 2nd ed. (Dubuque, Iowa: Wm. C. Brown, 1974), p. 29.

[21]From Harold P. Zelko and Frank E. Dance, *Business and Professional Speech Communication,* 2nd ed. Copyright © 1965, 1978 by Holt, Rinehart and Winston. Reprinted by permission of Holt, Rinehart and Winston, CBS College Publishing.

[22]Michael Doyle and David Straus, *How to Make Meetings Work: The New Interaction Method* (Chicago: Playboy Press, 1976), p. 32.

[23]There are numerous excellent parliamentary manuals. Some that might be consulted include: J. Jeffrey Auer, *Essentials of Parliamentary Procedure,* 3rd ed. (Englewood Cliffs, N.J.: Prentice-Hall, 1959); John W. Gray and Richard G. Rea, *Parliamentary Procedure: A Programmed Introduction,* rev. ed. (Glenview, Ill.: Scott, Foresman, 1974); Henry M. Robert, *Rules of Order Newly Revised* (Glenview, Ill.: Scott, Foresman, 1981); Alice F. Sturgis, *Sturgis' Standard Code of Parliamentary Procedure,* 2nd ed. (New York: McGraw-Hill, 1966).

[24]See G. M. Price, "How to Be a Better Meeting Chairman," *Harvard Business Review, 47* (1969), 98–108.

# 12

# Oral Reports

It is a near certainty in business that one day someone will ask you to prepare a report for oral presentation to a group. A manager must give a report to superiors about the production schedule. A personnel director is asked to report to a group of department heads on tardiness or absenteeism. A department head presents information on safety standards to employees. An executive vice-president indoctrinates managers on company policies. A manger reports on the economic outlook to company officials. The company president offers the annual progress report to the board of directors. A business employee lends expertise to a local civic group by presenting a report on current investment conditions. What happens when *you* receive such a request (or assignment) will depend on your personality, experience, and knowledge.

In this chapter a definition of the oral report is discussed first. Following that, a step-by-step development pattern is presented. The third major section treats the delivery of the oral report and, closely connected with that, the stage fright, anxiety, or nervousness that normally accompanies delivery. A means for handling these feelings will be offered. In the final section, a method for evaluating your oral effort will be examined.

## DEFINITION

An *oral report,* in its broadest sense, is simply the presentation of factual information using the spoken word. This occurs daily in informal interactions throughout any business. Thus, employees of any company give numerous oral reports—most in routine, conversational situations. See Figure 12–1.

Formal oral reports require skill and care in preparation. They are designed to convey business information that assists in the decision-making function of management or to present solutions to business problems. Whether they are presented to inform or persuade (discussed in the next chapter) or for the purposes of good will, decision, or record, the speaker must try to show the relationship between the research, data, or findings presented and management objectives. Sometimes data are presented without recommendations; in other cases speakers may present the results of an investigation with corresponding recommendations.

In most oral reports, speakers must convince their listeners that the findings are significant and relevant as well as valid, reliable, and useful to the organization. Often, in working with information over a period of time, speakers get so involved with it that its significance and relevance—or its validity, reliability, and usefulness—are so obvious, or so assumed by the speakers, that they forget that others do not share that same perspective. More on the role of the audience in oral report development in a moment.

Reports, whether written or oral, are keys to business success. They are the primary method by which objective information gets transmitted. Therefore, reports should be communication in its finest and most effective sense.

## DEVELOPMENT

People approach the task of speechmaking in different ways. As noted in the opening of this chapter, this may result from their personality. Extroverts generally love the spotlight. Because of their outgoing personality, they thrive on being the center of attention and welcome opportunities to speak. Introverts, being more reserved and withdrawn, do not relish being

**FIGURE 12–1.** The Oral Report. Although many of the characteristics of highly formal oral reports can be used in informal situations, the care and skill required to prepare the more formal reports underscores their need for study.

Informal Oral Reports
(routine conversations)

Highly Formal Oral Reports
(speeches or lectures requiring care and skill)

in the limelight; thus, for them, the request or assignment of an oral report is more traumatic. Most people fall somewhere between these two extremes. Although they do not cringe in horror at the thought of giving an oral report, they do become apprehensive about it.

How people approach the task of speechmaking may also relate to how much experience they have. There is no question that people improve as they gain experience. Further, they also find methods for developing speeches unique or peculiar to themselves. It is a good idea to adapt methods to your own needs. But how you adapt is often determined through practice. Practice does not make perfect; however, it certainly aids improvement.

How people approach public speaking is also dependent on their knowledge: (1) knowledge of the specific topic, and (2) knowledge of development techniques. The more people know about what they are going to speak on, the more confident they are likely to be. Development of the speech is likely to be easier; things will seem to fall into place naturally and comfortably.

How much people already know about speech development will also have an effect. Developing an oral report is a rather obvious process. That is, the things one must do to achieve success are logical and clear. When you think about it, they make sense. The more we know of these methods, the more likely they will appear instinctive. But often people think the methods are instinctive because they already know them through reading, using, or observing them.

This section will discuss the various aspects of speech development. Separate sections will treat the audience, purpose, obtaining information, and organization. Remember as you read that your perspective on each of these will be affected by your personality, experience, and knowledge.

### Audience

There is one essential feature that the oral report shares with all forms of communication: To be effective, it must "get through" to the listener. Thus, speakers must be concerned with the necessary background that needs to be provided, terms that should be defined, and how the thoughts would be best arranged.[1]

To get through to listeners is not something that automatically happens because people speak. Listeners understand because speakers do things to help them understand. What speakers do comes under the general category labeled *audience analysis.*

What is audience analysis? It is the process speakers engage in when they attempt to discover everything they can about their listeners. Areas that are important include (1) audience attitudes toward you, (2) audience attitudes toward the topic, (3) audience interests, beliefs, and values, (4) their intelligence, knowledge, and background, and (5) factors that surround the speaking situation itself.

An *attitude* is a feeling we have toward something. Audience *attitudes toward you* involve your credibility: How likely is it that you will be believed? Does your audience perceive you as competent? Sociable? Composed? Extroverted? Of high character or good reputation?[2] Do they trust you? And, too, how do you conceive of your position in this oral-report situation? Often, how you are viewed is in part a result of your role: Are you the boss? An authority? A superior? A salesperson?

How interested your audience is in the topic may also be a factor because *audience attitudes toward your topic* will affect how long you need to spend on a topic, how many facts or opinions are necessary, or how you should arrange your ideas. Your audience's interests or attitudes may also help direct you in choosing material. You may need more, or less, attention-holding material.

*Audience interests, beliefs, and values* are also important factors. What are your listeners' interests? When listeners are *interested* in something they give it their special attention. Are they the ones who will be directly affected by your ideas? If you are talking about using a new computer program, are they the ones who will benefit most? Can you tie your ideas to these benefits? Speakers must show listeners that their ideas will make a difference to or benefit them.

A *belief* is a conviction of the truth of something. We believe when we examine the evidence that supports something and feel that it is true. Beliefs are important to audience acceptance of speakers' ideas. How could you convince managers that a new advertising campaign should be introduced if the managers did not believe in advertising? But if increased sales records could be provided that coincided with the introduction of each new advertising campaign, perhaps reluctant managers could be swayed. Additional evidence might be that the new advertising could save sales presentation time by providing vital information currently offered by the sales staff. How many other facts could reluctant managers be given? Changes in the product, a new fad or value that could be appealed to, or new competition might be additional kinds of evidence.

*Values* have to do with what is important, useful, or worthwhile to us. Is the reputation of your company important to you? Is saving time useful to you? Would it be worthwhile to assign a new project to a study committee? Even this last item might depend on the value you place on committee work as a whole. Can you relate your ideas to things audience members value?

To know what motivates the audience can help speakers in slanting their material. Some listeners may be interested in money, others in status, still others in power. To know this helps when speakers relate their report to management objectives. Find out the impelling (controlling) needs of audience members; find out the attitudes and values that seem to guide their lives; find out what it is they want most. More on this in the next chapter on persuasion.

*Audience intelligence, knowledge,* and *background* will give you useful information. To know whether an audience is generally bright or dull, plain or sophisticated, can help speakers determine what level the oral report should be aimed at. Audience members do not like to be talked down to nor do they want material that passes over their heads. If *intelligence* cannot be determined, speakers should strike some reasonable middle ground.

Intelligence should not be confused with *knowledge.* People can be highly intelligent and unknowledgeable, or very knowledgeable and not terribly intelligent. Determining knowledge level will help speakers know if their audience is informed, uninformed, or misinformed. It will help them determine how much background needs to be provided and what jargon, if any, needs to be defined.

*Background* has to do with the total of a person's experience, knowledge, and education. Cultural background would involve such traditions as customary beliefs, social forms, and material traits of a racial, religious, or social group. When speaking, do you alienate certain audience members by not acknowledging their background? Using ethnic jokes, racial slurs, religious barbs, or sexual innuendo can unintentionally (or intentionally) alienate audience members and thus should be avoided. On the other hand, inclusion of audience members can be fostered by recognizing various background differences.

Audience analysis also must include an examination of the *speaking situation itself.* There are several factors that contribute to the makeup of the occasion. *Facilities* are an important consideration. Have you ever been annoyed because you had to stand, you could not see, it was too hot or too cold, or there were distracting noises going on while an oral report was being delivered?

How about *time?* Do you get annoyed when a speaker is late? Are you disturbed when speeches are too long? Are there certain times during the day when you find it easier to concentrate? What about the timing of this oral report with reference to other events that surround it?

This latter question on time also relates to *context.* There are situations surrounding every event that influence it to some extent. Have others spoken on the same topic either today or at some previous time? Have other speakers already created a mood, or generated feelings, that will affect your audience members? What current events bear on your speech? Are you presenting an idea that will require greater financial commitment in a time of economic hardship? Audience analysis that includes sensitivity to the present situation is more likely to be effective, immediate, and responsive to audience members' current state—how they are responding in the present speaking situation.

Earlier in this section I suggested that you should find out all you can about your audience. You might wonder what more is there. The status of listeners would be important. Who they are with respect to status may determine what the stakes are for you. Their influence may determine who else might be affected by your presentation. People talk to other people. Their age, sex, and background might help you in selecting examples or in choosing relevant and interesting information. As a final item, consider any peculiarities your listeners might have. That is, every audience is different. To know what makes this audience different can help you tailor your presentation even more while avoiding potential embarrassing or troublesome areas.

**Purpose**

Knowledge of the audience allows speakers to shape and mold their presentation at all points in the development of it. That is, to know the audience allows audience members to be an integral and important aspect of the speech, not just an element superficially considered or rather carelessly appended after the fact. That is especially true when one's *purpose* is established. What speakers need to know is what they hope to accomplish in their presentation. It follows the old saying that if you don't know where you're going, you might end up somewhere else.

In defining their purpose, speakers need to consider whether they want to (1) increase understanding, (2) change attitudes, or (3) get action. They may also wish to accomplish two or even all three. In a speech to increase understanding, the goal is to have listeners know something they don't know now. If it is to change attitudes, speakers may want audience members to adopt a certain feeling about a project, an idea, a department, an organization, or even themselves. Finally, if they want them to get action, they want them to do something as a result of the presentation: to adopt a proposal, increase the budget, extend a deadline, or sign a petition.

The point is, what you want your audience to do is an important part of speech development. If you don't know, or if you are unclear, how do you expect to get the intended result?

Once you have your purpose, write it down. Now check to see that it is

1. Specific—phrased in concrete, clear, and active words.
2. Measurable—offered in a way that you know when it is achieved. You got (will get) results to know that you achieved your purpose.
3. Realistic—have you limited your overall scope so that you can do what you plan to do in the time you have? Often, speakers bite off more than they can chew.

With respect to realism in your purpose, this is where your audience analysis can be especially important. When you know your audience, the question becomes: what can you reasonably expect to accomplish with *this* group of people? Are they decision makers? If not, you can hardly ask them to make a decision. How much background information do they need? You cannot ask them to change an attitude or take action if they have an insufficient knowledge base. Can you enlist their support to help influence the real decision makers? There is no way a purpose can be discovered without using your audience analysis to help shape and mold it.

It is best to state your purpose in sentence form. In that way you can check to make sure it is clear, complete, and not overly long.

**Weak:** Absenteeism over the period 1979–1983.
**Strong:** Absenteeism has decreased over the period 1979–1983 primarily because of worker incentives, improved conditions, and the demonstration of direct supervisory concern—to the point now where absenteeism is no longer a company problem.

The first version is general and incomplete. The second, although a little long, tells that the speaker will be trying to increase audience understanding; sets off the main points of the speech; and even presents the conclusion. It is useful because it can guide the speaker in obtaining information.

### Obtaining Information

Many speakers would probably go out and secure information, adapt it to the audience, and set forth a purpose. One problem with this has been pointed out: The audience is not an integral part of the development. But now an even more significant problem arises. Without a purpose, speakers may end up doing far more work than necessary or required. The purpose statement narrows the focus. If it includes the main points, as in the example above, speakers know exactly what they should be looking for. That is, during the process of obtaining information they can allow their selective attention to draw them to significant, relevant, and interesting material.

Speakers, however, may not be able to formulate a specific, narrow, fully developed purpose without having obtained some information. In those cases some preliminary investigation may be necessary to gain the broad picture. Speakers must be flexible enough to accommodate the various needs that arise. It may be that the three first stages of development are combined into one and are performed almost simultaneously.

Since most presentations you are asked to give will relate to your job, you really need little advice on where to find information. Knowing where to obtain it is a job responsibility. Personal experience, then, becomes an important resource. How much do *you* know? Other sources for obtaining information include your direct observations, reports that are on file, other printed materials, the knowledge and experience of associates, superiors, and subordinates, as well as data stored on computer tapes and microfilm. Some information you may have to gather by using information-seeking interviews, discussed in Chapter 9. Some may result from meetings or committees called to pool information.

In addition to these resources, your topic or purpose may call for additional information beyond immediate availability. For example, you might have to do library research, conduct a survey, arrange for interviews outside your organization, consult newspapers or magazines, listen to radio and television broadcasts, or even send away for specialized commercial or government publications. Most of the time information will be available to you within your organization, and it will be your job to get it. A well-organized filing system that allows you to preserve factual data as it arises is a major asset.

You are also responsible for the logic and validity of the evidence you present. Just because information is available does not make it correct. Not only can you double-check it for accuracy, you can also consult more than one source for the same information. Any one source of information (including your personal observations) may be inaccurate or biased. Thus, by increasing the number of sources you consult, you reduce the possibility of inaccuracy and bias.

As you prepare, a certain degree of ruthlessness is necessary. Ernest Hemingway once indicated that any writer must have a well-tuned, well-honed "crap detector." His point was that there is so much information available that you must be sensitive to that which is irrelevant and worthless. Only those items that relate specifically to your purpose, and to your audience, should be included. Everything else—no matter how fascinating or unusual—must be ruled out.

Intense, thorough preparation has several benefits. First, it aids self-confidence. You will feel better, stronger, and more in control. Second, it will help when it comes to the next stage of development: organization. The organization patterns needed or strongest for the material you have collected is often a natural outgrowth of it; that is, it is almost dictated by it. Third, it increases speaker flexibility. With more information at your fingertips, you can adapt to the specific, immediate needs of your audience as you are delivering your speech. (More on this in the section on delivery in this chapter.) Fourth, it activates the creative process.

*Creativity* is not usually something you do—it is something that happens. For example, you are working on a presentation and suddenly you find facts and ideas leading to other facts and ideas. A way to begin the report occurs to you just as a way to illustrate a set of statistics seems to pop into your mind. Words, examples, and relationships originate spontaneously, freely, almost without apparent effort. This is creativity at work. It is like a mysterious, driving force that propels you unconsciously.

It is because of this force that you must be prepared to benefit from it. *Preparation* is the first step of the creative process. It is the foundation upon which the other steps are built. Although creativity normally follows the steps briefly outlined here, it is important to understand that creativity cannot be regimented, confined, or predicted. That is, it is always working. As you drive to work, eat lunch, go to bed, shave, or apply makeup, the force is at work. (One business person told his secretary to hold all calls. "I'm on a creative binge," he said.) Prepare a file in which all ideas can be placed. Take a pencil and paper everywhere you go; be ready to respond to those momentary, fleeting ideas. An idea not captured is often an idea lost. You think it will return but it doesn't, or when it returns it is in a different form than when originally produced—but not as strong or effective.

The second step in the creative process is called *incubation*. When you engage in preparation you must allow plenty of time between the gathering of information and the delivering of the report. Part of this time is for incubation to occur: the time your subconscious needs to deal with the material. You have probably experienced it. You are working on a project for your boss and no ideas come to you. You put it down and go off to lunch. When you return from lunch and turn your attention to the project, you cannot believe your productivity. Suddenly, without explanation, the ideas flow.

You have given your mind a rest period following intensive involvement with the project. It is during the rest period that incubation works. Your mind mixes, interrelates, synthesizes, even generates new information. When this happens at night, it may wake you up. Having a pencil and paper on your nightstand may help you capture the product of incubation.

The product of incubation occurs in the stage called *period of insight*. This is when the solution, the decision, or the proper relationship results. "I have the answer," might be a typical response. These insights happen anywhere and anytime and need to be captured and recorded. If we allow the time for incubation, insights will surely follow.

But insights often come to us ineptly phrased, slightly inaccurate, or poorly supported. The final stage of the creative process is *revision*. When the insight comes, we must be willing to take the time to phrase it clearly and accurately, to check it for accuracy, establish its logic and validity, and find support for it. The revision process is the time to polish and perfect the product. It is often a process we cut short because of "not enough time," and yet when increased understanding, attitude change, or action are at stake, we must consider the importance of revision—to look over our product again for the purpose of correcting and improving it.

## Organization

There is no rule that dictates when preparation ends and organization begins. Sometimes it is an intuitive feeling—a feeling of comfort or confidence. Some researchers say, "You should gather *three times* the amount of material that you will actually use."[3] If your purpose is clear (or has been clarified as you have been gathering material), you have probably been organizing your material as you have been working. To organize your material is to arrange it into a coherent, unified, functioning whole. It is the difference between a jigsaw puzzle dumped onto a table from its box and one that has been put together.

Your purpose will help you structure your report. It may even dictate the main points. See Figure 12–2.

*Main points* are usually assertions or generalizations. They make a point but, left to stand alone, they have no support or substance by themselves. Thus, once you have selected your main points, you must think about how you plan to substantiate them.

Support for main points takes several forms. The more variety you can find, the more likely you will catch the attention of your audience and hold its interest throughout the speech. In a report, much of the support comes from *facts*. A fact is a piece of information that has actual existence: It can be observed. ("There has been a drop in absenteeism in our unit.")

*Statistics,* another form of support, are statements of fact presented in numerical form. "The drop in absenteeism across units over the past year has been 23 percent." *Expert testimony* involves statements made by people who qualify as experts or authorities in given areas. ("According to Bill Swift, personnel director, the drop has occurred because of a significant

**FIGURE 12–2.** The main heads of the report support the speech purpose. There should be a direct and obvious relationship. Again, this reaffirms the need to write out the speech purpose early. The clearer and more specific it is, the easier it will be to formulate the main heads of the report.

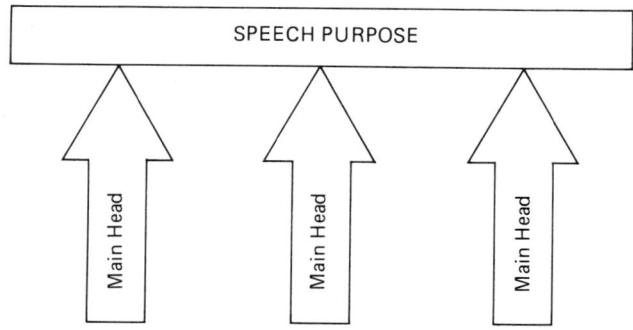

concern over job security. People do not want to take the chance of losing their jobs.")

Additional support comes from *examples,* particular incidents or instances used to illustrate, clarify, or explain an idea. An *illustration* is an extended example. *Personal experiences* are examples or illustrations that come from a speaker's private background or knowledge. See Figure 12–3.

What support has to do with organization must be clear, for it forms the substance or body of the report. How it is arranged may make a difference in how it is received by the audience. It influences both their attention and interest. It may also affect their retention because listeners tend to recall material placed either first (primacy) or last (recency) in a speech. How much time a speaker spends developing a point may also affect the importance that point may have in either the speaker's mind or in listeners' minds.

Supporting material proves, clarifies, and adds interest to main points. Thus, supporting material is subordinate to the main heads. (See Figure 12–4.) Now, the shape of the report is beginning to emerge.

**FIGURE 12–3.**

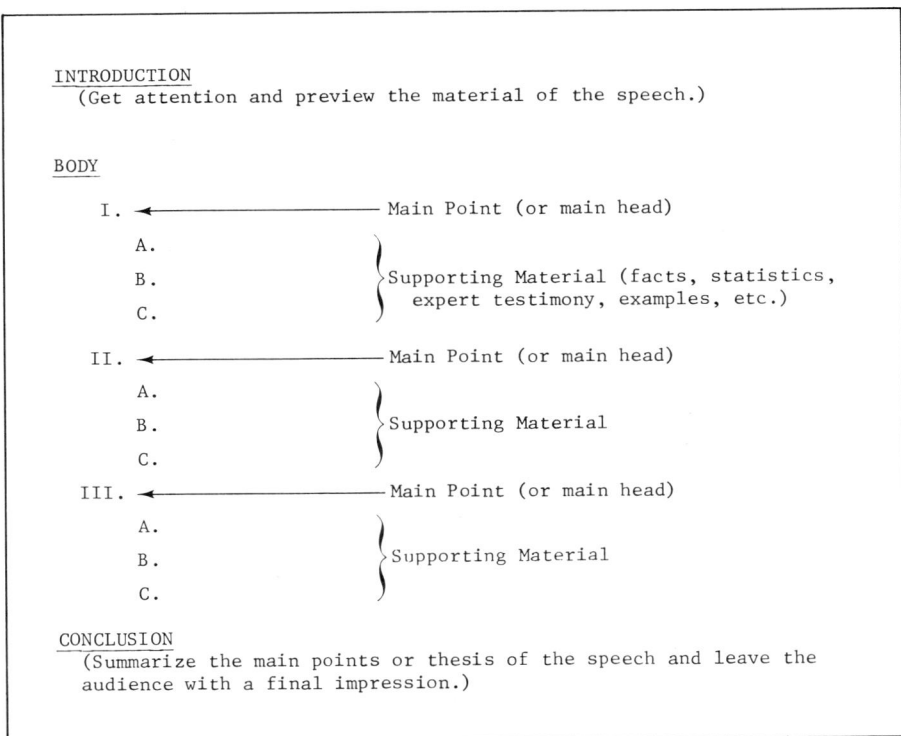

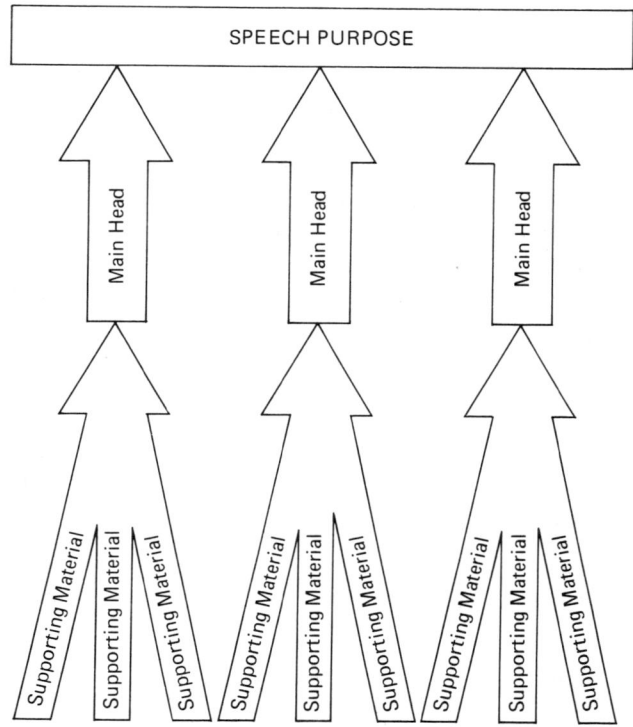

**FIGURE 12-4.** A main head may be supported by one or more pieces of supporting material. If one main head is supported by three pieces of supporting material, that does not mean that others must be supported by the same number. Supporting material could be facts, statistics, expert testimony, examples, illustrations, or personal experiences.

An important part of organization, too, is the relationship among the main points of the speech. A unified approach results when the main points are parallel with each other (have identical grammatical parts). And a unified approach also results when you consistently follow one of the different kinds of outline patterns. The most common is the *topical* pattern. When you have a topic like absenteeism and break down the main points into incentives, conditions, and supervision, you are using a topical pattern: the use of parallel topics.

There are several other useful patterns for reports. If the main points follow an historical or time sequence, a *chronological* pattern may be the most useful pattern. A *spatial* pattern is useful if the main points follow a physical or geographical arrangement. This might occur if you were reporting on the main parts of a photocopier: moving from the feed mechanism, to the control panel, to the way the copy mechanism operates, and finally to the output or collating mechanism. A *cause-effect* or *effect-cause* sequence works if the main points deal with antecedents, determinants, or reasons for certain results, or states the results first then moves to what brought about the event, circumstances, or conditions. *Problem solution* is another possible pattern. This will be discussed in the next chapter.

*Transitions* aid the organization by tying ideas together and helping to unify the report. In some cases a transition is just a word or phrase, a signpost that the speaker is moving on to another point. Examples are: "Next," "Second," "Further," or "In addition."

Transitions can also be *internal summaries:* "I have told you that absenteeism has decreased because of worker incentives, and because of improved working conditions, now let me show you how direct supervisory concern has also contributed. . . ." An internal summary, then, is both a flashback and a flashforward.

The final type of transition relates the material in the speech to the speech purpose. "Thus, you can see that improved working conditions have helped decrease absenteeism. . . ." It holds the report together because it keeps audience attention focused on the ultimate outcome.

Many speakers do not realize the need for transitions in oral reports. The main function of transitions emphasizes one of the essential differences between oral and written reports (to be discussed in the forthcoming section on delivery), namely, oral communication is a one-time event and listeners need help in understanding the material. Just because a speaker says it does not mean listeners will understand it. Transitions help keep listener attention focused on the location and direction of speakers: where they have been, where they are, and where they are going.

### Introduction

Most reports include a beginning, middle, and end. Surprisingly, the introduction (beginning) is best prepared last. It is only after the entire presentation is developed that speakers really know for sure what they plan to do. That is, the introduction should relate to the entire effort, but often it is incomplete when prepared first. To have to go back and adjust it may be a waste of valuable time.

As speakers prepare introductions, they should keep in mind the need to reach out and grasp listener attention, or the corresponding need to call attention to their subject. Speakers can spark attention by asking a rhetorical question, such as "Do you know what our new program can mean to you?" A startling statement can capture attention—"The most recent survey we have shows that we now have over 70 percent of the market share." Using a quotation also can be effective: "Kennedy said, 'Ask not what your country can do for you—ask what you can do for your country.'" Using a personal anecdote or story may work well. ("I am an alcoholic. I have a disease that is continuing to grow in business circles. There is no cure. But there is help.") Likewise, an illustration can be used: "When Sally Merchant, our top salesperson, asked little Tommy, who answered the door at the first call she made last week, whether he had heard of us, here is what Tommy said. . . ."

These are a few ways to get audience attention in the introduction. Others include referring to the occasion—"Today is the most important day in our history. . . ." Reference to the subject also may work, as in "You may not have heard of 'scoping it out' before, but you are about to now. . . ." When audience members are referred to, they are certain to pay attention—"Most of you heard the speech by our company president, and most of you were impressed. You should have been, because you were responsible. . . ." A personal reference also can be effective: "I, too, began my career as a salesperson. Do you know who received my very first sale?" A personal greeting can work, too, as when a speaker says, "I bring you the very warm, best wishes of management. . . ." Obviously, many possibilities exist; which ones to choose depends on your audience, subject, occasion, and resources.

An effective attention-getter also will stimulate interest in the subject. In some cases it may be helpful to reveal the speech purpose and main points of the speech in the introduction. Revealing the main points first is a process called *previewing, initial partition,* or *advance organizer,* and it serves as a guide to the speech. Also, it can be referred back to as the speech progresses to keep the speech unified.

**Conclusion**

Because your listeners are likely to remember what they heard last, the final impression you make is important. Your speech should not just end; rather, it should refocus attention on your purpose and main points. It could also make a special appeal to listeners for a specific response: to take action, for example.

There is no set way to conclude a speech. Many speakers forget that all of the techniques that could be used as attention-getters in the introduction can be used, too, as impression-makers in the conclusion. As they discover stories, personal experiences, quotations, and illustrations for the body of the speech, speakers need to plan ahead to preserve an impressive one, or two, for the conclusion. So many speeches fall flat because speakers have not had the foresight to plan their conclusion carefully with making that final, lasting impression in mind.

The point to remember is that the conclusion offers a final impression. Since it is the last thing listeners hear, it is the most recent thing in their minds when they leave your speech. This is the recency effect. It should make a clearly memorable impression, and it can if it is well planned with that in mind. Add a new piece of knowledge that expands even more what has been discussed in the speech. Make your appeal for comprehension and retention through the use of memorable material. Notice how this speaker draws a speech on suicide to a close. She is alerting business colleagues to the rise and importance of suicide in business circles:

> When you examine all these demographics, your most likely suicide victim will be a white male who tends to be over thirty and who may be an alcoholic, a homosexual, or divorced. Although I have provided the major clues that tend to predict suicides—verbal indicators and behavioral giveaways—most clues are recognizable only in retrospect. The key to treating potential suicide victims is availability: They need our understanding, our patience, and our respect. Many of us could help lower the suicide rate by becoming more involved with our co-workers. Can we help others feel understood, wanted, and needed? Can we help others find reasons for living? I wish I had known last year what I have shared with you today—maybe then I wouldn't have lost my best friend to suicide.

## DELIVERY

A close relationship exists between content and delivery. If you have analyzed your audience, gathered effective material, clearly defined your purpose, and organized your information, all this work can be nullified, virtually destroyed, if the delivery is ineffective or weak. Strong delivery of poor material is a sham. Weak delivery of strong material is a casualty: too often a speech is injured, lost, or destroyed through ineffective delivery.

In this section speech anxiety (stage fright) will be discussed. Written versus oral style, types of delivery, and the need for both flexibility and feedback will also be examined. The purpose here is not necessarily to make you an expert. Rather, it should help make you comfortable enough so that you can capitalize on your own talent and ability.

### Speech Anxiety

To experience nervousness before making a speech is both common and natural. But there are some things speakers do to help reduce this nervousness. There are few even experienced speakers who do not feel anxiety, or who do not do certain things to help reduce it. There are no panaceas, no sure-fire cures—just a common-sense approach that works under most normal conditions.

First, know your material. There is no substitute for knowing your material well. Not knowing it well has many drawbacks, including lack of confidence, uncertainty, and a sense of hesitancy, to name but a few.

Second, practice before the event. The more you practice, the more confident you will be. Use a mirror, tape recorder, video recorder, or any device that will encourage practice. Deliver the speech in the place where it will be given, in a sound booth, or in the shower. Don't be choosy; just *practice*.

Third, seek feedback. If you can get others to listen to your speech and to provide feedback, this will also be useful. It gives you important ways to adjust. It helps assure you that you are on the right track. Moreover, it provides an audience to perform before. Positive, constructive feedback is best, but any feedback is better than none.

Fourth, look at the speech situation as a cooperative one. Think of it as a time in which ideas will be shared. Listeners intend no harm. They want to hear you. They are supportive. If you cultivate the idea that you have information that will help them in some way, this will result in greater motivation to speak.

Fifth, be bold. Assume a "take charge" attitude. Strive to be assertive in the actual speech situation. State your concern clearly. Involve your audience. Assure them that you are satisfied with your approach, belief, or solution. Notice, in the conclusion by the speaker talking about suicide, how she said she wished she had the information earlier—letting her audience know she thought she had good, useful, practical information that could help even her. Another speaker, addressing a group of salespeople on developing trustworthiness, said, "Believe me, it is kindness, safety, friendliness, and pleasantness that develop trust between you and another person. Those are the precise qualities that got me off the porch and into the house when I was involved in a sale. You all know that you can't sell a product from the doorstep. You have to develop trust, and you have to develop it quickly."

Plan your ending (as indicated previously) carefully. End as if you are still in charge. That is, do not allow your speech to taper off. Make your ending strong and impressive. And make certain the final moments are crisp, clear, and to the point. Notice, once again, how the woman speaking on suicide concluded her speech. She knew what she planned to do, and she executed it skillfully.

Sixth, assume that you *can* make a difference. You must believe in what you are doing. Know that you have something to say, and that what you have to say can make a difference in the lives of your listeners. Believe that they really care and that because they care, there is an exciting possibility for improvement and change. If you don't believe this, it is unlikely you will get anyone else to believe it! Concentrate on your audience.

Seventh, keep active. It is the idle mind that gets into trouble. When we let our imagination dwell on past negative experiences or potential negative outcomes, nervousness and anxiety increase. Being active helps keep you optimistic and energetic.

Eighth, seek as many occasions to speak as you can. The more experience you get, the more improvement, self-confidence, and control you gain. The better you become at dealing with audiences, the more you will look forward to being in front of them.

Ninth, be flexible. Be willing to alter plans, change routine, or take a different approach. Life is not static. The effective speaker needs to stay loose. With experience, confidence, and an adequate reserve of material, flexibility should be no problem. It will allow you to be responsive to any situation that should occur. Do not allow the plans you make to be set in stone—unmovable, unshakable, and unalterable.

Tenth, do not be too harsh with or demanding of yourself. Nobody is perfect, and you cannot expect that of yourself. Remember, too, that your listeners do not expect perfection. If you forget your place, drop your notes, or say something you shouldn't, simply take care of the situation naturally but quickly, and continue as if nothing happened. Most listeners are forgiving and understanding; most also have short memories.

Finally, just before or during your presentation, take some deep breaths to relax your muscles. Gesture and move naturally and comfortably during the presentation to help channel your nervousness. Concentrate on developing a responsive expression that will reflect changes in emotions and sensitivity to audience responses. A frozen face is a serious barrier to communication because the face is a mirror for meanings, and a frozen face inhibits these meanings. Moreover, a frozen face usually is a clear sign of fear.

Gestures include the movement of hands and arms as well as posture and body movement. The goal of effective gestures is action that supports and advances the speech. It is a secondary support system designed to reinforce and underscore the words. The time to concentrate on effective gestures is during practice, and that effort should be focused on how gestures can punctuate and clarify your ideas. During the speech itself, your attention must be devoted entirely to your ideas and to your listeners.

**Written versus Oral Style**

The languages of writing and speaking differ. Sentences are longer and more complex when we write. We use short, simple sentences when we speak. We tend to be formal when we write, using statements, for the most part, and a straight (rather conservative) approach toward the topic. When we speak, we use more variety: questions, exclamations, and commands. Our approach toward topics can be more dramatic and colorful. In writing, we avoid repetition. If the reader needs to reread, he or she can go back over our material. But in speaking, since it is a first-time, once-only event, we must provide the repetition—both for increasing understanding and for emphasis.

There are advantages to an oral presentation over a written one. It is a personal situation. We can make our ideas clearer because of our use of vocal inflections, pauses, forcefulness, facial expression, and gestures. We also may have the advantage of immediate feedback from our audience. In that way we can adapt specifically and directly to our audience as we proceed. We have the advantage, too, of utilizing the full impact of our personality. Our vitality, credibility, and persuasiveness can have an effect on the success of our communication. Our friendliness, warmth, and genuine interest can also be demonstrated. Finally, oral communication is conversational and informal. We can use personal pronouns such as "I," "you," and "we," and we can also use colloquialisms and slang that may be common to the listeners or situation. Thus, it personalizes communication by placing our unique stamp on the message: "This is mine. It is intended for you."

**Types of Delivery**

There are four types of oral delivery, and in certain cases a combination of some of these types is used. In this section, the impromptu, extemporaneous, manuscript, and memorized types will be briefly discussed.

*Impromptu* speeches just happen. Someone asks you to make a few remarks, provide your reaction, or offer your suggestions or observations. An impromptu speech is one that is composed or uttered without previous preparation. It is distinguished because of its spur-of-the-moment nature.

As you gain more expertise in what you do, you will find impromptu speeches less threatening. This is because not only are you likely to command a large body of facts, but also with experience and knowledge often come self-confidence and poise. We not only feel better about the knowledge we command, but we also feel better about ourselves. Orienting new employees, giving on-the-job instructions, and responding to requests for information are examples of impromptu speeches. You are at work and your boss introduces you to a new employee. He then asks you to provide the employee with an introduction to the company and to the employee's new responsibilities.

Other opportunities for impromptu speeches occur in meetings. A report is given on a new product, a campaign, or approach, and a supervisor asks you, right there on the spot, "How do you think this will affect you and your division?" Time for an impromptu speech!

*Extemporaneous speaking* occurs when speakers carefully prepare their speech but deliver it from notes. Extemporaneous speaking preserves the directness and spontaneity of impromptu speaking but adds to that some of the preparation and documentation of memorized and manuscript speaking. Using this type, speakers prepare, outline, and, using notes, they practice their speech. But the exact wording is neither written down nor memorized. Although the ideas are well planned and structured, the words for the ideas occur spontaneously at the time of delivery of the speech: vivid realization of the ideas at the moment of utterance.

There are many different methods that can be used for delivery using an extemporaneous mode: the following is one possible method. After developing a complete outline, reduce the outline to key words. See Figure 12–5. Place these key words on several cards. Allow your words to be different each time you practice from the key-word outline so that when you get before the audience you will have several ways to phrase each of your ideas. To know the key words will help keep you from having to refer to your notes too often—something that can become distracting. With enough practice, you will come to know the key words well. It also increases your flexibility because it allows you to be in full, direct contact with your audience at all times.

*Manuscript* speeches require the most preparation next to the memorized type. In this type, speakers write out their presentation, then read it word-for-word. It is the best type for speakers to use when the subject is complex, controversial, or very significant. A public-information officer, representing an organization, may write out his or her ideas. Announcements to the press are often handled by manuscript. This assures careful wording.

Manuscript speaking has, however, several disadvantages. First, it often lacks directness with the audience. Speakers selecting this style should practice enough so that they can look at the manuscript about 10 percent of the time and the audience about 90 percent. There is no magic in these numbers; however, the point is that effectiveness in manuscript delivery comes from audience contact, *not* from manuscript dependence. Too often speakers use manuscripts as crutches when they do not know their material well enough. The 10 percent/90 percent formula drives

**FIGURE 12–5.**

Thesis: To gain personal power, you need to have a sense of time.

**OUTLINE (Body of Speech)**

I. Put "the monkey" where it belongs
   A. People want to put "the monkey" on others' shoulders.
   B. Personal power means putting "the monkey" where it belongs.
   C. We must ask for better treatment. (Personal example here.)
     1. Give a friendly fight.
     2. Ask for a better deal.
II. Eliminate the garbage of life.
   A. Stop waiting for others.
   B. Keep your priorities.
   C. Stop procrastinating.
   D. Evaluate everything.

**SPEAKER'S NOTES**

I. Monkey-shifting
   A. Others.
   B. Pers. power
   C. Example: "Come back tomorrow . . ."
II. Garbage
   A. Waiting
   B. Priorities
   C. Procrastination: Do it now.
   D. Evaluate everything: So what?

home the point that as the speaker increases the time he or she spends looking at the manuscript, the speaker takes time away from direct audience contact and, thus, effectiveness suffers. Speakers still should strive for vivid realization of the idea at the moment of utterance.

This is why this method—if used properly—requires so much preparation. Second, it may lack spontaneity and interest. Using a manuscript, speakers sound like they are reading, not conversing.

There are two additional disadvantages to manuscript speaking. Unless speakers are very familiar with their text, there is a strong likelihood of losing their place. Also, because the manuscript tends to be read rather than delivered freely, there is the possibility for decreased gesturing. Dependence on a manuscript tends to be inhibiting and restricting, and effective gesturing does not easily occur under these conditions.

*Memorized speaking* requires the most preparation of these four types. The material is learned by heart and, thus, committed to memory. It is an inflexible type because the words and sequencing of words are all planned. It is a useful style when the speaker is in a formal situation and full contact with the audience is desired. Perhaps the most common use of this type is when a speaker must introduce another speaker, accept a gift or an award, or make a presentation. When the speech is short, when the situation is precisely defined, and when the words that are to be said are important, a memorized presentation may be appropriate.

### Flexibility

Delivery is more than words and various vocal and bodily cues. Delivery is really a synthesis of all elements: It is the effective use of all factors in the conveying of ideas to listeners. And for delivery to be effective, it requires *flexibility*.

Flexibility is just one aspect of mastering ourselves. A flexible speaker is capable of responding or conforming to changing or new situations. Only in this way can a speech be interesting, spontaneous, appropriate, and direct.

Monitor your intentions and your behavior so that you are conscious of what you want as well as what you are doing. As Plato said, "The life which is unexamined is not worth living." This increased sensitivity will help you gauge how you are adapting. New information is found, a better way of saying something is discovered, or a useful insight about the audience is revealed. All require adaptation—flexibility. Realize that nothing is sacred (unchangeable); thus, everything can be varied, adapted, or made more appropriate. And this can occur from the moment preparation begins up to and including your delivery of the material before the audience.

## Feedback

Effective speakers are amazingly sensitive to the nonverbal cues of audience members. Facial expressions as well as body position and movement are signs to watch for approval and interest or disapproval and boredom. Even with a large audience in an unlighted auditorium, sensitive speakers receive feedback. Should I eliminate some material? Should I quicken my pace? Should I draw this example out? Should I pause for effect?

Feedback involves not only the response speakers get from audiences but also the adaptation they make to the response. And it is the response—even if it is an indication that everything is fine—that creates immediacy with an audience.

*Immediacy* is the feeling we get when we are a direct part of an event that is unfolding before us. When speakers adapt to feedback, audience members feel they are an important part of the effort. Speakers thus reach out and touch listeners (to use a cliché), and rapport is established. When there is rapport, there is a feeling of relationship between speaker and audience—harmony. And through feedback, rapport builds on itself in cyclical fashion. The better the audience feels, the better speakers feel about what they are doing, and when they feel better, they make audiences feel better. See Figure 12–6.

Thus, positive feedback begins when speakers have important messages to share and when they really believe in their message. In their delivery, then, they adapt that message to the particular audience in such a way that listeners feel the immediacy of the situation.

## EVALUATION

No matter how effective we are, there is always room for improvement. If our intent is to grow, change, and develop, then evaluation must be part of the whole process.

Sometimes the evaluation can occur as part of the immediate question-answer period following many oral reports. Often speakers can gauge their effectiveness by the nature of the questions asked. Did listeners understand? Did they listen well? Do they accept my position? My information?

Take advantage of any feedback you get from listeners. If you can ask for advice or suggestions, this can add to your improvement. It is often surprising how willing people are to share their insights with you when you ask—that is, when you place yourself in the role of learner or student. Feedback from a trusted associate may be even more valuable.

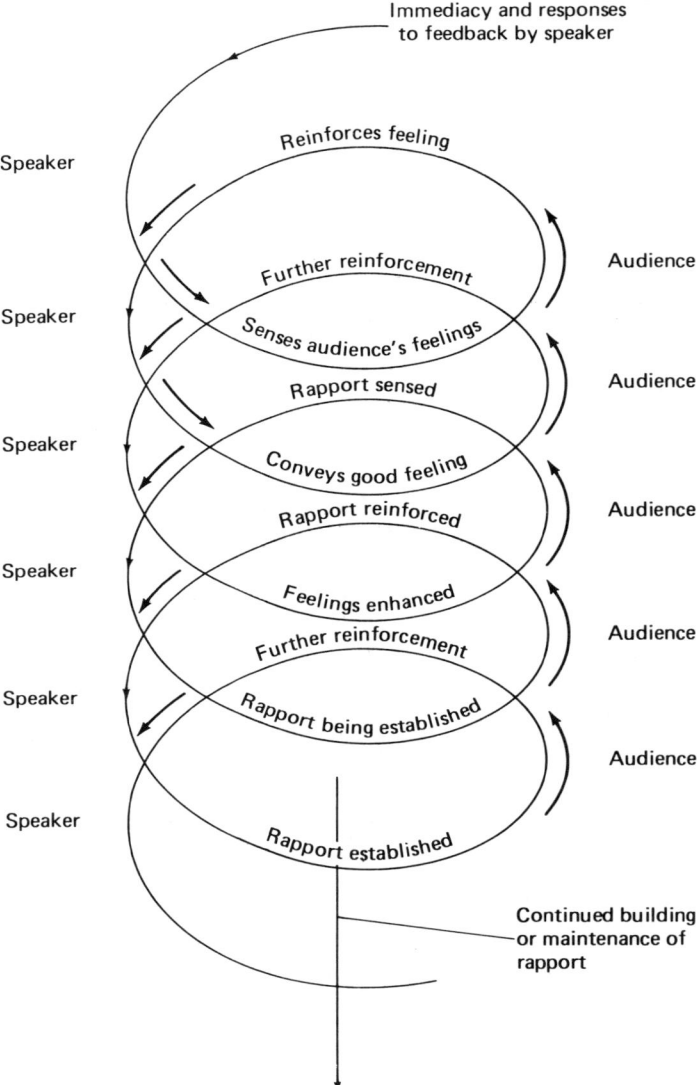

**FIGURE 12-6.** The cyclical building of rapport from feelings of good will. The cycle begins at the top.

### SUMMARY

Whole books have been written on the oral report process, for it is an important part of business. This chapter considered the definition of oral reports, their development, delivery, and a brief note on evaluation.

Oral reports are the primary methods by which objective information in business gets transmitted. Although there are both informal and formal oral reports, formal ones require skill and care in preparation and formed the focus of this chapter.

Various aspects of speech development were discussed. Speakers should adapt the suggestions and ideas presented to their own needs. Development was discussed with respect to analyzing the audience, obtaining the information, discovering the purpose, and establishing the organization.

As part of the section on obtaining information, speakers should be sensitive to creativity. The four steps of creativity—preparation, incubation, period of insight, and revision—can be an important aspect of oral-report development. It can help take an ordinary report and turn it into an outstanding, memorable event.

In organizing speeches, speakers must be concerned about main points, support for main points, transitions, introductions, and conclusions. Most organizing begins as one begins the development phase and continues (or is likely to continue) right up until the speech is delivered. To support a speech, speakers use facts, statistics, expert testimony, examples, illustrations, and personal experiences. The desired outcome is a coherent, unified, functioning whole.

Speech anxiety (stage fright) is a major element in the delivery of a speech. Other elements include the differences between written and oral style, and types of delivery. Speakers can choose between impromptu, extemporaneous, manuscript, and memorized types. Finally, the need for both flexibility and feedback in delivery was emphasized.

In evaluating our oral-report presentations, we should be concerned about improvement. We must learn to improve by learning from our failures (or weaknesses) and building on our successes. Seeking feedback helps us grow, change, and develop.

This chapter offered a foundation for the next one. Persuasion often takes place as a result of a base of information; that is, listeners need information before they can be asked to change their beliefs or to take action. Hence, persuasion is the subject of the next chapter.

## NOTES

[1]Roger P. Wilcox, "Characteristics and Organization of the Oral Technical Report," *General Motors Engineering Journal*, 6 (November–December 1959), 8–12, in *Readings in Interpersonal and Organizational Communication*, 2nd ed., eds. Richard Huseman, Cal M. Logue, and Dwight L. Freshley (Boston: Holbrook Press, 1973), p. 509.

[2]James C. McCroskey and Thomas J. Young, "Ethos and Credibility: The Construct and its Measurement After Three Decades," *Central State Speech Journal*, 32 (Spring 1981), 24–34.

[3]Susan Dellinger and Barbara Deane, *Communicating Effectively: A Complete Guide for Better Managing* (Radnor, Pa.: Chilton, 1980), p. 199.

# 13

# Persuasive Presentations

Persuasion is a natural part of business transactions. Whether it takes place in letters, interviews, small groups, or large assemblies, the principles are the same. When your goal is to influence and modify another person's behavior, your goal is persuasive. Through persuasion you are able to get decision makers to approve your suggestions, proposals, and recommendations. Through persuasion you are able to influence your superior's perceptions and evaluations of your job performance. Through persuasion you can also get people to buy a product.

In this chapter, the term *persuasion* will be used synonymously with *influence*. It will be used with reference to both formal and informal situations: speeches as well as day-to-day contacts. The chapter begins with an examination of attitudes, beliefs, and values. Then, in separate sections, emotional support, logical support, and support from credibility will be discussed. A persuasive organizational pattern will be presented as part of logical support. Then in the final section of the chapter, ways to resist the persuasion of others will be mentioned.

**ATTITUDES, BELIEFS, AND VALUES**

Erwin Bettinghaus defined *persuasion* as "a conscious attempt by one individual to modify the attitudes, beliefs or behavior of another individual or group of individuals through the transmission of some message."[1] Using his definition as a base, then, we are interested in intentional persuasion that affects attitudes, beliefs, and behavior. Values must be considered as well because attitudes and beliefs are centered in one's personal values.

### Attitudes

You are sitting in a meeting and a colleague raises the idea of beginning a campaign to enhance employee morale. You immediately respond, "I think the idea is sound. The feeling seems to be spreading that things haven't been going very well lately. I have sensed a certain complacency in employees." How did you respond in that way? Because of attitudes you hold toward employee morale. Attitudes are simply predispositions that cause you to think, feel, perceive, or behave in a certain way. Attitudes are usually aimed at an object, situation, event, issue, or person. In the above example, your attitude was directed toward the issue of employee morale. Attitudes usually have a direction, degree, or intensity. In this case the direction seemed to be one of support, the degree or intensity "strongly favorable." Attitudes, too, are learned responses. That is, we acquire attitudes through all the same means that we have for learning: our experiences, the experiences of others, reading, listening, seeing, and sensing. Attitudes are generally stable and enduring. That is, they differ from whim and fancy. An attitude is more substantive.

Substantiveness cannot easily be determined since attitudes are internal states, but the separation of whim and fancy from more in-depth responses may be easy for each of us to feel. For example, a co-worker tells you about how a problem was solved and asks you for a response. You say, "Sounds all right to me." Although there could be a solid, substantive base for this reaction, many such responses are based on whim and fancy—much as you would respond to someone who said, "How's it going?" and you respond with, "Fine."

Substantiveness engages our thinking processes. If a co-worker told you about a program of advertising and direct mailings designed to get better attendance at various industry meetings, and this matter touched you directly, you can see how your experiences, the experiences of others, as well as your reading, listening, seeing, and sensing might lead you to a more substantive response, such as, "Good idea. Let me see what you have in mind before we begin the program."

Communication researchers have identified three dimensions of an attitude. First, there is the *cognitive* dimension. That consists of the knowledge connected with objects, events, issues, situations, or persons. It is our information base. Second is the *affective* dimension. It consists of the feelings we have about objects, events, issues, situations, or people. The affective dimension is our emotional base. Finally, there is a *behavioral* dimension. That is, the cognitive and affective (our knowledge and feelings) often lead to action.

In the above example of employee morale, your knowledge is based on what you have experienced. It may also have resulted from talking to some employees. Your feelings may have been formed as a result of seeing productivity lessened. It could be that you noticed less employee commitment to their jobs. You know how that can affect your unit; thus, you are (or may be) directly concerned and involved.

These cognitive and affective dimensions serve as springboards to action. That is, with your knowledge and feelings, you may want to serve on a committee that formulates the campaign. You may want to promote it to others who have more power and authority to support it. You want to take action.

**Beliefs**

Attitudes come from *beliefs*. Beliefs are more deeply rooted than attitudes. They represent acceptance of information on both a mental and emotional level; we experience an internal state that acts as a degree of faith. ("I believe that management is basically good.") When you can precede a statement with "I believe . . . ," you have a belief.[2] Beliefs, just like attitudes, also have cognitive, affective, and behavioral dimensions. That is, beliefs are rooted in knowledge, feelings, and behavior.

Beliefs can be classified. At the center of Figure 13–1 are beliefs we accept because we have been socialized or enculturated to accept them. That is, we have been taught to respect our elders, to be courteous to others, and to support our country. These are beliefs reinforced by our family, the mass media, and what we see going on around us. *Enculturation* is the process by which we come to learn, accept, and even model the concepts, habits, skills, art, instruments and institutions of our culture. Some people are frugal—they carefully watch their finances—because they were raised in a frugal family. Belief in a particular religion or political party may result from *socialization*. The next ring represents *personal* beliefs. People may believe in honesty because of a run-in with the police early in their lives. They may believe in the value of automobile seat belts because a close relative was saved when using them.

At the third level are beliefs that result from *trust*. A friend convinces you that your vulgar and profane language is having a negative effect on your associates. An associate with whom you work has made you realize, by the model provided, that a clean, orderly desk is a virtue in your company.

At the next level is *authority*. Your doctor convinces you to stop smoking because of the belief in the harm it is doing to your body. Your boss has changed your belief in what "being on time" can mean to image, prestige, even promotion.

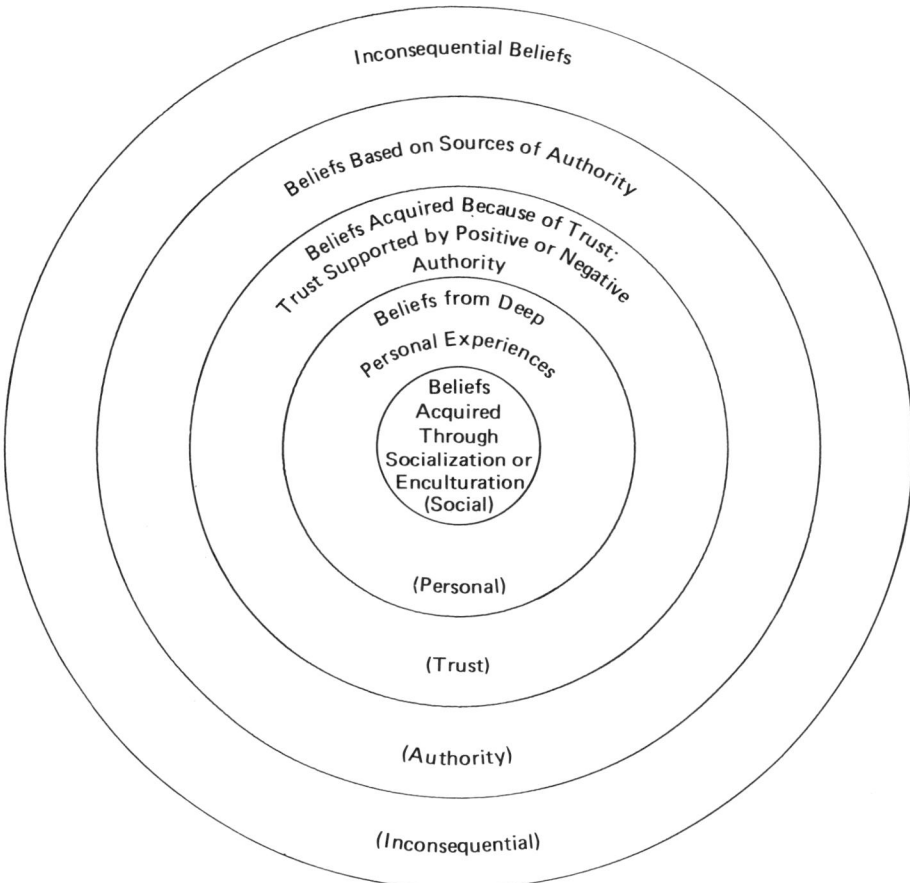

**FIGURE 13-1.**

In the final circle are *inconsequential beliefs*. You may believe that giving to charity is a good thing even though you may not do it. An office worker asks for a couple of dollars for a good cause. You give, realizing, of course, that everyone else has given, and whether you give or not may have an effect on your acceptance by colleagues. Inconsequential beliefs are beliefs that we hold but that do not really make a big difference to us. They do not really guide our lives, except, perhaps, momentarily, and they make little difference. Inconsequential beliefs might include believing that industrialized societies should help less industrialized ones, that the Presidency has become too powerful, or that people lack knowledge about nutrition. In most cases beliefs such as these do not touch your life directly, and yet they are still there.

**252**  *Persuasive Presentations*

Beliefs may move between the circles, but movement tends to be outward, not inward. Although I may have had a deep personal experience, I may find that trusted friends, even authorities, may deny or discount my experience until finally I am convinced it was unique—a "fluke"—and I determine that it is really inconsequential. Even socialized beliefs can be changed. But notice that beliefs toward the center of the circle are more firmly entrenched; thus, they are less likely to be changed.

### Values

Attitudes and beliefs are centered in one's *values*. That is, one's personal value system is the very core from which attitudes and beliefs emanate. Just how much of a core values form can be seen in the definition. *Values* are central psychological anchors or deep-seated standards. They guide our ethical conduct and determine whether to approach or avoid things. We value learning as an essential for growth; thus, we believe in books and newspapers as sources of knowledge, and our attitudes, as well, support the value. We might value good health. Then our beliefs about eating properly would likely support that value just as our attitudes toward junk food would likely correspond. See Figure 13–2.

Values, then, are deep-rooted. They guide our beliefs and attitudes. Some values might be the value of relationships with others, the value of competitiveness, independence, free enterprise, or free speech. They are often enduring and quite stable.

**FIGURE 13–2.** Note from this diagram that normally we have a few core values, like valuing efficiency. From these core values, beliefs will emanate and are likely to be greater in number than the core values—like beliefs in time management and productivity. Attitudes will be even greater in number, like attitudes toward "to-do lists," being punctual, starting meetings on time. or procrastination.

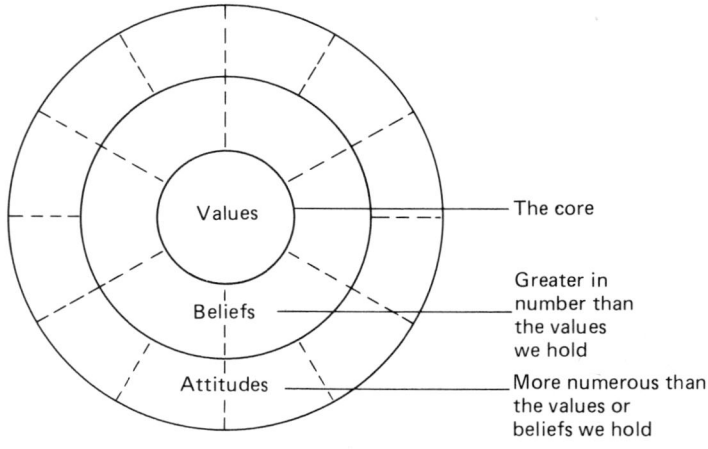

Attitudes, beliefs, and values are fused together—interrelated and interwoven. They not only reflect our personality but they also guide our behavior. They also affect our communication. Just as we are persuaded according to our attitudes, beliefs, and values, we persuade others according to theirs.

When we are persuading, we are not dealing with a blank slate. Rather, our words, whether written or oral, stimulate responses in readers or listeners that are part of this vast web (or system) of interrelated and interwoven attitudes, beliefs, and values. When a decision results from a persuasive attempt, it is likely to be based upon a vast array of interacting and interconnected variables (parts of the system). As much as we, as persuaders, would like to take credit for being persuasive, we must be realistic and view ourselves as part of a complex and highly individualized process.

For example, you are talking to a group of your committee members about getting to the meetings on time so that there will be more time for discussion. Notice in Figure 13-2 that attitudes toward getting to these meetings on time may or may not be rooted in a core value that has to do with "respect for time." For some, life is one big timetable with everything revolving around the clock; for others, time is not an essential value. As small as you may think the issue of starting meetings on time may be, in fact, the issue may be considerably more complex with roots that run down into core values that members hold.

Moreover, when you understand the nature and interrelationship of attitudes, beliefs, and values, you also understand the importance of audience analysis, discussed in Chapter 12. When you are dealing with change, and when the change desired is extremely important, the more you know about the attitudes, beliefs, and values of the persuadee(s), the more likely you will be successful.

## EMOTIONAL SUPPORT

Often, when people think of persuasion they think of a strong emotional situation. Persuasion and emotion seem to be closely linked. Emotional support, sometimes called *pathos,* refers to appeals a persuader makes to other people's needs, goals, or emotions. The purpose, once again, is to influence their attitudes, beliefs, or values and, thus, to influence their future behavior in some way.

*Emotional support* is the heart of persuasion. Persuaders, to be successful, must begin by asking the question, "What needs, goals, emotions, drives, or tensions can I stir up in these people that will motivate them to provide the response I want?" And their success at persuasion is likely to result from the proper link. That is, if I can link my proposal, suggestion, solution, recommendation, request, or item for sale with other people's needs, goals, or emotions, they are more likely to perceive the response I am after as desirable and will, likely, furnish it. The goal—not as simple as it sounds—is to motivate others to do what you want them to do.

For example, I am trying to get a company to pay a bill. I know that company (and the person I am addressing) is very concerned about its image. In the letter I write, I provide a clear deadline for payment, but I also add an additional statement. ("If this bill is not paid by November 1, a 'payment due' notice with complete explanation will be sent to Mr. Raymond Sontay, President, and Mr. Thomas Arons, Board of Trustees.") This would be contrary to that business's image-building goal, and might encourage payment.

In a sales presentation, as another example, a salesperson might indicate someone's concern for the education of his or her children as a basis for purchasing an encyclopedia. In a speech, a persuader might refer to the need for greater efficiency or productivity as a basis for purchasing a new piece of equipment.

**Needs**

People have many needs. These needs will vary according to the situation, other people, topic, and time. In one situation, for example, I might feel the need to express myself, but not in another. With some people I feel the need to be assertive, but not with others. On some topics I feel the need to be defensive (they affect me deeply), but on others the need is not present. At one time I feel the need to eat or sleep; at another time the need is not as great. As a persuader, the more I know about the various needs of those I want to persuade—especially as those needs relate to *my* goals—the more I can appeal to and depend upon them to help me.

Persuaders should know some of the major needs that motivate people. *Needs* refer to things requisite, desirable, or useful. They are not necessarily requirements or conditions that have to be relieved, but they could be. For example, most people need to *save time and effort*. Thus, appeals to effectiveness and efficiency often work. People need *adventure;* thus, appeals to get them to buy something new and different may be effective. People need *to have or know about what is new and current.* Appeals to their curiosity or to satisfying their quest for what is novel or "the latest" may work. People need *competition;* thus, appeals to excel or outdo others are often effective. People need *respect and admiration;* hence, appeals to what they consider to be worthy, or what they hold in high regard, can be effective. Sometimes this takes the form of imitation, and the appeal would be to what they consider admirable and imitable.

Other needs include the need to be *independent and individual.* Sometimes this appeal will take the form of what might make people stand out as unique. In other cases the appeal might be to what will allow them to make up their own minds. *Loyalty* is another need. Appeals could be made for allegiance to a group, faithfulness to other people, or a determination to help the organization for the benefit of everyone. *Personal enjoyment* is also a basic need, and a persuader could appeal to whatever might bring people pleasure, comfort, and relaxation.

People also have the need *to acquire money and material wealth.* Thus, appeals to their need to save, to become financially secure or independent, or to make wise investments are useful. And these needs by no means exhaust the list. Needs can be as unique and different as the people who hold them.

The point of this discussion is not to exhaust the list, but rather to sensitize you, as a persuader, to a variety of basic needs. For persuasion to take place, persuaders must (1) analyze readers or listeners to determine the dominant (commanding, controlling, or prevailing) needs, then they must (2) use those needs as the basis for the appeals employed in the persuasive part of the message. Persuaders must (3) use discretion and indirectness as the appeals are used. That is, most persuasion is subtle. Skillful persuaders consider their work delicate and elusive; they are perceptive and their techniques are refined. Like a surgeon, their skill is marked by keen insight and the ability to penetrate deeply and thoroughly but only to the degree necessary and only when necessary.

## Goals

A *goal* is an end toward which effort is directed. Most of your behavior is goal-directed. You engage in it to achieve an end. You do a job to get paid or to receive praise. You go to school to get a degree. You, as a persuader, can use others' goals as part of your persuasion, that is, to increase the likelihood that they will do as you wish.

Goals can be short-term or long-term. A respondent may want praise or recognition. These are short-term goals. Getting a raise or getting an account would also be short-term goals. Long-term goals might include achieving financial security, rising to the top of the organization, or satisfying one's philosophy of life. Other long-term goals could include helping to make an organization more responsive to human needs, or becoming a recognized, creditable spokesperson for a certain cause.

Goals can be the basis for emotional appeals. In some situations an appeal to short-range goals is most appropriate: "If we all get behind this project, I'm sure we can qualify for a substantial bonus at the end of this year." Sometimes, short-range goals lead to long-range benefits, as when a number of successfully completed projects lead to coordinate promotions. Also, short-range and long-range goals can be mixed.

As persuaders, we should make certain we show how our ideas tie in to our readers' or listeners' goals. Subtlety, once again, is important; however, as much as we recognize the link between ideas and goals, often readers and listeners do not. The guiding maxim (general truth or fundamental principle) should be: A link not made by the persuader is unlikely to be made by the respondent. That is, as persuaders, we should not assume that our listeners make the tie, complete the relationship, or take the intuitive leap we want them to take. Just because a persuader emphasizes the need for more personal and telephone contacts with potential buyers does not mean listeners will spend less time writing letters—which they are doing now—even though getting them to spend less time writing letters may be precisely the persuader's intent.

**Emotions**

When we think of the emotions we often think of being emotional: aroused or agitated in feeling. And persuaders should be sensitive to the need to arouse emotional states. But emotional states can vary dramatically from fear to love, or from guilt to affection. When effective persuaders use the emotions to gain an audience response, usually they make use of all the tools within their command: supporting materials, voice, body, and words. In a sense, they serve as a focusing element: a way to draw together all the potentially disparate elements. (See Figure 13–3.) Persuaders focus these elements to arouse the emotional state that will be most favorable for them to get the response they want. It could be altruistic feelings of charity, anger over injustices that have occurred, or sympathy ("poor so-and-so") for the plight of an individual or company.

Persuaders who use emotional appeals have (1) analyzed their reader or listener to determine which emotion (or emotions) would be most appropriate, (2) selected ways to arouse that emotion (or emotions), and (3) channelled that emotion (or emotions) to justify the response they are seeking. Once again, audience analysis is a crucial element. Further, they do not arouse emotions just for the sake of arousing them. They do it to get some kind of behavioral response: to give, contribute, help, cooperate, move, think, do. Readers and listeners are asked to engage in specific actions.

Some people might object to the use of emotional appeals suggesting that listeners should be presented with facts rather than with appeals to their emotions. This objection tends to be unrealistic. Emotion is one of the strongest motivators. Witness the effectiveness of advertising. Further, we cannot really distinguish between emotional and logical appeals. Emotions are internal states that occur within listeners; they are not part of the message.

If an audience understands a situation, reference to that situation in a logical manner can arouse a powerful emotional response. For example, a supervisor is addressing a group of salespeople who sell a coolant for large

Persuasive Presentations 257

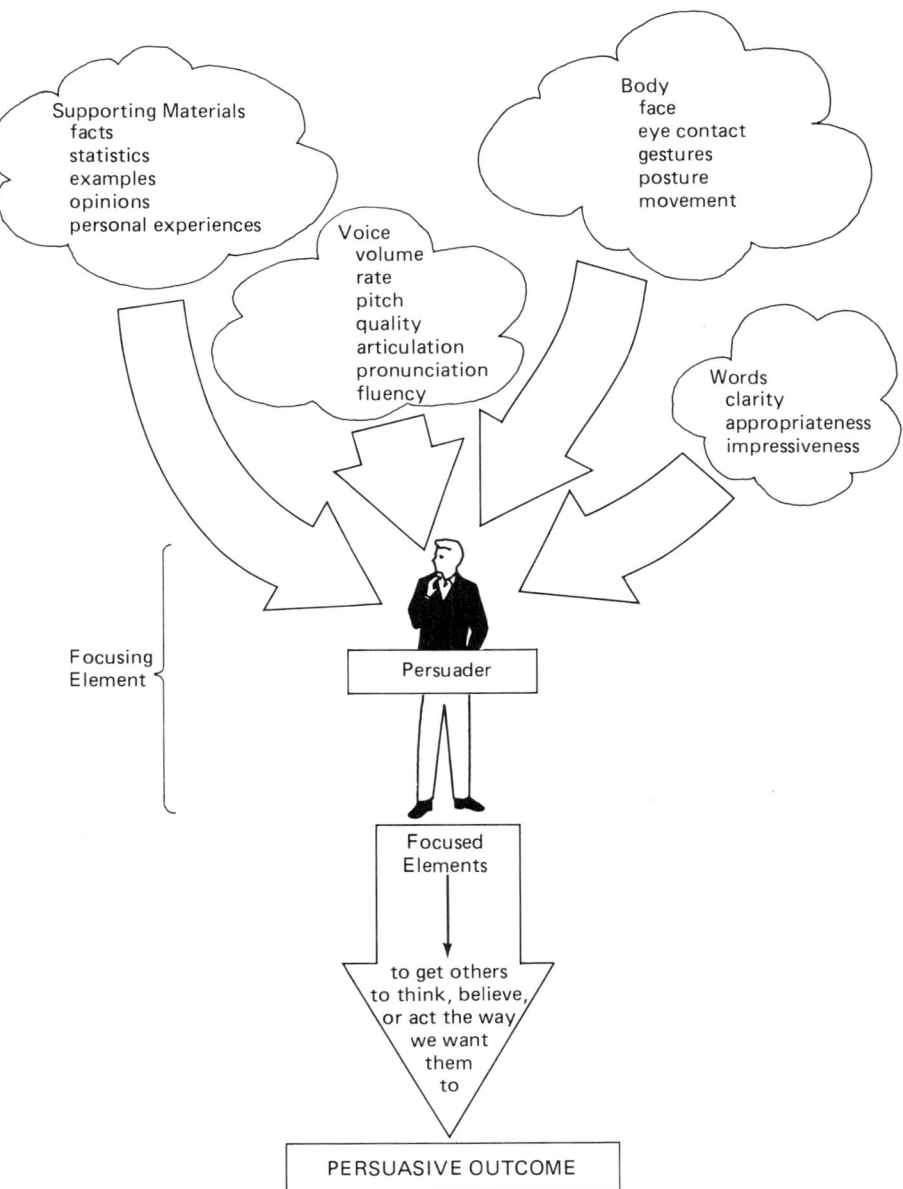

FIGURE 13-3.

machines. The supervisor logically explains a new pollution bill before Congress that is likely to render the coolant obsolete because of its significant contribution to pollution. Those salespeople quickly realize their jobs are in danger, since the coolant is their only sales product. Their adrenaline flow would be high. And yet the presentation is highly logical.

Often, persuaders can anticipate emotional arousal. It would be unethical for them to let sentiment substitute for reasoned judgment in making decisions. But it should be clear that there is nothing unethical about producing emotional responses in listeners. Think of the effectiveness, for example, of the supervisor in the previous example, if after producing this intense flow of adrenaline, he brought out and demonstrated the new antipollution coolant the company had just introduced.

The point of this discussion is that emotional responses can be a positive part of persuaders' planning. However, the best advice is that persuaders should aid listeners in arriving at fully informed responses; thus, emotional appeals are likely to be *part* of any approach—not *the* approach that is used.

## LOGICAL SUPPORT

One of people's basic needs is the need to believe that behavior is motivated by reason, not solely by emotion. That is, we need to believe that people do things for good reasons. Thus, in persuasion, something more than an emotional base must be provided. Emotional appeals often need logical underpinnings. Logic, sometimes referred to as *logos,* has to do with orderly, valid, cogent reasoning.

Persuaders must first analyze their audience. With the specific reader or listener (audience) in mind they can then formulate their purpose. In persuasion, a purpose statement is called a *proposition:* This is a simple declarative statement that clearly states the point to be discussed or what is offered for consideration or acceptance. It may or may not be stated in the actual persuasive presentation. Examples of propositions are:

> To have my listener finish the project on time.
> To get my reader to engage in negotiations at once.
> To encourage my audience to understand the company's position.

Once a proposition is framed, an intensive search for all available information to support it must be conducted. Remember to test your material for accuracy and recency. Go to a variety of sources so that information can be cross-checked. How do you know if a source is biased until you check it against other sources that say the same thing? Your search should be aimed at proving, clarifying, and adding interest to your main points, and these main points should directly support your proposition. Your intent is to get your audience to understand and remember your ideas—a logical response, or a response to the logic in your speech.

### A Persuasive Organizational Pattern

Because of its popularity and effectiveness, an organizational scheme for arranging the ideas of a persuasive problem-solving presentation should be strongly considered by persuaders. Its popularity can be measured by its mention and development in communication textbooks. Its effectiveness can be seen in its use by teachers, but even more so in its use by advertisers in commercial messages on television. It is called the Monroe Motivated Sequence, or simply the Motivated Sequence, and it was introduced in 1935 by Alan H. Monroe.[3] It works because it follows the normal process of human reasoning. The five steps of the sequence are: (1) attention, (2) need, (3) satisfaction, (4) visualization, and (5) action.

### Attention

At the outset of a persuasive presentation, persuaders need to be concerned about *attention:* (1) how to grasp it and (2) how to focus it on their topic. Why should a reader or listener be concerned about the topic?

### Need

Persuaders can show one of two kinds of *need:* (1) a need to change the status quo (present conditions), or (2) a need to change nothing—to keep conditions the same or preserve the status quo. For the first kind of need, persuaders must make the receiver dissatisfied with existing conditions. For the second kind, they must heighten receivers' satisfaction with the status quo.

A four-step sequence helps to organize this part of a presentation. First, state the need clearly, indicating what is wrong with present conditions or pointing out the danger if present conditions are changed. Second, illustrate the need by revealing incidents that clarify it or giving examples that demonstrate the problem. Third, reinforce the need by using additional facts to make it impressive. This part should clearly address and answer the question: How serious is this problem? Fourth, persuaders must point up the need by showing its specific and immediate importance to this particular receiver. How does the problem affect him or her?

Notice how the following persuasive speaker utilizes these four steps. She is speaking to a group of downtown business people about one of several special promotions designed to increase interest in her city as a convention site:

People don't think of our city as a convention site; thus, compared with other cities, we are losing a great deal of money. Notice, for example, when sites were chosen for the following conventions [she names several], our city was not considered. And yet a city just to our north *was* considered in each case. In the last seven years, our city has had 932 conventions. These brought 706,000 visitors who spent a total of $94 million. The record number of conventions during that period was 181 in one year when 122,000 visitors spent $31.1 million. But those figures, as low as they are when compared with other cities our size, have now tapered off. We are talking about money in *your* pockets. And when the demand tapers off, we are talking about money that is *not* in your pockets.

### Satisfaction

Persuaders should *satisfy* the need by presenting a solution. They need to state the belief or action being proposed. It must be explained clearly. Also, they need to show how it logically meets the need. There must be a clear and logical (valid) relationship between the need and the proposed solution to that need. How the proposal takes care of the problem is the main question that must be addressed and answered in this section.

Notice, once again, how the previous speaker satisfies the need:

> You may wonder what we can do to change our city's image among convention bookers. Here are some of my suggestions:
> —We will run "familiarization" tours for selected groups and individuals who can bring the highest results in visibility to our regional and national associations.
> —We will directly solicit conventions to our convention center, especially events that require multiple facilities and exhibit or banquet space.
> —We will increase our contacts with local members of national, regional, and state organizations to encourage groups to meet in our city at some future date.
> —We will sponsor luncheons for corporate department heads here to acquaint them with what our city has to offer them and to generate more support for future convention business.

To state a solution without sufficient support may weaken its potential acceptance. Thus, persuaders may wish to cite examples, facts, statistics, and opinions to reveal the soundness of the solution and its likely acceptance.

### Visualization

*Visualization* is one of the most important steps of the sequence and one of the most overlooked. Its purpose is to intensify audience desires for the proposal. Visualization, taken literally, will encourage the receiver to form a mental image of conditions—what they would be like—if the proposal were already in effect.

What would future conditions be like if the proposal were carried out? What would they be like if it were not? Here, persuaders could also contrast bad effects with good effects.

Once again, notice how our speaker, who is trying to help bring more conventions to her city, uses visualization:

> It isn't hard to imagine the results of such a campaign as this. The first, and most obvious, result will be a rejuvenation of our downtown area. There will be increased activity here.
>
> A second outcome will be increased sales. The more conventions, the more conventioneers buy. Not just room rents and food, but souvenirs, clothes, and other merchandise as well. Local concerts, dramatic events, and sports activities are likely to also benefit.
>
> A third outcome will be increased interest in further building and promotion of our downtown area. Interest generates interest. With our hotel and motel rooms near capacity from Thanksgiving through March, we will generate more interest to others in a growing, vital city.

The power of visualization in the sequence comes from creating a vivid, convincing, mental image. Persuasion occurs in the receiver. After all, that is where meaning lies. Thus, persuaders are really trying to get receivers to persuade themselves. With a mental image that is powerful and plausible, the likelihood of persuasion occurring becomes more realistic.

### Action

Persuaders capitalize on the creation of this vivid mental image by calling for a specific, definite, and concrete *action*. They do not leave action to chance. The action step channels and focuses the previous activities or processes toward a concrete outcome. This, after all, is what the persuader has been working or building toward.

The convention advocate has a powerful and direct action step as well:

> You may be wondering how you are involved in all of this. Obviously, you are. And obviously, too, such results are not magical; they don't just happen by themselves. Our city Convention and Visitors' Bureau cannot do it alone; we want to assist you—and we need your assistance as well.
>
> First, in all of your business contacts, we want you to include promotional material on our city. We have packets and mailers that include "I Love Our City" postcards and reprints of articles about our city.
>
> Second, we want to assist local organizations with membership drives. We will provide letters signed by the president of the Chamber of Commerce and the director of the Convention and Visitors' Bureau.
>
> Third, we want you to run city-oriented giveaways such as badges and posters. These can all be provided to you at no cost.
>
> Fourth, we want you to offer rate reductions and other special incentives during the Thanksgiving to March low-occupancy period.

Notice how our speaker outlined specific kinds of action. She was direct and to the point. If she had some of the promotional materials there to show her audience, this would have effectively reinforced her final points.

To see and understand the strength of this total, five-step sequence, apply it to the advertisements you see on television. You will find that it applies to most of them. As you do so, you will also find it easier to remember the various steps.

Getting a proposition, finding supporting material, and determining the organization for a persuasive presentation can be viewed as the logical foundation of the persuasive speech or letter. Superimposed on that base is the emotional support—which can also be part of it when you consider choosing supporting material for its emotional impact—and the persuader's credibility.

## SUPPORT FROM CREDIBILITY

*Credibility* has to do with the character (the aggregate of distinctive qualities characteristic of a person) of the persuader in the eyes of the reader or listener. It is sometimes referred to as *ethos*. It isn't what you've done, but what a reader or listener knows (or thinks about) what you've done. It isn't what you do in the speech or letter, but what a listener or reader thinks about what you do. There are two kinds of credibility: (1) What others know *before* this persuasive presentation or *extrinsic* ethos, and (2) What you do *within* this persuasive presentation to enhance your credibility, or *intrinsic* ethos. Thus, what credibility you bring to a situation is only half of what counts; it may be zero if the other person knows nothing of you. The other part is what happens within the encounter itself.

To show the difference, and what can happen as extrinsic and intrinsic interact, let's assume a well-known company executive writes you a personal letter. He enjoys high credibility because of what you know about him. But the letter is full of errors, inaccuracies, and an aggressive or dogmatic style that offends you. The intrinsic ethos counteracts the extrinsic and results in a negative impression. It shows, then, how credibility can be eroded during a persuasive encounter.

Credibility is composed of five separate dimensions.[4] They are presented here because of their importance in the persuasive process. Competence, character, sociability, extroversion, and composure will each be briefly discussed.

### Competence

Competent persuaders have a high level of expertise. That is, they know their topic well. This may come from their formal education, technical training, or vast experience. They appear to the reader or listener as trained, qualified, informed and authoritative. When you hear that someone has written numerous books and articles, is the president or chief executive officer of a major corporation, or has served for a number of years in his or her position, you assume competence. They often convey intelligence—people who have reasoning ability and a level of common sense. One quality highly prized in the world of work is the ability to deal with problems on a daily basis. And the extent to which this can be done with a balanced perspective—the avoidance of extremes—is also important to competence.

### Character

Character is an aggregate of distinctive qualities. Appearing trustworthy is an important part of character. Trust is often conveyed by persuaders through their kindness, friendliness, and pleasantness. Also, does a listener or reader feel safe with the persuader or safe regarding his or her ideas?

Honesty is another aspect of trustworthiness and, thus, character. Do persuaders have a reputation for being truthful and accurate? This would be a factor in extrinsic ethos. It shows the value of maintaining a good reputation.

Sincerity is another element in trustworthiness and character. Persuaders must believe in what they are writing or saying. Only when they sound like they believe in or really care about what they are saying, can they inspire belief in their listeners or readers.

Keeping promises is also important for persuaders. "Giving one's word" cannot be taken lightly. When you promise a subordinate to take action on a complaint or request, or when you pledge your cooperation on a proposal, you must follow through. Politics aside, not to follow through can result in a loss of credibility; following through on such promises and commitments helps build credibility.

Although following through on one's promises and commitments certainly builds a politician's credibility, there are many other factors that affect it as well—including immediate and sensational events—so that commitment or promise fulfillment is but one factor in the politician's ability to get reelected. Politicians often operate within a different arena in which a different set of criteria apply.

### Sociability

Persuaders who reflect sociability come across as warm, friendly, and pleasant. These same traits convey trustworthiness in others. Sociable people are those with whom companionship appears attractive. We like them, and we are generally more easily persuaded by them.

Sociable people also exhibit a concern for others, a feature that makes them attractive. They appear to be concerned about our interests and our welfare. If your reader or listener thinks you are as concerned about his or her interests and welfare as you are about your own, your credibility is likely to grow.

If you were trying to get a colleague to ask for release time to accompany you to a conference, you might show that person how the conference would be beneficial. You might also stress the need to take a break from his or her heavy workload. As an additional feature, you might even emphasize how your boss is favorably impressed with those employees who demonstrate an interest in furthering their education or knowledge—or, perhaps, that your boss will be going to the conference too.

Sociable people tend to be joiners. They associate with others and find cooperation to be an effective method for dealing with problems. In their letters, conversations, or speeches they readily and easily convey examples regarding their experiences and relationships with friends and associates. Sociability is an integral part of their personality, not something added on for effect.

### Extroversion

Persuaders who convey extroversion tend to command our attention. They are bold, forceful, and assertive, as opposed to timid, forceless, and nonassertive. Sometimes, they even scare us. They control a situation, not by manipulation or coercion, but by their presence.

Extroverted people are not afraid to express themselves, and they reveal their views comfortably and easily. They are people whose interests and attention are directed predominantly toward people, ideas, and objects outside of themselves. They reflect confidence, control, and a level of inner strength.

### Composure

Persuaders who convey composure reflect a calmness of mind, bearing (the way people carry themselves), and appearance. Composure is often revealed when people show they have gained mastery of their words, voice, and body. They convey an image of control.

Nervousness in an oral presentation can diminish or destroy an attitude of composure. Thus, it needs to be controlled and channelled into productive, positive behavior. Cues that are communicated to listeners should reflect your control of the situation: steady, direct eye contact; an erect, yet relaxed, posture; meaningful and purposeful gestures and movements, to name a few of these cues. In addition, a speech presentation should flow smoothly from point to point. Every cue should reveal control:

"I know what I am doing." Delivery should be smooth—devoid of unnecessary or awkward pauses.

In writing, persuaders follow the rules of appearance and format. They reveal control through their command of the language. The principles of writing, such as attitude, empathy, and a positive impression, are important. These will be discussed in Chapter 14, "Writing Principles."

To build credibility often takes time, yet it can be destroyed in an instant. Thus, all behavior and activity must be monitored. Building an image is a continual, step-by-step process that occurs in increments over a period of time. If you want to be a person with high credibility, you now know the kinds of behaviors and activities that need work. While some things can be mentioned in a letter or speech, a speaker often has the advantage of an introducer who can help establish a speaker's credentials. In a letter or speech, persuaders may need to (without bravado) cite personal experiences, examples, or experiences that indirectly allude to their credibility—to their character and competence.

## RESISTING THE PERSUASION OF OTHERS

Because of the prominence of advertisers, salespersons, and politicians in our society—not to mention teachers, ministers, priests, rabbis, the media, and others bent on persuasion—most people already have developed a built-in, natural, almost automatic resistance to persuasion.[5] People are inherently skeptical, and that is why persuading others is not an easy or direct process.

Most attempts at persuasion are aimed at feelings (the heart) rather than at the intellect (the mind). While sound reasoning, a careful, disciplined approach, and appeals to common sense may be the tools of many of those who exert influence, they are seldom as convincing or as quick to persuade as the well-placed, well-timed appeal to a receiver's emotions. Resistance to persuasion must be to both words *and* actions: to verbal and nonverbal influences. The former tends to be more logical (appeals to the mind); the latter tends to be emotional (appeals to feelings).

There are several ways receivers can resist the influence of persuaders. For example, some people avoid suspicious environments. They know that beautiful music, a sumptuous meal, or beautiful surroundings can lower their resistance. Other people make a public commitment to a position. Because the position is public—made to an entire group—they find it easier to stick to that position. One person always takes at least one other person, maybe more, into potential influence situations. Recognizing that there is safety in numbers, they protect themselves by being with others. People will also develop their own unique methods. Because of the profusion of persuaders, some people develop techniques they may not even be aware of; that is, they develop methods that may be unconscious or subconscious. For instance, a television advertisement comes on and, mentally, you turn it off. A manager says "equal opportunity" and the stereotypes you have regarding minorities come into play. A minister talks about tithing and you evoke your first, automatic response: "Yeah, that's easy for *you* to say."

**Perspective**

One of the first and most important needs of a resister is to gain perspective. Realize that when you are directly under the influence of a persuader, you are getting information from one source only. You have no perspective: the capacity to view things in their true relationship or relative importance.

To counter the influence, realize that opportunity rarely knocks only once, that the value of what you are being told is being exaggerated for effect, and that contrary issues are being avoided. Furthermore, question yourself regarding what you are hearing or reading: Is what you are hearing or reading correct? Is it the way you are perceiving it? Why are you being given this opportunity, or being exposed to this information? Do you have information that contradicts what you are hearing or reading? Finally, to counter the influence, ask for definitions, illustrations, clarifications, justifications, and supporting evidence.

**Eye Contact**

Eye contact can help the resister in several ways. First, it allows you to pick up various nonverbal cues that might be missed if you are not looking at the persuader. When people lie they often reveal it through nonverbal cues: by breaking eye contact or looking away or facial flush and body shift.

Additionally, maintaining eye contact gives others the impression that you are a mind reader. It makes persuaders feel uncomfortable—that you know what they are thinking. This may make them justify their idea or proposal or stop and ask you, "What's the matter?" or back up their ideas with more substance.

**Preparation**

The more you know about a topic, the less likely you are to be persuaded on that topic. Persuaders often rely on people's ignorance—their lack of information on topics. If you are knowledgeable, you will be able to meet their arguments with other arguments and counter their evidence with better evidence. The more people know, the more difficult it is to deceive them.

### Time

Allow time to work for you. When we give ourselves time to think about anything, we often discover new ideas that did not occur to us before. There are, no doubt, situations that demand our immediate attention. Most, however, can wait. Tell your persuader that you need time to sleep on it.

Suspending judgment has the same effect. Recognize that most persuasion does not occur instantaneously. Also, recognize that all ideas have many different sides to them. The best method is to hold off any decision. In that way you can talk with others, read more on the topic, or deliberate in your own quiet, personal way. There is always time to make a decision, and that time is usually not immediately.

### SUMMARY

Persuasion is a natural, active, and important part of business. It is used daily both informally and formally. This chapter focused on basic ideas relevant to all types of persuasion. The term *persuasion* was used synonymously with *influence*.

In the first section, attitudes, beliefs, and values were discussed. Attitudes are predispositions that cause us to think, feel, perceive, or behave in a certain way. They are usually aimed at an object, situation, event, issue, or person. There are three dimensions to an attitude: cognitive, affective, and behavioral. Beliefs are more deeply rooted than attitudes. Beliefs represent acceptance of information on both a mental and emotional level. They, too, have cognitive, affective, and behavioral dimensions. Beliefs can also be classified as social, personal, trust, authority, and inconsequential.

Values are central psychological anchors or deep-seated standards. They guide our ethical conduct and determine whether we approach or avoid things. They guide our beliefs and attitudes and are usually enduring and quite stable.

Attitudes, beliefs, and values relate closely to emotional support, sometimes called *pathos*, because we depend on them when we appeal to people's needs, goals, and emotions. Emotional support is at the heart of persuasion.

Emotional support, however, often depends on *logos*, or logical support, for its effectiveness. Logic has to do with orderly, valid, cogent reasoning. A logical presentation would involve a clear proposition, supported with relevant valid evidence, organized in a rational, effective manner. A persuasive organizational pattern called the Monroe Motivated Sequence was presented as a means to organize a persuasive problem-solving presentation. The five steps of the sequence were briefly outlined: attention, need, satisfaction, visualization, and action. Conclusions or inferences drawn from the material throughout the outline should be logical and valid.

The final type of persuasive support discussed was credibility—sometimes called *ethos*. Credibility has to do with the character of the persuader in the eyes of the reader or listener. Extrinsic ethos and intrinsic ethos were discussed. The five separate dimensions of credibility were examined: competence, character, sociability, extroversion, and composure.

Resisting the persuasion of others was the final section. Ways to resist such as perspective, eye contact, preparation, and time were revealed. Although people have a natural skepticism toward persuasive attempts, they must also learn to consciously resist it too.

Assumed throughout this chapter was a strong commitment to ethical conduct; that is, a commitment to honesty, accuracy, and fairness. It is unethical for persuaders to take advantage of less informed or less skilled communicators. Manipulation designed to selfishly advance persuaders' interests at the expense of readers or listeners is unethical as well. If your goal as a persuader is to arrive at results and outcomes that are mutually beneficial, you are more likely to be both effective and ethical.

When you cast doubt on your ethics, you are likely to affect your credibility. It may have short-term advantages, but the long-term effect may be ruinous. Thus, the best results will be achieved when persuaders combine ethical practices of fair play and respect for the interests and rights of others with the persuasive techniques and strategies discussed in this chapter.

## NOTES

[1] Erwin P. Bettinghaus, *Persuasive Communication* (New York: Holt, Rinehart & Winston, 1968), p. 10.
[2] Milton Rokeach, *Beliefs, Attitudes and Values* (San Francisco: Jossey-Bass, 1968).
[3] From *Principles of Speech Communication*, 9th ed. by Douglas Ehninger et al. Copyright © 1984, 1980 by Scott, Foresman and Company. Reprinted by permission.
[4] James C. McCroskey and Thomas J. Young, "Ethos and Credibility: The Construct and Its Measurement After Three Decades," *Central States Speech Journal*, 32 (Spring 1981), 24–34.
[5] Ideas in this section have been adapted from Abné Eisenberg's *Understanding Communication in Business and the Professions* (New York: Macmillan, 1978), pp. 314–18, and his *Job Talk: Communicating Effectively on the Job* (New York: Macmillan, 1979), pp. 158–61.

# 14

# Writing Principles

Successful business communication depends upon effective writing; thus, understanding business communication means understanding not only the principles of speaking, but also the principles of writing.[1] Effective writing is seldom the product of pure inspiration; rather, it is the result of careful preparation and logical organization. The techniques discussed in the preceding two chapters on "oral reports" and "persuasive presentations" must not be forgotten. That is, successful writers make use of many of those same skills. They must precisely define their purpose, then clearly determine the identity, needs, and goals of their specific reader. They gather facts and ideas to support their purpose, then organize their message by logically grouping those facts and ideas that the reader will need to understand the writer or to do what the writer wants done. Once the material is organized, the writer converts it to a rough draft, then polishes it into a final form. That is an overview of the entire writing process. How similar it is to the process of oral communication! Both require careful preparation.

In this chapter we will look at the various aspects of writing with the purpose of clarifying various writing principles. What are the elements that make writing distinctive? The first section, "Generating Ideas," helps writers overcome "writer's block" or the "blank page syndrome." To begin to write, one must know how to get started—a practical problem.

Words will be the first element discussed. Basic principles will be clarified, and several points not mentioned previously will be explained. In separate sections, sentences, paragraphs, and compositions will be examined. In the section on compositions, the Fog Index will be presented as a method for testing one's writing level.

## GENERATING IDEAS

"'Writer's Block' is a terrible thing," says Nancy Kuriloff, a business consultant who specializes in writing effectiveness. "It's a very real crisis when your livelihood depends on it."[2] Kuriloff helps writers unblock. She attributes most of the problem to the inner critic who is primitive, undeveloped, and unintegrated, and who often speaks in schoolyard language: "You're so dumb." Kuriloff tries to get writers to start a conversation with the critic—to reintegrate writer and critic. Her aim is to make writers autonomous, free to unlimber the imagination.

Writing is relatively new to the human experience. Kuriloff contends that, "Writing simply does not come naturally. It's an unnatural event. Most people who ever lived didn't write."[3] At least this helps put the problem into proper perspective, even though it offers little practical outlet.

The best way to start writing is by outlining in a very general way what the message is to be. Then go back over the outline and write a brief statement about each of the important points that needs to be discussed. Make sure that the ideas are in the order in which you want them. For example, a writer wanted to put together some information on donations. She wanted to address several issues: (1) how to get facts, (2) how to examine programs, (3) who watches charitable groups, and (4) the Internal Revenue Service rules governing contributions.

With the above ideas set down, she could now go over the list and write a brief statement about each point:

> **Getting facts:** We need to know everything we can about the organization—name and address as well as a financial statement.
> **Examining programs:** We need as much specific information as we can get—names of people, services rendered, staffing.
> **Watchdog groups:** Who are the agencies that publish lists of charities and that establish the standards they should meet?
> **IRS rules:** What are the limits of contributions? Are there any new rules or regulations of which we should be aware?

The next stage is to write topic sentences for the paragraphs you want to include. For example, topic sentences for two of the four areas discussed in the written piece on donations might be as follows:

**ON GETTING FACTS:**

1. Find out the name and address of the charity.
2. Write for, or secure, a financial statement.

**ON EXAMINING PROGRAMS:**

1. Who operates the program?
2. Examine the services.
3. Look at the staffing.

Develop each of the topic sentences into a paragraph. Each of the topic statements could be fleshed out. For the first one under the heading "On getting facts," the writer could provide names and addresses of some major charities and where these can be found. For the second item under the same heading, the paragraph might look like this:

> Now, write for or secure a financial statement. You may wonder what to do with it once you get it. You will need to ask at least three questions: First, how much was collected last year? This will give you an idea of its financial foundation and how well known it is. Second, find out how the money was spent. What you want to know is how much was spent on administration and how much on the programs the charity sponsors. This will give you a clue as to how much of your money supports charity administrators. You also can determine from this if the charity is adequately staffed and efficiently administered. Finally, find out if the charity has tax-exempt status. This is what would qualify your donation as tax-deductible.

After writing out a paragraph for each of your topic sentences, you will have a rough draft of your whole message. Go back and proofread this rough draft; check the dictionary for proper spellings, and insert the appropriate punctuation.

Revise the rough draft by arranging paragraphs in the proper order, eliminating repetition and redundancies, and correcting grammatical construction. Make certain that the communication satisfies both your reasons for writing it and your reader's reasons for reading it.

Your communication can be judged effective when your words, sentences, and paragraphs work together to achieve your objective. There should be no distraction. All of the elements become fused; none of these parts should stand out as unique or extraordinary or in any way call attention to itself.

## WORDS: A SUMMARY

Whole books have been written on words and uses of language. You might wonder why so much time is spent talking about words and language.

First, effective writing is not easy. Rather, it is tricky and demanding. It is also challenging. The challenge is the same as in oral communication: to compose a concise, precise message that will elicit the exact response you desire. A major principle of effective communication would be: *effective communication is concise and exact, eliciting the exact response a communicator wants.* But to achieve this requires a keen mind, a sharp eye, plenty of self-criticism, a lot of practice, and adherence to basic writing principles.

Second, effective writing can assure you of getting the results you want. Thus, effective writing may have a direct effect on your success or failure. Closely tied to this is that effective writing can make people's jobs easier. Since so much of business communication is written, effective writing adds a level of comfort and confidence to the job. The better people become at it, the easier and more rapid the task becomes. And this relates to the third reason for spending time discussing language.

With support from the cliché "time is money," efficient language usage means getting success quickly, without a lot of intervening letters, memos, or telephone calls. This is the third reason. One letter can settle a business transaction. Moreover, secretarial time is saved because secretaries do not have as much to type.

But the discussion of words can have other advantages as well. The more we understand words, the better chance we have of becoming skilled at using them—especially as we practice using them. We also learn basic principles of practical psychology. These principles help us to get along better with others both professionally and socially. Look, for example, at the principles highlighted in italics throughout this chapter. To use these in our everyday conversations will add a new dimension to our use of language.

Another advantage is that as we become skilled in any one mode of communication, it helps in other modes. That is, as we become skilled at phrasing our ideas in letters, this skill will aid us in speaking as well as in written communication. There are noticeable carryover effects.

Finally, the more we write, the more we realize the public-relations function that our writing serves. Letters and memos are part of the understanding others have of or the good will they experience toward us, our firm, or our institution. Thus, all our writing must be oriented toward winning instead of losing.

A winning style can be achieved by following basic principles of effective writing, and a summary of these principles follows. The first, and most important principle, a summary of the first major characteristic of language, is *words must be easily understood.*

One way to achieve this is through simplicity. Our *words should be plain, uncomplicated, and free from unnecessary elaboration or display.* For example, let us compare just the first paragraph of Lincoln's "Gettysburg Address" as he wrote it with the same first paragraph as it could be written in an excessively flowery or embellished style:

<u>The Gettysburg Address</u>
by
Abraham Lincoln

> Fourscore and seven years ago our fathers brought forth on this continent a new nation conceived in liberty and dedicated to the proposition that all men are created equal.

<u>The Gettysburg Address</u> (Flowery style)

> During those stimulating, excitement-filled years when our illustrious grandsires were hewing and carving out dwelling places among the Indian-infested forests, they paused in their mighty efforts for a period of time sufficient to enable them to innovate a new and powerful way of life for the common man. And what a way of life it was! Conceived in glorious and lasting liberty, and firmly (I say firmly advisedly), yes, firmly dedicated, established, and founded upon the ever-so-basic principle of the brotherhood and equality of all mankind.[4]

Simplicity is important because we, as writers, tend to know more about our subject than our reader. Thus, we and our reader are not equally equipped to communicate on the topic. We have no choice, if our goal is reader understanding, but to present our ideas in elementary words and concepts so that meaning is generated in our reader's mind. When it is necessary to use a technical term, it can be immediately, and briefly, defined.

Another reason for simplicity has to do with reader comfort. Writing that is slightly below reader level is more comfortable to read. It communicates best because the reader does not have to cope with deciphering difficult words. A little later in this chapter a way to determine your own writing level will be offered.

Another important principle regarding the use of words has to do with sincerity. *Words must be honest and genuine.* They should convey a warm, courteous, and friendly attitude. Admittedly, there are exceptions. A situation may demand strong assertion and, in such a case, warmth, courtesy, and friendliness may be less appropriate. (The author can envision no circumstance where warmth, courtesy, and friendliness would be totally inappropriate; after all, we *are* human beings dealing with other human beings.) For the most part, even a strongly assertive message can be conveyed in a warm, courteous, and friendly attitude. Take, for example, this message from management:

> It has come to our attention that an investigation of our business practices is under way. We welcome any such inquiry; however, to help us control the

image we project to the public, and to help us provide consistency, we would appreciate it if you would allow our public-relations personnel to be the major spokespersons for the company. We are not saying you cannot talk to reporters, and we are not limiting your freedom of speech—we have no right, nor would we even want to do that; we have nothing to hide. However, you could help the company as a whole if you would refer reporters, or any others requesting information, to our public-relations department. After all, that is what they are being paid to do!

This is also where the writer's credibility may have an effect on the message. Is the writer known to be competent, of reputable character, sociable, extroverted (a person willing to assert his or her ideas or position in a positive manner), and composed?

Emphasis in our choice of words allows us to stress certain ideas over others. *Words must be selected in such a way that certain ideas are given special impressiveness.* Every word chosen does not need to be emphatic, however. Positioning, space, sentence structure, and other mechanical means can be used to gain emphasis. Notice, for example, how this writer arranges ideas in parallel form for strong emphasis:

> Our company speakers bear a responsibility to the taxpayers and to the stockholders,
>
> —to the preferences of our chairperson
> —to the appearance of business harmony
> —to the vagaries of tax laws
> —to the pretensions of the city and state

Closely connected to emphasis is the need that *our words must also generate excitement.* But just as in choosing emphatic words, not every word we use need generate excitement. If all a person does is shout, we get so accustomed to the shouting that it has no effect. But our words must grasp and hold the reader's attention. If they do not, they are unlikely to serve any purpose at all. Excitement is generated by (1) selecting strong, vigorous words, (2) using concrete words, (3) preferring active verbs, and (4) avoiding overused expressions.

Notice in the following passage the writer's use of strong words. Active verbs also are used, and overused expressions are kept to a minimum.

> Free enterprise is based on freedom of choice, and business responds to this freedom in the ultimate pursuit of profits. To the extent that the political system dominates or distorts the economic system, freedom and the pursuit of profits may be restricted or diminished. When this happens there are consequences for both management and society.
>
> Management must be responsive to, and responsible for, the exercise of freedom, but this does not exempt the rest of society. In casting its votes—in the voting booth and the marketplace—society must have a greater awareness

of the impact of these votes and how they ultimately affect the decisions of management.

To help society use these votes more intelligently management cannot continue with its cosmetic messages. Instead, it needs to play a more active role in educating society of its available choices and their consequences.[5]

Strong words in the above sample include "dominates or distorts" and "restricted or diminished" in the first paragraph. The use of "must," "impact," and "ultimately affect" are strong in the second paragraph. The third paragraph includes "cannot continue" and "cosmetic messages." Concrete words include "pursuit of profits," and "the voting booth and the marketplace." This passage could be more effective with an emphasis on concreteness. The most overused expression in this passage is "pursuit of profits," which cannot be considered trite or a cliché, at least at this writing.

*Strong, vigorous words* produce an effect. They add personality and a sense of excitement. To call a person a "tycoon" instead of an "eminently successful business person" might be one example, depending upon who the reader is. Referring to a "bear market" instead of a "generally declining market" might be another example, just as "boom" could be used for a "period of business prosperity."

*Concrete words* are effective because they are sharp and clear in meaning. They are not abstract or vague. Concrete words tend to be more denotative than connotative. They represent things readers can see, hear, feel, touch, taste, or smell. For example, a reader can understand a 23 percent profit better than "a sizable profit," a student who graduated in the top 5 percent of her class of 500 students rather than one of "the best students," or by Wednesday at noon, rather than "in the very near future." In most cases, concrete words are short and familiar. Instead of "construction site," one could say "where they are building the new *skyscraper*"; "building" could be the "American Bank at the corner of Huron and Main"; "experience" could be anything from "a rock concert" to "a burned finger." An emotion can be "love," "jealousy," or "rage."

*Active verbs* generate excitement because they have the subject acting. Instead of saying "The proposal *was* passed by the committee," you say "The committee passed the proposal"—and to keep it concrete, you might add "by a margin of two-to-one." Preferring active verbs, however, does not mean eliminating the passive voice, for it, too, has a useful place in good writing. What it means is that you show a preference for the active voice by using it as much as you logically can. Why say "The books were inspected by the auditor," when you can say, with more excitement, "The auditor inspected the books"? Look at the differences below. On the left, the passive tense dulls the verb. On the right, the doer of the action acts and the verbs are short and clear.

## PASSIVE

The new merger is believed to be superior by the administration.

It is desired by this committee that the problem be brought before the board.

Recent procedures were reviewed by Mrs. Wilson.

## ACTIVE

Administrators believe the new merger is superior.

The committee wants the problem to be brought before the board.

Mrs. Wilson reviewed recent procedures.

*Overused expressions* have lost their impact because of excessive use. When we use them, it is like telling our reader that he or she is like everyone else and deserves nothing better. They also suggest that we are unwilling to think beyond the obvious. Instead of trying to be the least bit unique, we depend upon the cliché—the obvious. It is the easiest thing to do because it requires little thought. There are many overused expressions:

## OVERUSED EXPRESSION

"According to our records . . ."

"The question as to whether . . ."

"At your earliest convenience . . ."

"Enclosed, you will find . . ."

"Please contact me if you have any further questions . . ."

"This is a subject that . . ."

"I remain . . ."

"Permit me to say . . ."

"Take this opportunity . . ."

"Thanking you in advance . . ."

"The reason why is that . . ."

"Call your attention to the fact that . . ."

"Under separate cover . . ."

## POSSIBLE SUBSTITUTE

"We find . . ."

"Whether" or "The question whether . . ."

"Soon . . ."

State what is enclosed without the preface.

"For information, my phone number is . . ."

"This subject . . ."

Omit

Just say it without getting permission.

Just say it.

Omit

"Because . . ."

"Remind you . . ."

Omit[6]

Overused expressions generate no excitement, except, perhaps, enough to allow the reader to finish reading and quickly dispense with the letter or memo. Moreover, overused expressions contribute nothing to the unique, distinctive identity that is you.[7] *Words should reveal the personality of the writer.*

## SENTENCES

Choosing the right words is the first step in effective writing. Arranging those words into sentences that stimulate meaning in the reader's mind is the next step. There is no change in the overall principle that should guide us: *Sentences should be easily understood.* Once again, we are trying to adapt our message to our reader.

Although there are many principles for proper sentence construction, and there is no doubt about their importance or value to the writer, in the end, understanding between writer and reader is achieved through adaptation—the interpersonal process outlined in Chapter 2 and labeled "Communication as Transaction." We are guided by our mental image of who our reader is. The final choices we make will be based on the best judgments we decide upon; they are a product of our active, thinking mind as we fit and adjust our message to the exact, unique mental filter we feel best represents our reader. There is no doubt that this process is based on guesswork; however, the more we know of our reader, the more we reduce the amount of guesswork required.

In this section, principles of proper sentence formation are discussed. Since the sentence is the form of expression we have agreed upon to express our thoughts, we must learn to use that form effectively. Clear, orderly sentences reflect clear, orderly thinking just as vague, disorderly sentences reflect vague, disorderly thinking. Thus, if our concern is that our readers think that our writing is a product of good thinking (a good mind), we must follow the principles underlying sentence construction: (1) length, (2) economy of words, and (3) emphasis.

### Length

The most important characteristic of a sentence that contributes to reader difficulty is length. *Longer sentences are harder to understand than shorter ones.* This is a significant principle of effective writing.

There is also an aphorism that states that "anything taken to excess can become negative." Applied to the principle regarding longer sentences, this suggests that a letter or memo consisting of short sentences alone would probably have negative results. This is true. Many sentences of the same length become monotonous. Thus, another important principle of effective writing would be: *Varying sentence length makes writing more interesting to readers.* See how other authors have written about the length of sentences, using variety of sentence length:

> Variety in sentences can also be achieved by varying their lengths. No authority can say just how long a sentence should be. Ideas vary in complexity, so they need a varying number of words for expression. But surveys show that, for effective business writing, *average* sentence length should be somewhere between sixteen and twenty-two words. However, sentences with two words are appropriate; so are sentences with sixty words if they are clear. Mix them up. Variety is pleasant, and it helps to hold attention and interest.[8]

Notice the sentence lengths: eleven words in both the first and second sentences, then sentences of fourteen, nineteen, seventeen, three, and eleven words, respectively. A fairly good balance. The average length is just over twelve words. But the paragraph reads comfortably, and it seems appropriate for the ideas being expressed, does it not?

To determine sentence length, writers should keep in mind the readability level of the reader. *Writing must be adapted to the reader's readability level.* Writers aiming at the middle level of adult American readers should use sentence lengths averaging sixteen to twenty-two words. For more advanced readers, they can increase this average. It would be less for those with lower reading abilities. This does not mean that an occasional long sentence, say, of thirty words, or an occasional short one of only six, cannot be used. Writers must keep in mind the three essentials: (1) it is the readability level of the reader that must be considered, (2) it is the overall average length of sentences that counts, and (3) variety is what holds the attention of readers.

### Economy of Words

*Economy of words* refers to the ways writers choose to express their ideas. Of those ways (and there may be an endless number), generally the shorter ones are preferred. Shorter methods are clearer, more interesting, and vigorous. They also save the reader time. Thus, *in expressing ideas, the shorter ways usually are the best.*

How do writers gain economy of words? The best way is through practice. They are aware of the need and they carefully explore different approaches. Their sensitivity to the need makes them strive for economy in everything they write. They do not succumb to sloppiness or laziness, the two major obstacles to economy of words.

But there are also other ways to gain economy. Avoid needless phrases. Often, a phrase can be shortened. You may think that shortening a sentence or phrase by a word or two is insignificant, but over a long piece, the savings can be substantial. Notice the reduction (economy of words) between the long form and shorter substitutes that follow.

| LONGER PHRASE | SHORTER SUBSTITUTE |
| --- | --- |
| Along the lines of | Like |
| At an early date | Soon |
| At the present time | Now |
| Due to the fact that | Because |
| During the time that | While |
| For the purposes of | For |
| For the reason that | Because |

| | |
|---|---|
| In accordance with | By |
| In connection with | About |
| In the meantime | Meantime |
| In the neighborhood of | About |
| In terms of | Of |
| In view of the fact that | Since, because |
| On the occasion of | On |
| With reference to | About |

Writers can work toward an economy of words, too, by eliminating surplus words. When words add nothing to a sentence, eliminate them. Sometimes a sentence can be recast to eliminate verbiage:

| CONTAINS SURPLUS | SURPLUS ELIMINATED |
|---|---|
| *There are, essentially,* four principles *which* should be followed. | Four principles should be followed. |
| *In addition to these problems,* numerous other problems also plague the company. | The company is plagued by other problems as well.<br>or<br>Numerous other problems plague the company. |
| *During the period* between June and September we detected the problem. | Between June and September, we detected the problem. |

Economy of words can also be achieved if writers avoid needless repetition. When used for special effect or emphasis, repetition can be justified; otherwise, it should be avoided. Why? Readers can read a word, phrase, or sentence again to gain understanding if they need to. Repetition distracts and adds verbiage.

| NEEDLESS REPETITION | REPETITION ELIMINATED |
|---|---|
| *In my opinion,* I think the proposal is justified. | I think the proposal is justified. |
| The *important* essentials *of the* report must be included. | The report's essentials must be included. |
| *All* members *assigned to the* committee should be responsible. . . . | Committee members should be responsible. . . . |

### Emphasis

Just as words can be emphatic, so can sentences. But just as all words do not need to be emphatic, all sentences are not equally important to the message either. There are likely to be certain parts of a letter or memo that you want to stand out: a conclusion, a series of ideas, or the part that tells the reader what you want him or her to do. This intended importance must be conveyed, and to convey it requires that you control your information. What you want to do is control the impression the reader receives when he or she reads your message. But since you cannot enter his or her head, you control the stimuli (at least some of them) that have an effect on what goes on inside the reader's mind.

*Ideas can be emphasized through sentence design.* A short sentence is likely to carry more emphasis than a long one. The use of unusual word order, because it varies from what we commonly expect, may add emphasis. A sentence that covers one item will give more emphasis to that item than if it covers more items. For example, "We must look at how to dull alcohol's effect, alternatives to alcohol, and when to step in." As a preview or summary statement, this would be useful, but notice how the emphasis is increased when you say, "We must look at how to dull alcohol's effect." "Alternatives to alcohol will be considered next." "Finally, we will look at when to step in." Words or items that need emphasis should be placed at the beginning or at the end of a sentence or clause. For example, "*Starchy foods* will slow down the speed at which the body absorbs liquor." The last word in a sentence tends to be more emphatic than the first. For example, "What is served at a party and how it is presented can make a big difference in whether guests make it home without an *accident*." Finally, if you phrase an idea as a question, it is likely to be more emphatic than a statement. For example, a phrase such as, "Here are some tips that may help you deal with alcoholic beverages," could be rephrased for more emphasis: "Do you know how to deal with alcoholic beverages?"

*Ideas can be de-emphasized through sentence design.* If first and last positions in a sentence are emphatic, it follows that placing an idea in the middle of a sentence de-emphasizes it. Placing the idea in the middle of any cluster of thoughts will also de-emphasize it. Avoiding the use of the question also aids de-emphasis. Phrase the request politely, as a statement, and do not follow it with a question mark.

*Ideas can be emphasized through sentence arrangement with other sentences.* You can create anticipation by using climactic order. Begin with the least important idea and end with the most important. ("He began with the company as a stockboy. He then moved to warehouse manager. Following that he advanced to director of personnel. Now he is vice-president in charge of finance.") Emphasis is added at each step.

The writer can also introduce a sentence or series of sentences with one that indicates the importance of the idea or ideas that follow: "*Most important,* however, is an idea suggested to me by Mr. Raymond." Or, to arrange the sentence in a more emphatic order, "But Mr. Raymond suggested an idea I consider *most important.*"

*Parallelism* can also create emphasis. Words, phrases, or sentences can be constructed parallel with each other. Parallel structure requires that sentence elements that are alike in function be alike in structure as well.[9] Notice in this example that each sentence functions in exactly the same way; thus, it is structured in the same way.

> To be successful here you must be punctual. To be successful here you must be courteous. To be successful here you must be conscientious.

A writer could explain each element—punctuality, courteousness, conscientiousness—before continuing to the next. Then the writer could introduce each new element with the parallel clause. This would indicate to the reader the level of importance of the idea.

## PARAGRAPHS

Paragraphs also play a major role in our writing. When a number of sentences contribute to the same thought, we tie them together into a paragraph. Once again, we can depend on the same overall principle to guide us: *Paragraphs should be easily understood.*

Paragraphs help to organize information. They make it easier to understand a body of information because (1) they break it up into smaller bits and, while bits are digestible, big chunks are not, and (2) they offer us a rest stop between ideas. They give the mind a chance to pause, absorb, and reflect on what has been said as well as what is to come.

Although the actual techniques for designing paragraphs are not easy to explain, since much of it depends on the writer's mental ability to organize ideas and to relate facts logically, this section offers some practical advice. Principles of paragraphing include *unity, length, type,* and *sequence.*

### Unity

*Paragraphs should be built around a single topic or idea.* It is sometimes easier to think of writing paragraphs as "packaging ideas"—items that are similar are packaged together. Sentences that contain elements that contribute to a single topic or idea are grouped together in an easy-to-follow sequence. Unity means oneness.

It is not always easy to perceive the single thought or idea that is to make up a paragraph. You might say, for example, my whole letter, memo, or report deals with just one idea. Paragraphs, then, make up smaller units

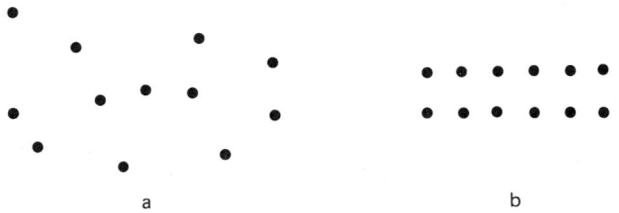

**FIGURE 14–1.** This is what unity, or coherence, looks like. (a) represents ununified material; (b) represents those same elements in a unified presentation. Unity affects the reader's perception of a communication. The way elements are fitted together is significant to the impact of the total written communication.

of that single idea; they usually include the lowest level of a detailed outline. You might ask yourself: Can my ideas in a paragraph be reduced to a single topic statement? If that statement does not refer to each part of that paragraph, that paragraph probably lacks unity.

There are other questions, too, writers can ask about their own writing that will help them achieve unity in their paragraphs. First, has the reader been led naturally from point to point? Second, do the ideas in the paragraph seem related? Third, can the relationship among the ideas be seen? If the answer to any question is "no," the package should be rewrapped (recast) for greater unity. See Figure 14–1.

**Length**

Just as words and sentences need to be of different lengths to prevent monotony, so do paragraphs. But because attention spans are short, *paragraphs should be kept short* as well. How short? Before writing a letter or memo, decide on the ideas to be included, then devote a paragraph to each idea. If one idea is too large, divide it into two or three parts and treat each in a separate paragraph, tying them together in the opening or closing sentences of each paragraph. When the discussion of each idea is complete, change paragraphs. Paragraphs will not be of uniform size because some items will need more discussion (space) than others.

What are some advantages of short paragraphs? First, they help readers follow the organizational pattern. The reader is less likely to get lost, or to lose the flow of thought. Second, short paragraphs emphasize the beginning and ending of the items covered. They help readers know when the discussion of one idea is complete and another one is beginning. With long paragraphs, ideas may become fused or mixed.

Third, short paragraphs are more pleasing to the eye. See Figure 14–2. This becomes an important factor in a reader's reaction to a letter, memo, or report. Open space between paragraphs also improves the overall appearance of a letter or memo. It adds a quality dimension. Notice, for

 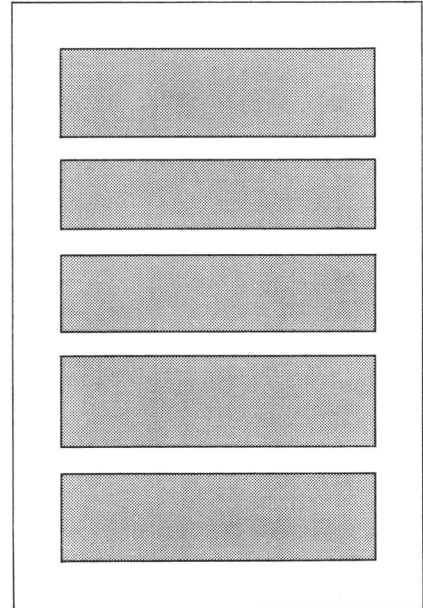

**FIGURE 14–2.** Paragraphs that look full of words are neither pleasing nor inviting. They look long and dull. Paragraphs of various lengths with numerous open spaces look both organized and inviting. They provide an encouraging, positive, psychological effect.

example, the amount of open space in a local discount-store advertisement compared with the amount of open space in an advertisement for a high-quality department store. Space may spell quality. But space may be even more important still. Readers may resist plunging into a letter or memo where there is no open space, only large sections of written copy. Open space assures readers they will have a rest break. People enjoy frequent breaks.

A series of paragraphs that are very short can have a negative effect as well. Nothing in excess! They can appear choppy. They can break up the flow of ideas. They can offer too many topics with little or no support or substantiation. They can be uninviting. However, a short paragraph occasionally can be used for emphasis. Even a two-word paragraph is acceptable. Usually very short paragraphs of a line or two are used as transitions connecting previous ideas to those forthcoming, summarizing ideas briefly, or relating material to the central idea of the letter, memo, or report.

Deciding paragraph length is a decision that should be based on the topic to be covered. However, most well-organized, well-paragraphed business letters, memos, and reports have paragraphs of eight or nine lines. As a paragraph grows beyond twelve lines, writers should begin to question its unity. Does it contain one topic only? If more, additional paragraphs should be used.

In business letters, writers should keep first and last paragraphs short. Short, in this case, means one to four lines. This makes the letter look more inviting. It becomes more likely that the recipient will begin reading it. It also lends a balanced and pleasing appearance to the letter.

**Type**

*Paragraphs need a topic sentence for both unity and coherence.* Topic sentences express the main idea of paragraphs. It is around topic sentences that details of support and elaboration are built. There are basically two types of paragraphs that can be used: the *deductive* and the *inductive*. Which one should be used depends on the material to be covered and how one plans to cover it. But both types gain their unity and coherence from a clear topic sentence with material that relates closely to it. *Paragraphs need to be organized.*

*Deductive* paragraphs present the topic sentence first, followed by the supporting material presented in some logical order. This is the most widely used paragraph plan, and it is the one used throughout this book. The strength of this format is that it gives strong emphasis to the major point of the paragraph.

The above paragraph is a deductive one. Note the difference between it and the next paragraph, arranged inductively.

The significant role of other paragraph formats should not be overlooked. One format especially is designed to build ideas in the reader. It prevents defensiveness because the material, or support, is presented first before the conclusion (the topic sentence) is presented. Thus, it attempts to prevent disagreement, or at least decrease it, before offering the main idea. Its strengths, then, come from the suspense it can build, or the persuasiveness it can provide. It is the *inductive* paragraph, where the supporting material is presented first *followed* by the topic sentence or conclusion.

In most business writing, the deductive style is preferred. Executives can read just the first sentence; if it makes sense they can skip the rest of the paragraph. Hence, the deductive style can save time.

One other note on paragraph types may be helpful. In most business letters, writers should strive for short paragraphs. For the sake of brevity, they may omit topic sentences. Letters are often so short that no grouping of ideas is necessary or required. Grouping becomes important in written reports.

**Sequence**

*Paragraphs should be sequenced to move readers toward the writer's objective.* Forward movement, then, is a good quality of paragraph design.

Sequencing can be assisted by the skillful use of transitions. Note the transitional paragraph inserted between the previous paragraphs on deductive and inductive paragraph types. Smoothness in writing style also assists in sequencing. Ideas should flow together in a natural, comfortable, unforced manner. Sentence design and word choice, of course, contribute to this smoothness and flow.

The order of paragraphs is usually dictated by a larger format. How writers arrange their main ideas is similar to how speakers choose to arrange theirs. Topical, chronological, spacial, cause-effect or effect-cause, and problem-solution orders can be used. These principles can guide us in arranging paragraphs as well. The essential point is that whichever format is used, it should be planned before the writing is begun. The format selected should be the one used throughout, as a guide for arranging the main ideas. Subordinate ideas can be arranged following other sequences as long as writers group subordinate ideas and follow a consistent pattern within that grouping. Finally, writers must review their paragraphs as an entire unit before the writing is completed. This will help assure unity and coherence.

## COMPOSITIONS

You would think that, having chosen proper words, arranged them in appropriate sentences, and designed logical, effective paragraphs, you would not need to be concerned about anything else—that you have a composition. That is not true. That would be like saying you have selected the trees, you have even grouped them according to their similarities, but you have no concern for the forest as a whole. And yet there is an environment that is most proper for that forest, just as there is an ambience (a surrounding or pervading atmosphere) conveyed by that forest. And to the degree that you have control over that ambience, you should exert that control. It is part of the whole message situation.

Once the composition has been constructed, look it over as a whole. Ask yourself questions about it, and try to be objective in your answers. For example, is this the right message? Is the material fair? Are the conclusions logical? Is the material arranged in the strongest way? Is it unified? Coherent? That is, does it all seem to be packaged well? Does the beginning properly introduce the message? Does the middle move the reader sensibly from part to part? Each sentence must grow naturally from the preceding sentence. Does the ending provide a final, positive impression?

Other questions about the composition as a whole also are useful. When you read it, are you bored? Your writing should have variety. Look for variety in word choice, sentence length and structure, and paragraph length. Check for grammatical, spelling, or punctuation errors. Does the tone of the writing reflect confidence? Writers should reveal confidence in their message and in themselves; they should come across as neither egotistical nor apologetic. Writing should accentuate the positive and subordinate the negative. This promotes good human relations.

Is your writing concise? Once again, you do not want to bore your reader, but you also want to cover your topic convincingly. Check to ascertain that you have not distracted the reader, and yet have used enough words to assure the proper foundation as well as courtesy.

As you read your composition, be sure that the ideas you want emphasized *are* emphasized. This may be done during paragraph formation; yet when the paragraphs are put together, ideas may be subdued or, in the other direction, too many may be screaming for attention. You may need to make adjustments. To make an idea stand out, you may need to remove nearby ideas, put a number next to the one you want remembered, change positioning to put it first or last, devote more space to it, or attach a label of significance to it: "This idea is most important," for example. Just as you work to make ideas stand out, other ideas can be de-emphasized by making them more abstract, using the passive voice, imbedding them in positions of less importance, reducing the space given to them, or using labels of insignificance.

One thing writers must keep in mind is that their writing style should always be subservient to their writing. That is, they must keep in mind that it is their *ideas* they want their readers to think about, not their way of expressing them. To have readers responding to writers' styles is distracting. Thus, when writers try to impress their readers rather than express their ideas in the most effective way possible, they are doing more harm than good. *Effective writing helps readers see our points without being aware of the writing itself.*

### Readability

One of the most important questions writers can ask about their composition as a whole is, Is it readable? *The level of writing of any composition should be easily read and understood.* Obviously, writing that is readable for readers at one educational level can be difficult for readers below that level. Readability levels exist for each general level of education. Those who read our writing should be able to understand it without rereading.

To be concerned about your readability is to be concerned about audience adaptation—a concept or process previously discussed in this book. In this case, however, formulas for determining readability are available. All are connected to qualities of writing that show the highest correlation to levels of readability, namely sentence length and word difficulty. Thus, if writers can determine the approximate reading level of their prospective reader, they can fairly accurately predict how close their own writing comes to that level. To measure our writing in an objective way, we can use a formula compiled by Robert Gunning, known popularly as the Gunning Fog Index.[10] There are other formulas, all accurate in measuring readability, but this one derives its popularity from its simplicity.

The Gunning Fog Index measures how difficult reading matter is. The results will help us estimate the school grade level for which our writing would be most appropriate. For example, an index of 8 means that the material tested is easy reading for one at the eighth-grade level. An index of 12 indicates writing appropriate for a high-school graduate level of readability. An index of 16 indicates the level of college graduate. To compute the index, follow these steps:

1. Select a sample. It should contain 100 to 150 words. For a longer piece, select a number of passages at random from throughout the piece. To count words, count each dictionary word as one word. "I" is one word; so is "computational." Count each word in hyphenated expressions, like "up-to-date," as separate words. "Up-to-date" is three words. Figures like "12" or "6" or "144" are also counted as one word each. Determine the total number of words in the sample.
2. Count the sentences. Treat as sentences all independent clauses. That is, in sentences with two or more independent clauses, count each clause (as long as it can stand independently as a sentence) as a separate sentence.
3. Divide the total number of words in the passage by the total number of sentences. This will give you the average sentence length.
4. Find the percentage of difficult words in the sample: the number of hard words per hundred. Difficult words are those of *three syllables or more*, but note these exceptions:
   a. Do *not* count as difficult words made up of two or more small words, such as bookkeeper, however, or nevertheless.
   b. Do *not* count as difficult a verb that becomes three syllables by the addition of -ed or -es, such as repeat*ed* or transpos*es*. On the other hand, verbs that become three syllables with the addition of -ing are counted as difficult.

   Now, allowing for the exceptions noted above, count the number of difficult words. Next, divide the total number of words in the entire passage into the total number of difficult words and move the decimal point two places to the right. You now have the percentage of difficult words in the sample: the number of hard words per hundred.
5. Add the figure that represents average sentence length to the figure that represents the percentage of difficult words.
6. Multiply the figure obtained in step 5 by 0.4. Drop the digits following the decimal point in the result. The product (result) is the minimum grade level at which the writing will be easily read, or the Fog Index.

Application of the Fog Index is illustrated with the following paragraph.

> The people doing the *receiving* in written *communication* are our readers. They are an *essential component* in the *communication* process, for without them there would be no need for us to write words on paper. Perhaps *creative* people such as poets write purely for the joy of writing rhythmic words, just as artists paint

pictures of scenes or sights that have *particularly* moved them. But you and I are very *unlikely* to transmit *information* without having a good reason for doing so. We must always keep the people who will be doing the *receiving* in written *communication* clearly in mind.

1. The passage has 100 words — 100
2. The passage has 5 sentences — 5
3. $100 \div 5$ = average sentence length = — 20
4. Percentage of difficult words = 100 into 11 = 0.11 = move decimal point two places to right (11.) to get number of hard words per 100 = — 11
5. Average sentence length (20) plus number of difficult words (11) = — 31
6. Multiply figure in step five (31) by 0.4.  $0.4 \times 31$ = — 12.4

The Fog Index is 12.

The Fog Index provides valuable information. It is widely used and has received much attention.[11] Remember when applying it that people generally prefer reading at a lower level than their capability. But that does not mean that writers should depend on overly simple words or a monotonous succession of short sentences. (There is no better way to make reading dull.)

Writing formulas are best used by unskilled writers. They can help improve the communication quality of their writing. Skilled writers often violate the formulas and still communicate effectively. There is no specific guideline for the level at which you should write; this depends on the subject matter and the audience for which it is intended. For most business-letter writing, however, a suitable score is between 8 and 11. If your business-letter writing readability score is above grade 12, you might consider using smaller words and shorter sentences. It is likely to improve your reader's understanding.

## SUMMARY

Successful business communication depends upon effective writing; thus, understanding business communication means understanding principles of writing. For that reason, some of the principles have been underlined throughout this chapter.

Like everything in business communication, the foregoing principles of effective writing must be tempered with good judgment. Writers who follow each principle blindly, to an extreme degree, are likely to produce bland or mechanical writing. Also, such principle adherence may cause the writer's style to become obvious. Readers will be distracted from the writer's content because the writer slavishly applied the rules with little intervention of common sense and good judgment. Principles are guides. Used with clear, logical thinking, they become useful aids in developing effective writing.

Material in this chapter is introductory. These are by no means all the principles that may be derived from communication theory. They are the most general and the most basic, but they are the principles that can be used in most business-writing situations. More specific applications are reserved for the next two chapters.

## NOTES

[1] For a listing of "Common Forms of Written Messages," see John J. Makay and Ronald C. Fetzer, *Business Communication Skills: Principles and Practice*, 2nd ed. (Englewood Cliffs, N.J.: Prentice-Hall, 1984), p. 194.

[2] "She Talks People Out of Writer's Block," *The Sunday Star Bulletin & Advertiser*, Honolulu, Hawaii (December 13, 1981), Sec. C, pp. 10, 14.

[3] Ibid., p. 10.

[4] Raymond G. Smith, *Principles of Public Speaking* (New York: The Ronald Press, 1958), pp. 150–52. Reprinted with permission of John Wiley and Sons, Inc.

[5] Dale A. Level, Jr. and William P. Galle, Jr., *Business Communications: Theory and Practice* (Dallas: Business Publications, 1980), p. 96. © 1980 Business Publications, Inc.

[6] For more overused expressions and an explanation of why each is weak, see William C. Himstreet and Wayne Murlin Baty, *Business Communications: Principles and Methods*, 5th ed. (Boston: Kent Publishing, 1977), pp. 23–27; Donald J. Leonard, *Shurter's Communication in Business*, 4th ed. (New York: McGraw-Hill, 1979), pp. 30–34; William Strunk, Jr. and E. B. White, *The Elements of Style*, 3rd ed. (New York: Macmillan, 1979), pp. 23–25.

[7] One author presents nine ways to avoid stereotyped language. See Howard Dana Shaw, "Are Your Letters Like the Surrey with the Fringe on Top?", *Sales Management*, 62 (1949), 58–62.

[8] Himstreet and Baty, *Business Communications*, p. 40.

[9] See Walter E. Oliu, Charles T. Brusaw, and Gerald J. Alred, *Writing That Works: How to Write Effectively On the Job* (New York: St. Martin's Press, 1979), p. 108.

[10] Adapted from Robert Gunning, *The Technique of Clear Writing* (New York: McGraw-Hill, rev. ed., 1968), pp. 38–40. Fog Index is a service mark of Gunning-Mueller Clear Writing Institute, Inc.

[11] Robert Gunning, "The Fog Index After Twenty Years," *The Journal of Business Communication*, 6 (Winter 1968), 3–13.

# 15

# Business Letters

As writing becomes a more frequent activity for business people, letters are likely to take up more and more time. Most people reserve a certain portion of the day just for responding to daily mail. Some, however, do not realize that responding to mail may be one of the most important services to the company. It may be the only direct and individual communication people have with a company. And yet, for many business people, letter writing ranks near the bottom of their business activities with respect to importance.

Although letter writing may be a small part of the total communication scene in business, it can serve several purposes. It can help a company meet its objectives. It can help customers by solving their problems or getting them a product they want. At the same time, it can build good will. Thus, as a communication medium, letter writing deserves attention.

In this chapter the advantages and disadvantages of business letters will be discussed first. Basic qualities will then be outlined, and beginnings and endings will be examined. Layout, the way a letter looks, or the nonverbal factors of business letters, will be considered in the section on "Metacommunication." In the final section, different kinds of letters will be considered: inquiries, claims, credits, collection, and sales.

## ADVANTAGES AND DISADVANTAGES

Whether or not to write a letter depends on a number of different factors. Some people are prone to dash off a letter at the slightest provocation; others tend to refrain from letter writing almost entirely. The purpose of this section is to make it clear that writing letters has both advantages and disadvantages, and the effective business communicator will weigh these before making a decision.

### Advantages

Letters can serve useful and valuable functions for business. Their first advantage, of course, is their main purpose—they are *effective communicators*. Why do we want to write letters in the first place? We write to make an inquiry, get some action, make a sale, or just transmit routine information. There is a definite need to communicate, and the fulfillment of that need becomes the main purpose of our letter.

But why letters and not face-to-face conversations or telephone calls? One advantage of letters is that *they do not interrupt* receivers as do conversations and telephone calls. True, they may not catch receivers' attention like a phone call might, but if a phone call catches someone at an inopportune moment, the opportunity to convey a message may be lost anyway! Recipients of letters may put them aside until time permits leisurely reading. This may allow more receptivity to the message.

Letters are also effective because *they serve as a reminder*. When people get a letter they usually file it for further reference, respond to it at once, or keep it in a place where they are reminded to respond to it. Often, a conversation or telephone call is forgotten. As they saying goes, "Out of sight, out of mind." But a letter has staying power, provided it is not promptly discarded.

Closely connected with this advantage is that *letters provide a written record*. It is a way to record a business transaction. And even after a face-to-face conversation or telephone call, those involved may commit what they have agreed upon to written record so that those involved can have a file copy (a permanent record) of the exchange. In business there is a need to record business transactions; thus, the proliferation of business-letter writing.

Letters also allow writers more time to think out what they want to say. *They enable writers to present their complete thoughts in logical sequence.* Usually writers of letters wait until they have time to write or until they are in the mood. Thus, their letters are likely to be more effective because they are carefully thought out and prepared. They can present these ideas in uninterrupted sequence. In face-to-face conversation and on the telephone, communicators are subject to interruptions and digressions that break the train of thought.

*Letters may save money.* Costs must be weighed. The cost of a business letter is more than just the combined costs of stationery, envelope, and postage. The cost of handling, filing equipment, space, as well as salaries for the letter writer and secretary must also be considered. The higher those salaries, the more a letter costs. This still may be cheaper, however, than lengthy long-distance calls. The money-saving element becomes even more evident as letters are transmitted via telephone lines from one computer to another.

### Disadvantages

Letters are not always the best way to respond. For example, *letters are slow.* The information float time is lengthy. If you want speed, letters are not the best system. A transaction could be concluded before a letter reached its destination. That is why the telephone or computer is used for urgent messages with letters as follow-ups. Slowness was a factor with the traditional letter; computers have largely erased this disadvantage.

**Letters lack instant feedback.** In face-to-face conversations, in telephone exchanges, and using electronics there is instant feedback that can provide the response you need. That instant feedback can even prevent the need for writing a letter in the first place. Moreover, through instant feedback (the nonverbal cues) you can find out how your message is being received. This can cause you to modify your communication to be even more effective. Computers are having a major effect here as well, as feedback time is reduced.

**Letters may not be answered.** Some people do not take letters seriously. They are careless or nonchalant in their care and handling of their correspondence. This may result in your getting no answer at all to your letters.

Even under favorable circumstances, answers to letters are likely to take a week or two. And when replies do not come promptly, it causes concern for writers. Maybe the receiver does not care, is on vacation, is irritated with you, has chosen to do business with someone else, and so on. Use of the telephone may avoid weeks of delay and resulting uncertainty.

**Letters may not get written.** Some people do not communicate well in writing, or they think that they do not do it well. Thus, when it comes to getting a letter out (or to replying to a letter received), they procrastinate. They wait until they know how to phrase what they want to say (which may

Involve your reader, and show him or her where he or she fits into the picture.
Try to understand and adapt to the reader's needs.
Forget your own ego and the part it plays in the letter-writing process.

To see how this you-viewpoint can be reflected in our letter writing, compare the lists that follow:

| WE-VIEWPOINT | YOU-VIEWPOINT |
|---|---|
| "We cannot comply with your request . . ." | "As a person well-versed in business procedures, you will surely understand why . . ." |
| "Send your order at once so we can fill it." | "As soon as your order reaches us, your new _____ will be on its way and you can begin to enjoy . . ." |
| "We are happy to have your order for . . ." | "Your selection of _____ should reach you by . . ." |
| "Our policy prohibits us from . . ." | "Because our office is financed by your tax dollars, you will appreciate our policy on . . ." |
| "We have been tolerant of your past-due account up until now. At this time we must demand payment." | "For you to continue to enjoy the benefits of credit buying, you should clear your account at once." |

Once again, caution is advised in using the you-viewpoint. Overuse of the technique can make writers appear insincere or manipulative. One author has pointed out the value of audience analysis with respect to its use. He suggests that friendly, sensitive people react positively to the you-viewpoint approach. Less sensitive people and those with harsh personalities may not.[1] The best advice regarding the use of the you-viewpoint is to use your judgment and common sense.

### Positiveness

There are many different ways of saying something, and each way is likely to convey a different impression or feeling. If we take time to phrase our message, we can make more certain that only that impression or feeling we want conveyed will, indeed, be conveyed. Just as all these aspects of letter writing do not just happen, positiveness, too, must be planned and emphasized. *Positiveness* is the quality of being confident and certain as well as explicit—in control.

In the last chapter brief mention was made of positiveness in the section on compositions. "Accentuate the positive and subordinate the negative" was stated there. Good advice, but how is positiveness achieved?

First, writers can choose positive words. Positive words put readers in the proper frame of mind. They place their emphasis on the pleasant aspects of a writer's objectives. They also create good will.

But this does not mean negative words cannot be used. Negative words are strong; they lend emphasis, and there are times when they should be used. However, in using them writers should be aware of the negative effect they are likely to produce. They may stir up resistance to objectives. They can also be destructive of good will.

To avoid words with highly negative connotations means avoiding words that convey meanings associated with unhappy or unpleasant events. Think of your own background and experiences when the words "error," "mistake," "failure," "problem," "loss," "wrong," and "damage" were used. Notice, too, how certain words have negative connotations because of the way they sound or because of experiences to which they relate: "slime," "sloppy," "grimy," "bloody," "guts," and so on. Words like these have no place in letters designed to convey a positive impression.

The second way to achieve positiveness is to emphasize the positive features of things we describe rather than the negative. This is demonstrated in the popular description of a "partly cloudy" day as "partly sunny," or of "getting old" as being "young at heart," or being "as young as you feel."

Negative elements do not disappear or go away when they are not mentioned or overlooked. But when they are ignored, they can be made to appear less important. If you were responding to a request for merchandise that your company does not handle, you could be negative and say, "I'm sorry, we do not carry the item you requested." This simple phrase of the "we-viewpoint" has two negatives within it: "sorry" and "not." It might be better phrased to read, "The merchandise you requested is carried by the Willett Company, also located in this city. Our company specializes in Wilson cutlery." Other examples of the positive approach will be offered when the various letter types are discussed later in this chapter.

### Coverage

In the opening section of this chapter on advantages and disadvantages of letters, the first advantage of letters mentioned was their effectiveness as communicators. But they do not serve this purpose effectively if information that should be included is not. Readers should not need to follow up letters with more letters or with telephone calls. Careful planning of letters means including all necessary and pertinent information.

Sometimes in our attempts to be concise, we reduce our letters to only the barest of essentials. If, by doing this, we give a matter a brusque, hurried treatment, we lose both our effectiveness and good will.

To gain coverage, writers must be concerned about *completeness*. First, writers should make certain that when writing in response to a query, all questions are answered. To leave questions unanswered raises further questions, even doubts, in the reader's mind. Questions that cannot be answered should not be ignored. Writers should tell why the question cannot be answered. Completeness inspires readers.

A writer has written to our company for information on our summer rental units. She has asked which of our three locations is the most secluded; if rental units are still available for the last week in June; the cost range for one week; and if other companies have better prices. She's also requested a catalogue. The rental company could respond by just sending a catalogue—assuming that would answer all the questions, and it does. It could send back the inquirer's letter with a catalogue and brief answers to the questions in the margin of her letter. Both responses are inappropriate. Each of the questions should be answered in a separate letter that will accompany the catalogue:

1. All of our locations are essentially the same with respect to seclusion. The third, however, is closer to the shopping area than the others.
2. Many rental units are still available. They are filled on a first-come, first-served basis. You should make rental requests as soon as possible since this is the time most people make their summer plans.
3. Cost range for our units varies considerably with respect to size and distance from the beach. Rates vary from $160 to $350 per week.

(The fourth question is one the company prefers *not* answering and thus handles in this manner:)

4. I am sure that you will find our prices very competitive with those of other rental companies in this area.

Coverage also means explanations and justifications. True, it is sometimes easier—and certainly shorter—to say "no" to a request that cannot be fulfilled or for information you are asked to provide but cannot. There is a certain assertiveness in being strong, definite, and curt. But this approach is unlikely to win many friends. The writer conscious of generating good will takes the time to explain and justify his or her response.

"Coverage-and-then-some" would be explaining and justifying and then suggesting some alternative course of action. Writers should be human-relations conscious. One sales representative explained the reason for being successful in three words: "and then some." The sales representative would always do what was necessary, "and then some." Writers use this approach when they add a brief extra sentence wishing a newly promoted employee good luck in his or her new position. Or when an insurance agent adds congratulations to a policyholder who just earned some distinction. Can you add some additional remarks concerning the guarantee on a product? Other related and helpful products? Some suggestions for using the product? How about a few words about some new merchandise? Other services your company provides? Recent price reductions? Such information helps build good will.

*Shortness* concerns the number of words writers need to say what they have to say. It does not involve leaving out information vital to reaching your objectives. Do not take these ideas, however, as carte blanche to add any amount of additional information. Once again, your discrimination here will be greatly appreciated by your reader. Only that which is necessary to reach your goals should be included.

### Organization

The structure of a letter should serve two purposes: (1) to move your reader step-by-step through the various points you want to discuss, and (2) to help accomplish your objectives. To do this, planning must be done.

The *organization* of the letter depends on several things. The purpose of the letter may help determine its structure. For example, is the purpose to convey a favorable, neutral, or unfavorable response? Are you going to be persuasive? Once you have determined your approach, structure will become easier.

Moreover, once you know what you want to say, the structure will become clearer. Some things will need emphasis; other things will be de-emphasized. Some items will need more space; others will need less.

*Purpose* and *message* are two important elements in determining structure. Another is the reader. How will your reader react to your strategies? Can you anticipate how his or her mental filter will work with reference to your organizational decisions? What you need is a reader-specific plan that will accomplish your goals effectively.

More will be presented on letter organization when various types of letters are discussed in the final section of this chapter. It will become clear at that point that structure is very important, and that there are specific organizational schemes that can be followed.

## BEGINNINGS AND ENDINGS

The beginning and ending of a letter are important spaces and should be reserved for news you want to give great emphasis to.[2] They create first (primacy) and last (recency) impressions.

### Beginnings

The problem with the beginnings of letters is that they usually lack creativity. They follow stereotypical, cliché, or format phrasing and, thus, do not serve writers' purposes in the best way possible. The beginnings of letters stump many writers as they try to avoid typical rubber-stamp openings. That is why some attention to how to begin a letter will help us be creative and provide us with a specific way to begin.

To be realistic, it is reasonable to assume that recipients of business letters are busy people with numerous claims on their time and attention. They probably receive many letters, which means that any one letter will tend to blend in or merge with the others. Consider, too, the phenomenon of junk mail and the skepticism this creates in readers' minds. This phenomenon tends to create a knee-jerk response that causes readers to toss letters aside after a quick glance. Also, because of the nature of the business letter as a practical and functional form of communication, there is the expectation that it will be concise and direct. These circumstances and expectations provide certain guidelines within which writers of business letters must work. Letters have many different purposes; thus, letters have many different openings:

1. Orientation
2. Gain attention
3. Set tone
4. Offer a link
5. Provide a buffer

A *buffer* is a device used for reducing or cushioning against shock—bad news, for example. A buffer needs to be pleasant, relevant, equivocal (avoiding any implication that the answer is yes or no), and transitional. It should not, however, be misleading.[3]

The other four letter-opening functions are to follow. First, however, some overall guidelines that govern the construction of letters and that pertain to all the other functions that follow.

The most obvious factors that must guide the letter beginning are *brevity* and *importance*. First, *it must be short*. Brevity leads readers to the rest of the message. It should be like a headline that attracts readers and causes them to continue. Try to keep the beginning paragraph to an overall length of two or three sentences; the fewer the better.

Second, the *letter beginning should say something*. It should announce what the letter is about, to arouse reader interest. Anything else should be subordinate. The opening position of the letter should not be wasted by telling the reader what he or she already knows or by relaying trite or ineffective information.

Ideally, then, there are several functions that the first paragraph of a letter can perform. First, *the opening paragraph should indicate what the letter is about*. "You need not pay anything to examine this line of products," "The catalogue you requested on March 21 was mailed today," "Thank you for your helpful suggestions about our recent sales conference," are examples of good letter beginnings that tell what the letter is about. Beginnings can also be phrased as a question. ("When can we expect to receive your payment for the five copies of *The Business Communicator,* which we shipped on February 12?" "Did you know that we have many other items similar to the one you ordered?" "Would you like to know other ways we can save you money?") Even phrased as an exclamation, the first sentence or paragraph can indicate what the letter is about. ("Many people have taken this opportunity to invest in their future!" "July 10 is a great day! It is the day you first contacted us and began a great business adventure!")

*It can gain favorable attention.* A letter opening can gain favorable attention by starting out positive: "Here is your refund." "Your order has been mailed." "Yes, you are welcome to use our meeting facilities."

But what if there is no favorable element in the writer's letter plan? Then writers should begin by creating good will or through resale. Good will was discussed in the section on tone. It has to do with treating others as human beings and using pleasant words.

*Resale* is the process of keeping people sold. It states, in effect, that their decision to purchase a product was, indeed, a good one. Because there is often a one-week to two-week delay between the order of a product and its receipt, some people need to be told again how wise they were in the decision they made to purchase a product. Resale simply helps purchasers overcome any lingering doubts they may have about their decision.

The point is that letters should seldom begin negatively. Even overdue payment requests begin positively in the early stages; in later stages they become more negative. A negative response can turn off readers. This may make it unlikely that they will read the rest of the letter. Of course, if the first line summarizes the purpose, little more may be needed. An inductive approach, discussed in the last chapter under paragraph types, will first lead readers step-by-step through the explanation and presentation of alternatives and then leave them with a solid understanding of why their request must be rejected. They will have read the evidence and will more likely be left with a positive impression.

*The first paragraph should set a friendly tone.* Since we have already discussed tone, and since gaining good will has been an underlying goal throughout this chapter, little more needs to be said. Let this merely serve as a reminder that friendliness is conveyed by warmth, concern, appreciation, support, and a humanness conveyed through sincerity and genuineness. How would you want to be treated in similar circumstances? ("You were thoughtful to enclose your cancelled check. It made processing your request much easier." "This may not be the best time to request your help because we are all busy at this time of year, but you did such an outstanding job last time you spoke before our group. . . ." "Thank you for writing to us about your experience with our pens. We are always happy to hear from our customers. . . .")

Finally, *the beginning of a letter should link up with previous correspondence.* Lapses of time between letters may cause confusion. The fact that your letter may be one of many different letters received may cause people to forget about it or its contents. Also, some people may receive many letters on the same topic or idea, which may also create confusion. In some cases, too, one person may have many different contacts with the same company. To identify the subject or date may help the reader to zero in on the specific contact under consideration. Thus, writers should include a reference to the date or to the subject. It should be done more creatively than "This is to answer yours of September 23," "We have received yours of September 23," or "Referring to yours of September 23. . . ." The reference to the date of earlier letters should always be subordinated. In each of the preceding cases it is emphasized. Thus, an important part of the letter is being wasted merely to tell the reader that his or her letter was received. Notice how subordination of the date can occur with the use of techniques already considered: "Our research and development office shipped material today that will help you answer the questions raised in your inquiry of September 23." "We have enclosed a useful brochure entitled, 'Exercises for Successful Selling,' which you requested on September 23." "Thank you for writing to us about your typewriter. The problems you cited in your letter of September 23 were unfortunate ones. . . ."

**Endings**

The end of a letter should be designed to leave a positive final impression. Once again, this is a recency effect because the last thing mentioned will be the most recent thing in a reader's mind. After applying the ideas presented regarding beginnings, and after careful wording and structuring of your ideas, you will want to maintain the same strength in the ending. The most important principle to use to guide your phrasing of the end of your letter should be to *stop writing when your message is complete.*

There are many ways to end letters. Unfortunately, most writers use the same method over and over, or they rely on trite, well-used phrases that reveal little thought or creativity: "If I can be of further assistance, please let me know," "We look forward to your response," "Once again, thank you for writing," "Thanking you in advance," or "Trusting that we have your cooperation in this matter," tend to be some of the overused ways of ending letters. It is not that they do not work; obviously they do work, and that is why they are overused.

Using trite, well-used phrases reflects the laziness of writers unwilling to take the time to think. Such endings show little regard for readers. Writers are not treating readers as individuals since all readers get the same response as everyone else. And these responses reveal no originality. Writers miss an opportunity to imprint their unique personality on the letter as part of the final impression they can make.

Let us look at some other methods for ending letters that serve the purposes of leaving positive final impressions, and yet offer some alternatives to stereotypical final phrases. Some are designed to get action, some to resell, some to establish or reinforce an attitude. All must be phrased in such a way as to maintain good will.

*Getting action.* The last paragraph of a letter should make it easy for readers to take the action writers want taken. Writers can use the final paragraph, for example, to show readers how easy it would be to do what needs to be done: "Just sign and return the enclosed postcard and you will receive our company brochure free of charge." "Your check in the enclosed envelope will enable you to continue enjoying a high credit rating with our company." "You may call our company collect to receive an estimate at no cost or obligation to you."

A direct question can also be used to get action. "May I have an interview with you at your convenience?" "Would you allow such a small amount to jeopardize your credit rating?" "Can you telephone me next week to verify this information?" Or the question could be as simple as, "May we hear from you?"

*Resale.* Obviously, resale can be part of letter beginnings *and* endings. When writers feel the need to reassure their reader or to strengthen their confidence, *resale* is an appropriate method. "We sell only quality merchandise. The appliance you purchased will give you many years of excellent service. It is the finest in our line."

*Establishing or reinforcing an attitude.* Like an ending that is designed to get action, this one treats readers' attitudes. The "you-viewpoint" discussed earlier in this chapter should be employed. "All of us wish you every success in your new business adventure." "I know you will find the arrangements made for you at the Sutton Inn comfortable and convenient." "I know you realize our predicament, and we appreciate your understanding of the problem." Attitude establishment or reinforcement could also be phrased as a polite question: "May we have the opportunity to serve you in the future?" "May we join all your business friends in wishing you continued prosperity?" "You will feel free to contact us in the future, won't you?"

Endings should be framed with friendliness in mind. Writers should strive to be polite, courteous, and appreciative. It is only with this kind of attitude that they can get the action they want or change the attitude in the direction they desire. But such a mood should not be overdone. Again, the best advice is for writers to stop when their message is complete. Overdone friendliness begins to sound syrupy, sweet, even sickening.

## METACOMMUNICATION

Writers sometimes forget that it is not the words alone that communicate. When recipients read letters they are affected by all aspects of the communication from the envelope to the smallest typographical error. They are sensitive to what is going on around the words, or beyond the words, as well. That is, readers notice what is said soundlessly: without words. The prefix *meta*, from the Greek, means "beyond" or "in addition to." So, when we examine *metacommunication*, we must look beyond the obvious communication—beyond the words themselves.

Metacommunication involves, then, the nonverbal aspects of letters. Anything in written communication that does not include the words selected is nonverbal. You receive a memo and the paper it is written on, whether it is typed or handwritten, how hurriedly it appears to have been transcribed, or how many errors are included (which may reflect haste) can be important silent messages that help you gauge the seriousness or, perhaps, the importance of the memo. Thus, nonverbal communication is anything other than the words themselves that either communicates or affects (enhances or hinders) the flow of the message among people.

In many cases the responsibility for the neatness and attractiveness of written communications is assumed by secretaries. But when you sign your name at the bottom of the letter, you assume responsibility for everything from the content to the layout, from the spelling and grammar to the mechanics of the letter. If there are problems in any of these areas, the reader judges you—the one who signed the letter—not your secretary. In this section we will discuss *appearance*—the outward aspects of business letters. We will discuss the envelope, address location, stationery, letterhead, standard parts of the letter, and special parts of the letter.

### Envelope

An envelope is an advertisement. The quality of the paper, pictures, slogans, and company logo all contribute to the company image. Envelopes should show the sender's return address in the upper left corner and should either be in a format identical to the letterhead or typewritten and should be about one-half inch from the top left edge of the envelope.

### Address Location

The addressee's name and address must appear in a specific location—the "read zone"—so that post office electronic mail sorters can use the information. Optical Character Readers (OCR) require dark print on a light background that is parallel (within 5°) to the bottom of the envelope. See Figure 15–1.

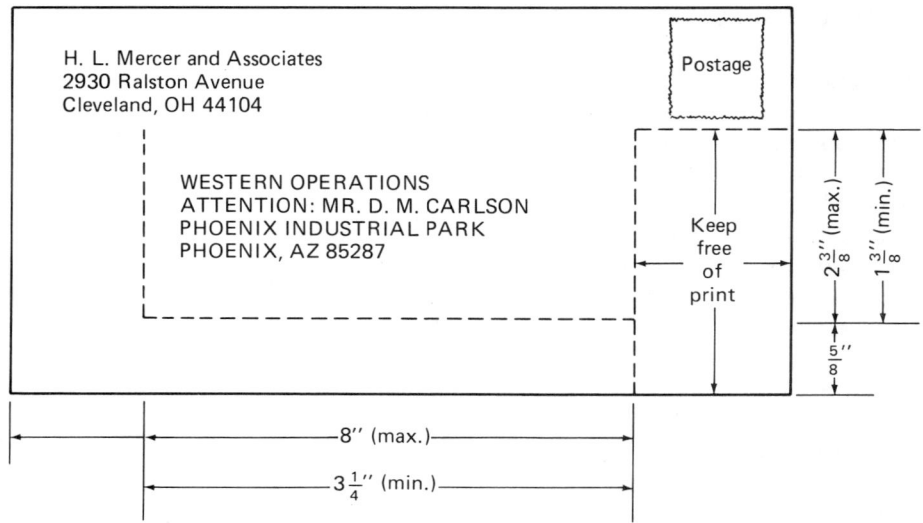

**FIGURE 15-1.** Envelope with measurements indicated for OCR readability. It is suggested that all capitals be used in the address.

Other requirements for OCR reading include a single-spaced blocked format; typewritten capital characters without punctuation (recommended); city, state, and ZIP code on bottom line; street name or box number on the line above city, state, and ZIP code. The number of an apartment, room, suite, or other unit of a multiunit building should appear after the street address and on the same line. Any instructions such as "Confidential," "Attention Mr. Frank," or "Please forward" must appear within the "read zone" on any line above the second line from the bottom.

People who use the mails often know this information. Not to know it reflects on one's credibility and image. To display proper form here conveys a positive first impression.

### Stationery

It is true that the purchasing department may be responsible for selecting the stationery you use, but you may have an opportunity to suggest a change. Once again, the company's personality is reflected by the quality, size, and color of the paper as well as the letterhead itself.

The appearance of your letter is like your appearance; the less attention it calls to itself, the better. A reader may reject a written message that calls attention to its format. A personalized letter sent by first-class mail will nearly always get a reading. Thus, an excessively heavy or light quality, an unnecessarily large or small size, a lavish color, or a flashy design is like yelling at a person whose attention you already have. When the writer violates the conventions of letter form, the reader's attention is distracted from the message.

If your stationery is inappropriate, it will be noticed. The most common business stationery, and therefore that which is least likely to be noticed, is 16–20 pound white bond paper. It should contain at least 25 percent rag content and be $8\frac{1}{2}$-by-11 in size. The main off-standard size is $7\frac{1}{2}$-by-$10\frac{1}{2}$.

White is the most common and popular color, but your imagination and the rainbow itself set the limit of possibilities. Some firms achieve a distinctive quality and warm touch by using pastel stationery and envelopes. There is marked movement toward more color in stationery. One must also consider what is appropriate. It may be wise to run your own test on a small sample to test appropriateness for particular situations. Whatever the choice of paper, the same color and weight should be used for first and second pages as well as the envelope.

### Letterhead

The letterhead on a piece of stationery is the signature of the company or organization. It should take no more than two inches at the top of the page, or it may occupy just a corner.

Minimum amount of information to be contained here includes name and company address, ZIP code, telephone number, cable address, nature of the business, and the name of the department or branch office sending the correspondence. Sometimes the nature of the business is conveyed by an added trademark or slogan.

Although modern letterheads generally do not include the names of officers and directors, pictures of the company and its product, slogans, and starting date of the firm, these are available options. The trend today is toward simplicity. Whatever the choices in letterheads, tasteless designs, garish colors, and strange combinations should be avoided.

### Standard Parts of the Letter

The problem here is *convention*—what is expected or standard practice. To break with convention may distract or cause the reader to wonder about the writer. It is best, when writing letters, to adhere to the seven standard parts, using a single space within parts and a double space between parts. The seven standard parts are: (1) heading, (2) inside address, (3) salutation, (4) body, (5) complimentary close, (6) signature area, (7) reference section. The letter in Figure 15–2 includes additional information.

**Heading** ↕ 2″    LETTERHEAD

------

January 18, 198_

**Inside address**
Mr. John J. Hunter
Director of Marketing
Mathus Manufacturing Company, Inc.
619 South Main Street
Springfield, OH 45321

**Salutation**  Dear Mr. Hunter:

**Body**  It is this letter form, the modified block, that is used most frequently in business. Notice that all parts of the letter except the date, complimentary close, and signature begin at the left margin.

In this example, the date (placed 13 lines below the top of the page) ends at the right margin. Begin the complimentary close at the horizontal center of the page, or to the right of center so that the longest line in the signature ends at the right margin.

In the signature area, the company name may be included. The signer's typed name and business title should appear four lines below the complimentary close. The signer's business title may be typed on the line below the name or may be split and typed on two lines.

**Complimentary close**                                Sincerely,

                                                        *Weldon L. Murdock*
                                                        Weldon L. Murdock
                                                        Director, Customer Service

**Reference initials**  WLM:vm

**FIGURE 15-2.**

### Special Parts of the Letter

There are also six widely used special parts of a business letter. You may, in your writing, find use for any one of them.

The first special part is an *attention line*. This is used in a letter addressed to a company if you want a certain individual to read your letter: "Attention Mr. Smith." If you do not know the person's name, you may use the job title: "Attention: Sales Department." This line is placed between the inside address and salutation, with a double space above and below, flush at the left margin or centered. The attention line has no effect on the salutation; the salutation relates to the inside address.

Some writers use a *subject line* to quickly tell the reader what the letter is about. It can also be used to refer to previous correspondence for necessary background. The subject line appears flush at the left margin a double space below the salutation. When space is at a premium, it can appear on the same line as the salutation, only centered and underscored, or in solid capitals to make it stand out. The writer may use "About," but "Re" and "In re" are old forms and "Subject" is redundant since the position and wording make it clear what the subject line is.

Below the reference initials by a single or double space, the writer may include an *enclosure notation*. This is simply a reminder to the person putting up the mail to make the enclosure. Its presence in the letter reminds the reader that there is more than just the one item. Enclosure may be spelled out, abbreviated *Encl.*, or *Enc.*, followed by a colon and a number indicating how many enclosures, or by a colon and words indicating what the enclosures are.

If individuals other than the addressee should be informed of the contents of the letter, the writer indicates *copy* designations by *CC* (or *Cc*, *cc*, or *Copy to*) a single or double space below either the reference initials or the enclosure notation. If it is necessary to keep the addressee from knowing that others are receiving copies, *Bc* (for "blind copy"), a colon, and the name can be typed on the copy only.

*Postscripts* are afterthoughts. But they are rare in business communication because they reflect poor planning. If a postscript is necessary, the writer has two options: to have the letter retyped, or to add a handwritten note. Such handwritten notes may increase the effectiveness of the letter by adding a personal touch. They can increase effectiveness especially if the note ties in with the development of the whole message and stresses an important point.

A postscript should be the last thing on a page, a doublespace below the preceding parts. A "P.S." is optional since both position and wording clearly indicate what it is.

*Second-page headings* are useful when it comes to filing or reassembling multipage letters. A second page should be blank (without a letterhead) but of the same weight and quality as the first page. For identification, a second page should include the addressee's name, the date, and the page number. This could be typed in any of three styles: (1) across the top:

Mr. N.L. Styles           - 2 -           June 23, 19__

or (2), typed down the left margin:

```
Mr. N.L. Styles
June 23, 19__
Page 2
```

or (3), for speed and equal acceptability:

```
Mr. N.L. Styles, June 23, 19__, page 2.
```

The body of the letter on that page contains a quadruple space below this last line. See Figure 15–3. This letter is designed to include the six features discussed here. Again, read the letter for some additional insights.

Many companies have adopted a format for writing letters that is used throughout the company. In that way, all letters written contribute to an attractive, uniform image. Writers should be aware that such policies exist.

All the letters you write should be designed to work for you. Even grammar, spelling, punctuation, and syllabication contribute to the overall effect and thus should be treated seriously. Although you may say, "Oh, those are secretarial responsibilities," you still assume the final responsibility for correctness and accuracy. The elements of metacommunication carry significant weight in determining final impressions.

## DIFFERENT KINDS OF LETTERS

Business communicators write many different kinds of letters, and they tailor each one to fit a specific need. Thus, one essential prerequisite for successful letter writing is to study each situation. In this section, some of the major types of letters will be examined: (1) inquiries, (2) claims, (3) adjustments, (4) credits, (5) collections, and (6) sales. Letters that relate to employment were discussed in Chapter 10, "Getting a Job."

### Inquiries

The letter of inquiry is the one most frequently written to business firms. This kind of letter seeks information on a wide variety of matters including the operation of a piece of merchandise, the price of certain products, the uses to which an item can be put, or any of an infinite variety of other similar concerns.

The *solicited letter of inquiry* usually results from an advertisement inviting readers to write for more information. Writers of solicited letters should be specific about what they want. They should also include their name and address if they use paper without a letterhead. See Figure 15–4 and Figure 15–5.

```
                            LETTERHEAD
  2"


- - - - - - - - - - - - - - - - - - - - - - - - - - - - - - - - - -

September 14, 19__

Accounting Department
Eastern Manufacturing Company
9732 Fifth Avenue, SW
Washington, D.C. 20261

Attention Ms. Arlene Smythe

Ladies and Gentlemen:      Account #136409114

This is a full block form, which means that all parts of the letter
begin at the left margin. A full-block letter is never double
spaced.

In this example, the complimentary close includes the name of the
company. This occurs when you are writing about company business,
and the company is to be legally responsible for the letter.


Cordially,

LOEB AND BRILHART
Michael J. Morrison
```

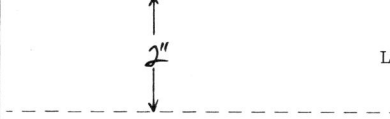

```
Michael J. Morrison
General Manager


MJM:ltd


Enclosures:  3
CC:  Mr. Thomas Acredited
     Miss Teresa Lever
```

**FIGURE 15–3.** In addressing a person, try to use the courtesy title he or she prefers. Traditional titles are "Mr.," "Mrs.," "Miss," or "Ms." *Ms.* may be used for all women, regardless of their marital status, unless they have a professional title or insist on "Mrs." or "Miss."

```
Nikon, Incorporated
Garden City, New York 11530

Gentlemen and Ladies:

Please send me information on the Nikon EM
which was mentioned in your Time advertisement
last month.

                    Sincerely yours,

                    James C. Young
                    James C. Young
                    2734 Seaside Drive
                    Seattle, Washington  98114
```

**FIGURE 15-4.** A Sample Letter of Inquiry

**FIGURE 15-5.** Another Sample Letter of Inquiry

```
                    LETTERHEAD
- - - - - - - - - - - - - - - - - - - - - - - - - - -

Electra Company
International Business Office
Suite 102, 1828 Swift
North Kansas City, Missouri  64116

Gentlemen and Ladies:

Please send me information about the Freedom Phone
Cordless Telephone Model FF-3500 which you advertised
in Nation's Business for March 1982.

                    Yours truly,

                    Adam Connault
                    Adam Connault
                    Vice President
```

*Unsolicited inquiries* are those in which writers take the initiative for asking for information. They must also be direct. Writers must get right to the point of the letter. Sometimes this can be handled outright with a question: "Can you provide me information about . . . ?" Again, writers need to be as specific as possible about the information they want. If there are several parts to a request, they should be tabulated, which helps assure

**FIGURE 15-6.** A Sample Unsolicited Letter of Inquiry

---

Gentlemen and Ladies:

   Would you please help us make <u>Business Universe</u> more beneficial to you? We hope this monthly publication has been useful, but now we want comments from readers to make the publication even more valuable. Your comments will guide us in making improvements.

   Just a minute of your time will be necessary to answer the questions below. A stamped, self-addressed envelope is enclosed for your convenience. Your response will help us keep <u>Business Universe</u> practical and specific.

Sincerely,

*Howard H. Montclair*

Howard H. Montclair<br>
Editor

1. In which are you most interested?

   ___ foundations of business     ___ production
   ___ social responsibility        ___ marketing
   ___ management                   ___ promotion
   ___ human resources              ___ pricing
   ___ labor-management             ___ finances
              ___ government

2. Which of the following sections has proved most useful to you?

   ___ future directions            ___ employment trends
   ___ regulations                  ___ business headlines
              ___ letters

3. Would you be interested in an expansion of the "Business Tips" section?

   ___ Yes                          ___ No

4. Is the address to which <u>Business Universe</u> has been sent correct? If not, please correct the address here.

that readers will not overlook items asked about. If the request is short, the questions can be placed in separate sentences. If all questions are grouped in one sentence, readers may see only the first and fail to respond to the others. Also, if the means for the reader responding is reduced to "yes" and "no" responses in which readers can simply check a box, this helps make responding easier. With any inquiry, courtesy requires that a stamp, or a self-addressed, stamped envelope be enclosed when addressed to an individual or small firm. For a large firm, doing so may interfere with mailing procedures.

A letter of inquiry should be clearly structured. Writers should make a clear statement of the information desired: what is wanted, who wants it, and "why" can also be included. A tabulation of questions or reference to an enclosed questionnaire should be the second item. The letter should close with a statement of appreciation. See Figure 15–6.

**Answering Inquiries**

Answering inquiries is a serious activity. First, you know the respondent is serious. Few people who take up a pen to write a letter are not serious. Second, you know the respondent is interested. Whether it be in a product or in a bit of information, your answer will be important to the person responding. Remember, the writer took the initiative to respond. Third, you know this is an opportunity to promote good will and the company image. Someone who takes the time to write is engaging in an interpersonal (one-on-one) relationship with a business firm. There are few better situations for showing how human-centered a company is. A thoughtless response is likely to offend the writer of the inquiry just as if you had offended him or her in person. Just because a response is written does not make the effect of that response any less important, effective, or immediate.

When people write, they are engaging in the same transactional-communication experience as when they are talking to others. They are communicating with an image of the firm or an image of the other person that to them is real and present. Chapter 2 discusses communication as transaction.

There are several major problems that occur in answering inquiries. The first is tardiness. Often, responses take weeks. Prompt responses promote a good company image; they reflect concern. They also reflect good organization. Someone who can take action quickly comes across as a disciplined, organized person. Prompt replies also reflect a business that cares about what people think of it.

The second problem that occurs in answering inquiries is sloppiness. Addresses are wrong. Incorrect material or information is enclosed. Something is missing. No special care is taken; rather, inquiries are handled as if no one is on the other end. Or, perhaps the guiding principle is, "Some response is better than no response at all."

The third problem is error-ridden answers. This problem could be part of sloppiness. People do not check their work or their information. Closely related to this problem, and sometimes part of it, is the answer that is unclear or written in confusing words, abstract language, or business jargon.

The final problem has to do with forgetting to enclose the material, catalogue, or brochure requested. Usually, mention of it in the letter will prompt enclosure. Thus, respondents should always refer specifically, in the letter, to anything either enclosed or sent separately.

### Claims

Claim letters are designed to bring errors to the attention of those responsible for them. They are usually written by individuals asking for something to which they think they are entitled: refunds, replacements, exchanges, and payment for damages are some examples. Letters written to take action on such claims are called *adjustment* letters, which are discussed in the next section.

Writers of claim letters should take the direct approach. They have everything working for them. It is as if the dice are loaded in their favor. Most businesses want to please customers; thus, they want to make adjustments to keep customers happy. Further, directness lends strength to the claim. It emphasizes it and shows your confidence in reporting it. See Figure 15–7.

Claim letters should be fair. They should not be written in a time of anger. Writers should also refrain from sarcasm and accusations. Negative words such as *unfair, false, untrue, worthless, disgusted, dishonest, disreputable, no good,* or *disgrace* should usually be avoided. When writers let their emotions run away, their letter stands less chance of gaining a response. They are more likely to get a response if they can be fair.

Claim letters should stress facts. Writers should provide a clear, straightforward explanation of what is wrong. All specifics should be included: dates, amounts, model numbers, sizes, colors, or any other information that will make it easier for the reader. Writers need to indicate the inconvenience or loss resulting from the problem. They can attempt to motivate action by appealing to the reader's sense of fair play, honesty, or pride. Threatening loss of business at the first error is excessive and emotional. Writers should state specifically what adjustment would be considered fair. Writers who do not know exactly what they want or what constitutes a fair settlement should stimulate prompt investigation and action and let the adjuster suggest a satisfactory settlement. Finally, conditions or consequences for nonfulfillment of the request should be mentioned.

> Seeing your advertisement in <u>Business Reports</u>, I wrote for the book, and enclosed a check for $15.95. Your advertisement said "satisfaction guaranteed, or your money refunded."
>
> Although I like the book, <u>Career Opportunities</u>, it was badly damaged in transit. Also, pages 52-65 are actually missing. I feel that I have not gotten my money's worth from this book.
>
> I am returning the book to you hoping that you will stand behind your guarantee. I would like you to send me the same book. If you do not have any more, a refund will be fine.

> Please send another copy of <u>Career Opportunities</u> to replace the one in the attached mailing folder.
>
> This book was badly damaged in transit. Also, pages 52-65 are missing.
>
> The enclosed invoice was packed with the book when it was mailed to me.
>
> I shall appreciate an exchange (or a refund if your supply is gone).

**FIGURE 15-7.** Claim Letters. The direct approach (bottom) requests the action to be taken in the first sentence. Details supporting the request are presented next. Finally, the writer closes with an expression of appreciation for the action being taken.

### Adjustments

How adjustments are handled reflects company policy toward claims. For example, granting all claims reflects the policy that the customer is always right. Granting adjustments when the claim seems fair reflects the policy that adjustments are decided based on the merits of the claim. Finally, granting no claims at all reflects the policy of *caveat emptor,* or "let the buyer beware"—a policy no company can afford to adopt.

Fairness must be the guiding principle for writers of adjustment letters. They must realize they are handling a delicate situation. Customers are disgruntled and upset, and they believe sincerely that they have a grievance. In trying to be fair, adjusters must not side too much with the claimant for that may exaggerate the claim and make it seem greater than it is. And yet adjusters must never argue with or accuse customers of making unjust claims. They should, however, listen to customers' positions. Fairness requires a straight course between the extremes of company position and customer complaint. Many companies have clear positions on how to handle grievances.

Adjusters must realize that every claim, no matter how trivial it may seem, is important to the person who makes it. People require a prompt answer or acknowledgment. Answers must be factual, courteous, and fair. Such writers must offer no argument and refrain from taking a critical attitude. Throughout the letter, a spirit of good will must be promoted.

The best format for *granting an adjustment* is to directly present in the opening of the letter the news in which the reader is most interested. Begin by granting the adjustment if that is possible. Second, include any necessary explanation. Include with this the information that any recurrence of the situation is likely to be minimal. Writers could assure readers of a change in operations or procedures or of increased vigilance regarding similar problems. Finally, writers should resell the product, the service, and the company. This is their opportunity to regain the reader's faith. See Figure 15–8. If the claim is not going to be granted, or if the claim is not real, a buffer (mentioned previously) can be presented in the opening followed by the necessary explanations and ending with a resale of the product. For example, "We understand the difficulty you have had with the Weegee Calculator. Unfortunately, we are unable to replace it because the Weegee Calculator is no longer made. We would be willing to send you the name, address, and phone number of the distributor nearest you, who might be able to repair your product. The Weegee is, after all, a prized item, and we appreciate your reluctance to move to a more complicated product."

**FIGURE 15–8.** Letter of Adjustment

```
       You are perfectly right in expecting merchandise from our
  company to be in perfect condition.  For that reason we are sending
  you a new replacement for your Phone-mate 900 on Tuesday.

       If you will put your first Phone-mate 900 into the new box
  and mail it back to us C.O.D., that will help us evaluate the
  situation.

       Apparently the problem occurred because of a slip-up in
  inspection.  We have taken steps to reduce the likelihood of it
  happening again.

       Your record of patronage of our company is outstanding, and
  we want to keep it that way.  We want to make every transaction
  satisfactory for you.  If it is not, we will make it right.
```

*Refusing an adjustment* is more difficult. Even a partial adjustment, from the customer's viewpoint, may be taken as a refusal. The best guidance for writing the refusal of adjustment is taken from the Bible: "A soft answer turneth away wrath." It will be the overall tone of the letter that maintains good will and continued association between the company and the claimant.

Refusing an adjustment can be handled in various ways; however, the overall goals should be the same: Convince readers they are being treated fairly, gain their confidence in the products, services, or policies of the company, and retain their good will. To do this successfully requires both tact and self-control on the part of writers. It is not a job for the neophyte.

Even when customers are at fault, they should not be blamed. Any negative connotation must be avoided. Customers should never feel like shamed, naughty children. People *do* make mistakes. Furthermore, they fail to follow instructions; they do not read instructions; they misinterpret instructions. But that does not diminish the need for tact and for being positive. People should always be treated as adults.

Writers should begin by getting on common ground with readers. See Figure 15–9. They must agree with the reader in some way. Such an opening establishes good will from the outset and assures continued reading. Readers are not put off by an opening that contains a negative refusal.

The second part of an adjustment refusal should be a clear explanation of the situation from the adjuster's point of view. Here, there is no need for defensiveness. A simple description is required. Customer claims or perceptions should not be negated or refuted. This comes across as defensiveness. Once again, avoid negatives where possible. Phrase the entire explanation in positive language.

The third part of the letter should be the complete refusal of adjustment or statement of partial adjustment. This part of the letter should not be avoided. Fortunately, by the time readers reach this part, they have your complete explanation; thus, the blow is somewhat softened. Also, by its

**FIGURE 15–9.** Communication is a transaction. This figure represents the writer's ability to identify with the reader. This may simply be his or her degree of agreement with the reader's position.

Overlapping area of common ground

```
Dear Mrs. Goldsmith:

Thank you for your letter of January 18. You are right to expect
your new designer jeans to fit perfectly, even after they have been
washed. The ultimate goal of Rubisahn's is to provide customers
with the finest in designer fashions at reasonable prices. When
someone feels our goal has not been met, we want to hear about it.

Your letter noted the $34.95 sale price, which represents a thirty
percent reduction from the original price at which the jeans were
marked. We are able to bring such reductions to our customers by
eliminating the cost of returns. This is only done during major
clearance sales. The policy of no returns is marked on sale
stickers throughout the store as well as at all cash registers.
Because you are a valued customer, the best we can do is to invite
you to use the enclosed $10.00 gift certificate. It may be used
on any item in our store.

You will note that the gift certificate must be used between now
and the end of February. Fortunately for you, this coincides with
our new "spring-in-winter" sales. Designer fashions -- including
jeans -- have been marked down twenty to thirty percent off our
regular stock. These savings are advertised only by mail to our
preferred customers. We hope you will take advantage of the gift
certificate and the savings from our "spring-in-winter" sales.

Sincerely,

Robert Fitchberg

Robert Fitchberg, President
```

**FIGURE 15-10.** A Sample Letter Refusing an Adjustment

position in the letter, the actual refusal is de-emphasized. Sometimes bad news can be softened if writers offer readers an alternative. Is there anything else that can be done to help their situation? Adding alternatives further de-emphasizes the bad news.

The letter should end on a positive note. This may help maneuver the reader's mind away from the disappointment resulting from the refusal. This will also help to rebuild the good will established in the opening paragraph of the letter. See Figure 15-10.

### Credit Letters

*Credit* is a means by which a person may have something now and pay for it later. For the grantor of credit, it is an estimate of someone else's ability and willingness to pay later. Credit becomes important when you consider what good credit can get a person: an education, a car, or a house, to name some of the major items. It is based on the principle, "Have now, pay later."

Routine applications for credit, requests for credit information, giving of credit information, and final letters granting or refusing credit are usually handled by form letters or simple office forms. When they are not, such letters should be direct and to the point. See Figure 15–11 for sample application, acknowledgment, and granting letters.

*Refusing credit* is one of the hardest letters to write. Most letters of this type follow a routine format: "This is to inform you that we are unable at this time to extend credit." They usually end with a more positive expression that things may be different in the future. To end a refusal this

**FIGURE 15–11.**

```
Gentlemen and Ladies:

Please consider opening a line of credit for our company with an
initial limit of $1,500.

We have enclosed a recently compiled financial statement that should
give you an idea of our current solvency.

Listed below are companies that can serve as references regarding
our repayment performance:

                        Littleman and Company
                        673 Allmass Boulevard
                        Brooklyn, NY   11210

                        Pohlmart Enterprises, Inc.
                        13120 Cedarville Avenue
                        Baltimore, MD   21212

                        Englewood Products
                        4593 Summers Place
                        Decatur, IL   62522

We are currently putting together our first order.  We will send
it after we hear from you.

                                          Sincerely,

                                          _____
```

Dear Mr. Cameron:

We certainly appreciate the opportunity to do business with your firm. Your expression of confidence is gratifying, and we will do everything in our power to live up to it.

We look forward to your first order. As an expression of our confidence in you, we will ship it by express as soon as it is filled.

So that we will be able to handle your future needs without delay, we would appreciate a complete financial statement. If you prefer, just fill out and return the enclosed credit form.

Credit information is always kept confidential. We are looking forward to having you as a regular customer. May we have your credit information soon?

                                        Sincerely yours,

---

Dear Mrs. Long,

We are happy to grant you credit with a top limit of $1,000, in accordance with your request of March 22.

Our bills are sent on the 10th of each month and are payable by the end of each month. We charge $1\frac{1}{2}$ % interest.

We hope you enjoy shopping in our store, and we look forward to your continued patronage.

---

way serves none of the purposes discussed throughout this chapter except, perhaps, directness. It lets readers know they are poor credit risks and it lets the whole matter end with an indefinite refusal. There is neither good will nor pleasantness reflected. This is an easy way out for a credit manager, but makes little sense for a business.

    Rather than simply refuse credit, writers of refusal letters should try to get the applicant's business on a cash basis. Sound incentives for cash

> Dear Mrs. Long,
>
> We appreciate your request for credit at our store, dated March 22. We take all such requests very seriously and do a thorough investigation before granting any.
>
> We are unable to extend credit to you at this time; however, all our stores grant discounts of up to ten percent for cash purchasing. This is because cash reduces the processing and overall paperwork with which our staff must deal.
>
> Continued cash purchases over a period of time at our stores, will, I am certain, establish your reputation so that another request for credit can be processed in the very near future. We look forward to such a request if based on continued cash purchasing over the next several months.

**FIGURE 15–12.** Sample Credit Refusal

buying could be proposed in the letter: discounts for cash buying, savings on interest charges, purchases in small quantities for cash and thus keeping up-to-date merchandise in stock, or the pleasures of end-of-the-month freedom from bills. They could even propose that cash buying over a period of time will establish a reputation so that credit may be granted in the future.

Credit refusals need to follow a fairly clear format. Writers should open on a neutral note expressing appreciation for the application. They must then explain the refusal. This explanation must not turn into a lecture. The refusal itself should be brief but clear. Negative terms must be avoided. Writers should then move readers away from the refusal. Trying to get orders on a cash basis is one way of doing this. Finally, project an optimistic outlook toward doing business in the future. See Figure 15–12 for a sample credit-refusal letter.

### Collection Letters

The process of collection is closely related to credit. Collection letters become important when the use of credit has been abused. When the credit department is expertly managed, the work of the collection department is easier. In most companies, both functions operate out of the same department.

Collecting debts is a touchy undertaking. True, you want to collect the

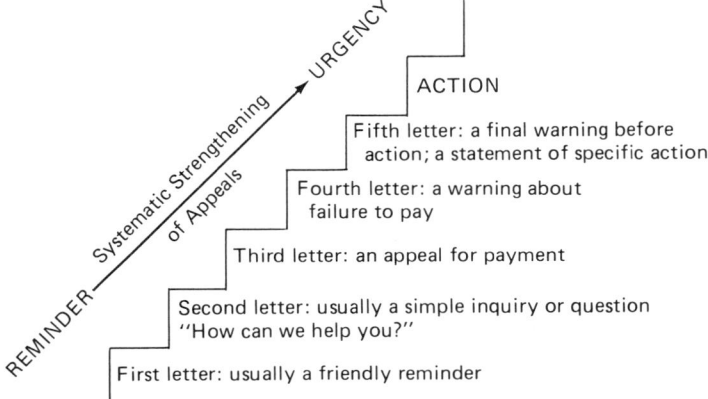

**FIGURE 15-13.** Company Collection Procedures. The actual number of steps depends on the company.

debts owed your company, but you do not want to lose valuable customers during the collection process. Dealing with single individuals is difficult, but dealing with giant corporations is even more troublesome. Although they demand payment from others immediately, they want to retain their own money as long as they can, especially when interest rates are high. Thus, the writing of collection letters requires both good judgment and a clear plan of action.

Most company collection procedures follow a clear step-by-step method based on one, clear, supporting principle: Customers will pay if they are reminded regularly. See Figure 15–13. Guidelines that are important during the collection process include the following:

1. Give customers the benefit of any doubt:
   bills may have been paid
   there may have been serious intervening circumstances
   bills get lost or misplaced.
2. Maintain a friendly, pleasant disposition while sounding a note of urgency.
3. Only as the process continues should you make persuasive appeals. In the third letter you can appeal to readers' honor, pride, and self-interest.
4. Always reveal a willingness to help, a firm but helpful attitude. Examples of collection letters are shown in Figure 15–14.

There are so many possible credit and collection situations. Tones, styles, and structures will vary according to the type of business writers work for, their credit policy, industry practices, and the customer's payment (credit) record. As in all communication situations, it is important that all relevant variables be considered before starting to communicate.

Dear Mr. Jamison:

We have an outstanding balance of $31.50 in your account due January 6 of this year.

We have enclosed an addressed, return envelope for your convenience.

If this bill has been paid, forgive this reminder and disregard this notice. We appreciate the payment.

---

Dear Mr. Jamison:

Our account still indicates an outstanding balance of $31.50 due January 6 of this year. Our first notice was sent February 6.

We are enclosing a second, addressed, return envelope for your convenience.

If you need to call us regarding this balance, our phone number is (419) 874-3135. If payment has already been made, please disregard this notice; we appreciate your payment.

---

Dear Mr. Jamison:

We have not received the $31.50 due January 6. Our reminders were dated February 6 and March 6.

As a customer in good standing with our company, I am certain you are interested in maintaining that good credit rating. Payment of bills is a matter of trust and good will between businesses and their customers.

If payment has been made, please disregard this notice, but if you have not paid, please put it in the enclosed envelope at once and mail it promptly.

**FIGURE 15-14.**

Dear Mr. Jamison:

$31.50 is the outstanding balance of your account with us. This is the fourth notice.

Failure to pay will terminate your credit with our company, and your account will be turned over to a collection agency, thus affecting your credit rating in the community.

Place a check or money order in the enclosed envelope and mail it now. If payment has been made, please disregard this notice.

---

Dear Mr. Jamison:

This is our <u>final warning</u>.

If payment of $31.50 is not received in our offices within <u>ten days</u>, your account will be given to a collection agency and will be out of our hands. Please mail it today.

The enclosed envelope will facilitate your <u>immediate</u> payment. If payment has been made, please call our office at once to assure proper credit: (419) 874-3135.

### Sales

The sales letter is the most often used persuasive, written communication. They are selective because they can reach almost any age group, financial class, professional category, geographical area, or occupation. They gain concentrated attention because when recipients read the letter no other items are competing for their attention at that moment. Finally, they are a high-percentage sales message because they can carry much more advertising than other media. Sales letters concentrate on material bearing directly on the product or service; thus, no space is wasted on irrelevant entertainment or attention-arousing pictures.

Sales letters have greatest effectiveness in certain situations. For example, when the product or service has specialized appeal, or when it is being offered at a fairly high price. Also, when the product can be classified as a "novelty," sales letters may be effective in moving that product. Thus, writers of sales letters are addressing readers who can be picked out from the many uninterested ones.

Writers should structure their sales letter. First, they must capture the attention of the reader. Second, they must create a desire for the product or service. This was labeled "need step" in the Monroe Motivated Sequence. Third, they must convince the reader the product or service is as good a value as the writer claims it to be. This is where logical support is essential. As a fourth step, writers can show readers how the product or service, once purchased, will help them. What will it actually do for the purchaser? Finally, writers must motivate action. Some of these functions can be combined. Usually, however, each is treated in a separate paragraph. See Figure 15–15.

Just as in any persuasive presentation, writers must begin by analyzing their product. What are its basic features? What are the buyer benefits? Next, they must analyze the market. It is a combination of the basic data of

**FIGURE 15–15.** A Sample Sales Letter. The letter closely follows the Monroe Motivated Sequence. The Sequence is an effective method for organizing a persuasive sales letter because it follows the normal process of human reasoning.

| | |
|---|---|
| 1. *Attract Attention* (Attention) | Can you believe, over 100 miles per gallon? |
| 2. *Create Desire* (Need) | Do you realize how much money that would save you just getting to and from work? Think about all those short errands that you run. Imagine the savings there! |
| 3. *Convince Reader Product Is Good* (Satisfaction) | Amergo has been making two-wheeled vehicles for more than twenty-five years. And the Amergo Moped has the same quality and easy-maintenance performance as our whole line of products. Amergo Mopeds use a two-stroke engine that speeds you along at 30 mph for 125 miles on a mere gallon of gas—even farther if you pedal part way. |
| 4. *Show How Product Will Help* (Visualization) | Picture yourself taking trips to school, to the beach, to the store, or to almost anywhere sitting atop an Amergo Moped. You get a smooth, fun-filled ride with no clutching, no shifting, and no parking problems! |
| 5. *Motivate Reader* (Action) | Ride one on us. Drop in to your local Amergo dealership for a free trial ride. You won't believe it until you ride it. |

the product and various market analyses that are used to determine market strategy for a product. The planning and creating of an effective selling campaign then begins. The point of this campaign is to bring the buyer and seller together for their mutual benefit. Because of the expense of effective advertising campaigns as well as the potential results, the process is usually not handled by beginners.

## SUMMARY

The planning and construction required to write a business letter take both care and time. Care is necessary because of the importance of the activity; time is necessary because it should not be left to chance. This chapter put the entire business-letter writing process into perspective.

Whether to write a letter or not depends on a number of factors. Advantages of a letter included effectiveness. Letters do not interrupt the recipient; they serve as a reminder, provide a written record, enable writers to present their complete thoughts, and can save money. These must be weighed against disadvantages, such as a letter's slowness, lack of feedback, possibility of no answer, and chance it may not be written.

Basic qualities of business letters all revolved around the planning that must go into them. It is only through planning that good will can be assured as well as effective sale of the company image. The qualities required are tone, you-viewpoint, positiveness, coverage, and organization.

Because the beginning and the ending of a letter are so important, a separate section treated each of these. Letter beginnings must be short, should say something, must gain favorable attention, should indicate what the letter is about, must be friendly, and should link up with previous correspondence. Endings must also be short. They should get action, resell, and either establish or reinforce an attitude.

Metacommunication is what occurs in a letter beyond the words. Basically, in business-letter writing, it involves the nonverbal aspects of letters: all their outward aspects. Those factors that can make an impression include the envelope, location of address, and stationery. Also discussed were the letterhead, standard and special parts of the letter.

Business communicators write many different kinds of letters, but only the major types were discussed in this chapter. These included inquiries, claims, adjustments, credit letters, collection letters, and sales letters.

Writing is one of the most important business-communication skills. The greater the job responsibility, the more important writing skills are. Weak writing costs valuable time and money because it creates misunderstanding. Weak writing may affect good will by fostering an unfavorable impression. Speed and accuracy are important in business-letter writing because of the volume of mail that needs answering, but writers who are effective write with courtesy and tact and a clear understanding of who they are writing to, namely, the reader of their effort.

## NOTES

[1] Sam J. Bruno, "The Effects of Personality Traits on the Perception of Written Mass Communication" (doctoral dissertation, Louisiana State University, Baton Rouge, 1971).

[2] Jessamon Dawe and William Jackson Lord, Jr., *Functional Business Communication* (Englewood Cliffs, N.J.: Prentice-Hall, 1974), p. 38.

[3] C. W. Wilkinson, Peter B. Clarke, and Dorothy Colby, Menning Wilkinson, *Communicating Through Letters and Reports*, 7th ed. (Homewood, Ill.: Richard D. Irwin, 1980), p. 80.

to hundreds of people? Will there be primary as well as secondary readers? (Will the people who get the report first pass it on to others?)

3. *Determine the major ideas.* This will help guide the stages of research. For short reports, just write down the general ideas (main points) you are going to want to include. These are the points that will need development if the report is going to fulfill its objective. For longer reports, some collection of data might be necessary to help establish all the points to be covered.

4. *Collect necessary material.* This is the process of gathering facts and figures. For some reports, writers have all the information in their heads. For others, research is necessary.

 a. Primary research involves using first-hand unpublished material. It's first-hand because it was written by the person involved—like a handwritten speech or report. Writers using primary sources depend on organization records, original letters, diaries or minutes, questionnaires, interviews, personal experiences, or experiments.

 b. Secondary research involves using published material. Writers can often save time by consulting books, magazines, newspapers, pamphlets, government documents, atlases, and encyclopedias first. Make certain material is unbiased and accurate.

Researchers are advised to collect all the data that might be needed. Careful records should be kept on file cards or sheets of paper. Usually only one fact or idea is put on each.

5. *Sort and interpret the data.* Whether you do primary or secondary research, the material collected must be put into some understandable form. Shorter reports require less work at this stage. Longer ones may require weeks of study, rearranging, and analysis. Keep material objective by freeing it from your own personal biases. Always keep your potential audience (readers) in mind as you work. This is the stage at which preparation of charts, graphs, and tables becomes appropriate.

6. *Organize the material.* An outline helps you to structure your thoughts and to better analyze the problem. It clarifies thinking and allows writers to evaluate their ideas more objectively. The purpose of the outline is to show the relationship between the parts of the report and the whole. Making an outline allows writers to arrange and then rearrange parts. Key points can then be placed in positions of importance. Organizing ideas first saves much time in later writing because it (1) provides structure to the writer and (2) provides a starting point from which you can proceed through the beginning, middle, and end.

Material can be organized in several ways. It can be arranged by order of time (chronological), by order of location (spatial), by order of importance, by order of familiarity (putting simple, familiar ideas first and moving to the complex and unfamiliar), or by sources (using your prominent experts as key points).

In outlining, some system of symbols will be used to designate the levels of importance of the outline parts. The most common system is:

I. First degree of division
   A. Second degree of division
      1. Third degree of division
         a. Fourth degree of division
            (1) Fifth degree of division
               (a) Sixth degree of division
               (b) Sixth degree of division, second item
            (2) Fifth degree of division, second item[3]

The second form, called the *numerical* or *decimal* form, uses whole numbers to designate the major sections. The decimals and additional digits after the first whole number indicate subsections of the major sections. Each additional digit to the right of the decimal designates each successive step in the subdivision.

1. First degree of division
   1.1 Second degree of division
      1.11 Third degree of division, first item
         1.111 Fourth degree of division
         1.112 Fourth degree of division, second item
      1.12 Third degree of division, second item
   1.2 Second degree of division, second item
2. First degree of division
   2.1 Second degree of division, second item
      2.11 Third degree of division, first item
      2.12 Third degree of division, second item
      2.13 Third degree of division, third item
         2.131 Fourth degree of division, first item
         2.132 Fourth degree of division, second item[4]

Numbers over ten may cause confusion. First, realize that 1.19 indicates that this is item 9 of the third degree of division. It is not the 19th item of the second degree. To indicate the 19th item of the second degree write 1.(19).

*7. Write the report.* One of the hardest parts of report writing is putting those first words on paper. Writers generally write a rough draft first. A rough draft allows them to make errors—knowing they will be corrected later. Moreover, adjustments can be made later in the logical sequence of ideas. The purpose of any early writing (rough draft) is just to get ideas, facts, and conclusions down on paper. It is easier to delete material then add it later; thus, include all material at this stage even if you are in doubt about it. Write in a manner that is comfortable for you.

Formal reports generally require the use of the third person. It is an impersonal style. Personal writing uses first-person pronouns. Memoranda and reports to be distributed within the company among employees of the same rank or lower usually use this informal style. To decide which style to use means you must know who your readers will be, whether or not the content lends itself to a style (formal or informal), and the length of the report (for long reports, the formal style is more appropriate).

A major consideration in level of formality of a report should be whether or not the writer's superiors will read it. Just as anyone would dress appropriately for a meeting with superiors, the writer should consider the "dress" of his or her report. Every part of a report will reflect on its author, and how well the report is received depends on how well writers present their packages.

A philosophy of my own may be of some use here. In writing reports, memos, or letters, I would make it a practice to present my very best effort—assuming in the process that a superior's eyes will see my work at some point. If we believe that we are always "on focus" (the center of activity, attraction, or attention), then we are always more careful about the way we look, act, and present ourselves. A report is simply an extension of ourselves.

The headings of writers' outlines will guide them in determining headings in the final report. Headings are used to direct readers through the report. See Figure 16-1 for a sample of the various types of report headings.

## QUALITIES

What should be the qualities writers work for in preparing their reports? First, writers should *strive for completeness and conciseness*. All facts must be included. The questions who, what, why, when, where and how need to be addressed.

> *Who* will read the material? (audience)
> *What* needs to be included? (material)
> *Why* does it need to be included? (justification)
> *When* does it require inclusion? (time orientation)
> *Where* should it be included? (placement priority)
> *How* should it be included? (word choice)

---

FIRST-DEGREE HEADING

If your report requires four or five degrees of headings, then a first-degree heading can be used for the title of the report -- as shown above. It is centered and typed in all capitals with or without underscoring. It should be triple spaced above the first line of the report, and no other headings in the report should be typed in this form.

Second-Degree Heading

If the title of your report is in the all-capitals first-degree form, then the second-degree heading is used for main sections (introduction, main points of text, and conclusion) of the report. This heading is centered and typed with or without underscoring. All important words are capitalized. Use triple spacing above it and double spacing below.

Third-Degree Heading

The third-degree heading begins at the left margin. Once again, important words are capitalized, and it is underscored. Use triple spacing above the heading and double below.

Fourth-degree heading. This is sometimes referred to as a run-in heading. It is indented the same as a paragraph. It begins with an initial capital letter, and the balance of the heading is typed in lower case. A run-in heading is always followed by a period. It is also underscored.

The Fifth-degree heading consists of merely the underscored first key word or words of the first sentence in the paragraph. From looking at the outlining suggestions, you can see that most reports, unless very complex, do not get to this level.

---

**FIGURE 16-1.** First-Degree Headings

Writers need to make certain they are filling the requirements of the assignment. They need to trim their report to the essentials, omitting irrelevant material. They must avoid wordiness, triteness, and repetition. Wherever they can they should present both favorable and unfavorable viewpoints. Whatever prefatory and supplemental parts that are necessary must also be added.

Writers must also *strive for concreteness, conviction, and objectivity*. Specific words and figures must be used. Sources of information must be identified and source reliability established. Writers must maintain objectivity in quotations, paraphrasing, and abstracting. On what basis were conclusions drawn? They should check the logic of the writing as well. Emotional writing must be avoided and facts must be presented impartially. They need to use concrete nouns, active verbs, and the present tense.

Writers must *show consideration and courtesy.* Consideration can be revealed through the integrity of writers' research, analysis, interpretation, organization, and presentation of all facts, figures, and comments. You are giving your reader the basis for making an informed decision. Consideration and courtesy also are reflected when writers choose their organizational scheme for the most effective reader reaction. Also, they must organize their topics after considering what would be most effective for readers' understanding. Writing style and the formality of the approach also must be reader-related. Writers help reinforce their own credibility through their tone and their logic.

Writers achieve clarity by *phrasing all statements so that readers can easily understand them.* Definitions must be included. Clarity can be aided, too, if writers round off figures, percentages, ranks, and ratios. Graphic aids also help clarity. They should be discussed briefly before presented. Clarity is also reinforced with headings and transitions. Transitions hold introductions, main points, and conclusions together. Transitional phrases reflect movement from one part to another: "Another consideration," "Let's now look at," or "Second," are examples. They also can indicate the completion of one part of the report: "Let me sum up this idea," "Before stating my next point," or "What I have been saying adds up to this." Material can also be listed wherever reader understanding will be benefitted.

Finally, writers must *check for correctness.* They should verify the accuracy of their facts, grammar, spelling, and the parallelism of headings. They need to distinguish clearly between facts, opinions, and inferences. Wording must be checked too. Prefatory and supplemental parts should also be examined for accuracy. Correctness also means making sure the layout of the report is attractive and uncrowded.

## STRUCTURE AND FORMAT

Reports are far from standardized with respect to their physical arrangement—their structure and format. In this section some of the possibilities for report structure and format will be discussed. If all the various parts were included, a workable, attractive formal report would be the result. Few of the reports that are submitted are likely to follow all these steps, but most fit in with the framework of the whole pattern, and knowledge of this pattern will help you plan reports. As the report gets longer and more formal, more of the parts are likely to be included. As length and formality decrease, parts will be eliminated.

The full report pattern includes the following parts:

Prefatory Pages
    Title fly
    Title page
    Letter of authorization
    Letter of transmittal, preface, or foreword
    Table of contents
    List of illustrations, tables, or charts
    Summary
The Body of the Report
    Introduction
    Findings
    Conclusions, recommendations, or summaries
Appended parts
    Bibliography
    Appendix
    Index

## Prefatory Pages

Letters and memoranda require no prefatory pages because they are informal and short. Generally, however, as length and formality increase, so do the number of prefatory pages.

*Title fly.* This is the first among possible prefatory pages, but it serves little purpose except to indicate formality. The title is typed slightly above the center of the page. If no cover is used, the title page protects the text. As the formality of the report decreases, this would be the page eliminated first.

*Title page.* Like the title fly, the title page presents the report title. It is necessary for any report other than a memorandum or letter report. In addition to a clear, concise, and complete title, the title page also mentions the name and position of the person or persons who prepared the report. If the report will be sent outside the company, the name of the preparing company should be included. Finally, the date on which the report is completed is included. See Figure 16–2.

*Letter of authorization.* When a report is authorized in writing, a copy of this document should be inserted after the title page. This letter provides a direct, clear authorization of the investigation. It clearly explains the objective and describes the area of the problem requiring investigation. It may also mention time and cost limitations and any other special instructions.

```
              RECOMMENDATIONS FOR
              COMPANY IMPROVEMENTS
                  FOR 19__




                   Prepared for

                 Nancy L. Wingard

           Vice President, Masindon Co., Inc.









                    Prepared by

                  Robert L. Anders
                 Associate Director
               Midwestern Research, Inc.
         1643 Montcalm Avenue, Chicago, Illinois  60607

                     May 10, 19__
```

**FIGURE 16–2.** Sample Title Page

*Letter of transmittal, preface, or foreword.* Whichever one of these is selected, it provides the writer of the report with an opportunity to communicate personally with the reader, even if the report is formal. The letter of transmittal, as the name implies, transmits the report to the reader. The letter follows the same format as any other company letter. See Figure 16–3 for a sample of a letter of transmittal.

**FIGURE 16–3.** Letter of Transmittal

---

Midwestern Research, Inc.
1643 Montcalm Avenue
Chicago, IL 60607

May 10, 19__

Mrs. Nancy L. Wingard, Vice President
Masindon Company, Inc.
34127 Lake View Drive
Chicago, Illinois 60613

Mrs. Wingard:

Subject: Recommendations for Company Improvements for 19__

Attached is the report you asked us to prepare for your company. This series of recommendations, authorized on December 20, 19__, was completed with the assistance of Ray Newcomb, James McCleary, Saundra Manners, and Linda Moriarty.

Recommendations are included for each of the major divisions of Masindon: production, marketing, and finance. In addition, we provided recommendations for those in both sales management and sales directorship positions. The report range is broad, but the recommendations are specific.

My staff and I appreciate your confidence in us. If you have any questions concerning this study, please contact me.

Sincerely,

*Robert L. Anders*

Robert L. Anders

cp

Attachment

Prefaces and forewords, although a bit different from each other, provide preliminary messages to readers and are designed to help readers understand the report. They can include helpful comments about the report and expressions of indebtedness to those assisting in the research. There is no established pattern for arranging the contents of prefaces and forewords; they are usually written in the first-person but are not usually as informal as some letters.

*Table of contents.* If a report is over five or six pages long, and sections have been broken down into subsections, readers will be helped by a table of contents. The final outline of the report becomes the table of contents, and each section and subsection is listed with the appropriate page numbers. Leader lines (dots with a space between) help readers clearly align sections with corresponding page numbers.

*List of illustrations, tables, or charts.* Usually these items do not require a separate contents section, but if the report contains many of them, they could be listed individually. Such lists become reader aids. This is especially true if certain illustrations, tables, or charts might be used independently from the report. In some cases this list can be combined with the table of contents—especially when it is short—or at other times it can be done on a different page. Illustrations, tables, and charts are usually numbered throughout reports.

*Summary.* Writers must condense their entire report into a summary. Summaries are sometimes called briefs, synopses, abstracts, or epitomes; whatever the label, summaries save readers time by giving insight into the findings and conclusions of the report. They are used by some to make quick decisions. Summaries are often sent to interested people who would not need to read the whole report.

Writers of summaries should try to include parts of all the sections of a report, but they should place their emphasis on conclusions and recommendations highlighting their important findings. Summaries can be single-spaced with double spaces between paragraphs, but they should be condensed to one page only, if possible.

### The Body of the Report

Three major sections comprise the body of the report: introduction; findings; conclusions, recommendations, or summaries. Writers who follow this order conform to the conventional or traditional sequence. It is the one understood and accepted by most companies.

*Introduction.* The introduction serves as an orientation for readers to the problem at hand. The first few paragraphs of a report may determine its acceptance or rejection. Writers need to catch the attention of readers quickly, and anything that will help readers understand and appreciate the problem should be included. For example, writers could review the facts of authorization for the report (its origins), its purpose, scope, or limitations. Historical background or sources and methods of collecting data could be included. Definitions could be provided or a report preview could be offered.

Writers can also indicate their methodology in the introduction. How they conducted their research should be clearly and completely explained, and any research limitations or delimitations should be indicated. The introduction can be tailored to the report.

*Findings.* This is the part of the report where writers present the information collected and relate it to the problem in the report body. The findings represent the time and effort spent on the research. It must be given sufficient preparation time since its existence supports the reason you were given the assignment. Writers must present their findings clearly, concisely, and completely.

Data in the findings section must be presented objectively. Writers must refrain from expressing their opinions in this section. Furthermore, they should attempt to show all sides of the issues presented. If opinions of others are used, the sources for those opinions should be cited in the findings.

Graphics can help to explain the writers' findings, but writers who use illustrations, tables, or charts should also discuss the information contained in each of these in the text. Tables and other graphic aids should appear as soon after this discussion as possible. Small illustrations, tables, and charts can be placed in the body of the report. Use a separate page if the aid requires it.

*Conclusions, recommendations, or summaries.* Reports may be ended in a variety of different ways. Conclusions, recommendations, or summaries can be used, or a combination of these.

*Conclusions,* simply inferences that writers draw from their facts and discussion in the body, should flow logically from the facts. For easy reference, conclusions may be tabulated. Sometimes the most important conclusions can be listed first; otherwise, they should follow the order of presentation of the facts in the body.

*Recommendations* are presented only if writers are asked to present them. If asked, they state their opinion based on the conclusions. Recommendations include who should do what, when, where, why, and sometimes how.

Recommendations may also include alternative courses of action. But writers presenting alternatives should also state their own preferences. Writers should remember when presenting recommendations that they are the closest to the information; thus, they are in the best position to give advice. They must state the desired action then leave readers to determine their own course.

*Summaries* are a gathering together of the major findings of a report. They are useful when the body of the report does little more than present facts. Often, such reports have minor, internal summaries at the end of each major division of the report. The final summary then recaps these internal summaries. This form of summary is not a synopsis. Although a synopsis presents a review of major findings, it contains the gist of the major supporting facts as well.

### Appended Parts

Many reports do not require appended parts. The presence of these parts depends on the specific needs of the problem addressed. A bibliography should be included if information has been cited from other sources. An appendix can include writers' working papers, questionnaires, or cover letters. Supplemental graphic information can also be placed in the appendix. An index is important only when the report is lengthy.

*Bibliography.* Bibliographies are required when writers depend on the contributions of other writers. Even though writers have properly documented their sources in footnotes or in text citations, they include a bibliography to list all the published material they consulted: books, magazines, journals, and other sources. Personal interviews used in the research are also included. An interview citation includes the name of the person, position within the company, and addresses. When the number of citations is lengthy, the bibliography should be divided up: Sections could be designated "books," "magazines," government publications," and "other references." Cards prepared during research can be placed in alphabetical order for ease in typing the bibliography.

Writers preparing a bibliography should be careful of their bibliographic form, for there are specific guidelines that should be followed. First, authors' names should begin at the left margin. The second and succeeding lines of each entry are indented five spaces. Second, author's names are listed alphabetically, last name first. When there is more than one author of a source, writers should reverse only the last name of the first author. If a source is edited, the name or names of the editor(s) is followed by a comma and *ed.* When no author's name is listed, the name of the book or article is alphabetized. Each entry ends with a period.

Third, writers include the title of the article or book. Titles of articles are enclosed in quotation marks, ending in a period. Titles of books are underlined. They should include the complete title, including the subtitle, and end with a period.

The fourth guideline regarding bibliography preparation includes providing complete publication information after the title. For books, writers should give the location of the publisher (including the state if the city is not well known). This is followed by a colon. The name of the publisher, shortened only if no confusion will result, follows the colon. It is followed by a comma. The date of publication is last, followed by a period.

Information for a magazine differs from that of books. The name of the magazine is underlined and followed by a comma. Next is the volume, number, year (in brackets), and the pages. The final part of the entry, the pages, includes inclusive pages for the complete article, preceded by p. or pp., and ending in a period. Page numbers are not given for books.

Here is a sample bibliography that illustrates most of the principles outlined in this section:

DIDSBURY, HOWARD F., JR., ed. *Communications and the Future: Prospects, Promises, and Promises.* Bethesda, Md.: World Future Society, 1982.

EVANS, CHRISTOPHER. *The Micro Millennium.* New York: Washington Square Press, 1979.

KAPLAN, STEPHEN, AND RACHEL KAPLAN. *Cognition and Environment: Functioning in an Uncertain World.* New York: Praeger, 1982.

*MANY VOICES, ONE WORLD.* London: Kegan Paul Ltd., 1980.

MONTGOMERY, CLAYTON. "Communication and Technology: A Transformation in the Making." *U.S. News & World Report, 96,* No. 4 (1984), pp. 87–88.

*Appendix.* The appendix is a section tacked on to the report. Writers use it for supplementary information that supports the body of the report, contributes to an understanding of it, but has no logical place in it. An appendix might include supporting tables, charts, or graphic aids. Questionnaires, working papers, and additional references can also be included. Other reports, raw data from questionnaires, and observation sheets may appear there too.

Usually, writers include charts, graphs, sketches, or tables that directly support the findings of the report in the main body of the report. Writers should always keep their readers in mind as they arrange their material. Readers should not have to thumb through many pages of an appendix to locate an illustration, chart, table, or graph for the facts they require.

*Index.* Few business reports require an index. Only in a long, detailed report would an index help readers locate specific pieces of information. *Indexes* are alphabetical guides to the subject matter within a written work. If a report you are preparing requires an index, one of the most reputable and complete sections on indexing is contained in:

A MANUAL OF STYLE (12th ed.). Chicago: The University of Chicago Press, 1969.

## STYLE

The way in which writers express their thoughts is their *style*. In most cases, the style of business reports tends to be impersonal and formal. Most business reports make dull reading. Contributing to this dullness is the fact that writers generally use the third-person and the passive voice.

Whether or not your report makes dull reading depends upon your audience. If you believe that your readers will prefer a formalized, impersonal style, then you should accommodate that style. Generally, however, readers prefer a livelier, more active style, and that style is likely to result if writers follow these guidelines: easy understandability, simplicity, sincerity, impressiveness, and excitement. These suggestions can help promote a personalized style characterized by directness and the use of the active voice.

Perhaps the worst fault in report writing is wordiness. It creates both expense and waste. It results from writers trying to say too much (not narrowing their focus), from writers who spend little or no time reviewing what they have written (polishing and revising to remove wordiness), and from the impression that a long report is somehow better than a short one. Submitting reports that are excessively wordy suggests that writers are tired, lazy, busy, or vague; they haven't the time to think clearly or revise.

Once again, the best thing to stress in writing is a readable, unobtrusive style that is adapted to the reader. Making your writing interesting will increase reader attention, understanding, and conviction. Remember, the process of report preparation and writing is a human one: one human being writing to other human beings. Concentrate on those qualities you would want to see in a report that you would read: accuracy, conciseness, soundness, and, above all, readability.

## SHORT REPORTS

Most of the foregoing discussion concerns long reports—the more formal types. While these formal types are important in business, most of the reports written tend to be shorter and more informal. Although much of what preceded refers to both types, certain differences exist. For example, short reports usually deal with day-to-day problems, are primarily intended for only a few readers, and those readers usually know the problem and its background. Readers of short reports, then, are more interested in the findings and the actions recommended in the report. Thus, there are major differences between long and short reports, and in this section, the differences are pointed out. The emphasis throughout is on the shorter report. Differences emphasized include: (1) introduction, (2) order, (3) style, and (4) plan.

**Introduction**

In the shorter, more informal report, fewer parts are considered necessary. Most of these reports are intraorganizational (within the organization); thus, they are constructed with a more personal, informal tone and format. It could even be that all the prefatory parts are reduced to a single title page, if, indeed, that is even needed.

The length or brevity of any given report depends on situational factors. That is to say, not all short reports have no need for introductory material. No rule can be applied that covers them all. The idea of an introduction is to prepare your readers. If a report requires some introductory reference to the problem or mention of the authorization for the investigation, then these can be included in an opening paragraph. Reports that cover personnel action, weekly sales, inventory, or progress may need no introductions.

**Order**

The decision about the order that reports should follow also hinges on situational factors. Once again, there are no formal rules that apply. If writers feel that their readers need information first and then a recommendation, the traditional logical order (introduction, body, and conclusion) is a natural, comfortable one.

Typically, however, short reports are more goal-oriented. That is, they are written to handle specific, immediate problems and to make definite recommendations or to supply specific suggestions. Often, the recommendations and suggestions are so important that they outweigh the analysis and information that support them. In these cases—determined by situation analysis prior to writing the report—writers should take a direct approach and lead off with the most important information first.

Leading off with the most important information first will also assist readers who want to use that particular information as the basis for action they must take. A direct approach speeds their efforts and saves time for busy executives.

People with a high level of credibility in the eyes of their readers may choose to use the direct approach too. Readers want the writers' recommendations or suggestions; they know that the material that comes from people with a high level of credibility is likely to be clear, concise, and logical because they have full confidence in the people responsible for it. Should the readers decide to question the support, it is there for their inspection. For people without this credibility or for those new on a job, the logical (indirect) order may be preferred.

### Style

Very often in shorter, informal reports, writers use personal pronouns such as "I," "we," and "you," rather than a more formal third-person approach. When writing short, informal communications, writers should stress the humanness of the communication situation. This is often easier in shorter reports because the situations that call for these reports usually involve personal relationships. Also, the reports are written between people who know each other and who, on a daily basis, address each other informally. The finished reports, too, reflect personal observations, analyses, and evaluations.

Just as short reports are used in day-to-day communications, relating day-to-day occurrences, they should reveal day-to-day informality. It is logical to report such occurrences informally, and a personal writing style successfully accomplishes this.

Two important governing factors control writers' choice of style. The first, stated and restated throughout this book in a variety of different contexts, is reader preference. Writers must first consider who will be reading the report. The second major consideration involves the circumstances. If the situation calls for formality, then write in an impersonal style. If writers are in doubt about which style to use, it is usually safer to proceed with the more conventional, impersonal, formal style—at least at first—until it is clear who the readers are or will be and which situations can be labeled "formal."

### Plan

Length is a major factor creating a need for clear organization. The longer a report is, the easier it is for readers to become confused. Parts do not stick together as well for them, and important relationships are missed. When a report is both long and complex, coherence (the way a report hangs together) may suffer. Writers then plan longer reports carefully so that main points are parallel, internal summaries and transitions are included, and every part is related to the whole.

Short reports gain coherence because of their brevity. It is not that they do not need coherence, because they do, but without as many parts there are fewer words required to relate the parts. The information is often so simple that a logical and orderly presentation clearly reveals the plan of the presentation.

Length is not the only criteria for determining the need for a plan. Writers should also consider the material of the report. If it is complex, or if it contains organizational problems, writers should consider using introductions, summaries, and transitions to help relate the parts—a clear plan for holding material together. Need is the major determinant, and need is likely to vary so dramatically from situation to situation that writers must be the final arbiters regarding the need for including coherent elements. But there is little doubt that the need increases as length and complexity increase.

## SUMMARY

This chapter was different from others in this book because much of the information presented here appeared in earlier chapters. Thus, it served more as a review and synthesis than as a source of new information. As a summary, the major aspects of each section have been gathered together below. This will serve as a useful, practical checklist or guide for writing written reports.

### Purpose

\_\_\_\_ Does your report aid in decision making?
\_\_\_\_ Does your report present needed information?
\_\_\_\_ Does your report allow information to be kept on file?
\_\_\_\_ Does your report point out strengths and weaknesses in the organization?
\_\_\_\_ Does your report help solve problems?
\_\_\_\_ Does your report provide a means of communication among employees?
\_\_\_\_ Does your report provide a means of communication between your business and people outside your business?
\_\_\_\_ Does your report serve to alert people to the progress of your company?
\_\_\_\_ Does your report serve an analytical function?

### Preparation

\_\_\_\_ Have you defined the problem and purpose?
\_\_\_\_ Have you considered who will receive your report?
\_\_\_\_ Have you determined the major ideas?
\_\_\_\_ Have you collected the necessary material?
\_\_\_\_ Have you sorted and interpreted the data?
\_\_\_\_ Have you organized the material?
\_\_\_\_ Have you been careful in the writing of the report?

## Qualities

___ Is your report complete?
___ Is your report concise?
___ Is your report concrete?
___ Is your report convincing?
___ Is your report objective?
___ Is your report considerate?
___ Is your report courteous?
___ Is your report clear?
___ Is your report correct?

## Structure and Format

___ Does your report require prefatory pages?
___ a title fly?
___ a title page?
___ a letter of authorization?
___ a letter of transmittal, preface, or foreword?
___ a table of contents?
___ a list of illustrations, tables, or charts?
___ a summary?
___ Have you structured the body of your report?
___ Did you include an introduction?
___ Are the findings clearly presented?
___ Does your report require a section for conclusions, recommendations, or summaries?
___ Does your report require appended parts?
___ Do you need a bibliography?
___ Are appendices necessary?
___ Is the report long and detailed enough to require an index?

## Style

___ Have you analyzed who your reader or readers will be?
___ Have you narrowed the focus of your report to avoid wordiness?
___ Have you spent time polishing and revising your drafts to remove wordiness?
___ Have you kept your report as short as is necessary to convey your information completely?
___ Have you checked the readability of what you have written?
___ Is your writing interesting?

## Short Reports

___ Is your report short enough to eliminate the need for an introduction?

____ Do your readers need to be prepared?
____ Do your readers need information first, then the recommendation? (the traditional, logical order)
____ Would it be better to lead off with the important information first? (a direct order)
____ Do you know who will be reading your report and whether or not this person prefers an informal style?
____ Does the situation you are writing about call for formality?
____ Is your report short enough that it will stick together (cohere) logically and easily?
____ Is the material of your report complex, or does it have organizational problems that require introductions, summaries, and transitions to relate the parts?

## NOTES

[1] For a discussion of classification schemes and report types, see J. Menning, C. Wilkinson and P. Clarke, *Communicating Through Letters and Reports* (Homewood, Ill.: Richard D. Irwin, 1976), Chapter 13.

[2] Raymond V. Lesikar, *Business Communication: Theory and Application* (Homewood, Ill.: Richard D. Irwin, 1980), p. 311.

[3] If this outline were continued, the next point could be "(2) Fifth degree of division, third item," or "b. Fourth degree of division, second item"—*only!* These are the only two possibilities available with the outline set up as it is illustrated. Only after "b. Fourth degree of division, second item" would "2. Third degree of division, second item," be appropriate. And only after the latter would "B. Second degree of division, second item" be appropriate.

[4] In this outline, the writer has three choices if he or she continues: (1) 2.133 Fourth degree of division, third item, and (2) 2.14 Third degree of division, fourth item, and (3) 2.2 Second degree of division, second item. Whatever the writer's choice, a 2.2 must occur in the outline before a "Part 3, First degree of division, third point" can be used. This simply follows proper outlining procedure.

# Glossary

**Action step**  The final (fifth) step of the Monroe Motivated Sequence; designed to call for specific, definite, and concrete action.

**Ad hoc committee**  Like a special committee in that it deals with noncurrent—or, one-time—special tasks. Ad hoc committees typically handle noncontroversial tasks.

**Adjustment letter**  Letter written to take action on claims.

**Advance organizer**  The process of revealing main points first in a speech. Also known as *previewing* and *initial partition*.

**Affective dimension**  Of attitudes—consists of the feelings we have about objects, events, issues, situations, or people.

**Aggressor**  Fills negative group roles by revealing discontentedness and disapproval. Distrusts and dislikes others and reveals this through criticism, jealousy, and ill-will.

**Analogic communication**  Unlike digital communication, involves analogues to words, or the feelings and attitudes that are similar to what is being expressed verbally. Analogic communication is generally conveyed nonverbally by tone of voice, facial expressions, gestures, posture, and distance.

**Anecdoter**  Fills negative group roles by getting carried away in the stories and personal experiences he or she tells.

**Antecedent conditions**  Those circumstances that precede. Events or causes that are characteristic of situations that increase the likelihood of conflict are antecedent conditions to that conflict.

**Appendix**  Often tacked on to reports; includes additional or supplementary material that is related, but not essential, to the report.

**Appraisal interview** Interview used to evaluate the quality and quantity of employee work. Sometimes called *performance* interview.
**Attention line** A special part of a business letter designed to direct the letter to a certain individual, as in "Attention Mrs. Smith."
**Attention step** The first step of the Monroe Motivated Sequence, designed to grasp attention and focus attention on the topic.
**Attitude** Feeling we have toward something, or predisposition that causes us to think, feel, perceive, or behave in a certain way.
**Behavioral dimension** Of attitudes—consists of action.
**Belief** Conviction of the truth of something; it represents acceptance of information on both a mental and emotional level.
**Belongingness and love needs** Include our need to belong, to be accepted, liked, and respected by friends. They include affection, affiliation, and group identification needs.
**Bibliography** List of books and other writings that deal with a certain subject. Often attached to reports.
**Bipolar questions** In interviews—restrict interviewee responses to only two choices—such as yes/no, like/dislike, approve/disapprove, or high/low.
**Bipolar thinking** Reduces complex phenomena to simple either-or, good-or-bad, black-or-white dimensions. It represents a two-value orientation where something is divided into two diametrically opposed views.
**Blocker** One who fills negative group roles by being totally negative and preventing group progress. Blockers object to the ideas and suggestions of others.
**Brainstorming** In conflict situations—a means of finding alternatives by spontaneously and vigorously developing solutions.
**Buffer** In letter writing—a device for reducing or cushioning against shock—bad news, for example.
**Bypassing** Occurs when a message source and a receiver attribute different meanings to the same words or use different words though intending the same meaning.
**Candor** In interviews—reflects interviewees' forthrightness.
**Catharsis** The alleviation of problems or fears by giving them expression.
**Cause-effect outline patterns** Those in which the main points deal with antecedents, determinants, or reasons, for certain results.
**Character** As an aspect of *ethos*—in persuaders includes appearing trustworthy, honest, and sincere.
**Chronological outline patterns** Those in which the main points follow an historical or time sequence.
**Claim letter** Designed to bring errors to the attention of those responsible for them.
**Clarity of language** Using language that is easily understood.
**Closed question** In interviews—one that limits interviewee's flexibility of a specific response.
**Clown** One that fills negative group roles by using jokes, antics, and irrelevant comments to entertain the group.
**Cognitive dimension** Of attitudes—consists of the knowledge connected with objects, events, issues, situations, or persons.
**Cohesiveness** The attractiveness a group has for its members.
**Committee** Small group with specific task, mission, or charge.
**Common definition** One that recognizes the problem as a mutual one—not a win–lose situation.
**Communication** The purposeful sharing of information through symbols—words or other types of messages.

**Competent** As an aspect of *ethos*—a quality demonstrated by persuaders that makes them appear to others as trained, qualified, informed, and authoritative.
**Complementary relationship** Emphasizes differences, where one person's behavior complements another's by filling in or providing things the other does not or cannot.
**Composure** As an aspect of *ethos* in persuadees—includes reflecting calmness of mind, bearing, and appearance.
**Compromiser** In conflict situations—seeks to find a position that allows all sides to win.
**Conference** Formal gathering of a number of people for consultation and discussion. Conferences are more formal than meetings, and may last from a full day to even a week; they require extensive planning.
**Confessor** One who fills negative group roles by too readily revealing his or her fears, needs, and shortcomings.
**Confidence** In interviews—revealed when interviewees convey faith in their own skills, powers, or circumstances.
**Conflict resolution** Bringing the conflict to an end.
**Congruent communication** Occurs when verbal and nonverbal cues communicate essentially the same meaning.
**Connotative meaning** Of a word—lies in the mind of the person using that word.
**Consistency** An agreement or harmony of the parts or features of the interview as they relate together and are perceived as a whole.
**Counseling interview** One directed toward personal considerations.
**Credibility** The character (the aggregate of distinctive qualities characteristic of a person) of the persuaer in the eyes of the reader or listener. Sometimes referred to as *ethos*.
**Deductive paragraph** Presents the topic sentence first, followed by the supporting material.
**Denotative meaning** Of a word—derived from the dictionary.
**Diagonal communication** When an employee in one division goes to the manager of another division of an equal level.
**Digital communication** Unlike analogic communication—involves discrete (individually distinct or separate) units. Words are a form of digital communication.
**Disciplinary interview** Used by supervisors to confront and correct employee behaviors such as tardiness, reduced or lack of productivity, or unethical or tasteless behavior.
**Dominator** One who fills negative group roles by trying to monopolize group interaction.
**Downward communication** That which occurs between managers and employees.
**Ectomorph** Person with a thin physique.
**Effect-cause outline patterns** Those in which the results are stated first, then the outline moves to what brought about the event, circumstance, or condition.
**Effective communication** Is concise and exact, eliciting the precise response a communicator wants.
**Egalitarian distribution of power** Represents a belief in human equality with respect to social, political, and economic rights and privileges.
**Elaborator** One who fills group task roles by helping to clarify and expand the ideas of others.
**Embedded sentence** Occurs when one full sentence can be found within another.
**Emblem** Nonverbal cue that has a consistent verbal translation.

**Emotion**  Strong, generalized feeling. Being *emotional* involves having one's feelings aroused or agitated.
**Emphasis**  The force or intensity given to an idea.
**Employment interview**  One used to select applicants for jobs. Also called *selection interview*.
**Enclosure notation**  As a special part of a business letter—a reminder to the person putting up the mail to make the enclosure.
**Encourager**  One who fills group maintenance roles by showing support for the other members of the group.
**Enculturation**  The process by which we come to learn, accept, and even model the concepts, habits, skills, art, instruments, and institutions of our culture.
**Endomorph**  Person with a fat physique.
**Energizer**  One who fills group task roles by motivating group members to reach decisions, solve problems, and become more involved.
**Enthusiasm**  In interviewing—the excitement or inspiration that is manifest.
**E.R.G. theory**  Created by Clayton Alderfer to compress Maslow's five need categories into three: existence, relatedness, and growth.
**Esteem needs**  Operate on two levels: self-esteem and other esteem. *Self-esteem* needs include personal worth, competence, achievement, independence, and freedom. *Other esteem* includes the need for prestige, respect, admiration, and recognition.
**Ethos**  The character (the aggregate of distinctive qualities characteristic of a person) of the persuader in the eyes of the reader or listener. Also known as *credibility*.
**Evaluative listening response**  Involves judgments regarding the goodness, appropriateness, effectiveness, or rightness of another's idea, behavior, or comment.
**Evaluative thinking**  Involves placing a judgment of relative goodness, appropriateness, effectiveness, or rightness.
**Example**  Supporting material (particular incidents or instances) used to illustrate, clarify, or explain ideas.
**Exception report**  Report that treats aspects of the business that are exceptions to (excluded or separate from) normal business operating procedures.
**Exit interview**  Interview conducted at the time employee is ready to leave a company.
**Expert testimony**  Statements made by people who qualify as experts or authorities in given areas.
**Explicit norms**  Those norms that are formal and usually verbalized.
**Extemporaneous speaking**  Occurs when speakers carefully prepare their speeches but deliver them from notes.
**External communications**  Those communications with individuals and groups outside the business.
**External feedback**  The openness and sensitivity we express toward the reactions of other people, and how we use this information to guide our future action.
**Extrinsic ethos**  What others know of the persuader *before* the persuasive presentation.
**Extroversion**  As an aspect of *ethos*—in persuaders, includes being bold, forceful, and assertive.
**Facts**  Pieces of information that have actual existence. They can be observed.
**Feedback**  The reactions one gets from audience members while in the process of communicating. Effective communicators notice it, respond to it, and use it to further guide their communication efforts.

**Felt conflict**  Is personal and is usually expressed in feelings of threat, hostility, fear, or mistrust.
**Flexibility**  In speechmaking—means being able to respond or conform to changing or new situations.
**Fog Index**  Measures the difficulty of reading matter.
**Follower**  One who fills group maintenance roles by acquiescing to the wishes of others. Followers serve as a neutralizing element in small groups.
**Forcer**  One who, in conflict situations, seeks to meet his or her own goals at all costs.
**Forms of business communication**  Include: memos, bulletin-board messages, company publications, letters, video programs, public-address systems, reports, grievance systems, suggestion systems, attitude surveys, exit interviews, telephone, business meetings, employee counseling, social events, managerial visibility, and electronic communication.
**Functional (or strategic) conflict**  Has to do either with the way the organization functions or with strategies used in resolving issues.
**Gatekeeper**  One who fills group maintenance roles by controlling the flow of communications in a group by opening or shutting channels.
**Goals**  The end toward which effort is directed.
**Good will**  Reflected in kindly feelings of approval and support that occurs between people.
**Grapevine**  An informal communication channel that is both well-established and well-known.
**Grievance interview**  Interview that allows employees to voice their discontent.
**Group maintenance role**  Role that, when performed, helps a group build and maintain interpersonal relationships among members.
**Group task role**  Role that, when performed, helps groups accomplish their task or the purpose for which they are meeting.
**Gunning Fog Index**  Also known as the Fog Index—measures the difficulty of reading matter.
**Harmonizer**  One who fills group maintenance roles by helping reduce conflict by aiding in mediating differences, introducing compromise, and reconciling differences.
**Hearing**  The physical process of receiving auditory stimuli. Hearing involves the ear and the other physical mechanisms necessary to receive sound.
**Hitchhiking**  In conflict situations—a means of finding alternatives by taking an idea of one person further or finding another idea as a result of the first suggestion.
**Homophily**  The degree of perceived similarity or correspondence between one's own attitudes, morals, values, appearance, status, and class, and those of others.
**Honesty**  In interviewing—fairness and straightforwardness of conduct.
**Horizontal communication**  Communication that exists between employees who are on the same organizational level, but not necessarily in the same department or area.
**Illustrations**  Extended examples—supporting material that are instances or incidents used to illustrate, clarify, or explain ideas.
**Immediacy**  The feeling we get when we are a direct part of an event that is unfolding before us.
**Implicit norms**  Those norms that are understood and accepted and never specifically or directly stated.
**Impromptu speech**  One composed or uttered without previous preparation.

**Incubation** The time your subconscious needs to deal with the material. The second step of the creative process.
**Index** Alphabetical guide to the subject matter within a written work.
**Inductive paragraph** Presents the supporting material first followed by the topic sentence or conclusion.
**Information giver** One who fills group task roles by offering facts, examples, and personal experiences.
**Information seeker** One who fills group task roles by asking for facts, opinions, and examples from others.
**Initial partition** The process of revealing the main points first in a speech. Also known as *previewing* and *advance organizer*.
**Initiator** One who fills group task roles by getting groups started and keeping them going by proposing new ideas, procedures, goals, and solutions.
**Inquiries** Letters that seek information on a wide variety of matters.
**Integrator** One who fills group task roles by tying together elements of a discussion.
**Internal feedback** The feedback we provide ourselves. It is intrapersonal communication.
**Internal summaries** Flashbacks and flashforwards that draw together what has been covered before moving the reader or speaker to a new point.
**Interpersonal communication** Communication that occurs between oneself and others. In this book, interpersonal communication is treated as dyadic—between two people.
**Interpretive listening response** A desire to teach or to impart meaning.
**Interview** A meeting between two people in which there is a predetermined and serious purpose, planning is involved, and oral interaction occurs between the two parties.
**Intrapersonal communication** Communication *within* an individual.
**Intrinsic ethos** Based on what persuaders do within their persuasive presentation to enhance their credibility. It contrasts with *extrinsic ethos*, which is developed before a speech.
**Levels of communication** Includes downward, upward, horizontal, and diagonal communication. It also includes intrapersonal, interpersonal, group, public, mass, and intercultural communication.
**Listening** A physical, emotional, and intellectual process of receiving auditory stimuli in our search for meaning and understanding.
**Logos** Refers to logic and has to do with orderly, valid, cogent reasoning or presentation of material.
**Lose–lose strategy** Results when neither side gets what it wants, or gets only a fraction of what it wants.
**Manifest behavior** Overt action that results from perceived or felt conflict.
**Manuscript speech** Occurs when a speaker writes out the presentation, then reads it word-for-word.
**Maslow's need hierarchy** Identifies and orders basic needs according to their strength.
**Meaning** That which is intended to be—or actually is—conveyed, evoked, signified, or understood by acts (nonverbal cues) or language (words).
**Meetings** Assemblies or gatherings of people especially to discuss or decide on matters.
**Memorized speech** A speech committed to memory and then delivered without notes or manuscript before the audience.

**Mesomorph**   Person with a medium or athletic physique, as contrasted with ectomorphs (thin people) and endomorphs (fat people).
**Metacommunication**   Communication *about* communication. In letter writing, it is anything beyond the words themselves.
**Mirror questions**   In interviews—either restatements of interviewee responses or exact recapitulations of their responses.
**Monroe Motivated Sequence**   A persuasive organizational pattern that includes the five steps of attention, need, satisfaction, visualization, and action.
**Need**   Something requisite, desirable, or useful.
**Need hierarchy**   Identifies and orders basic needs according to their strength. Created by Abraham Maslow.
**Need step**   The second step of the Monroe Motivated Sequence; designed to establish a need for change.
**Negative role**   A role that, when performed in groups, is less than desirable.
**Noise**   A barrier to communication that may be physical, psychological, physiological, semantic, syntactic, organizational, or societal.
**Nonverbal communication**   The exchange of messages primarily through nonlinguistic (or nonword) means. It refers to signals transmitted by voice, appearance, face and eyes, touch, the body, personal space and distance, silence and time, and environment.
**Norms**   Sets of assumptions or expectations held by members of groups about the kind of behavior that is right or wrong, good or bad, appropriate or inappropriate, allowed or not allowed by the members of that group.
**OCR**   Stands for *Optical Character Reader,* which is the electronic mail sorter used by post offices.
**Open question**   In interviews—one that gives the interviewee freedom to answer as she or he pleases.
**Opinion giver**   One who fills group task roles by offering his or her beliefs, attitudes, and judgments about relevant issues.
**Opinion seeker**   One who fills group task roles by soliciting beliefs, attitudes, and judgments from others.
**Organizational noise**   Disturbance that originates with the administrative or functional structure of our work place.
**Organizing**   As a function of communication—involves the integration of resources: drawing together in some systematic manner the personnel, materials, equipment, and processes with the business's goals.
**Orienter**   One who fills group task roles by helping to keep groups on track. Orienters remind groups of their goal, clarify purposes and positions, and help identify distractions, irrelevancies, and digressions.
**Other-esteem needs**   Include the needs for prestige, respect, admiration, and recognition.
**Paralanguage**   How a message is said.
**Parallelism**   In sentence structure—requires that sentence elements that are alike in function be alike in structure as well.
**Parliamentary procedure**   The rules governing the proceedings of deliberative assemblies.
**Parsimony**   Finding the simplest explanation for a behavior or set of behaviors.
**Pathos**   Refers to emotions; it is the emotional support a speaker provides by appealing to other people's needs, goals, or emotions.
**Perceived conflict**   Happens in people's minds; it is highly individualized and subjective.

**Period of insight** The time when the solution, decision, or the proper relationship results. The third step of the creative process.
**Personal experience** A type of supporting material that includes examples or illustrations that come from a speaker or writer's private background or knowledge.
**Persuasion** A conscious attempt by one individual to modify the attitudes, beliefs, or behavior of another individual or group of individuals through the transmission of some message.
**Physical noise** Noise that enters the communication channel from an outside source.
**Physiological needs** Include food, water, air, sleep, shelter, and sex. They are at the bottom of Maslow's need hierarchy because they are the most basic.
**Physiological noise** Noise that occurs within our body.
**Positiveness** The quality of being confident and certain as well as explicit—in control.
**Postscript** As a special part of business letters—is an afterthought.
**Preparation** In interviewing—being in a state of readiness.
**Presiding officer** Conducts meetings in a fair, impartial, and efficient manner.
**Previewing** The process of revealing the main points first in a speech. Also known as *initial partition* and *advance organizer*.
**Primacy** The state of being first. Material coming first in a communication is perceived as being important.
**Primary research** First-hand unpublished material.
**Probing listening response** Gathering further information or provoking discussion. Such a response occurs in the form of questions designed to draw out others.
**Probing question** In interviews—is used to explore more fully responses that appear to be incomplete. They are usually follow-up questions.
**Problem solver** In conflict situations—an ideal type because he or she has a high concern both for people and for the task.
**Proposition** A simple declarative statement that clearly states the point to be discussed or what is offered for consideration or acceptance.
**Proxemics** The study of personal space and distance.
**Psychological noise** Noise that occurs in one's mind.
**Recency** The state of being most recent (last) in the receiver's mind. For speakers and writers, recency would involve placing some of their most important ideas last in a speech or report so that receivers remember them better.
**Recognition seeker** One who fills negative group roles by demanding the recognition and sympathy of others.
**Recording secretary** One who keeps accurate records of the business transacted in large meetings.
**Resale** The process of keeping people sold. In the beginning or ending of a business letter, the writer should reinforce the reader's commitment to the product.
**Resolution aftermath** The consequences of the conflict.
**Responsiveness** In interviews—the interviewee's willingness to take an active oral part in the interview.
**Résumé** Sales tool written and designed to obtain interviews with employers and to summarize one's qualifications for a job. They are concise outlines highlighting personal, educational, and work experiences as they relate to a particular position.

**Revision** The time necessary to phrase the outcome clearly and accurately, check it for accuracy, establish its logic and validity, and find support for it. The fourth step of the creative process.

**Safety and security needs** Include our desire to be free from danger, and the need for physical, psychological, and financial stability. Part of Maslow's need hierarchy.

**Satisfaction step** The third step of the Monroe Motivated Sequence; designed to satisfy the need or to provide the solution or answer necessary to accomplish the need provided in the second step.

**Screening interview** Interview used to eliminate applicants who do not meet the qualifications for a job.

**Secondary research** As opposed to primary research—using published material as the basis for the proof or evidence that supports ideas.

**Second-page heading** As a special part of business letters—includes the addressee's name and date, and page number.

**Selection interview** Interview used to determine which applicants are most appropriate for certain jobs.

**Selective attention** The process of selectively turning our senses to part of the environment.

**Selective retention** The ability to preserve certain ideas in one's mind.

**Self-actualization needs** Involve our drive toward self-fulfillment or the realization of our potential. Part of Maslow's need hierarchy.

**Self-disclosure** The process of sharing information about your private world with another.

**Self-esteem needs** Include personal worth, competence, achievement, independence, and freedom. Part of Maslow's need hierarchy.

**Semantic noise** Results from difficulty understanding the meaning of the words used.

**Sergeant-at-arms** One whose duty it is to be sure no members become disorderly, and to deal with those who do.

**Simplicity** Means being natural and direct. In communication, this means messages that are plain, uncomplicated, and free from unnecessary elaboration or display.

**Sincerity** In communication—that communication marked by honesty and genuineness.

**Slang** Language peculiar to a particular group—usually nonstandard language.

**Smoother** In conflict situations—one who places a high priority on maintaining relationships with others, and who is less concerned about the achievement of their own or company goals.

**Sociability** As an aspect of *ethos*—in persuaders, includes coming across as warm, friendly, and pleasant.

**Societal noise** Originates in the neighborhood, community, state, or nation.

**Solicited letter of inquiry** Usually results from advertisements inviting readers to write for more information.

**Spatial outline patterns** Those in which the main points follow a physical or geographical arrangement.

**Special committee** Committee designed to deal with a single and specific issue that cannot be handled within ordinary company procedures.

**Special-interest pleader** One who fills negative group roles by pleading for favors and attention toward groups outside this immediate group for which he or she has loyalty and group affiliation.

**Speech anxiety**  The nervousness one experiences before making a speech. Sometimes referred to as *stage fright*, it is both common and natural.

**Standing committee**  Permanent part of an organization; is assigned work to do on some regular basis.

**Statistics**  A form of supporting material that are statements of fact presented in numerical form.

**Status**  The degree of importance members attach to roles.

**Stereotype**  A fixed impression or unchangeable reaction to something.

**Style**  The way in which writers express their thoughts.

**Subject line**  A special part of a business letter that quickly tells readers what the letter is about.

**Supportive listening response**  Involves trying to reassure others or reduce the intensity of their feelings.

**Symbol**  Something that stands for or suggests something else. Words are one form of symbols.

**Symmetrical relationship**  Relationship based on equality of behavior.

**Syntactic noise**  Noise having to do with problems with phrasing, clauses, and sentences.

**System**  An organization of regularly interacting or interdependent group of parts that together form a unified whole.

**Tension reliever**  One who fills group maintenance roles by decreasing the formality in a situation by interjecting humor.

**Theory X**  Assumes that people are basically lazy; they dislike work and avoid it if possible. Created by Douglas McGregor.

**Theory Y**  Assumes that people like to work and that it is natural and fulfilling to accomplish tasks. Created by Douglas McGregor.

**Theory Z**  Focuses on a style of managing people that emphasizes a strong company philosophy, a distinct corporate culture, long-range staff development, and consensus decision making. Created by William Ouchi.

**Third ear**  Our ability to listen to the meanings behind words—the area where true listening occurs.

**Tone**  A manner of speaking or writing that shows a certain attitude on the part of the speaker or writer consisting in the choice of words and phrasing.

**Topical pattern**  An outline pattern that uses parallel topics or subjects—subjects that are equal in their likely effect on the audience.

**Transactional communication**  A view of communication which suggests that we construct images of others on which we act when we communicate with those others and, further, that effective communication depends on the amount of information (and the number of images) we share in common with those with whom we communicate. Emphasizes the relationship between senders and receivers.

**Transition**  A signpost that a speaker or writer is moving on to another point. It serves to tie ideas together.

**Trite language**  That which has grown stale from excessive use. Trite expressions are also called hackneyed words, clichés, stereotyped expressions, deadwood, or whiskered words.

**Trust**  The reliability of a person's character, ability, strength, and truthfulness.

**Truth**  In interviewing—sincerity in action, character, and utterance.

**Understanding listening response**  Involves gaining understanding. This approach depends on paraphrasing what the other person has said.

**Unsolicited letter of inquiry**  A letter in which the writer takes the initiative of asking for information.

**Upward communication**  That which flows from employees to their superiors.
**Values**  What is important, useful, or worthwhile to us. Values are central psychological anchors or deep-seated standards.
**Visual aids**  Instructional devices (such as charts, maps, or models) that appeal chiefly to vision. Also known as *graphic aids*.
**Visualization step**  Step that is designed to intensify audience desires. The fourth step of the Monroe Motivated Sequence.
**Vocalics**  Aspects of the voice such as pitch, volume, quality, and rate; the nonverbal aspects of vocal communication.
**Win-lose strategy**  Results when one party fails to achieve his or her objective.
**Win-win strategy**  Focuses on acceptable gains for all parties.
**Withdrawer**  In a conflict situation—wishes to maintain neutrality at all costs.
**You-viewpoint or you-attitude**  Seeing situations from your readers' viewpoint and choosing words and strategy that will most directly affect them.

# Index

Accenting, as function of nonverbal communication, 81, 82, 93
Accuracy, and improving perception, 100
Achievability, and motivation, 5
Action, 261–62, 268, 302, 347
   as a step in the Monroe motivated sequence, 261–62, 268, 347
   in business letters, 302
Active verbs, in writing, 275–76
Ad hoc committee, 221, 347
Adjectives and adverbs, and sincerity, 72–73
Adjustment, 100, 314–17, 325, 347
   and improving perception, 100
   letters of, 314–17, 325, 347
Advance organizer, 238, 347
Affective dimension, of an attitude, 249, 347
Aggressor, as negative group role, 215, 347
Alderfer, Clayton, 33
Analogic communication, 30–31, 347
Analysis, in small-group problem solving, 211
*And then some*, coverage in business letters, 297–98
Anecdoter, as negative group role, 215, 347

Antecedent conditions, as conflict stage, 117–18, 122, 129, 347
Anticipation, in improving listening, 60
Appearance, 84–86, 138–39, 303–8
   of business letters, 303–8
   nonverbal communication and, 84–86
   of visual and graphic aids, 138–39
Appended parts, of business report, 339–41
Appendix, in business report, 340, 347
Application letters, 184–88
   asking for action in, 186
   cautions regarding, 186
   format of, 184–85
   getting attention in, 185
   identifying specific preparation in, 185
   offering convincing evidence in, 185–86
   positive features of, 186–88
   sample of, 187
Applying for jobs, 184–88, 198
   asking for action, as part of, 186
   attention-getting, as part of, 185
   cautions in, 186
   evidence in, 185–186
   letter of inquiry for, 187
   positive features in, 186–88
   preparation in, 185

Appraisal interview, 151–52, 348
Apprehension, in making speeches, 239–41
Arousal, in nonverbal communication, 93
Asking for action, in applying for jobs, 186
Assertiveness, 240
Attention, 185, 259, 268, 300, 306–7, 348
  applying for jobs and, 185
  business letters and, 300
  line, in business letters, 306–7, 348
  as step in the Monroe motivated sequence, 259, 268, 348
Attitude, as part of interviewer role, 155
Attitudes, 228, 248–50, 252, 267, 302, 348
  beliefs, and values, 248–253
    relationship of, 252
  business letters and, 302
  oral reports and, 228, 348
  surveys of, as form of upward communication, 13
Attractiveness, 263–64
  (See also Sociability)
Audience, 227–30, 328–29
  analysis, definition, 227
  and developing oral report, 227–30
  analysis, as part of business reports, 328–29
Authority, as an aspect of beliefs, 250, 251
Availability, and improving perception, 100
Avoidance, as lose-lose strategy in conflict resolution, 120
Axioms of communication, 29–31
  and transactional communication, 31

Background, audience, in oral reports, 229
Bar graph, 136, 140, 141
Barriers, 52–54, 96–112
  and bipolar thinking, 103–4, 111
  and bypassing, 106, 111
  and evaluative thinking, 104–6, 111
  and lack of understanding, 106, 111
  and noise, 106–7, 111
  and poor listening, 107, 111
  and selective attention, 97–100, 110–11
  and selective retention, 100–103, 111
  to listening, 52–54
Bars, 136, 141
Behavioral dimension of an attitude, 249–50, 348
Beliefs, 248–49, 250–52, 267, 348
  audience, in oral reports, 228, 348
  classification of, 250–252
Belongingness and love needs, 32, 348
Bibliography, as part of business report, 339–40, 348
Bipolar questions, in interviews, 166, 348
Bipolar thinking, as a barrier, 103–4, 111, 348
Blanchard, Kenneth, 5–6, 88–89

Blocker, as negative group role, 215, 348
Body language, 30–31, 79–95
  (See also Nonverbal communication)
Body:
  and nonverbal communication, 89–90
  and the business report, 337–39
Boxes, 102
Brain, 51
Brainstorming, 127–28, 212, 348
  hitchhiking, 212, 354
  leapfrogging, 212
Brevity:
  and business letters, 299
  and business reports, 332
Bubble, personal, 90–91
Buffer, in business letters, 299, 348
Bulletin-board messages, as form of downward communication, 10
Business:
  communication and, 1–2
  definition of, 1
  meeting, as form of communication, 16
  web of, 1–2
Business letters, 290–326
  advantages of, 291–92, 325
  basic qualities of, 293–98, 325
  different kinds, 313–25, 347–48
    adjustments, 314–17, 325, 347
    claims, 313–14, 325, 348
    collection, 320–23, 325
    credit, 317–20, 325
    inquiries, 309–13, 325
    sales, 323–25
  disadvantages of, 291, 292–93, 325
  format, 308–25
Business meetings, 200–224
  (See also Groups; Committees)
Business reports and memoranda, 327–46
  advantages of, 328
  preparation of, 328–32
  purposes of, 328
  qualities of, 332–33
  short form of, 341–44
  structure and format of, 333–34
Bypassing, as barrier in business communication, 106, 111, 348

Candor, and interviewee role, 162, 348
Capitalizing on thought speed, as part of improving listening, 60
Causal interviews, 169, 170, 171
Catharsis, 115, 348
Cause-effect pattern of organization, 237, 348
Cautions in applying for jobs, 186
Caveat emptor, 314
Chalkboards, as visual aids in oral reports, 143

Disciplinary interviews, 153–54, 349
Distance, in nonverbal communication, 92
Dominance, in nonverbal communication, 93
Dominator, as a negative group role, 215, 349
Dots, 282
Downward communication, 7–11, 22, 35
 definition, 7, 349

Ear, 51
Economy of words, in writing, 278–79
Ectomorphs, and nonverbal communication, 86, 349
Effect-cause pattern of organization, 237, 349
Effective communication, 349
Egalitarian power, as part of upward communication, 11–12, 349
Egospeak, 106, 108
Elaborator, as a group task role, 214, 349
Electronic communication, 17–18
 potential problems with, 18
Embedded sentences, 70, 349
Emblems, and nonverbal communication, 87–88, 349
Emerson, Ralph Waldo, 160
Emotional support, 253–58, 350
Emotions, and persuasive presentations, 256–58, 350
Empathic listening, 58
Empathy, and improving listening, 58
Emphasis:
 in language use, 74–75, 350
 in writing, 274, 279–81, 286, 350
Employee counseling, 16–17
Employees, as communication payoff, 20
Employment interview, 150–51, 188–99, 350
 (See also Job interview)
Enclosure notation, in business letter, 307, 350
Encourager, as group maintenance role, 215, 350
Enculturation, 250, 251, 350
Endings of letters, 298, 301–2, 325
Endomorphs, and nonverbal communication, 86, 350
Energizer, as a group task role, 214, 350
Enthusiasm, as part of interviewee role, 160–61, 350
Envelopes, for business letters, 303–4
Environment, in nonverbal communication, 92–93
Equal Employment Opportunity Commission (EEOC), 196
E. R. G. theory, 33, 350
Esteem needs, 32–33, 350

Ethical behavior, 256, 258, 268
Ethics, 256, 258, 268
Ethos, 262–65, 267, 350
Euphemisms, in language use, 73
Evaluation:
 in interviews, 165
 in oral reports, 245
 in small group problem solving, 212–13
Evaluative response style, 54–55, 61, 350
Evaluative thinking, as barrier in business communication, 104–6, 111, 350
Examples, as supporting material, 235, 236, 350
Exception reports, 12, 350
Existence needs, in E.R.G. theory, 33
Exit interviews, 13–14, 154–55, 350
 as a form of upward communication, 13–14, 350
Expert testimony, as supportive material, 234–35, 236, 350
Explanation, in using visual and graphic aids, 137
Explicit norms, as characteristic of groups, 207, 350
Expressing, as nonverbal communication, 82, 93
Expressing feelings, in group problem solving, 209–10
Extemporaneous speaking, 242–43, 350
External communications, 19, 22, 350
External feedback, 41, 350
Extrinsic ethos, 262, 350
Extroversion, as part of credibility, 264, 350
Extroverts versus introverts, 226–27
Eye contact, 59, 87–88, 159, 266
 improving listening and, 59
 interviewer tone and, 159
 nonverbal communication and, 87–88
 resisting persuasion and, 266

Face, in nonverbal communication, 87–88
Facts, as supporting material, 234, 350
Fashion, and nonverbal communication, 85
Feedback, 6–7, 11, 15, 39, 40–41, 54–57, 350
 barriers in business communication and, 108
 bipolar thinking and, 104
 control and, 6–7
 and delivery, in oral reports, 240
 diagram, as an aspect of the controlling stage, 6
 letters and, 292
 listening and, 54–57
 oral reports and, 245
 organizing and, 6–7
 response styles and, 54–57
 transactions and, 28

Feedback (cont.)
  upward communication and, 11
  value of, 57
Felt conflict, 117, 119, 129, 351
Findings, as part of a business report, 338
First-degree headings, 329–32
Flexibility, 100, 104, 241, 244, 351
  delivery of an oral report and, 241, 351
  improving perception and, 100, 104, 351
  oral reports and, 244, 351
Flip chart, in oral reports, 144
Focused interviews, 169, 170, 171
Fog Index, 270, 287–88, 351
Follower, as group maintenance role, 215, 351
Follow-up letter, and job interviews, 192–94
Forcers, in conflict situations, 120, 123–24, 351
Foresight, in using visual and graphic aids, 134
Foreword, in business report, 337
Forms of business communication
  (See Attitude surveys; Bulletin-board messages; Business meetings; Company publications; Electronic communication; Employee counseling; Exit interviews; Grievance systems; Letters; Managerial visibility; Memoranda; Public-address systems; Reports; Social events; Suggestion systems; Telephone; Video programs)
Frame of reference, 157–58
Functional conflict, 114, 351

Gatekeeper, as group maintenance role, 215, 351
Gathering data, in small-group problem solving, 211
Generating excitement, in writing, 274–75
Generating ideas, in writing, 270–71
Genuineness, in writing, 273–74
Gestures, 90, 241
  in nonverbal communication, 90
  in oral reporting, 241
Getting action, in business letters, 302
Getting a job, 173–199
  applying, 184–88
  communication skills and, 173
  evaluating yourself, as an aspect of, 174–76
  getting information for, 181–84
  interviewing, 188–99
  résumé preparation, 176–81
Getting job information, 181–84, 198
  levels, 182–84
  sources for, 182–83
Gettysburg Address, 272–73

Giving information, in interview, 149–50
Goals, in persuasive presentations, 254–55, 351
Goodwill, 246, 351
Granting an adjustment, 315
Grapevine, as communication, 18–19, 35, 351
Graphic aids, in written reports, 139–42, 146, 357
  values of, 131–33, 146
  (See also Visual aids)
Graphic communication, 131–47
Grievance interview, 153, 351
Grievance systems, as upward communication, 12
Group communication, 37, 200–224
  (See also Groups)
Group maintenance roles, 214–15, 351
Groups, 200–224
  advantages of, 201, 222
  characteristics of, 203–8, 222
  cohesiveness in, 208, 348
  committees as, 221, 223, 348
  conference agenda, as aspect of, 219–21 sample, 220
  conference as, 219–21, 223, 349
  conflict in, 221–22, 223, 349
  definition of, 200
  disadvantages of, 201–2, 222
  ideal conditions for, 208
  improving, 218–21, 222–23
  leaderless, 205
  leader-member participation and, 213–18
  leader-oriented small, 204–6
  leadership functions in, 216–18, 222–23
  maintenance roles in, 214–15
  meetings as, 218–19, 223, 352
  membership functions in, 213–16, 222
  norms in, 207
  participant-oriented small, 204–6
  personality of, 206–7
  problem solving in, 209–13, 222
  size, as a factor in, 203–4
  structure of, 204–6
  task roles in, 214
Group task roles, 214
Growth, as communication payoff, 20
Growth needs, as part of E.R.G. theory, 33
Gunning Fog Index, 287–88, 351

Hall's distances, 90–91
Harmonizer, as a group maintenance role, 215, 351
Hearing, 50, 51, 351
Hemingway, Ernest, 232
Hidden agenda, 210
Highly structured interviews, 169
High technology, 146

Hitchhiking, 212, 351
Homophily, 99, 351
Honesty:
  in interviewee role, 161–62, 351
  in writing, 273–74
Horizontal communication, 14, 22, 351

Ideas, generating them in writing, 270–71
Identifying interests, in resolving conflicts, 127
Illustrations:
  in business report, 337, 351
  as supporting material, 235, 236, 351
Immediacy, 5, 245, 351
  motivation and, 5, 351
  oral reports and, 245, 351
Implementing the result, 125, 128–29, 213
  conflict resolution and, 125, 128–29
  small-group problem solving and, 213
Implicit norms, 207, 351
Impressiveness, in writing, 274
Impromptu speaking, 242, 351
Improvement in quality, as communication payoff, 21–22
Improving listening, 57–60
Improving meetings, conferences, and committees, 218–21
Improving perception, 100, 104
Inconsequential beliefs, 251
Increased competition, as communication payoff, 21
Incubation, 233, 352
Index, as part of business report, 340–41, 352
Index, Fog
  (See Gunning Fox Index)
Inductive paragraphs, in writing, 284, 352
Influence, 248–68
  (See also Persuasion)
Influencing behavior, in interview, 149, 150
Informal reports, 341–44
Information explosion, as communication payoff, 21
Information float, 16, 18, 292
Information giver, as group task role, 214, 352
Information overload, 136
Information seeker, as group task role, 214, 352
Initial partition, 238, 352
Initiator, as group task role, 214, 352
Inquiries, 309–13, 325, 352
Intangibility, and motivation, 5
Integrator, as group task role, 214, 352
Intelligence, audience, in oral reports, 229
Intended meaning, 26
Interest, and visual and graphic aids, 133
Interests, audience, in oral reports, 228

Intermittency, and motivation, 5
Internal feedback, 41, 352
Internal summaries, 237, 352
Interpersonal communication, 37, 39–43, 352
Interpersonal processes, 39–44
  feedback, 40–41, 350
  listening, 41–43, 352
  metacommunication, 43–44, 353
  self-disclosure, 40, 355
Interpretive response style, 55, 106, 352
Interviewee, 159–64, 171
  confidence and, 163–64, 171
  consistency and, 162, 349
  enthusiasm and, 160–61, 171
  honesty and, 161–62, 171, 351
  nervousness and, 163
  positive mental attitude and, 161
  preparation and, 160, 171
  questions to ask in job interviews, 196–97
  responsiveness and, 162–63, 171
  role and responsibility and, 159–60
Interviewers, 155–59, 171
  attitude and, 155, 171
  climate and, 156–57, 171
  eye contact and, 159
  frame of reference for, 157–58, 171
  objectivity and, 158, 171
  orientation for, 157, 171
  questions to ask in job interviews, 194–96
  tone and, 159, 171, 356
Interviewing for jobs, 188–99
  conduct of interview when, 190–94, 199
  follow-up letter, 192–94
    sample, 193
  frequently asked questions, 194–96
  negative factors, 197–98
  preparation, 188–90, 199
  questions for interviewees to ask, 196–97
  questions for interviewers to ask, 194–96
Interview, 148–72, 352
  appraisal, 151–52, 348
  arrangement of, 157
  casual, 170, 171
  counseling, 154, 349
  definition of, 148
  disciplinary, 153–54, 349
  distance in, 156
  evaluation in, 165
  exit, 154–55, 350
  focused, 170, 171
  formality in, 156–57
  interviewees in, 159–64, 171
  interviewers in, 155–59, 171
  listening in, 164–65, 171
  purposes of, 149–50, 171
  questioning in, 165–68, 171
  selection, 150–51, 355

Interview (cont.)
  structured, 169–70, 171
  structure of, 169
  structuring, 168–70, 171
  types of, 150–55, 171
  understanding in, 165
Intimate distance, 91, 92
Intrapersonal communication, 36–38
  definition of, 37, 352
Intrinsic ethos, 262, 352
Introductions, 237–38, 298–301, 338, 342
  business letters and, 298–301
  business reports and, 338, 342
  oral reports and, 237–38
Introverts versus extroverts, 226–27
Involvement, 59, 104
  improving bipolar thinking and, 104
  improving listening and, 59
IRS (Internal Revenue Service), 270

Japanese system of business, 11–12, 17, 35–36
Jargon, 68, 106
Job, getting a, 173–99
  and communication skills, 173
  applying for jobs, 184–88
  evaluating yourself, 174–76, 198
  getting job information, 181–84, 198
  interviewing, 188–99
  preparing a résumé, 176–81, 198
Job information, sources of, 182–83
Job interview, 188–99, 350
  conduct of, 190–94, 199
  follow-up letter, 192–94
  frequently asked questions, 194–96
  negative factors, 197–98
  preparation for, 188–90, 199
  questions for interviewees to ask, 196–97
  questions for interviewers to ask, 194–96
  (*See also* Employment interview)
Junk mail, 299

Key-word outline, 243
Knowledge, audience, in oral reports, 229

Lack of understanding, as barrier in business communication, 106, 111
Language, 63–78
  characteristics of, 68–77
  connotative meanings, 67, 349
  denotative meanings, 67, 349
  importance of, 63–64
  jargon and, 68
  needs and, 63–78
  overview of, 64–68
  parsimony and, 71, 353
  stereotyping and, 64–65, 356

transactional communication and, 66
transactional perspective and, 68–69
you and, 65–66
Leadership, in groups, 216–18
Leadership style, 217–18
"Leapfrog," 212
Letterhead, for business letters, 305
Letter of authorization, 334
Letter of inquiry, sample, 187
Letter of transmittal, 336–37
  sample, 336
Letters, 308–325
  adjustments, 314–17, 325, 347
  beginnings of, 298–301, 325
  claims, 313–14, 325, 348
  collection, 320–23, 325
  credit, 317–20, 325
  as form of downward communication, 10–11
  inquiries, 309–13, 325, 352
  motivated sequence in, 324, 353
  sales, 323–25
Letter writing, 290–326
  (*See also* Business letters)
Levels of communication, 7–15, 352
  diagonal, 14–15, 349
  downward, 7–11, 349
  horizontal, 14, 351
  upward, 11–14, 357
Line graph, 135, 140
Listening, 41–43, 46–62, 107–8, 352
  barriers to, 52–54, 61
  "between the lines," to improve, 60
  competence and, 51
  feedback and, 54–57, 61
  hearing and, 50, 51, 351
  importance of, 47–49
  improving, 57–60, 61
  interference and, 51, 52
  interviews and, 164–65, 171
  message problems in, 52–53
  mind problems and, 53
  myths about, 49–51, 61
  nature of, 49–52, 61
  people problems in, 53–54
  poor, as a barrier, 107–8
  problems, 52
  process, 51
  quiz, 49–50
  response styles in, 54–57
  three-part process of, 50, 51
Listening and feedback, 54–57
  evaluative response style, 54–55
  interpretive response style, 55
  probing response style, 56
  supportive response style, 55–56
  understanding response style, 56
  value of, 57

Logical support, 258–62
Logos, 259–62, 267–68, 352
Lose-lose, as a conflict resolution strategy, 120–21, 352

Main heads, 234, 236
Managerial visibility, 17
Manifest behavior, 117, 119–20, 129, 352
Manuscript speaking, 243–44, 352
Maslow, Abraham, 31–34, 35
Maslow's need hierarchy, 31–34, 352
Mass communication, 37
McGregor's Theory X and Theory Y, 34–36, 44
Meaning, 26, 352
  definition, 26
Meetings, 200–224, 352
  advantages of, 201, 222
  characteristics of, 203–8, 222
  cohesiveness in, 208
  dealing with conflict in, 221–22, 223
  definition of, 218
  disadvantages of, 201–2, 222
  ideal conditions for, 208
  improving, 218–21, 222–23
  norms in, 207, 353
  parliamentary procedure in, 218–19, 353
  presiding officer in, 218, 354
  problem-solving in, 209–13, 222
  recording secretary in, 219, 354
  sergeant-at-arms for, 219, 355
Membership, in groups, 213–16
Memoranda, 341–44
  business, 327–46
  example, 9
  (See also Business reports)
Memorized speaking, 244, 352
Memos, 9, 12, 341–44
  as form of downward communication, 9
  as form of upward communication, 12
  (See also Business reports; Memoranda)
Mesomorphs, and nonverbal communication, 86, 353
Message, of business letters, 298
Message problems in listening, 52–53
Metacommunication, 37, 43–44, 303–8, 325, 353
  and business letters, 303–8, 325, 353
  and communication process, 43–44
Mind problems, in listening, 53
Minimally structured interviews, 169–70
Mirror questions, in interviews, 167, 353
Moderately structured interviews, 169
Monotony, as vocal problem, 84
Monroe motivated sequence, 259–62, 267–68, 324, 353
Motivating, and communication, 5, 22

Motivation, 5, 58–59
  definition, 5
  and improving listening, 58–59
Movie projectors, in oral reports, 145–46
Multilevel communication, 37

"Narrowing the problem," in small group problem solving, 210–11
Need, as step in Monroe motivated sequence, 259–60, 268, 353
Need hierarchy, 31–34, 352, 353
  (See also Maslow's need hierarchy)
Needs, 31–34, 254–55, 353
  in persuasive presentations, 254–55, 353
Negative factors, in job interviews, 197–98
Negative roles, in groups, 215–16, 353
Nervousness, 163, 239–41, 264–65
  in interviews, 163
  in oral reports, 239–41
  (See also (Composure; Speech anxiety; Stage fright)
Noise, 106–7, 111, 353
  definition of, 107
  physical, 106–7, 354
  psychological, 107, 354
  types of, 107
Nonverbal communication, 30–31, 79–95, 353
  business letters and, 303–8, 325
  definition of, 80
  distances and, 90–91
  functions of, 80–82
  importance of, 79–80
  nature of, 80
  types of, 82–93
Nonverbal cues, as symbols, 26–27
Norms, of groups, 207, 353
Numerical order, in business reports, 330

Obesity, 86
Objectivity:
  in business reports, 332
  and interviewer role, 158
Obtaining information, and developing oral report, 231–33
OCR (Optical Character Reader), 303–304, 353
OCR readability, 304
One-way communication, 15, 48
Opaque projectors, in oral reports, 145
Open mindedness:
  and improving listening, 60
  in interviews, 164–65
Open questions, 105, 165–66, 353
  in interviews, 165–66
Opinion giver, as group task role, 214, 353
Opinion seeker, as group task role, 214, 353

Optical Character Reader (OCR), 303–4, 353
Oral communication, 225–47
  advantages of, 241–42
  (See also Oral reports; Persuasive presentations)
Oral reports, 225–47
  audience analysis and, 227–30
  audience attitudes and, 228
  audience beliefs and, 228
  audience values and, 228–29
  definition of, 226
  delivery in, 239–45
  development of, 226–39
  evaluation in, 245
  informal versus formal, 226
Oral versus written style, 241–42
Order, and business report, 342
Organization, 3, 4–5, 22, 234–39, 247, 284, 298, 325, 329–30, 353
  definition, 4
  business letters and, 298, 325
  business reports and, 329–30
  communication and, 4–5, 22, 353
  oral reports and, 234–39, 247
  writing and, 284
  (See also Business)
Organizational noise, 107, 353
Organizational patterns, for oral reports, 236–37
Organizational patterns, for persuasive speeches, 259–62, 267–68
Orientation, and interviewer role, 157
Orienter, as group task role, 214, 353
Osmosis, 147
Other-esteem needs, 32–33, 353
Ouchi, William, 11–12, 36
Ouchi's Theory Z, 36
Outline skeleton, 235
Outlining, 234–39, 259–62, 267–68, 284, 329–30
Overcoming barriers, in business communication, 108–10, 111
  feedback in, 108
  multiple channels in, 109
  repetition and, 109
  reinforcement and, 109
  simplicity and, 109–10
Overhead projector, in oral reports, 144–45
Overused expressions, 276

Paragraphs, 281–85
  length of, 282–84
  sequence of, 284–85
  types of, 284
  unity in, 281–82
Paralanguage, 83, 353

Parallelism, 236, 281, 333, 353
  organization and, 236, 353
  reports and, 333, 353
  writing and, 281, 353
Paraphrasing, 56, 105–6, 164
  and listening, in interviews, 164
  and listening response styles, 56, 105–6
Parliamentary procedure, 218–19, 353
Parsimony, in language use, 71, 353
Passive versus active verbs, 275–76
Pathos, 253–58, 267, 353
Patience, 57–58, 100
  and improving listening, 57–58
  and improving perception, 100
Patterns of organization for oral reports, 236–37
People problems, in listening, 53–54
Perceived conflict, 117, 118–19, 129, 353
Percentage of time spent listening, 47, 49
Perception, 96–112
  as barrier in business communication, 96–112
  improving, 100, 104
  process of, 101
Performance interview, 151–52
Period of insight, 233, 354
Personal:
  beliefs, 250, 251
  bubble, 90–91
  distance, 91, 92
  experiences, as supporting material, 235, 236, 354
  reality, 97
  space and distance, 90–91
Personality, 175, 206–7, 276
  as a characteristic of groups, 206–7
  as part of writing, 276
  qualities (a list), 175
Perspective, and resisting persuasion, 266
Persuaders, 248–68
Persuasive presentation, 248–68
  attitudes and, 248–50, 267, 348
  beliefs and, 248–49, 250–52, 267, 348
  emotional support and, 253–58, 350
  goals and, 255–56, 351
  logical support and, 258–62, 352
  needs and, 254–55, 353
  organizational patterns in, 259–62, 267–68
  proposition in, 258, 354
  values and, 248–49, 252–53, 267, 357
Persuasion, 248–68, 354
  definition, 248–49
Physical:
  noise, 106–7, 354
  reality, 97–98
Physiological needs, in Maslow's need hierarchy, 32, 354

Physiological noise, 107, 353
Pictograms, 141–42
Pie graph, 141
Placement, and visual and graphic aids, 135–36
Plan, and business report, 343–44
Planning:
  and business letters, 293
  and communication, 4, 22
  definition, 4
Pleasure, and nonverbal communication, 93
Poor listening, as a barrier in business communication, 107–8
Position of information, as emphasis, 74–75
Positiveness, in business letters, 295–96, 325, 354
Postscripts, in business letters, 307, 354
Practice, and delivery of oral reports, 239–40
Precision, in writing, 272, 286
Preface, in business reports, 336
Prefatory pages, in business reports, 334–35
Preparation, 160, 176–81, 185, 188–90, 198, 233, 266, 328–32, 344–46, 354
  applying for jobs and, 185, 354
  business reports and, 328–32, 344–46
  creative process and, 233
  interviewee role and, 160, 354
  job interview and, 188–90
  resisting persuasion and, 266
  résumé and, 176–81, 198, 354
Presentation of speeches, 242–44
Presiding officer, of meetings, 218, 354
Previewing, 238, 354
Primacy effect, 74–75, 237–38, 298, 354
Primary research, 329, 354
Principles of writing, 269–89
  (See also Writing Principles)
Probing response style, 56, 105–6, 354
Probing questions, in interviews, 167–68, 354
Problem-solution pattern of organization, 237
Problem solvers, in conflict situations, 120, 123, 124, 354
Problem solving, in groups, 209–13
Proposition, and persuasive presentations, 258, 354
Proxemics, 90–91, 354
Psychological noise, 107, 354
Public-address system, as downward communication, 11
Public distance, as nonverbal communication, 91, 92
Public speaking, 37, 225–47
  (See also Oral reports; Persuasive presentations)

Punctuation, and communication, 30
Purpose, 230–31, 298, 327–28
  business letters and, 298
  business reports and memoranda and, 327–28
  oral report development and, 230–31

Qualities of business reports, 332–33, 344–46
Questioning, 165–68
  interviews and, 166–68
    closed questions and, 166–67
    mirror questions and, 167
    open questions and, 165–66
    probing questions and, 167–68
    summary of, 168
  listening in interviews and, 164
Questionnaires, as a form of upward communication, 13–14
Questions interviewees should ask, 196–97
Questions interviewers should ask, 194–96

Rapport:
  cyclical building of, 246
  in oral reports, 245
Reaching an agreement, 125, 128
Reacting to ideas, and improving listening, 59–60
Readability, 278, 286–88, 304
  of OCR, 304
  and writing, 278, 286–288
Reality, 65, 97–98
  personal, 97–98
  physical, 97–98
Recency effect, 74–75, 238–39, 298, 354
Recognition seeker, as negative group role, 215, 354
"Recognizing the difficulty," in group problem solving, 209
Recommendations, in business report, 338–39
Recording secretary, for meetings, 219, 354
Reformulation, in small-group problem solving, 211
Refusing an adjustment, 316, 317
Refusing credit, 318–20
Regulating, in nonverbal communication, 81, 82, 93
Regulation, as communication payoff, 22
Reinforcement, and visual and graphic aids, 134–35
Relatedness needs, in E.R.G. theory, 33
Relaxation, in delivery of oral report, 241
Repetition, in writing, 279
Reports, 12, 327–46
  business and, 327–46
  upward communication and, 12

Resale, as an aspect of business letters, 300, 302, 354
Resisting the persuasion of others, 265–67
  eye contact and, 266
  perspective and, 266
  preparation and, 266
  time and, 267
Resolution aftermath, 117, 122, 129, 354
Response styles, 54–57
  evaluative, 54–55
  interpretive, 55
  probing, 56
  supportive, 55–56
  understanding, 56
  value of, 57
Responsiveness, as an aspect of interviewee role, 162–63, 354
Résumé, 176–81, 198, 354
  conventional format, 177–78
  list of possible sources, 181
  practical guidelines for preparing, 178
  preparation of, 176–81, 198
    format for, 177–81
    sources for more information on, 181
    things *not* to include, 181
Retention, and visual and graphic aids, 132–33
Revision, 233, 355
Rhetorical questions, 237
Rumors, 18–19, 22

Safety and security needs, 32, 355
Sales letter, 323–25
Satisfaction, in the Monroe motivated sequence, 260, 268, 355
"Saying what you mean," 66
Screening interviews, 151, 355
Secondary research, 329, 355
Second-page headings, in business letters, 307–8, 355
Securing information, in interview, 149
Seeking causes and interests, 126–27
Selection interviews, 150–51, 188–99, 355
  (*See also* Job interviews)
Selective attention, 97–100, 110–11, 355
Selective retention, 100–103, 111, 355
Self-actualization needs, 32–33, 355
Self-awareness, 59–60
Self-disclosure, 40, 355
  definition, 40
Self-esteem needs, 33, 355
Self-evaluation, in getting a job, 174–76, 198
Semantic noise, 107, 355
Sentence, 276–81
  length of, 277–78
Sentence design, 280
Sentence structure, 75

Sequence, motivated, 259–62, 267–68, 324, 353
Sequencing, in writing, 284–85
Sergeant-at-arms, for meetings, 219, 355
"Setting the stage," in resolving conflict, 125
Shared meaning, 28–29, 158
Shortness, and business letters, 298
Short reports, 341–44
  introductions in, 342
  order in, 342–43
  plan for, 343–44
  style in, 343
Simplemindedness, 71
Simplicity, 71–72, 138, 273, 355
  language and, 71–72, 355
  visual and graphic aids and, 138
  writing and, 273, 355
Sincerity, 72–74, 263, 355
  language and, 72–74, 355
  (*See also* Character)
Situation, in oral reports, 229
Size, 137–38, 203–4
  groups and, 203–4
  visual and graphic aids and, 137–38
Slang, 76, 176, 355
  job interview and, 176, 355
  language usage and, 76, 355
Slide projectors, in oral reports, 145
Smoothers, in conflict situations, 120, 123, 355
Smoothing, as lose-lose strategy, 120
Sociability, 263–64, 355
Social context, 38–39
Social distance, 91, 92
Social events, 17
Socialization, 250, 251
Societal noise, 107, 355
Solicited letter of inquiry, 308–10, 355
Space, in language use, 75
Spatial order, in business reports, 330, 355
Spatial pattern of organization, 236, 355
Special committees, 221, 355
Special-interest pleader, as negative group role, 215, 355
Specificity, and motivation, 5
Speech anxiety, 239–41, 247, 356
Speech delivery, method, 243
Speech purpose, 230–31, 234, 236, 237, 243
Speech speed, 42
Stage fright, 239–41
Stages for preparing business reports, 328–32
Stages of conflict, 116–22
Standing committees, 221, 356
Stationery for business letters, 304–5
Statistics, 234, 236, 356
Status, 207, 356

Steps for interviewees to gain confidence in interviews, 163
Stereotypes, vocal, 83–84, 356
Stereotyping, 64–65, 356
Strategic conflict, 114
Strength, in writing, 275
Strokes, 49
  definition, 49
Structure and format of business reports, 333–34
Structure, of groups, 204–6
Structured interviews, 169, 171
Structuring interviews, 168–70, 171
Style, 85, 341, 343, 345, 356
  and business report, 341, 343, 345, 356
  of clothing, in nonverbal communication, 85
Subject line, in business letter, 307, 356
Submitting an issue to a third party, as lose-lose strategy, 120–21
Substituting, in nonverbal communication, 81, 82, 93
Suggestion systems, 13
Summary:
  in business report, 337, 338–39
  in improving selective attention, 100
Superlatives, 73
Support from credibility, 262–65
  character as, 263, 348
  competence as, 262–63, 349
  composure as, 264–65, 349
  extroversion as, 264, 350
  sociability as, 263–64, 355
Supporting material, 234–37
Supportive response style, 55–56, 106, 356
Suppression, as a lose-lose strategy, 120–21
Surprise, in language use, 74
Suspending judgment:
  in improving listening, 58
  in improving perception, 100
Symbol, 26–27, 63, 356
  definition, 26
Symbolic communication, 26–27, 63–78
Symmetrical relationship, 31, 356
Syntactic noise, 107, 356
System, 3, 22–23, 356
  definition, 3
Systems approach, 3

Table of contents, in business report, 337
Tables, 139–40, 337
  business reports and, 337
  visual or graphic aids and, 139–40
Telephone, 16
Temper, and interviewer role, 156–57
Ten percent/ninety percent formula, 243–44
Tension reliever, as group maintenance role, 215, 356

Theory:
  X, 34–35, 36, 44, 356
  Y, 35–36, 44, 356
  Z, 36, 356
Third ear, in listening, 41, 356
Thought speed, 42, 60
Three-part process of listening, 50, 51
Time, 91–92, 136, 229, 267
  nonverbal communication and, 91–92
  oral reports and, 229
  resisting persuasion and, 267
Title fly, as part of business report, 334
Title page, as part of business report, 334–35
Tone, 159, 293–94, 300, 325, 356
  business letters and, 293–94, 300, 325, 356
  interviewer role and, 159, 356
Topical pattern of outlining, 236, 356
Touch, 88–89
Transactional communication, 27–29, 31, 69, 191, 277, 312, 316, 356
  axioms and, 31
  implications of, 29
  job interview and, 191
  writing and, 277, 312, 316, 356
Transferring information, 26–27
Transitions, 237, 285, 356
  in writing, 285, 356
Triteness, 75–76, 356
Trust, 250, 251, 356
Trustworthiness, 263
  (*See also* Character)
Truth, and interviewee role, 161–62, 356
Two-way communication, 15, 48, 52, 59
Type of paragraph, in writing, 284
Types of delivery, 242–44


Understanding, 56, 58, 61, 105, 132, 165, 272, 276–77, 281, 286–88, 333, 356
  business reports and, 333
  improving listening and, 58
  interviews and, 165
  response style and, 56, 61, 105, 356
  sentences and, 276–77
  visual and graphic aids and, 132
  writing and, 272, 281, 286–88
Unity, in writing, 281–82
Unpredictability, and motivation, 5
Unsolicited letter of inquiry, 311–12, 356
Upward communication, 11–14, 22, 35, 357
  definition, 11, 357


Value of feedback, 57
Values, 248–49, 252–53, 267, 357
  of audience, in oral reports, 228–29

**372** *Index*

Variety:
  as vocal need, 84
  in writing, 277–78
Verbal communication, 30–31
  (*See also* Language; Words)
Video programs, as downward communication, 11
Visual aids, 142–46, 147, 357
  oral reports and, 142–46, 147, 357
  use of, 133–39, 146
  values of, 131–33, 146
Visual communication, 131–47
Visualization, in the Monroe motivated sequence, 260–61, 268, 357
Vital statistics, 68
Vocalics, 83, 357
Vocal stereotypes, 83–84
Voice, 83–84

**W**eighing evidence, in improving listening, 60
We-viewpoint, in business letters, 295, 325
Who, what, why, when, where, and how, in business reports, 332
"Why" questions, 105

Win-lose, as conflict resolution strategy, 120, 357
Win-win, as conflict resolution strategy, 120–21, 357
Withdrawers in conflict situations, 119–20, 122–23, 357
Words, 26, 63–78, 271–76
  a summary, 271–76
  symbols as, 26
  usage and, 63–78
  (*See also* Language; Verbal communication)
Writer's block, 270
Writing principles, 269–89
Written reports:
  checklist, 344–46
  guide for writing, 344–46
Written versus oral style, 241–42

**Y**ou-attitude, in business letters, 294–95, 325, 357
You-viewpoint, in business letters, 294–95, 325, 357

**Z**IP code, 304, 305

## LIBRARY OF DAVIDSON COLLEGE

Books on regular loan may be checked out for **two weeks**. Books must be presented at the Circulation Desk in order to be renewed.

A fine is charged after date due.

Special books are subject to special regulations at the discretion of the library staff.

MAR -9 1987
MAR 24 1987
DEC 1 1988
DEC 16 1991